REA

ACPL ITEM
DISCARDED

S0-BWW-717

JUN 24 '70

MRS. EDDY

By the Same Author

THE IMPATIENCE OF A LAYMAN
THE VISITOR
AND I WILL GIVE HIM THE MORNING STAR
CHRISTIAN SCIENCE AND ORGANIZED RELIGION
MRS. EDDY AS I KNEW HER
ARISE SHINE

Mrs. Eddy

HER LIFE, HER WORK
AND
HER PLACE IN HISTORY

by Hugh A. Studdert Kennedy

THE FARALLON PRESS
58 SUTTER STREET
SAN FRANCISCO 4, CALIFORNIA, U.S.A.

Copyright 1947

Copyright under International Copyright Union

All Rights Reserved under Inter-American Copyright Union (1910)

by

The Farallon Press

Printed in United States of America

L'Esperance Sivertson & Beran

San Francisco

1532521

Contents

Foreword

TRUTH OR TRADITION? A straightforward and factual account of one of history's most colourful characters, or another excursion into calculated fiction? Immediately the biographer lifts his pen to write the life story of Mary Baker Eddy, he is confronted with two urgently sponsored but conflicting versions of Mrs. Eddy. There is the first-sly-then-violent demand for the legendary creature of ecclesiasticism, painted from a palette of disclosure, suppression and distortion to represent an oracular but pale nonentity. Then there is thrust upon him, by her avowed and unavowed detractors, a villainess made equally repellent by a different admixture of the same colours of disclosure, suppression and distortion. The clamour raised by these contenders is so great as to divert attention almost entirely from the long-recognized need for an unslanted record of the extraordinary figure that was the real Mrs. Eddy, one that will place her in true historical perspective and one that will live because of its authenticity.

"All biographies of Mrs. Eddy," as my husband, the late Hugh A. Studdert Kennedy, has observed, "have hitherto been put out by the Church as propaganda in defence of Mrs. Eddy, or they have been vicious attacks on her by her antagonists. Why not relate the whole story quite simply, as in the case of any important character, and let the facts speak for themselves? I have always felt it was something very like presumption on our part to attempt to steady the ark of Mrs. Eddy's life story by suppression of relevant information—especially in the face of her public proclamation that 'nothing has occurred in my life's experiences which, if correctly narrated and understood, could injure me'."[1]

As far back as 1914, when he set sail from England to become Foreign Editor of *The Christian Science Monitor* in Boston, there was close to Mr. Kennedy's heart the desire to write a genuine portrait, one so untainted by either apology or recrimination as to win the respect and interest of Christian Scientists and non-Christian Scientists alike. But years were to slip by before he felt ready to undertake the monumental task. It was not until the Fall of 1938 that the work began in earnest. Convinced that such a book could go out with the goodwill of all concerned, Mr. Kennedy confided his vision to his friend, Mr. William P. McKenzie, Chairman of the Board of Directors of The Mother Church. "Now is the time for collating of fact and the retiring of falsehood," Mr. McKenzie was to write enthusiastically, and "Whenever you come here, you will be welcomed and have any help we can give."

An interview with the Board on October 10, 1938, served to highlight the need for total independence from official pressure and partisan considerations for the historian—in short, the demand for absolute integrity of authorship. When Mr. William P. Rathvon asked, "To what extent will you have us interested?" Mr. Kennedy replied: "I think it would be a most dangerous thing for the success of the book if you had anything to do with it. I think this has been the charge against all the books [the biographies of Mrs. Eddy]. They have been procured books for a purpose. . . . I want your help and approval, your advice and recommendations, and I am eager to give the fullest consideration to anything you have to say; but I must safeguard my book from any suggestion that it has been written to order or is in any sense at any point 'dictated' or 'procured.' "[2]

It may be asked why the Board was consulted at all. The vast archives of The Mother Church, the First Church of Christ, Scientist, in Boston, contain most every document of importance relating to the life and work

[1] *Miscellany*, p. 298.
[2] The Board's official transcript of the conference.

of its founder, Mrs. Eddy, either in original or facsimile. Mr. Kennedy felt that the custodians of this treasure in historical material would hardly expect him to make bricks without straw, especially when the only sufferer would be Mrs. Eddy's memory, and he entertained the sanguine hope that they would welcome an opportunity to correct from their data any historical inaccuracies which might arise.

About this time there came into Mr. Kennedy's hands authenticated copies of all the documents and other records needed for a full and rounded biography, the absolute reliability of which was attested by Judge Clifford P. Smith, Editor, Bureau of History and Records of The Mother Church, official representative of the Board and generally conceded authority on the incidents of Mrs. Eddy's long life and the development of her organization. In his letter to Mr. Kennedy of December 1, 1938, he states categorically that the source material in question, even in most of its detail, is authentic and that "The Mother Church has most of the documents which are quoted" therein. Thus it became possible to do the book independently of officialdom, yet without sacrificing the advantages of officialdom's resources.

The lengthy manuscript was completed by the Fall of 1939 and copies were submitted for comment to several whose opinions were highly valued.

To Mr. McKenzie, the author wrote: "I place great emphasis on the obstacles which Mrs. Eddy had to overcome in establishing her great work, for I want quite definitely to get away from the dangerous pseudo-serenity which pervades some previous biographies. The net effect of such an attitude [as theirs], as I am sure you will agree, is to present Mrs. Eddy not as one like Jesus tempted in all things like as we are, but as a being that never was in earth or heaven, and so affording the ordinary human no points of sympathy or contact. To me Mrs. Eddy is nowhere more vivid in her claim to what men call grandeur than in just this, the way she rode the storm. I come back to it again and again."

If there was any lingering doubt as to the fairness of the biographer who would bring right out into the open the pertinent facts—with nothing at all withheld—it was dispelled by Mr. McKenzie's response on reading the manuscript: "I think the strongest feeling that is in our minds is that of gratitude. It would take too many words to express our feelings, and so I will say no more at present. I am sure there is a place for the work of a friend to our Leader who writes from the standpoint of observation, evaluation and goodwill."

The propriety of discussing the sensational charges levelled against Mrs. Eddy by her detractors and of telling frankly the whole story of the fascinating and significant Quimby controversy received the unqualified endorsement of Lord Lothian, who will be remembered as the British Ambassador to the United States and a pre-eminent Christian Scientist. In a letter dated June 14, 1940, he stated his reaction to the book: "I think I have read all the hostile lives of Mrs. Eddy and I have always thought, as you have done, that they ought to be answered—or, at any rate, that a biographer should take into account what they have alleged and deal with it indirectly if not directly. These hostile books are the mine from which opponents of Christian Science and of Mrs. Eddy are going to dig out their material for decades to come and it is essential that there should be in existence and available a satisfying answer. That, I suppose, is why I enjoyed reading your book so much. It is by far the best account that I have yet read of what one might call the human aspect of Mrs. Eddy's life."

The answer to the question of what the book might mean to the all-important "outsider," the impartial non-Christian Scientist, was indicated by Mr. Constant Huntington, President of Putnam's in London, the publisher who had undertaken to issue the work abroad: "I want to tell you that I continued to enjoy my reading of the book to the end, and when I had finished it, I felt that you had achieved what we both set out to do. . . . Throughout the work, you have consistently kept yourself in the background, and let the facts of the life of Mrs. Eddy speak for themselves. This is a great achievement."

Lastly, the manuscript was submitted for expert editing to Mr. Arthur Corey, who is perhaps the best qualified authority today on the life and work of Mrs. Eddy and the history of her movement, because of his access to and familiarity with an unmatched wealth of source material and—what is of infinitely more consequence—because of his clearly judicial attitude on the subject.

"The only major point which Mr. Kennedy's book does not discuss," Mr. Corey writes, "is the widely-publicized charge that Mrs. Eddy was guilty of frequent plagiarism. However, I am inclined to agree with the author that this is a somewhat extraneous matter, bearing little if at all upon the basic trend of her life and the attainment of her goal. There has never been a writer of moment, apparently, who has not made generous use, either consciously or unconsciously, of the writings of others. As Emerson points out, even Shakespeare owed debts in all directions, for out of 6043 lines in one play, 1771 were written by some author before Shakespeare, 2373 by him on the foundation laid by his predecessors, only 1899 being entirely his own. It is the use that greatness makes of such material which gives the material a greatness it did not before have and it is in this that the value of great writing lies. Within the limitations of human language, nothing else is possible. Mrs. Eddy used what she found where she found it. Hegel and Swedenborg accommodated her with apt expressions—although they would undoubtedly have been surprised at the meaning she gave their words; before Mrs. Eddy's advent, Ann Lee was 'the woman of the Apocalypse' to her followers, who called her 'Mother,' referred to her foundation body of Shakers as 'the Mother Church' and began the Shaker version of the Lord's Prayer with 'Our Father and Mother which art in heaven'; while from *Lindley Murray's English Reader* (page 118) came most of what Mrs. Eddy has to say in *Miscellaneous Writings* (page 147), word for word, about 'the man of integrity.' But, lo, with what magic does she transform these obscure and previously moribund expressions! Whatever their original impulsion, the thought that now lies behind them vivifies and invests them with immortality.

"Because she was driven by the all-absorbing conviction that hers was a holy cause, Mrs. Eddy's use of what she found where she found it was not confined to her literary activities, for everything else and everyone else and even herself she used without hesitation to further her crusade. In this light it is no mystery that she demanded unquestioning loyalty from her followers, for this meant loyalty to Principle as she saw it."

So it is with the hope that my husband's endeavour to paint with words an objective, accurate and uninhibited portrait will place the heretofore enigmatical Mary Baker Eddy in true historical perspective that this, his fondest work, goes forth.

CLARISSA HALE STUDDERT KENNEDY

La Mirada
Saratoga
California

A New England Ancestry

THE LONG LIFE of Mary Baker Eddy extended from 1821 to 1910. Times have changed since 1910, so that looking back upon those years seems like looking back upon the age of innocence. It was an age when the tempo of life was still unhurried, when a bicycle was still for the most part the fastest thing on the road, certainly in New Hampshire, where in and out of the hills the roads wound,

> Narrow ribbon strips
> Of white, amidst the green,

and no man thought of traffic save when he thought of the great city and its busy streets. Oxen ploughed the fields, and the "moving picture" was still something for the small town boy, who had gone to the big town, to tell about on his return.

But if New Hampshire of thirty years ago represented an unaccustomed scene, the New Hampshire of one hundred years before that was in another world; not so much in the outward and visible sign as in the inward and spiritual grace. The New Hampshire of 1910 had a century of peace behind her. On both sides of the Atlantic men and women were beginning to talk of how best might be celebrated the great fact that for nearly one hundred years no strife had risen between the two great branches of the English-speaking peoples, and New Hampshire in common with the rest of the country was taking part in the discussion.

It was very different in the New Hampshire of 1821 when our record opens. The War of 1812 was still a vivid memory; the War of the Revolution not so long past but that fathers who had fought in it and mothers who had waited through it could be telling the story once again to their children's children. New Hampshire had been in the midst of it all.

Running up as it does to the Canadian frontier, the Granite State, as it came to be called, early learned the stern realities of war and that demand for watchfulness which is the price of liberty. The French wars, the Indian wars swept through her valleys, and among the earliest recollections of the child, Mary Baker, must have been the story of how her great-great-grandfather, Captain John Lovewell, lost his life in a desperate struggle with the Indians at "Lovewell's Fight", and of how General John McNeil, cousin of her venerable grandmother, was the hero of the battle of Chippewa in the War of 1812.

By 1821 the noise of war had died away in the distance; but the men and women of those days had known about it, and the hills and the vales and the meeting-houses, even the trees, had their tales to tell.

Life was hard and rugged. In winter, it was a constant struggle with the elements, in the spring and summer with the soil. The winters in New Hampshire are winters indeed. From the day that the first snowflake drifts aimlessly down to a frost-bound earth early in November, well on into April, winter has it all its own way. The magic of October with its forthfaring of unbelievable colour gives way to the lighter glory of November; the crimson and the orange and the purple merge gently into the pale grey and gold. And then one day, as Longfellow has it:

> *Out of the bosom of the Air,*
> *Out of the cloudfolds of her garments shaken,*
> *Over the woodlands brown and bare,*
> *Over the harvest fields forsaken,*

> *Silent, and soft, and slow*
> *Descends the snow.*

Thence onwards it snows hard and often. There are days of splendour, with the sun shining from a cloudless sky. Then there is more snow, until stone-wall and fence have vanished and roads are no more and even the houses seem to have pulled white sheets and blankets around them.

And cold! Whittier knew all about it and in his "Snowbound" has left an ineffaceable picture of a New England winter and how it was met in a New England home one hundred years ago.

> *A chill no coat, however stout,*
> *Of homespun stuff could quite shut out.*

His story as presented in "Snowbound" was the winter story of any farm in New Hampshire, when, after a night and a day and a night of storm and snow, nothing is left of the familiar landscape, "no cloud above and no earth below," just sky and snow everywhere, with all familiar sights taking on strange shapes.

But the work of the farm had to go on. Paths had to be dug through the drifts. Wood had to be brought in, stalls had to be littered. Hay had to be pitchforked down from the hay-loft for the cows. The horses had to have their corn. Milking, skimming, churning had to go on, and at night the women folk had still their spinning and weaving and knitting to do.

In vivid contrast to all this was the spring and summer. Those accustomed to the gradual, almost imperceptible, oncoming of spring in milder climates, can have no idea of the sudden burst of trumpets which heralds spring in New England. For weeks, underneath, the snow has been "going". Outwardly, all is much the same, but underneath the warm blanket of the snow the soil has been quickening with countless sturdy growths. Then suddenly all nip and eagerness seem to vanish from the air; what breeze there is is mild and warm, and in a day or two the melting snow reveals a world of life well on its way. Lush new green is suddenly everywhere and each morning finds a new phalanx of wild flowers in the woods and by the brooks.

Soon it is high summer.

The setting was the same a hundred years ago, but in those days the machine age was still a long way off, and the farmer and his hired men went forth to their work "in the morning until the evening" in a very real sense.

Indeed, work, hard work to which no limit was set or expected, was a characteristic of everyday life. There were few pleasures as the present world understands them, but in their place was the glamour of the pioneer life with its opportunity to wrest something new from the earth every day, and the vision of a new country like a growing child coming daily into fulfillment. In the soul of the New Englander there was a passionate joy in thrift, and in the visible achievements of his own hands. The digging up of another tree stump, the reclaiming of another acre of land, gave a zest to the days and a deep-toned content to his night's sleep. The life was, and had to be, tremendously self-contained. In a large household, and many of them were very large, there had to be a large measure of organization. With a great multiplicity of things to do, everyone had to perform his part faithfully, and the efficient housewife had a place and a time for everything, and her daughters and hired girls—often the daughters of neighbouring households—had to be faithful.

A bright cleanliness was characteristic at all times, but especially in summer; open doors and open windows, with well-scrubbed tubs and churns drying in the sun, and everywhere a sense of brightness and light.

So it was no doubt on July 16, 1821, when Mary Baker was born in Bow, New Hampshire, a little township some four miles south of Concord, the State capital.

Mark Baker, her father, lived on his own farm, an upland tract of some five hundred acres which had been cleared by his father and elder brother. For six generations there had been Bakers in New England. The first immigrant was one John Baker, who, as the records show, was a freeman of Charlestown in 1634. He came from Kent where his people had for generations been substantial yeomen in the parish of Lyminge. Lyminge is not far from Folkestone, and the low square tower of the old parish church was a landmark on the way to the coast when Edward the First was king.

The first Baker of whom anything is known, is one Robert, a native of Lyminge, whose life's span spread itself over the greater part of the fifteenth century. Of his long story nothing is known for certain save one thing. When he lay a-dying and bethought him of the things he had done or left undone, he made provision in his will that "twelve pence" be paid to the church for "tithes forgotten", another twelve pence for the maintenance of the church building and a bushel of wheat "to all the lights of the said church".

Perhaps it may be too much to picture from this an all too scrupulous honesty combined with a deep religious feeling and a strong sense of public spirit and responsibility. And beyond this a fundamental generosity, which lay however so deeply buried under the demands of thrift and care that it only emerged when these demands had been fully met.

Be this as it may, such a fashion of a man might well be held as a composite picture of all the Bakers. So they were in Kent and so they were when they crossed the Atlantic and settled on the New England seaboard.

The next Baker in succession in Lyminge was John, the son of Robert. It is possible that his father's tardy payment of tithe represented an incipient rebellion against the demands of the Church, which only approaching death could reverse. But whatever the father's attitude, there can be no doubt about the son's. He openly flouted the ecclesiastical demands by attempting to administer his wife's estate without paying tax to the Church. He was tried and condemned, condemned "to march before the Procession in church on two Sundays, clad only in ragged shirt and breeches, bearing a lighted candle worth a penny".

There is more than a little reason to conclude, especially from the penance imposed upon him, that John Baker was a Lollard. The teachings of Wycliffe, in spite of all that ecclesiastical authority could do to suppress them, had spread steadily through England. Wycliffe's "poor preachers" went everywhere. Carrying portions of the newly translated Bible with them, they "constantly did mingle among the poor" and found great favour with them.

So much was this the case, and so strong did feeling run, that in the early years of the fifteenth century, in many places, "Processions" were abandoned and the worship on saints' days ceased to be observed. The abandonment of the Procession, such an integral part of pre-Reformation worship, was a specially sore point with the ecclesiastical authority, and when renewed persecution had resulted in its inevitable flood of recantations, one of the first signs of the return to orthodoxy was the restoration of the Procession, and one of the favourite penances imposed on "repentant" heretics was to walk in it.

John Baker's was evidently a particularly bad case, for he not only had to walk in the Procession, but to do so "with contumely and discredit". He did not resist to the point of martyrdom, as did so many, but he must have gone much further than his fellows, to be placed, as he was, in the forefront of the Procession.

In any event, whatever may be thought of Robert's forgetfulness in the matter of tithes or John's contumacy in the matter of taxes, there can be no doubt as to the open rebellion of their descendant in the fourth generation, one John Baker, who after much discussion and "earnest persuasion", by which he "refused to be exercised", was finally excommunicated as an "obdurate separatist".

That was in 1634. Some four years previously the great migration to the New World had begun. The Massachusetts Bay Company was chartered in 1629. In sharp contrast with the little company of settlers, humble farmers, labourers and artisans, long immortalized as the Pilgrim Fathers who had landed on the bleak shores of Cape Cod nine years before, the new company was a magnificent enterprise. The Plymouth Colony was an outlawed religious band. In the eyes of orthodox England its members were contemptible troublemakers. In the opinion of the Bishop of London they were "men of no account instructed by guides fit for them, cobblers, tailors, felt-makers, and such like trash".

On the other hand the Bay colony was literally a cross section of English society transferred bodily to the New World. All strata, with the exception of the peerage, were represented. Not a few possessed large landed estates in England; some were wealthy merchants; others were prominent men of learning. On the roll of the company were such names as Sir John Young, Sir Richard Saltonstall, John Endicott, John Winthrop, and many other well-known landowners and men of substance.

The great mass of the new colonists, however, were yeomen farmers and freeholders from East and South-eastern England. And they came with their livestock, their tools, with great stores of supplies and goods for trading with the Indians. Above all, they brought with them the Established Church. They were not "Separatists" in the strict sense of the word, although orthodox England may so have regarded them. They greatly desired that the "English form" might be purified, but they did not say on leaving England, as did the Separatists, "Farewell Babylon, Farewell Rome," but rather in the words of one of them, "Farewell dear England! Farewell the Church of God in England and all the Christian friends there."

It was to a ship's company setting out for this New England that John Baker attached himself after his excommunication at Lyminge.

Meanwhile throughout all the years stretching back into centuries, four other families, afterwards destined to come together, were moving from one generation to another in England, the Ambroses of Suffolk, the Goodhues of Kent, the Chandlers of Hertfordshire, and the Lovejoys from Buckinghamshire, weavers and millers, candle-makers, blacksmiths, people of much solid worth who about the same time and for the same reason as did John Baker of Lyminge, decided to throw in their lot with the Massachusetts Company and seek a larger freedom in the New World. Henry Ambrose, Nicholas Goodhue, John Lovejoy and William Chandler, all set out on the great adventure about the same time.

Of the ways and means of John Baker's journey nothing is known. What time of the year or hour of the day he left the little village where his people had lived and laboured for so long, who, if anyone, went with him, where he took ship and who were his companions on the voyage, there is no record. When next we meet John Baker, he is a freeman of Charlestown, a little settlement on the other side of the Charles Estuary from

Boston. The fact that he was registered as a freeman shows that he was able to bring some small fortune with him and so had a status above the hired labourer or indentured white servant, large numbers of which came out with every company. A few years later he was in Boston, had evidently put his substance to good account and was the owner of a profitable grist mill which derived its power from the rise and fall of the tides among the fens to the west of the city.

He died in 1684 full of years, "well loved and worthy," as may be gathered from the Roxbury church records wherein he is referred to as Father Baker and described as "old and blind and godly".

But while John Baker was thus prospering, accommodating himself to a larger freedom, settling himself into a groove which no Baker seems to have been able to tolerate for long, the religious views of the colony were not being allowed to remain undisturbed.

Three years before John Baker reached Charlestown, there had landed in Boston one Roger Williams, a scholar of Cambridge. He came to New England not at all with the moderate hopes and demands of his fellow immigrants. He was a refugee in the fullest sense of the word from the tyranny of Archbishop Laud, and he threw a bombshell into the settlement of Boston by insisting that religious toleration, far from being merely a matter of practical expediency, was a demand of Christian principle. In other words, he sought to defend everyone's right to think for himself and to enjoy in so doing the respect of his fellows. Williams was quite emphatic in the matter. He insisted that persecution for cause of conscience was "most evidently and lamentably contrary to the doctrine of Christ Jesus", that no one should be bound "to worship or maintain a worship against his own conscience", that the church and state should be separated, that to limit a choice of magistrates to church members was like choosing a pilot according to his "plan of salvation" rather than to his skill in seamanship, and finally, that the magistrate could not have and should not have "any power in matters of conscience".

Such a thought in the land of "the last word and the final good" was indeed a square peg in a round hole. But even worse than Williams was

Anne Hutchinson. That a man should hold such views was bad enough, but in a woman they were simply baffling. Moreover, Mrs. Hutchinson was clearly no fanatic, but a woman of calm judgement, of good family, "of ready wit and bold spirit," as Governor Winthrop admitted in no little dejection. And yet here she was, he added, "like Roger Williams or worse". She not only insisted that the Holy Ghost "dwelt in every believer", but stoutly maintained the inalienable right of private judgement in religious matters against all authority, ecclesiastical or civil.

Such doctrines cut at the very roots of established Puritanism, and so in the end both Roger Williams and Anne Hutchinson were banished. Williams was the first to go. He could not return to England where Laud was dealing more hardly than ever with nonconformists. He had no choice but to go out into the wilds. And so, when the glory of the fall had well passed and night brought an ominous breath of cold, he set out for the vast stretches of wooded lands, which lay then as now at the head of Narragansett Bay.

The winter which followed was one of terrible privation, but when spring came again he had gathered five companions around him, and together they founded the settlement of Providence. That was in 1636. Two years later, Anne Hutchinson was banished, and joined Williams in the Providence settlement.

Thereafter for many years a steady stream of people who chafed under the ever-increasing intolerance of the Massachusetts clergy and land-owners, followed the two pioneers into the wilderness. They had fled to the New World from the tyranny of Charles I and Archbishop Laud. And so when they saw the same "intolerable errors" "taking root downwards and springing upwards" all around them, they picked up and went out once more.

Throughout the seventeenth century the settlement of Providence (Rhode Island, as it came to be) and later New Hampshire were havens of refuge for all who could not do with the "form" of Massachusetts and longed for still freer and more individual life.

This came to be specifically true of New Hampshire, and so it is not surprising that the Bakers ultimately found their way there. About the middle of the eighteenth century a great-grandson of old Father Baker, one Joseph Baker, took the road north and settled in Suncook, now Pembroke, New Hampshire.

Joseph Baker is the first of his house of whom a succinct life story is preserved. He prospered greatly. Like so many other of the pioneers in these new lands, he had a considerable knowledge of surveying. Suncook was then in territory claimed by both Massachusetts and New Hampshire, and when the dispute came up for definite settlement, Joseph Baker was employed to survey the disputed areas, and to make the necessary reports. It was not an easy job, especially in such a matter where feeling was likely to run high, but Joseph Baker acquitted himself well, and, later on, we find him becoming a selectman, a deacon of his church, and a collector of taxes.

He also made a happy and fortunate marriage to Hannah Lovewell, daughter of Captain John Lovewell, whose name, as has been seen, was a household word throughout New England as the hero of Lovewell's fight in the Indian Wars. Captain Lovewell was killed in battle, and the "Song of Lovewell's Fight" became one of the folk songs of the day.

Hannah Lovewell brought Joseph Baker two hundred acres of good farm land, and into his home a remarkable character. She inherited all her father's courage, and stories of her fearlessness where Indians were concerned were recounted by New England firesides long after the Indian menace had ceased. She was the mother of eleven children, and like all New England mothers of those days her work was never done.

Meanwhile, her husband was becoming a figure of some importance, not only in the little town where they lived but in the state, or province as it was then, of his adoption. In 1758, Governor Benning Wentworth of New Hampshire appointed Joseph Baker Captain of the militia. It was in those days a more than ordinary trust. The fourth and final struggle between the French and English for supremacy in North America had reached its most acute stage. The French had overrun the Ohio valley, and this together with the building of Fort Duquesne, where

Pittsburgh now is, clearly revealed their intention to shut off the English from the Mississippi valley and confine them to the Atlantic Seaboard.

New England colonists were, to an ever larger extent, taking part in these wars, and the experience thus gained was fitting them for the great struggle for independence, which, at the time when Joseph received his captain's commission, was less than twenty years away. When this struggle did come, Joseph Baker marched with the rest. He was also a member of the local Committee of Safety and a delegate to the Provincial Congress of New Hampshire.

It was probably at the close of the Revolutionary War that Joseph Baker's eldest son, also named Joseph, moved across the Merrimac River and settled in Bow.

There in the uplands, high above the river valley, he had acquired his five hundred acres, and now set about the great task of clearing the land. There he married Marion Moor McNeil. Ultimately Scots, both the Moors and the McNeils had come to New England by way of northern Ireland from the county Antrim, and they brought with them all the fire and fight in religious matters for which Ulstermen, even then, were well known. Mark Baker, Mary Baker's father, was their younger son.

Meanwhile, through the years since their arrival in the New World, the Ambroses, the Goodhues, the Lovejoys and the Chandlers had been coming together. In sharp contrast with the Bakers, the Ambroses and the families that went to their making were a mild and peace-loving people. If the Bakers were all Michaels, the Ambroses were all Gabriels. They united as did all New England in those days on the basis of religion, but their approach was that of the meek rather than the mighty. It was Nathaniel Ambrose, Mary Baker's grandfather, who after serving faithfully in the Revolutionary War, devoted all his savings from his calling as a carpenter to the building of a meeting-house in Pembroke, New Hampshire. It survived for many years as "the Ambrose meeting-house".

Nathaniel Ambrose married Phebe Lovejoy, whose family on both sides, the Lovejoys and the Chandlers, had for many generations enjoyed a special reputation for "gentle godliness". It was of the first Chandler to arrive in New England, namely, William, of whom John Eliot, his pastor, wrote that he lived "a very religious and Godly life" and that when he died he left "a sweet memory and savor behind him".[1]

Nathaniel Ambrose and his wife, Phebe Lovejoy, had a daughter Abigail, and early in the nineteenth century the strangely contrasting lines of the Bakers and the Ambroses were united when this girl, Abigail Ambrose, was married to Mark Baker.

To these two, Mark and Abigail Baker, was born, on July 16, 1821, a little girl, the subject of this record, their sixth and last child. The old grandmother, Mark's mother, Marion Moor McNeil that was, was asked to choose a name for her. She named the child Mary.

[1] Roxbury Lane and Church Records, p. 83.

C H A P T E R 2

The Early Years

ABIGAIL BAKER WAS in her thirty-eighth year when her youngest child was born. Early marriage was the rule in New England in those days where a woman, still unmarried at twenty-five, was looked upon as already an old maid. But no matter how early she married, the young girl became a matron in the fullest sense of the word on her wedding day. Thence onwards her life was her home and her children. Her children were wont to come quickly and regularly, and her family would be complete in the early thirties. Thirty-eight would be regarded as rather past the usual age of childbearing.

It is not surprising, therefore, that to the thought of a deeply religious woman as Abigail Baker was, the coming of this child in her "old age" should take on some special significance. In the Bible which she loved and studied so earnestly were many stories of children destined to greatness being born to women in later life, and although her essential meekness and modesty caused her to view such thoughts with disquiet, she could not, as she confessed in distress to a friend, avoid their coming.

In the spring of 1821, Mrs. Baker and this friend and neighbour, Sarah

Gault, were much together. She was "a devout and pious woman", and the two would frequently and regularly meet and talk over religious matters and pray aloud together. As runs one account of the matter which seems to be traditional, "During these meetings, Mrs. Baker many times told her neighbour, Mrs. Gault, that she felt herself to be a most wicked woman, because of the strange thoughts she had regarding her youngest child, which was yet unborn. She told Mrs. Gault that she could not keep her thoughts away from the strong conviction that this child was holy and consecrated and set apart for wonderful achievements, even before her birth. She said, 'I know these are sinful thoughts for me to entertain, but I cannot shake them off.' Then these two devout women would talk the question over and pray together."[1]

However this may be, there can be no doubt that between the little girl Mary and her mother, there existed from the first dawnings of the child's consciousness a more than usually deep spiritual bond. Abigail Baker was in every sense of the term a mother in Israel. Writing of her many years afterwards, Mrs. Eddy said, "Of my mother I cannot speak as I would, for memory recalls qualities to which the pen can never do justice."[2]

She seems to have been a remarkable woman, not only in point of culture, but because of a certain calm and patient wisdom which rose serenely above the many besetments of a working day and was found almost mystically at hand when help was needed. She was well named Abigail, for between her and her namesake in Israel there was a bond clear enough. The "iron-willed" Mark Baker, unrelenting Calvinist as he was, must often in spite of himself have called her blessed. She had a way of softening the rigours of his faith without hurting him, and, with a fine heresy in the presence of which the voice of protest was often stopped, "dwelling on the all embracing love of God" in an age committed to the "horrible decree" of predestination, as John Calvin rightly called his own tenet.

All his long life Mark Baker was a veritable Boanerges in matters of religion. Instant and effective in argument, he found the task of convinc-

[1] Adam Dickey: Memoirs of Mary Baker Eddy, pp. 133-4.
[2] Retrospection and Introspection, p. 5.

14

ing a waverer or confronting a backslider particularly congenial to him, while he gloried in the sternness of his faith and in its demands for scrupulous obedience. "My father's relentless theology", Mrs. Eddy wrote of him many years afterwards, "emphasized belief in a final judgement day, in the danger of endless punishment, and in a Jehovah merciless towards unbelievers."[1] But if Mark Baker was a true Baker, Abigail Ambrose was a true Ambrose. If the church militant was most in evidence in Mark, the "earnest of things hoped for" was the prevailing spirit of Abigail. If Mark was wont to get up and out and shake the dust from off his feet, Abigail was wont simply to stand, for she could not otherwise— "so help me God".

It might seem at first difficult if not impossible to fashion from such stuff a home characterized by "the open hand", and at which "the needy were always welcome", and pervaded by a love long remembered by its children. Abigail Baker did it, but the adjustment demanded in the coming together of these two heritages was tremendous, only exceeded in difficulty by the task of making the adjustment in the soul of a single individual.

That adjustment, the little girl who had been named Mary was destined to undertake and carry through with portentous effect.

As we have seen, she was the youngest of six children. Three brothers, Samuel, Albert, and George Sullivan, and two sisters, Abigail and Martha, awaited her in the farmstead at Bow. The three boys at any rate and possibly Abigail were old enough to take note of it all and to receive the new sister with that eager interest and competition in affection which in large families seems only to increase with each new arrival. If the little girl was to be spoiled she was destined to it. From the first she seems to have been regarded as a much-prized possession by all the family, but especially by the old grandmother, who had named her Mary.

Grandmother Baker was a typical New England grandmother. If Abigail was the mother of her children, Grandmother Baker was the Mother Emeritus, and the same gracious spirit which gave her the naming of the youngest child consigned that child specially to her care. It was

[1] Retrospection and Introspection, p. 13.

Grandmother Baker who rocked Mary's cradle in those first few months as she sat by the open window, and it was Grandmother Baker who, later on, took the child on her lap, and told her wonderful stories of her people, about the Indian wars and other wars, of the mighty deeds of mysterious ancestors who far away, and longer ago still, had done things worthy of remembrance.

Like all families that have wandered far from their homelands, the Bakers were full of traditions, some of them well founded, others not so well. In her book, *Retrospection and Introspection,* Mrs. Eddy recalls how among her earliest recollections was a great sword in a brass scabbard which her grandmother told her had been given to one of her ancestors by Sir William Wallace. It lay in an old chest in the garret at Bow, along with some worn leather-bound books and papers yellow with age, relics from the Moor household, which Marion Moor McNeil had brought with her, many years before, when she was married to Joseph Baker.

Grandmother Baker had many other tales to tell Mary. She showed her the old newspapers which Mrs. Eddy, with all the vividness of a childhood memory, recalls, contained, among other things, stories of Valley Forge, of the surrender of Lord Cornwallis, of Washington's farewell to his troops, and most vividly remembered of all, "a full account of the death and burial of George Washington".

Among the papers in the chest were "certain manuscripts containing Scriptural sonnets, besides other verses and enigmas which my grandmother said were written by my great-grandmother".[1] It was the cherished conviction of Grandmother Baker that Hannah More was in some way among her forebears, but, inasmuch as Hannah More lived and died a spinster, this was clearly one of the traditions not so well founded. But there had been no doubt in the mind of the little Mary Baker. That her grandmother told her so was enough. There was, moreover, the poetry in her great-grandmother's own writing to prove it.

No portrait or description of Mary as a little girl remains, but from descriptions of her in young womanhood and some incidents in her childhood it is not imagining too much to picture her as a child of more than

[1] Retrospection and Introspection, p. 1.

ordinary beauty, with large blue-gray eyes, a singularly clear skin—she never lost that—and an abundance of curly chestnut hair. She was a happy, eager child, one who gave the impression at all times of listening with all her ears, and her family early came to learn that no conversation was really over her head. She did not always get things right, but, right or wrong, she always got something, and she had a way of putting fragmentary sayings and vivid expressions to strange and unexpected uses.

Like most children she loved long words—she loved them all her life—but as a child it was specially noticeable, and she sometimes brought them out with telling effect. One instance, which is traditional, is worth recalling. Mark Baker, as has been seen, was a great man in a dispute. At no time was he more in his element than when elucidating some matter of "strange doctrine" or preparing with the help of "Priest" Burnham from across the river to administer a "seemly rebuke" to some recalcitrant church member. Priest Burnham was a man after Mark's own heart. Like Sarah Battle in Lamb's famous essay on Whist, he really enjoyed "the rigour of the game". It would almost seem that he must have felt grateful to backsliders for the satisfaction their summary confounding brought to him. Mark Baker felt very much the same. The very word backslider would at any time galvanize him into satisfying action. And so whenever Priest Burnham crossed the river and drove up the hill from Pembroke to the Baker farmstead, he was sure of a welcome. There were other disputes of an entirely secular nature which Mark Baker was called upon to settle. He was known as a man who loved an argument too much not to see fair play, and he set his face sternly against bad language and against any display of heat calculated to impair the satisfying unfoldment of the theme.

Mary was often the silent observer and auditor of these battles of words. Her sisters, Abigail and Martha, or the boys, would probably not have been admitted to the parlour where they took place, but Mary was still so small that she was overlooked. And so it happened on one occasion, when a more than usually heated argument was under way between two farmers who had brought their case to Mark Baker for arbitration, that one of the disputants raised his voice beyond the point at which Mark usually intervened with some restraining order. On this occasion he did not intervene, and Mary from her corner became alert and anxious. At last she could bear it no longer, and in a sudden lull remarked quietly but firmly, "Mr. Bartlett, why do you articulate so vociferously?"

There was silence for a moment, and then everyone burst out laughing, and it was not long before the matter was settled and all concerned were discussing good humouredly the child's quaint speech. It passed into a "family saying", and years afterwards whenever discussion ran too high the spell could at once be broken by some reference to Mary's quiet rebuke.

It was not, however, only in the matter of quaint speeches that Mary began to stand out in the family circle. She had queer ideas about animals. Incidents that the rest of the farm household took inevitably as a matter of course, occasioned her deep concern—whether the horses were too cold in the snow, or the hens were warm enough at night, or the ducks distressed because the pond was frozen. Grandmother Baker did her best to comfort the little girl, assuring her that God "cared for all his creatures", but Mary was never quite assured, and one chill evening in November, her brother Albert found her singing softly to the pigs at the other side of the pasture wall because she felt sure they were lonely.

Abigail Baker, it is to be imagined, must often have wondered—as she recalled her talks with Sarah Gault—at these traits of difference in her youngest child. None of her other children had made problems of such matters as lonely pigs, inadequately warmed horses, or ducks barred from the enjoyment of their natural element by the forces of nature. Yet to Mary they were quite obviously real problems.

Such fancies are not uncommon with sensitive children, and it is doubtful if they would have been even remembered if it had not been for another development which brought no little perplexity to Grandmother Baker and Abigail, and deep concern to Mark. "Mary's Sayings" had always amused him, even as they often puzzled him, but the story he was to hear now from Abigail about Mary's hearing a voice calling her seems to have filled him with a doubt which bordered on fear. To the solid, intensely concrete mind of Mark Baker, in spite of the fact that he accepted the story of Samuel in its entirety, there could be nothing but "something wrong", when told of Mary's "voices".

Whatever the actual explanation may be, the account of the matter given by Mrs. Eddy herself in her book, *Retrospection and Introspection*,[1] is her honest recollection of the matter, undoubtedly.

Whether Mrs. Eddy in childhood heard the voice of God by audible sound, in any literal sense, is surely irrelevant to the question of her own personal integrity and irrelevant to the larger question of whether she was divinely ordained to be mankind's saviour in this age. But it is interesting enough to warrant some consideration here. Surely with all the marvels which tax our credulity anew each day, only the reckless or the incorrigibly ignorant would deny the possibility of such supernormal occurrences as Mrs. Eddy describes from her childhood, although conservatism would prompt the average reader to a few reservations. Fairness demands that allowance be made for the inevitable infusion of biblical concepts and comparisons by this narrator of pious bent.

"Many peculiar circumstances and events," Mrs. Eddy writes in later years, "connected with my childhood throng the chambers of memory." Then she goes on to recall having heard a voice during her eighth year calling her repeatedly, and of having gone to her mother only to be told that no one had called. She recites that her cousin, Mehitable Huntoon, overheard the voice on one occasion and that her mother was troubled by their account of the strange phenomenon. Steeped as she was in scriptural lore, it is not surprising that the then little Mary and the later Mrs. Eddy sought an explanation in the story of the voice of the Lord coming to Samuel. The sincerity of this colourful account cannot be questioned, but many will challenge the reliability of human recollection in such things. Psychologists insist that everyone is subject to paramnesia, the unintentional falsification of memory, and few are likely to concede Mrs. Eddy to be the world's sole exception to this universal tendency. For those who cherish the prophet version, the voice will come three times and will thus

---

[1] Retrospection and Introspection, pp. 8-9.

foreshadow sainthood. We need not take sides—in this question of no fundamental consequence—in considering the words of one who has proved herself a truly great leader. We can plumb the depths of her undeniable genius and marvel at her spectacular achievements without hanging her on a tradition which can do no less than discredit her and her work in the eyes of a skeptical age.

But what about Mark Baker? Accepting without question the full teaching of Calvin as to God and Heaven and Hell, he nevertheless was overwhelmed at such an outrage on probability as Mary's voices. Brushing aside impatiently Abigail's less material explanation, he declared that the child's brain was too big for her body, that she must drop all her books, have done with questionings which caused him so much vague uneasiness, and go out into the fields and romp and play like other girls and boys.

And so the child went out, not at all averse, but her questionings went with her. Already, for Mary, the world was not the simple place it was for her sisters, Abigail and Martha, and the boys.

One of the boys, however, seems to have understood Mary better than the others. Albert Baker was eleven years old when she was born, and from the first seems to have held his little sister in special regard. Her questionings evidently did not disturb him as they did his father, and as the years passed and the little boy of eleven had come to be a big boy in his teens and the little girl was rising eight or nine, there began to develop between the two a relationship of rare sympathy and understanding. About the time that Mary was listening in scared silence for her "voices" or slipping out of the kitchen door in the gathering darkness to sing to the lonely pigs, Albert was preparing to enter Dartmouth. All the Bakers were well taught, sufficiently well taught, as Mrs. Eddy herself has recorded, to teach school "acceptably at various times,"[1] but Albert quite evidently from his subsequent history was more than ordinarily a student and a thinker. Along with his brothers, and later on with his sisters, Abigail and Martha, he attended the common school nearby, but whereas the brothers went no further, Albert moved on to the Pembroke Academy and thence to Dartmouth.

[1] Miscellany, p. 310.

Mary was an eager repository for Albert's learning. How early the two began that "discursive talking", which Albert alludes to in a later letter, it is not possible to say, but if the boy is, as he clearly was, father to the man, the future lawyer and congressman-elect, Albert Baker, friend and law partner of Franklin Pierce, was ready to share what he knew with an audience always ready to ask questions. And so with the old grandmother's valiant stories and the mother's simple faith, and Albert's unfolding record, "new every morning," and her own forever questions, the little girl had much to do and many things to straighten out.

One thing especially began to trouble her about now, the question of religion, she later writes. From the first moment that she was able to apprehend anything of the matter, Mary seems to have taken her religion seriously. Hers was a serious day and religion was the most serious topic in most households of that day. But as a small child her approach to it was not at all the accustomed one. The unquestioning acceptance of a tutored attitude not only did not commend itself to her, but never seems to have occurred to her as anything like what should be required. She devoted herself obediently to the task of learning the Westminster Catechism, and actually could say it by heart before she was ten. She went to church and Sabbath school and sat or knelt with due devotion through the prayers and Bible reading with which Mark Baker exercised himself and his household, morning and evening. But such fulfilling of all righteousness was not at all enough for her. To her brothers and sisters, and even to Mark himself, the due fulfilment of such obligations constituted the essential part of their religious life. To Mary they were only incidents. As far as the Bible was concerned, she not only listened dutifully to what was demanded of her, but she was actually found studying it at all times with absorbed interest. This, combined with the fact that while she was willing and eager to believe in the love of God, she did not seem to be at all reconcilable to the wrath of God, caused Mark no little misgiving. The wrath of God was, of course, his great standby. The love of God was well in its way, but the wrath of God was the real thing, and Mary's apparent conviction that the care, which she was convinced from

21

her grandmother, God bestowed on lonely pigs and cold horses, must be extended to all men regardless of sect, Mark Baker viewed with increasing disquiet.

Already, as he saw it, he had had more than his share of trouble with his children in this matter of religious conviction or lack of it. Up to the time that he began to be concerned about Mary, none of them had made any formal profession of faith, and Mark was not only greatly troubled but completely at a loss to understand what it could mean. To him religion was essentially a grand thing, a mighty exercise, an exulting and exalting conflict, with enemies worthy of his weapons. He could not understand any man worth the name not being eager to throw his hat in the ring and go to it. With backsliders to be found in every community and grand differences of doctrine constantly arising, any failure to take advantage of such opportunities was to Mark Baker simply incomprehensible.

It was not that his children, but especially his sons, were in any sense of the word irreligious or even lax in the meeting of their religious obligations. On the contrary, they all seem to have been even scrupulous in doing so. Only they had never "found religion" in the almost unctuous fullness of that term, as Mark had done.

Mary had always been his hope. True, her exceptional devotion occasioned him some uneasiness. The stories Abigail told him, from time to time, of long Bible readings, of prayers carefully written out and composed, of brave determinations on the part of his small daughter to emulate her hero Daniel, and pray seven times daily with her face towards the east, all this was not as it should be. Abigail does not seem to have been troubled by it. Neither, it is to be imagined, would Mark have been had it not been for Mary's growing tendency towards restless inattention, if not open dissent, whenever, in their discussion of religious matters, he touched upon the subject dearest to his own heart, the great doctrine of "unconditional election". Predestination, endless punishment, inexorable decrees. Many a time, no doubt, had he and Priest Burnham rejoiced over them together. Mary obviously shrank from them. Naturally joy loving and light hearted, as one contemporary has described her, she seems to have rebounded from the grave and distressful view of things, as Mark would have them, with a most unseemly ease. There was nothing morbid in her childish devotions. No doubt she shared in the "luscious gloom" of the period, and could sigh with the best of them over "withered joys" and "perished hopes", over graveyards and upturned sods and what not. But when faced with a real issue such as her father was propounding to her so vigorously, she came out every time quite emphatically on the side of the cared-for animals, rather than that of the eternal punishment of unbelievers. It was clearly her father's duty to do something about it.

Mary was in her twelfth year when they finally came to grips. Mark was satisfied that it was about time that she made a formal profession of faith, and, after the fashion of those days, he felt that it was laid upon him to prepare her for the exercise and to see to it that she was "sound in doctrine and of good understanding".

This brought the matter, the whole question of predestination and the "horrible decree" of endless punishment, right out into the open between the two. Mark quickly found his worst fears confirmed. To his utter perplexity, he discovered that the doctrines that filled him with such exaltation, aroused in his daughter nothing but dissent. She was unwilling to be saved, if her brothers and sisters were to be doomed to perpetual banishment from God.

Nothing that Mark Baker could say or do would change her. He spoke of the final judgement day, of the dangers of endless punishment, and of a God utterly merciless towards unbelievers. Mary stood her ground.

But she sank physically under the struggle. She could not sleep at night, and grew worried and anxious. Whether Abigail actually intervened at this point, it is not possible to say, but that something happened to awaken Mark to a sense of what he was doing, is certain. For the next time we see him, he is rushing from the house towards the stable, hitching a horse to the wagon, and driving recklessly down the hill towards Pembroke to fetch the doctor. The story seems to be well founded that someway down the road he met a neighbour, who hailed him with concern, asking him where he was going in such a hurry. But all he got for an answer, as Mark urged his horse to greater efforts, was the agonized shout, "Mary is dying."

But Mary was not dying. And although the old doctor, who knew Mark Baker, declared she had a fever, and must be kept quiet, he made it clear to a much chastened and sobered Mark that there must be an end to his great missionary work. The old doctor guessed, but it was Abigail Baker who really understood, and in her handling of a difficult situation disclosed a rare sympathy and wisdom. At a moment when a mother's advice to submit or compromise would have been easy to give and obvious, Abigail refrained. She told the child simply that God would guide her and make the way clear for her.

Writing of the incident many years afterwards, Mrs. Eddy says: "My mother, as she bathed my burning temples, bade me lean on God's love, which would give me rest, if I went to Him in prayer, as I was wont to do, seeking His guidance. I prayed; and a soft glow of ineffable joy came over me. The fever was gone, and I rose and dressed myself, in a normal condition of health."[1]

And then she goes on to relate how from that moment the horrible decree of predestination, the dread of the day of judgement, and of a God "merciless towards unbelievers," "forever lost its power."

But the small heretic had to go through one more ordeal before she could reckon herself to have won her first great battle for freedom. She loved her church and was not at all averse from her father's wish that she should become more closely united with it. But not at the expense of her convictions. How the gap was finally bridged is best told in her own words. Writing of her examination before the church members, she says:

"The pastor was an old-school expounder of the strictest Presbyterian doctrines. He was apparently as eager to have unbelievers in these dogmas lost, as he was to have elect believers converted and rescued from perdition; for both salvation and condemnation depended, according to his views, upon the good pleasure of infinite Love. However, I was ready for his doleful questions, which I answered without a tremor, declaring that

[1] Retrospection and Introspection, p. 13

24

never could I unite with the church, if assent to this doctrine was essential thereto."[1]

She then goes on to relate what followed, how she stoutly maintained that she was willing to trust God and take her chance of spiritual safety with her brothers and sisters, not one of whom had taken the step she was taking, even if her creedal doubts left her outside the doors.

Nonplussed for a moment, the pastor tried another way; he asked her to tell him when she had experienced "a change of heart", to which the child could only tearfully reply that she could not remember any precise time. The pastor, however, insisted that she *had* been truly regenerated, and begged her to say how she felt when the light dawned upon her.

"I replied", Mrs. Eddy has written, "that I could only answer him in the words of the Psalmist: "Search me, O God, and know my heart: try me, and know my thoughts: and see if there be any wicked way in me, and lead me in the way everlasting."[2]

This was so earnestly said, so the story continues, that even the oldest church members wept. After the meeting was over, they came and kissed her, while to the astonishment of many, the old pastor relented and received the little girl into communion and her protest along with her.

So was the first victory won, and it is perhaps significant that it was won without compromise and without bitterness, with "satisfaction and tears of gratitude", achieved no one knew how, as the final outcome.

[1] Ibid., p. 14.
[2] Ibid. p. 14.

Growing Up

"WHEN I HAD finished my business, passing from Stoddard through Hillsborough, I called at a log-hut, and after a few words, asked the farmer how he lived? As other farmers. Where do you get your meat? In yonder brooks. Where your meal? At Lichfield. I asked him if he would sell. He replied that he would. I told him to go along with me to a Justice of the Peace, and I would purchase his farm, which was about fifty acres. After the deed was executed I continued my journey to Chelmsford, and the spring following, 1786, in company with a soldier, my companion in the Army, I came to Hillsborough, and took up my residence in the log-hut I had lately purchased. Here I commenced cutting and clearing away the trees, lying on a blanket with my companion, and living as best we could."[1]

So does General Benjamin Pierce, veteran of the Revolutionary War, and an old friend of the Bakers, record in his quaint autobiography the founding of the family fortunes in New Hampshire. At the outbreak of

[1] From an autobiography of General Pierce preserved among the papers of Albert Baker now in the possession of the Longyear Foundation. The paper carried the title: *Being an account of the life and adventures of General Benjamin Pierce in his own words such as was oft told to his son Franklin in his earliest years.*

the war of revolution, he was working on his uncle's farm at Chelmsford, a little town not far from Concord, Massachusetts, and on the historic day of April 19, 1775, when the British marched out of Boston to take possession of the stores and arms at Concord, the news reached young Pierce as he was ploughing in the field. "The British", shouted a passing horseman, "have fired on the Americans at Lexington and killed eight men."

Like so many others, young Benjamin did not hesitate a moment. "I stepped between the cattle," he writes, "dropped the chains from the plough, and without any further ceremony, shouldered my uncle's fowling-piece, swung the bullet-pouch and powder-horn, and hastened to the place where the first blood had been spilled. . . . Next morning, I enlisted in Captain John Ford's Company, which was stationed at Cambridge."

The end of the war found him covered with honour, but "destitute of money", so when he was solicited by one Colonel Stoddard to explore lands which he, Colonel Stoddard, owned in New Hampshire, he accepted gladly and went on his journey. It was on his way back from this expedition that he made the quick purchase just mentioned of a log hut and fifty acres of land at Hillsborough.

In this same log hut, some twenty years later in 1804, Franklin Pierce, the future President of the United States, and life-long friend of Albert Baker, was born.

At that time Benjamin Pierce was coming to be a man of consequence, not only in his little community but in the state. In the year Franklin was born, the log hut was exchanged for a "new and elegant home" in Hillsborough Lower Village, and Benjamin Pierce began to take a vigorous part in State and National politics. His education had amounted to very little—what he could gather before he entered the Army "by attending school from the age of ten to sixteen years, three weeks in each year"—but he was a man of rugged forceful personality, wise and generous. If his long years of soldiering had made him somewhat domineering, he was quick to see his own limitations and to acclaim the virtues of his fellows. Known throughout the countryside as Squire Pierce, he was a "squire" in every sense of the term, as it had come to be used in New England.

At the time when Mark Baker was beginning to wrestle with the religious problems of his youngest child, Benjamin Pierce, now a General —he had taken an active part in the War of 1812—was Governor of New Hampshire, and when attending to his duties at Concord he would often ride over of an evening to see Mark Baker at Bow.

Bow was just a pleasant ride from Concord, and although there were in those days no telephones to escape from, Governor Pierce evidently found the Baker home at Bow a welcome retreat from official duties, and Mark Baker a congenial companion. Even after he had retired finally into private life, as he did in 1830, the General would often on occasion drive over from Hillsborough "along the winding Contoocook river" to visit his old friend.

The two had much in common. Indeed it is to be imagined that after Priest Burnham, there was no one Squire Baker loved to talk with more than Squire Pierce. The old General may not and probably did not share Mark's militant strength in religious matters, but when it came to denouncing a Federalist or maintaining the principle of States' Rights, the two veterans went along together without a hitch.

Mary seems to have been particularly interested in these visits, not only because "grown up conversation" always had a fascination for her as a child, but no doubt chiefly because, sooner or later, in the course of the visit, she would be sure to hear something about her much-loved brother, Albert, then—about 1832—at Dartmouth, and about the General's son, Franklin. Albert had been a guest several times at the Pierces, and between him and Franklin Pierce, just then establishing himself as a lawyer at Hillsborough, there early existed a very real bond of sympathy. Franklin was six years older than Albert, just about the right disparity in age to produce devotion on one side and lively interest on the other, and there can be no doubt that when Albert returned home at vacation time he brought back with him glowing tales of his friend and of the household at Hillsborough.

Mary, of course, would be all ears. The Pierce family—five boys and three girls—was, as a whole, some five or six years ahead of the Baker family. The youngest child was nine years old when Mary was born. To a little girl of twelve or thirteen they represented attainment in the fullest sense of the word, and Albert, so definitely on his way as to be at Dartmouth, gained much reflected glory to Mary's mind in having Franklin for a friend.

Almost from the first, Mary's education seems to have presented a problem. At the usual age, she began to go with her brothers and sisters to the little country school at the cross roads close by. But whereas Abigail and Martha thought nothing of it, taking everything as a matter of course, the long trudge down the hill and the long climb back again, the noise of the school sessions, and the still greater noise of the play hours, Mary seemed to wilt under it. So much so that on the advice of the old family doctor, Nathaniel Ladd of Pembroke, she was ultimately kept at home most of the time, and depended for education upon what she could learn for herself with the aid of her mother—and Albert.

Albert was her great resort and standby. In those days, Dartmouth, like most other colleges, aimed at giving its students what used to be called in England "a gentleman's education". The specializing of today was unknown, and, before he graduated, the student had to be well grounded in the classics, mathematics, physics, rhetoric, and mental and moral philosophy. The college year was a long one, at any rate for the faculty. Instead of terminating as now in June, it went on into August, an arrangement which enabled students, who needed to do so, to take two or three months off during the winter to "teach in the country schools at home or elsewhere".

To the student who needed to work his way through college or to supplement an insufficient allowance, this was a great boon, and it was probably on such vacations as these that Albert and his small sister studied together, as she has recorded in her book, *Retrospection and Introspection*.

Summing up the matter, she writes: "My father was taught to believe that my brain was too large for my body and so kept me much out of school, but I gained book-knowledge with far less labour than is usually requisite."[1]

And then she goes on to tell how that at the age of ten she was "as familiar with Lindley Murray's *Grammar* as with the Westminster Catechism; and the latter I had to repeat every Sunday." Her favourite studies with Albert, she tells us, were "natural philosophy, logic, and moral science", while she also "received lessons in the ancient tongues, Hebrew, Greek, and Latin".[2]

It seems a formidable order indeed, but, on the other hand, exactly the kind of "education" one would expect an eager child to get from an undergraduate brother whose thought was necessarily entirely occupied with just such studies. It need not be supposed that any of it was very deep or very thorough, but, combined with the Westminster Catechism and the sonorous eighteenth century literature of Lindley Murray's *Grammar*, it helped to lay a sure foundation for that precise style which was to be characteristic of Mrs. Eddy's writing all her life.

Lindley Murray's *Grammar*, if thoroughly studied, as books were studied in those days, read and re-read and read again, was a liberal education in itself, especially when combined with the *English Reader*. Mary had both books, and her original copies, much worn and copiously annotated, are still preserved. They are strangely revealing, for although they were in her possession all her life and might have been annotated at any time, still the character of the handwriting in these notes shows clearly enough the little girl in her teens.

The *English Reader*, first published in America in Alexandria, Virginia, about 1810, is truly grand in its sweep and in the catholicity of its taste. The *Grammar*, which was the standard text book for fifty years throughout England and America, is excellent, but the *Reader* is just grand. In the four hundred or so pages which comprise the two books, Lindley Murray in the seclusion of his Yorkshire home managed to secure a truly remarkable selection of all that is best in eighteenth century literature. Goldsmith, Addison, Pope, Hume, Cowper, Samuel Johnson, to mention only a few at random, have liberal scope, while the Bible,

[1] Retrospection and Introspection, p. 10.
[2] Ibid., p. 10.

especially the Book of Proverbs, and the ancient classics are well represented. With the help of Lindley Murray, the little girl learned that there were such people as Socrates and Sallust, Cicero and Marcus Aurelius, and read a few of the things they said.

Lindley Murray was, moreover, much interested in questions of the day. As a lawyer in New York before he determined to retire and make his home in England, he had been brought in contact with the rising question of slavery. When he reached England he found Wilberforce thundering against the practice in the British colonies, and so into his *Reader* went several articles on the subject, and poems by Cowper and Addison. That was some fifteen years before the Missouri Compromise of 1820, whereby slavery was made a kind of local option in the United States. Fifteen years after the Compromise, with Lloyd Garrison in turn fulminating against slavery in his abolitionist paper, *The Liberator*, in Boston, Mary Baker, in the farmhouse at Bow, was reading her Lindley Murray, marking the verses by Cowper and Addison, carefully studying the articles and evidently being specially impressed with the paragraph which runs: "It may not be improper to remind the young reader, that the anguish of the unhappy negroes on being separated from their country and dearest connections, with the dreadful prospect of perpetual slavery, frequently becomes so exquisite as to produce derangement of mind, and suicide."

The extracts from the Bible, if one is to judge by the markings, were studied with special care. This verse from Proverbs has a mark and a number all its own: "Happy is the man that findeth wisdom. Length of days is in her right hand; and in her left hand riches and honour. Her ways are ways of pleasantness, and all her paths are peace."

And so as the little girl studied with her mother and Albert, Lindley Murray was a great help.

Books, moreover, were only a small part of her means to the desired end. There were the hundred and one things she could read, mark, and learn, every day in the life around her. Very early, she seems to have developed that aptitude for learning from the most unpromising things and circumstances which was so characteristic in her later life.

31

As soon as she could read at all, she read the newspapers. The New Hampshire *Patriot and State Gazette* came regularly to the house, and, in the early thirties of last century, the New Hampshire *Patriot and State Gazette*, like all other papers in America, was full of the great question of slavery and how best it might be dealt with. That she read all about it and much else besides, is perhaps sufficiently attested by the family record that, when her father had settled down to read the family paper at night, she would, on occasion, steal downstairs in her nightgown and inveigle him into letting her read the paper to him. In spite of her occasional difficulty with long words, Mark seems to have suffered her gladly.

In this matter of education, Mark Baker was a typical New Englander of that generation. With the greater part of their own young lives spent amidst wars and rumours of wars, in blazing new trails and clearing new lands, the New Englanders of the Revolutionary period had little time or opportunity for education. Education, however, was part of their heritage. Living in a less troubled period their fathers and mothers had it more than they. And so when more settled times came again, the Mark Bakers and Benjamin Pierces of New England determined that whenever possible and wherever their children were ready to accept it, they should be given a good education. They wanted a good groundwork for all their children, but if any one of them should show any special ability and reveal the possibility of becoming a "scholar", that was the fulfilling of a great desire, and he was afforded every opportunity.

The achievements of Franklin on the one hand and the promise of Albert on the other were a great bond of union between the two fathers, and Mary's quiet insistence that she must learn things "like Mr. Pierce" Mark evidently found hard to gainsay.

It was about this time that an arrangement was come to between the two families, which was to bring them still more closely together. To Mary especially it meant new day dreams for her two heroes.

A case had come up for decision in the Court House at Concord involving the townships of Bow and Loudon, a small town some four or five miles at the other side of the State capital from Bow, concerning a question of pauperism. The case for Loudon was pleaded by young Franklin Pierce; that for Bow by Mark Baker, and Mark Baker won. There is no record as to the rights of either party. It is possible that Loudon had such a bad case that Bow could not have lost, no matter who had conducted the case; but the outcome appealed to the sporting instincts of old General Pierce with a special keenness. He lost no time in driving over to Bow to congratulate his old friend, and to enjoy with him the thought that the young people did not have it all their own way after all.

The story is one that finds a place in many records and shows how the two men seem to have vied with each other in generosity, Squire Pierce maintaining that Squire Baker was the hero, a man who, without benefit of law learning of any kind, could go into open court and win his case against a man specially equipped, as was his son, Franklin. Squire Baker in return dilated upon young Pierce's generosity, telling how he had come up to him after the trial and "swept him a bow", and congratulated him with all his heart. And then, so the story goes, Squire Pierce not to be outdone began to talk about Albert and how full of promise he thought the lad and how they had been glad to welcome him into their home at Hillsborough, and how he would go far, and Mark should get him into politics, and how Franklin, who was a good Democrat, would be glad to show him the way. In fact, after he left college, what Albert should do was to come over to Hillsborough and get to reading law in Franklin's office.

And so it was virtually settled and seems from that time to have been taken for granted by the family at Bow as one of the happy developments that might be looked forward to in the future.

Whether Mary actually overheard the conversation which settled the question, as she did so many, it is not possible to say, but it is evident from her subsequent references to the matter that the plan filled her with deep satisfaction. Her first letters, which began to appear about this time, show how eagerly—if sometimes, a little self-consciously—she welcomes any and every opportunity to learn both for herself and others.

A letter she wrote at this period or a little later to her brother Sullivan makes this clear enough. She thanks a "Dear Brother" for "friendly advice and council" and for "lively interest in my welfare", tells him how much she misses his help and encouragement, chides herself with the reflection that there is "no philosophy in repining", and begs in conclusion that he will "excuse all mistakes".[1]

But it was not only absent brothers—Samuel had by this time gone to Boston to learn the building business and Albert was at Dartmouth—that tempted repining. The burden of ill-health which Mary was to carry through so many weary years began even then to press hard upon her.

What exactly was the nature of this ill-health or its cause is not easy to determine. It was nothing that Doctor Nathaniel Ladd could give a definite name to. At best he could only observe the things and circumstances, especially the circumstances, that seemed to make the child better or worse. Some of it was simple enough. When he found that the rough and tumble of the country school was evidently too much for her, he advised that she be kept at home as much as possible; when he found that Mark was launching one of his grand crusades to rescue a soul from the burning with his small daughter as the objective, he could put his foot down and insist that it stop. But there were other things not so clear, and even Doctor Ladd found it hard to believe that the theoretical sufferings or inconveniences of animals or such abstruse and far-away questions as unconditional election could have a serious effect on the little girl's health. And yet somehow they seemed to be conjoined, to operate as cause and effect.

At first, it was no more than a low fever at times, long restless nights, alternating with radiant joy and complete freedom. Later on, it took physical shape in some form of indigestion, until at the age of about fourteen we find a passage in a letter to her brother Sullivan which indicates clearly enough that the long struggle had begun.

"I must", she writes—the phraseology is typical—"extend the thought of benevolence further than selfishness would permit and only add my health at present is improving slowly and I hope by dieting and being careful to sometime regain it."[2]

[1] Letters of Mary Baker to her brother Sullivan, Sept. 7, 1835.
[2] Ibid.

1532521

The Last Year at Bow

IN THE AUTUMN of 1832, when Mary was in her twelfth year, her eldest brother, Samuel, married Eliza Glover, daughter of John and Nancy Glover of Concord. It was the first wedding in the Baker family of that generation and a great occasion. Friends came to it from far and near. For several years previously, Samuel had been living in Boston, where he was doing well as a builder and contractor, and the fact that he came back to Concord to claim a bride from among his own people made the match a popular one. Among those present at the wedding was the bride's young brother George, just past his majority, and in the merry-making which followed the ceremony he and Mary seem to have been thrown very joyfully together.

George Washington Glover was a happy eager boy who loved to talk and be talked to. He was full of fun and just the type and just the age to appeal to a little girl, who, in spite of all the deeps of a strangely questioning mind, had an almost exuberant capacity for enjoyment. Mary Baker, too, loved to talk. Her mother in a letter written several years later, indicates rather pathetically how much she misses her "chatter"; and in the way of such gatherings the little girl and the big boy became the best of friends. George was going back with his sister and his brother-in-law to Boston to learn the building business, so the wedding feast at Concord was, for him and Mary, a veritable hail and farewell. However, they made such good use of their time, that, when the party finally broke up, George hoisted the laughing curly-headed Mary on his knee and swore that he would be back in five years' time to marry her.

The incident was recalled afterwards when the two actually were married, but for the time being George Glover went away to Boston, and to new adventure. And Mary went back to the farm at Bow to wrestle with herself and her father over the question of unconditional election, to study Lindley Murray's *Grammar* and the *English Reader,* and to acquire through her brother Albert and through her own untrammeled studies a kaleidoscopic mass of general knowledge, to which only the years could give coherence.

The next clear glimpse we get of Mary—and thereafter all is more clear —she is a few months over fourteen. It is a Monday afternoon in September, 1835—September 7, to be exact—and she is writing to her brother Sullivan, who a few months previously had gone to Wethersfield, Connecticut. For some time his health had not been good, and it was evidently thought that a change from the rigours of Bow to the comparatively mild climate of Wethersfield might be helpful. And Mary is writing to him. It is the letter already referred to.

As the letter shows, she is alone in the house. Her father and mother and her sister Martha have gone to attend a funeral, and—but, since it is the first letter preserved out of the many thousands destined to be written by the same hand in the future, perhaps it should be quoted with all its mistakes upon it. Writing from Bow, Mary begins:

"As I have an opportunity of sending you a letter by Mr. Cutchins without putting you to that expense which any intelligence that I could communicate would ill repay I improve it with pleasure."

Then there is the passage already quoted, wherein she thanks Sullivan for his "friendly advice and council", tells him how much she misses him, and reports her own improvement in health and the hope that she would with care "sometime regain it". After rambling through various commonplaces, she quaintly concludes:

36

"Although I did not receive the toothpick I shall take the will for the deed and think much of them for coming from you. Write every opportunity excuse all mistakes as this is the second letter I ever wrote and accept the well wishes of your affectionate sister Mary Baker."

The picture that such a letter conjures up and the story that goes with it are both distinct. Years afterward, from her wide balcony window at Pleasant View, Mrs. Eddy could look down the valley of the Merrimac towards the high lands of her childhood's home at Bow, and in her book, *Retrospection and Introspection*, she wrote of the changes fifty years or more had made, how where once were "broad fields of bending grain waving gracefully in the sunlight, and orchards of apples, peaches, pears, and cherries shone richly in the mellow hues of autumn,—now the lone night-bird cries, the crow caws cautiously, and wandering winds sigh low requiems through dark pine groves." And then filling in the details of the picture, she recalls "green pastures bright with berries, singing brooklets, beautiful wild flowers", and large flocks spreading themselves over rich acres.[1]

So it would have been on this Monday afternoon in September when Mary wrote to Sullivan.

Perhaps the most important part of the letter from the point of view of subsequent events is the reference to the journey of her father and mother to Sanbornton to look at a farm, for within the next six months the family were to move there, and the little town on the Winnepesaukee River was to see some of the most important events in Mary's early life. But for the moment the chief value of the letter is the picture it affords of Mary herself, a queerly bookish, rather wistful little girl, already all too familiar with the handicaps against which she was to struggle through so many years. That the letter is decidedly solemn and sententious in parts, reveals nothing of importance, save that Mary followed the fashion of the day, which demanded pathos in some form, at some point in a letter, as almost a first requisite. No well brought up girl of a hundred years ago could have written to an absent brother at any length, without

[1] Retrospection and Introspection, p. 4.

a reference of some kind to the uncertainties of life, and the wanness of the outlook generally.

There is reason, moreover, to suppose that the letter does not fairly represent Mary as she generally was. Something not accustomed was influencing her. She had remained at home alone when the rest of the family had gone off for the day. True, one purpose of the excursion was not very cheerful, to attend a funeral, but, after the funeral, there was the new farm to be inspected, and the new farm represented to the family at Bow the possible culmination of a change which had evidently been under discussion for some time. The three sons had left home. Mark had prospered and his three daughters, all distinguished for their beauty, were growing up. Bow was small, so small as to be hardly a village. Concord was only four miles away, but four miles was a long way, especially in winter, and it would be easier for everyone to be in a larger community where neighbours were separated by only a few yards instead of a few miles and a "handed tea" or a "reception" did not involve a long cross-country journey. Sanbornton had just the facilities necessary.

In ordinary circumstances, the prospect, one might suppose, would have been especially exciting to a young girl of Mary's age and temperament, but for some reason she was not specially interested, indeed she evidently regarded the proposed move with such scant favour as to prefer remaining at home to taking any active part in its consummation.

There was a reason, of course, for this apathy, and that reason was one Andrew Gault.

Very little is known of Andrew Gault, save that he was the son, or as some authorities maintain, the nephew of that same Sarah Gault, who was Abigail Baker's friend and confidante in the weeks and months before Mary was born. He was six years Mary's senior and, as may be gathered from a letter of Martha Baker's to Mary several years later, he had known Mary all her life. And so, if he was in love with her, as Mary was or thought she was with him, it must have been just about this time that the young man of twenty was beginning to realize that the little girl of short skirts and waving hair was growing up.

As to Mary's feelings, the only testimony, indeed the only record of the incident at all, is to be found in two short poems. But they tell a great deal. The first she wrote and sent to Andrew or perhaps—as was quite commended in those days—gave to him on parting just before the family left Bow. The second she sent to him from Sanbornton. Neither of them is great poetry. In fact they are no better nor no worse than any girl of fourteen or fifteen in those days might have written in the circumstances. There are the same desperate dilemmas in the matter of rhyme and the same fabulous solutions. In the first line of the opening verse she finds it hard "to take a final leave", and the nearest she can go to a rhyme in the third line is "with unaccustomed grief my bosom heaves". The problem she had to solve was a difficult one and the solution was not perfect, but one can think of many worse, and Andrew, it may be ventured, thought the whole thing just perfect. A vernal feeling thrills her "very breast," and clasped hands linger fondly.

> But go—those finer feelings riven
> Which through my bosom shot
> And with thee take this flower of Heaven
> The flower forget-me-not.

And so Andrew got his forget-me-not and his good-bye, and one day, soon afterwards, he saw Mary drive down the hill from Bow and out of his life. For so it really was. No doubt his thoughts followed her with many vows as he watched the wagon disappear round the bend towards Concord, and equally no doubt Mary was firm in her constancy. In the poem she sent him soon after they had settled in their new home at Sanbornton, there is no doubt as to where her heart is, or as to where she thinks it is. It is in Bow with its "running brooks" so restful to the soul wearied with "studying worn-out books". There it was she had lost her heart, and there, too, had she learned the sad truth, "We live, we love, we part."

Andrew, no doubt, received the poem with tears—it was the only way in those days he could have received it. And Mary, no doubt, meant every word of it. But although they may have seen each other occasionally in the years which followed, they drifted quietly and happily apart. He married and Mary married, and the curtain never rose again on the old scenes.

Sanbornton Bridge

"THEY REMEMBER MARY BAKER as a most interesting and beautiful child, dainty and fragile. . . . As a young woman she was slim, alert and graceful. Of medium height, she had a well-formed figure. Her feet and hands were exquisitely fashioned. Her features were regular and refined—a delicately aquiline nose, a rather long and pointed chin, a firm mouth and a high broad forehead. But her most striking beauty lay in her big grey eyes, deep set and overhung by dark lashes."[1]

Some thirty years or more ago, seeking data for a series of articles on Mrs. Eddy which subsequently appeared in *McClure's Magazine,* Georgine Milmine, a New York newspaper woman, journeyed to New Hampshire and succeeded in finding quite a number of people who remembered Mary Baker as a young woman and had "heard speak" of her as a child. The foregoing description is from the record of what she found. It fits in very well with what little can be learned or inferred from early letters and other sources.

She was a beautiful child and a beautiful woman. Indeed, all the Bakers were remarkable for their good looks. There is no early picture of Mary, as there is no picture at all of her mother, but one that is preserved

[1] "Mary Baker G. Eddy": Georgine Milmine, *McClure's Magazine,* vol. xxviii, p. 235.

of her eldest sister Abigail shows a woman of statuesque beauty and grace, while her father, as is seen from a picture taken in middle life, was tall and erect, with high brow and clear piercing eyes.

Mary always seems to have had the knack of dressing well. In practically every account that has been given of her this fact is recorded, together with some comment expressing wonder as to how, in an out of the way place like Bow or even in Sanbornton, she could have kept abreast as she did with the fashions of the day. In Sanbornton some thirty or forty years ago, it seems still to have been a matter of lively recollection how Mary Baker, Mark Baker's youngest girl, introduced to the little town the "French Twist", evidently a form of hairdressing which, in those days, was the last word.

Sanbornton, or more correctly, Sanbornton Bridge—the Tilton of today—was in the middle decades of last century a thriving little mill town with woollen mills, grist mills and cotton mills straggling up and down the Winnepesaukee River. The first settler was one Nathaniel Tilton, who came there in 1768, and, a hundred years later, when the town was incorporated, its name was changed to Tilton in his honour. At the time the Bakers arrived, the Tiltons, descendants of the original Nathaniel, were the most substantial people in town. Alexander Hamilton Tilton was a prosperous mill-owner. The "Tilton Tweed" which he had invented was known everywhere and brought in to him a large and increasing revenue. The fact that within two years of the Bakers' arrival Alexander Tilton married Abigail Baker, Mary's eldest sister, would seem to show that from the first the two families were thrown much together and that the Baker girls would have, in the way of social intercourse, all that Sanbornton had to offer.

And Sanbornton apparently could do very well. It was no more than a small town but, after Bow, it must have seemed to Mary and her sisters a veritable whirl of social life. For Sanbornton did not depend only upon itself. All round about, wherever there was a stream with a good volume of water and a suitable fall, a dam had been laid and a mill had been built and a little settlement had sprung up, and Sanbornton Bridge visited friends in Sanbornton Square or Franklin Falls or Tin Corner or

42

the Chapel and vice versa. The "Bridge", as it was generally called, had a fine wide street lined with shade trees and flanked by white houses with green shutters. It had a large church with a typical Bullfinch Steeple, while, away above the town on Academy Hill, was Sanbornton Academy whose hundred or more students, boys and girls, formed a social centre in itself.

To Mary it meant a new world. There is, it is true, the backward glance to Bow and Andrew already noted, but it is not long before Mary is writing to Sullivan of the various parties and weddings and excursions and what not, in which she and her sisters are taking part, and of the many new people she is meeting and the new friends she is making. In all, she expresses a natural and wholesome attitude in such typical tid-bits as this:

" . . . I will give you an abridged sketch of a gentleman recently from Boston, now reading medicine with a doctor in this town, a perfect complet gentleman, I met him a number of times at parties last winter. He invited me to go to the Shakers with him but my superiors thought it would be a profanation of the Sabbath, and I accordingly did not go."[1] And so it goes.

Then there is the tremendous event of Abigail's wedding. It was to be a great affair, a real June wedding with all the friends of both families gathered together. But, as was only proper one hundred years ago, Mary, in writing about it to her brother Sullivan, had to express some due feeling of regret, if not actual sorrow, at the approaching separation. "She will be lost to us irrevocably, *that* is *certain*," she writes. And then, as if reluctant to surrender the luxury too quickly, she adds: "How changed is one short year. Dear brother can you realize it with me? If so take a retrospect view of home, see the remaining family placed round the blazing ingle scarcely able to form a semicircle from the loss of its numbers."[2] However, it is not long before she is herself again, quoting Burns and begging Sullivan to come and see them before long, when she promises not to be as sleepy as she and Abi were the last time.

[1] Mary to Sullivan, April 17, 1837.
[2] Ibid.

43

And now letters from Albert begin to appear. He is in practice at Hillsborough, and, with Franklin Pierce more and more preoccupied with politics, he is very busy, too busy in fact, for it is clear from his letters that he has already embarked upon that reckless spending of his energies which brought an untimely end to a more than ordinarily promising career some four years later.

The relationships which existed between Mary and Albert, and Mary and Sullivan present an interesting contrast. Sullivan was her gossip. She wrote to him about the little day to day happenings and knew he would be interested. But Albert was evidently reserved for more serious questions. Thus on one occasion the two sisters, Abigail and Mary, had evidently been the objects of some kind of village talk and Abigail had written to Albert about it, and then, before he could reply, had written again to say that the matter had been cleared up. And so Albert writes to Mary to tell her how glad he is. "You cannot be too careful or too sensitive," he adds, "to any breath of slander; though you need never fear so long as you are innocent. The things always work their own way clear."[1]

It is sound advice, but the letter is chiefly interesting for the light it throws on Albert's outlook at that time. In the spring of 1837, Sanbornton Bridge had been the scene of one of those unbelievably vigorous revivalist missions which were wont periodically to descend on a New England town and sweep all before them. Abigail had evidently mentioned it in her last letter to Albert and so Albert comments on it in this letter to Mary.

"Abi informs me", he writes, "that there has lately been a *protracted meeting* at Sanbornton, and that you cherished a hope, that you had been brought to embrace the doctrines of that religion, the strange influences of which have thus far puzzled philosophy to solve." Albert says he knows Mary will be anxious about how this information will affect him, but says there is no reason for her timidity as he does not wish to discountenance religion. For that matter, "a woman can hardly live without it," he adds naively, and then he strikes a timely warning:

[1] Albert to Mary, March 27, 1837.

44

"One thing, do not allow yourself to be suspected of bigotry or fanaticism. They are as distant from true religion, as from true philosophy—its very antipodes."[1]

In order to appreciate the full significance of such a statement it is necessary to understand in a measure the attitude at that time of the orthodox New England evangelical religionist on this question of "conversion". According to his view, a community was divided into three classes; the definitely converted, the hopefully inclined, and the finally lost. The finally lost were beyond the pale.

As already noted, when Mary was twelve, none of her brothers and sisters had made any definite "profession", and it is evident from this letter that Albert is still very far from doing so and that Mary is still holding out, although wavering. The letter clearly shows that the brother and sister must have talked the matter over many times, and a just inference seems to be that, while Mary steadfastly remained among the hopefully inclined, Albert had gone over to the finally lost. He had no desire, however, that Mary should follow him, and probably less positive now than he was in his Dartmouth days, is even anxious that Mary should feel free, if she should so desire, to cross over the border into the fold of the definitely converted. His only hope is that she retain that freedom from bigotry and fanaticism which the two had evidently agreed was the only fitting attitude on religious questions.

At Dartmouth, Albert had been much interested in Mental and Moral Philosophy. As has been seen, he was an excellent scholar, a member of the Phi Beta Kappa, then as now a very definite gauge of scholarship. He was also a member and at one time vice-president of the United Fraternity, a literary and debating society, whose discussions on such subjects as "Is the evil of underrating our abilities greater than that of overrating them?" and "Have the people the right to instruct their representatives?" attracted wide attention. It is interesting to note that, quite typically, Albert took the affirmative side in the first of the specific subjects mentioned and the negative in the latter. In discussing such questions he was evidently in his element.

[1] Ibid.

45

As his opponent for Congress, the Hon. Isaac Hill wrote of him just after his death in 1841: "He was fond of investigating abstruse and metaphysical principles, and he never forsook them until he had explored their every nook and corner however hidden and remote."

Thus in Albert is seen all the elements which, years afterwards, were to compel his sister Mary into new fields in the realms of religion. He could not accept orthodox faith; but he was convinced that, without that something which religion professed to give, man was "a stranger in a strange land", and so he had the will to explore and the courage to keep on.

Meanwhile, he writes to reassure Mary. If there was any further correspondence on the matter between the two during the year which followed, it has not been preserved. Anyway, in the summer of 1838, Mary took the step she had so long delayed. In that year, under date July 26, was inscribed in the Clerk's Book of Sanbornton Congregational Church, this notice:

"Received into this church, Stephen Grant, Esq., John Cilly and his wife Hannah, Mrs. Susan French, wife of William French, Miss Mary A. M. Baker, by profession, the two former receiving the ordinance of baptism. Greenaugh McQuestion, Scribe."

Mary's letters during this period show that she was passing through a period of stress and doubt and that continued ill-health was beginning to raise questions in her mind, the answer to which was still thirty years or more away. It is, however, almost startling to find in one of her letters—a letter to Sullivan in the spring of 1837—the following passage:

"Martha has been very ill since our return from Concord. I should think her in a confirmed consumption *if I would admit the idea,* but it may not be so, at least I hope not."

The italics are Mary's and, in view of the fact that this thought was to appear some thirty or forty years later as a fundamental mental attitude in the practice of Christian Science, the statement is interesting and significant enough.

However, it was not all sickness or religious questionings with Mary in those days. She was living the life of a normal girl of her age and time, and in the early summer of 1838, her health evidently much improved, she attended Holmes Academy at Plymouth and set about the work of learning, with that eager vigour which characterized her all too few opportunities for regular study. Mary was now seventeen and for a brief time was able to be a typical school girl of that age. She made friends easily, inspired "devotion", and returned it wholeheartedly, and although, as was then only proper, it was always "Miss Burnham" or Miss Howard or Miss Shedd or Miss Sutherland in her letters, such studied restraint had no concord with the normal abandon of her attachments. It was at Holmes Academy that she met Augusta Holmes, daughter of Nathaniel Holmes, a prominent mill owner of Sanbornton. The two girls were attracted to each other from the first, and the correspondence which passed between them after Augusta left Sanbornton and went to live with her family at Haverhill is refreshing for the way it runs true to form. At Sanbornton the two were devoted to each other with a passion which only school girls of seventeen or eighteen can compass. Mary is Augusta's "Little Spouse" and Augusta is Mary's "Husband", and a younger girl—who appears only as "Betsy R."—is their daughter. It lasted as do all such "passions" through a summer day, and when Augusta returned to Haverhill and a certain "Enoch" began to weave his disturbing way in and out of her letters, Mary, after a few doleful expressions of regret, resigns herself plaintively to the inevitable and the relationship moves easily on to more solid ground.[1]

And the ground was solid enough. There is the usual gossip in the letters about parties and people, clothes and what not, but such questions as literature and religion occupy the greater part of them. Mary and Augusta are at the age when they are reading everything in sight and it is a new world. They ask excited questions back and forth in a way suggestive of nothing so much as a slow motion picture of a telephone conversation if such a thing can be conceived. Had Mary read Byron's *Prisoner of Chillon*? No, but she had read *Corsair* and *Winifred*, and did Augusta ever see *Godey's Lady's Book*? And did she possess a copy of Surwalt's grammar, and, if so, would she lend it to her, as she heard

[1] Mary Baker to Augusta Holmes, Jan. 6, 1839.

47

that it was easier than Levizac's, and is she well, and did she get home safely?[1]

Mary's reading about this time was wide enough in its scope. In the scrapbook of her poems which is still preserved are many pages of manuscript devoted to extracts from Shakespeare, Milton, Wordsworth, Scott, Mrs. Hemans, Byron, and so on. Of these, Milton seems to have been her first and most lasting favourite. Literally pages are devoted to transcribing portions of *Paradise Lost*. The main theme of it all is, of course, the joys of solitude, the pathetic beauty of nature and the uncertainty of human life.

Mary, however, was gaining an education in another way, by listening to and talking with other people. All her life she had an extraordinary faculty for doing just this, for hurdling the elements of a new subject and using with assurance information acquired perhaps only a few moments before. In early life, it is safe to say, she uniformly thought and talked beyond her years, and if she sometimes got out of her depth, her very daring had an evocative effect on her auditors.

Thus one of her "teachers" about this time was the Reverend Enoch Corser of Tilton Church. It was Doctor Corser who received her into church membership, and many years afterwards, his son Bartlett recalled the long religious discussions his father had had with Mary Baker, and how much the old Calvinist had admired her.

"Bright, good, and pure, aye brilliant," he declared to Bartlett one day, as they walked back from a visit to the Baker home. "I never before had a pupil with such depth and independence of thought. She has some great future, mark that. She is an intellectual and spiritual genius."

To what extent Bartlett Corser's memory was irradiated by Mrs. Eddy's subsequent attainments, it is impossible to say. But there is evidence enough that Mary was thinking for herself, especially in the realm of religion. She passed through periods when she sought to whip herself into orthodoxy, when the orthodox idea of God as the great Afflictor to the ends of good, seemed the only possible view of the matter, and on one occasion we find her begging Augusta to pray for her, declaring in true

[1] Ibid.

Jonathan Edwards style that she could not but be amazed at God's forbearance towards her.

Indeed, she was getting religion from all sides now, and this, combined with increasing ill-health and the tendency of the period to take a pseudo-pathetic view of life in general, plunged her often into the depths.

She was really ill at times. The rigours of winter, which modern invention has done so much to modify, pressed hardly upon her, and her letters are full of colds and yet more colds, taken for granted as an inevitable accompaniment of the frost and snow of the dark days of the year in New Hampshire. Albert is often sorely anxious about it. In one letter home about this time, he speaks of how saddened he is to hear that Mary's health is again in danger.

"I pray she will be more careful," he adds, "I fear she has exposed herself. Don't breathe these awful frosts. It is enough to break up the health of the stoutest. I have suffered from them of late, but am recovered."

Albert, in fact, at times felt the strain very much. He had never spared himself and his election to the State legislature in 1839 threw upon him a load of work which, in addition to his practice as a lawyer, was at times more than he could carry. He was never very robust. In a letter to his brother George while he was reading law in Boston, under date of April 28, 1837, he tells him how he had just left hospital a day or two previously, and that he had "done nothing since the first of March". Several times in his letters occurs the phrase, "if my health continues," and mention is made, as in the quotation above, of sickness from which he has recovered.

After his election to the legislature, he took a prominent part in the business of the House. He was chairman of the select committee appointed to deal with the ever-present question of slavery and was undeviating in his Democratic devotion to States' Rights. Sympathetic as he undoubtedly was towards the sentiments which advocated Abolition, he favoured the resolutions which rebuked abolitionist agitation, and recommended that Congress should not interfere with the slave trade between any states that desired this trade to continue.

49

He was, moreover, in great demand as a speaker and lecturer, and when his friend Franklin Pierce went to Washington as Senator, the care of his practice, both at Hillsborough and Concord, devolved upon Albert. He is clearly being overworked, and it is not surprising to find him writing in a letter to Mary about this time, "I set out for Boston this morning. I am almost worn out. I have scarcely slept two hours for the last two days."

Like Mary, however, he has periods when his health is "unusually good", and then he forges ahead with redoubled energy. In the three years he was in the legislature he piloted several important reforms through to the State statute book. Among these were the abolition of imprisonment for debt, the revision of the election laws, the protection of graves from molestation, the powers to be conferred on corporations including railroads, whether a town should be allowed to buy stock in a railroad, the holding of courts at convenient times, and so on.

And all the time, Senator Pierce from Washington was writing to his young partner not only about laws but about politics, and it began to be clear that Albert Baker had his feet definitely set on the road to Congress.

It ought to have been a happy and inspiring period for both Albert and Mary, and so to a certain extent it was. Albert "loved to work", as he himself often put it, and as long as he could work even under difficulties his natural buoyancy of spirit asserted itself. In his student days he had written home to his brother Sullivan how that he had sold his college classics "for the round sum of ten dollars", and when that was gone he would sell his shirt. "By the Gods," he added, "I am as rich as a prince. What a glorious thing, this idea of borrowing money and dying insolvent."[1] There is a laugh, of course, in every line of it, and there were many times later on when Albert could get back to where he was then, but the last few years of his life were overshadowed by ill-health.

In this respect the brother and sister undoubtedly reacted unfavourably on each other. They worried over each other's health. His joy is "saddened" many times by the news from home, and his letters show him turning more and more "for help and consolation" to religion. He never seems to have reached the standpoint of the definitely converted, but he

[1] Albert Baker to Sullivan, 1838.

had quite evidently ceased to find any satisfaction in numbering himself among the finally lost. Thus in a letter to Mary during one of her periods of sickness, he says he hopes his sister is enjoying good health, but even if not, she should maintain an attitude of calmness and resignation, since providence is inscrutable. He adds that he sees the hand of God in events good and evil. "God rules, let the earth submit."[1]

That was in 1840. The following year he was nominated to Congress in a district where election was certain, but he died some two weeks before election day, on October 21, 1841.

His death was a cruel shock to his family and friends, but to no one more than to Mary. One rather pitiful little poem in which she expects soon to follow her brother, and wonders whether her friends will miss her or forget her, is the only reference to her sorrow that has been preserved.

[1] Albert Baker to Mary.

51

George Washington Glover

GEORGE WASHINGTON GLOVER, the boy of twenty-one, who had companied so well with the little curly-headed Mary at Samuel Baker's wedding, was curiously enough true to his promise or, at any rate, to a part of it. He did return in five years. But whether he had the courage to ask the radiant young person on the edge of seventeen, whom he found in place of his little playmate of eleven, to marry him and was refused, or whether he did not ask her, because the whole incident had been long since forgotten, as seems most likely, it is not possible to say.

But it was just five years after Samuel's wedding, in 1832, that George was again a guest in the Baker household. The occasion was Abigail's wedding to Alexander Hamilton Tilton, and George came up with Samuel from Boston to attend the ceremony, and join in the great family reunion which marked the occasion.

There is no record of his meeting with Mary at this time, or what they thought of each other, and when he said good-bye to her after the great event was over and the guests were departing, it was to go further afield than ever. After Samuel's wedding he was leaving Concord for Boston; now he was to leave Boston for Charleston, South Carolina.

There is very little in the way of direct record of George Glover, but a clear enough picture of him—more clear than is usually the case—can be had from what there is. The one portrait of him which is preserved shows a young man of about thirty, well groomed in the style of the day, with the inevitable wealth of wavy dark hair, a fine broad brow, long straight nose, and forceful but not overly determined jaw. It is a portrait which seems to fit in very well with what may be gathered of his character from his few letters, or inferred from what he did. That he was vigorous and enterprising, in an age when vigour and enterprise were so essential to success, is clearly shown, if only by the fact that he was ready at twenty-one to leave his native Concord for Boston to seek his fortune, and, not content with that, was eager later on to adventure further afield still, into the almost alien land—to a New Englander—of South Carolina.

It is, however, in his letters, as is so often the case, that George Glover reveals himself most clearly. One written from Concord, while evidently on a flying visit home from Charleston, is specially interesting. It is addressed to Samuel Baker in Boston. Samuel was then a widower, his wife, George's sister, having died some years previously. Dated Concord, April 20, 1841, the letter runs along gaily, in a sort of pseudo-sophistication, with the grown-up salutation, "Friend Baker," and a postscript telltale of a young man just finding himself: "Sir, will you visit the South for a wife—if you do I will present you with a Lady, plantation and ninety negroes." He states he is in the height of prosperity as a contractor, having just undertaken the construction of thirteen houses. Jestingly, he says that if Abi will name her first son for him, "I will give him a negro servant worth a thousand." He extends his "respects" to "all young Lady's now in the market," and asks to be remembered "to your sisters and the rest of the family, Friend Baker."

It is a cheery, swaggering kind of letter, pervaded by that badinage and that atmosphere of hail-fellow-well-met, which, from all that can be learned of him, was the essential George Glover. He loved to talk and meet new people. He was a born promoter in the best sense of the word, one of those men who, starting from nothing, would inevitably have made

53

his fortune in a big way if he had had time. He would build and borrow and buy and sell, and, at each turn, add a little more to his actual capital. He probably always kept at the right side of a forced liquidation, but, no doubt, the margin of safety was often small, and, in order to steer such a business to success, his own personal attention was requisite all the time.

Records in Charleston show that the land on which the thirteen dwelling houses mentioned in this letter were erected was actually conveyed to him. The probabilities would seem to be that the purchase was financed by the sale of something else and that the thirteen dwelling houses, when completed, were in turn sold and the proceeds of the sale immediately reinvested in the purchase of materials to build the cathedral at Haiti which was his great unfinished enterprise at the time of his early death. Only thus can the fact be accounted for that the equity in his estate, when all claims had been met, was comparatively small.

However, his greatest assets were his vigour and enterprise, and these are clearly enough in evidence in his letter. He is "at the heighth of prosperity."

As to Mary, the nearest the letter gets to any mention of her is to ask Samuel to convey his, George's, respects to his sisters. And yet in a curious way, it does shed some light on the course of his courtship, if so it can be called. Among the few papers relating to Glover preserved among Mrs. Eddy's effects, is a "reading" of George's character by a phrenologist of Charleston named William P. Heberd, in the course of which he is described as "naturally cheerful and fond of enterprise, yet too cautious to venture much himself, without he is sure of success." Below this description, in Mrs. Eddy's handwriting, are the words: "in proof thereof Sept. 5—1841."

The presumption seems excusable that George did actually spend the summer, as in his letter he was hoping to do, in the North, with his people at Concord, or even, for a time, at Sanbornton, that the courtship of the two moved slowly forward, as courtships were wont to do in those days in New England, and that when the time came early in September for George to return for the winter to Charleston, he proposed and was accepted; that Mary was willing to risk an immediate marriage, but that George, with a characteristic final caution, wanted to wait until his position was more secure.

Be that as it may, he did return to Charleston with no more than a promise, if that, and a few weeks later, Albert Baker's death had overshadowed all else in Mary's mind.

It was a bitter blow. But the girl is just twenty and, sickness and bereavement notwithstanding, the joy of living and a vital interest in a thousand things struggle eternally out into the open. Everyday life at Sanbornton is quickly resumed. Her friend, Augusta Holmes, now married, not to the disturbing Enoch but to one Samuel Swasey, a rising attorney in Haverhill, New Hampshire, destined one day to become Speaker of the House of Representatives, is Mary's never-failing resort. She writes to her about everything, moving easily if somewhat disconcertingly at times from the most earnest consideration of religion and kindred topics to the latest marriages and the latest engagements and the latest possibilities among their mutual friends at Sanbornton.

In a typical school-girlish letter, she rambles on about Miss L. Howard attending a singing school and a dancing school, about Miss Shedd being engaged, about Caroline Dean getting letters from George Merrill, about Miss Delano hurrying preparations for an early marriage. Of these events she admits she does not know first hand, and then, rather tardily, she concludes that if "everyone would be cautious in reporting flying stories, a great deal less of falsehood would be reported."

Then, in other letters, the two girls bandy names back and forth, as girls have always done. There is a Mr. Noyes who has called on Mary, but "only to be polite", and a Mr. L. who is "incoherent about Diana". Mary asks Augusta to say "something nice" for her to "Mr. Dickey", is more than willing to do what she can towards "making cold hearted man raise his standard of female excellence still higher. But", she adds —and this perhaps may after all be the true explanation of George's return empty handed to Charleston—"as to my being married, I don't begin to think much of that decisive step, neither do I intend to be married at present. I am sure I feel as though I should like my liberty a little while longer."

Long courtships were very much the rule in New England, one hundred years ago. The relationship of an engaged couple always had about it an air of "limited permanence". It was a transitional stage, of course, but one to be traversed slowly and all its amenities explored. There is nothing to show that Mary and George were engaged, but that there was some kind of understanding between them and had been for several years seems most likely. Their actual marriage, when George returned to Charleston in the fall of 1841, was still more than two years away.

In those two years, if the joy of Mary's life sometimes heightens, the depression often deepens. Keenly appreciative of beauty wherever she might find it, she is carried up into the seventh heaven by a trip she made with her brother Sullivan through the White Mountains in the summer of 1842. A little journal she kept shows how much she revelled in it all —"The hue of my feelings are painted on all objects," she writes; and then a little later, showing how inexorably the cloud of ill-health overshadowed her outlook, she adds, "O if I felt well, *then* might I be happy."

She found no little comfort and joy in writing poetry, and her poems found a place in the local newspapers and magazines to an increasing extent. She even got as far as *Godey's Lady's Book*, one of the most popular magazines of the day. None of it is great poetry. Many years afterwards, Mrs. Eddy was to write of herself, "From my childhood I was a verse-maker," and this exactly describes these earlier efforts. Nevertheless, in these poems will every now and again appear a line of no little beauty and power, shadowing forth that vigour of expression which was to appear so emphatically later on in her prose.

Then there is another picture of Mary about this time which has its own charm. It is supplied by a certain Martha Philbrick, who, as a little girl at Sanbornton, was taught by Mary in Sunday School. Writing many years afterwards, Martha Philbrick, then Mrs. Weeks, says: "Then we did not have a question book but I learned a few verses from the Bible, and after repeating them to her, she would explain them to me.

She was very pretty to look at; her cheeks were red, her hair was brown curls, she had beautiful eyes. She wore a crepe moire silk. . . . Her bonnet was white straw and had a pink rose in each side, with her curls she was just lovely."

So, one may be sure, did George Glover find her when at last he felt himself sure enough, and came back to Sanbornton to claim her for his wife.

Mary's wedding was a great occasion. Time had wrought many changes since Samuel was married. Old General Pierce was dead and Grandmother Baker long since, and Albert's death was still a sad memory. The Pierce home at Hillsborough, so long the scene of joyous goings and comings, was closed, and Franklin Pierce, supposedly retired from public life, had removed to Concord, opened spacious offices almost opposite the Court House—they are still there much as he used them—and was devoting himself to building up his practice as a circuit lawyer. Mark Baker, grown older, but still erect and emphatic, more militantly religious than ever, has prospered greatly. Already he is contemplating selling the farm outside the Bridge and acquiring one of the most favoured homes on the main street. Martha has been married to Luther Pillsbury of Concord a year or more, and Abigail, now a mother, is climbing with her husband Hamilton Tilton to new heights of importance. Hamilton is becoming a wealthy man, and Abigail, with that remarkable executive ability which she was later to put to such good purpose, is helping him.

And so Mary's wedding was a great occasion. There were, of course, the usual tears, but in all cases, except perhaps one, they were concessions to the demands of the times. The exception was the first Abigail, Mary's mother. All her life, Mary had meant very much to her, but it was not until after Mary married and left home that the full extent of Abigail's devotion is revealed.

"Dear Child," she writes to her youngest daughter when the two had been separated about six months, "Your memory is dearer to me than gold. Everything reminds me of you. . . . Do you remember our twilight meeting? It is a precious time for me for there I feel like meeting with you and sometimes I fear I worship Mary instead of the great Jehovah."

Such a message is poignant and eloquent enough, and throws a vivid light on the character and personality of the young girl who could inspire such devotion in the heart of a woman as poised and possessed as was Abigail Baker. In an earlier letter full of happy gossip, Abigail presents a picture of the Baker household about this time and especially of Mary which outshines in value many pages of description.

"And now Mary," she writes, "I will visit you in your own room, at your fireside with dear George."

Is Mary happy? Are her anticipations fulfilled? Are her surroundings pleasant? She answers for Mary, "Yes, dear mother, perfectly." Does Mary muse on their doings back home during the cold of the winter? But things are as always. Martha is sewing, Mahala is braiding, father sits reading. But they miss Mary's cheerful presence. "I look out at the window and say how I wish I could see George and Mary coming over the hill."

The Mary that emerges as the result of it all is perhaps clear enough at last. In spite of her sickness and her day by day questionings, cheerful and helpful, one who uniformly made the best of things and had that in her which made her presence at twilight, for her mother—a benediction.

It was deep winter, two weeks before Christmas that they were married, with snow covering the mountains and deepening in the valleys. The company came in pungs[1] and sleighs and on foot from far and near. Dr. Enoch Corser, Mary's special friend and teacher, performed the ceremony, and when it was over and the last good-byes said, George and Mary bundled into a sleigh and took the road along the Winnepesaukee River towards Concord, where the first break in the long journey to far-off Charleston was made.

Next morning, Mary drove round with her young husband for a last look at her old haunts. They drove over to Bow and up to the old farmstead, past the country school and down the hill to Pembroke, and then, later on in the day, took the stage to Boston. From Boston, a few days later, they sailed for Charleston.

As they were leaving Sanbornton, Abigail Baker handed George a

[1] A large sleigh to accommodate a number of people.

little package. It was carefully sealed and marked with the injunction that it was not to be opened until the two were well on their journey.

They had a rough passage, more than usually rough, and Mary was very sick, but, as they sailed south, the storm abated, and so it was that they opened the package together. There was no letter inside, only a little book, a copy of Lydia Sigourney's poems, one of which Abigail had marked. It is in Lydia's best style. The Mrs. Hemans of America, as Lydia Sigourney has been well called, has no counterpart today. She belonged to an age that is past, but it is not difficult to believe that her poem conveyed to George all that Abigail wanted to tell him out of the fullness of her heart.

> A mother yields her gem to thee
>   On the true breast to sparkle rare,
> She places "neath thy household tree"
>   The idol of her fondest care;
> And by trust to be forgiven.
>   When judgement wakes in terror wild
> By all thy treasured hopes of Heaven
>   Deal gently with my darling child.

So runs one of several verses. If the exact meaning is sometimes obscure, its message gains dignity and pathos as coming from Abigail to George.

And so, in due time, the spire of St. Michael's in the Queen City of the South rose up all white and glistening out of the blue sea, and before long the packet was moored to the wharf at Charleston.

Charleston

CHARLESTON, LIKE MANY other cities in the South, divides its history into three periods. "From the earliest times" to the Revolutionary War; from the end of that war to the War of 1812; and from the end of the War of 1812 to the outbreak of the great civil conflict in 1861. After that, for many decades, there is no story.

In the Forties of last century, Charleston had reached the peak of its third and most brilliant period. The South was still the senior partner in the great federation, for although the North was beginning to feel its growing industrial power and was ready to assert it, the real Southerner in the real South never believed for a moment that such assertion would ever amount to anything.

Charleston was the crown jewel of the South. All through her long history of nearly three hundred years she seems to have had a unique facility for surprising her visitors. "Behold the half was not told me," is a common summing up of the matter even today.

Beautiful for situation on a narrow strip of land between the Ashley and the Cooper rivers—really arms of the sea—the town, like New York, runs south and north, a vivid picture at all times, especially in the sunlight, of primitive colour. Blue and green and dazzling white, with a nearer view of endless shipping stretching up to the skyline.

Josiah Quincy, sailing up the Ashley river from Boston in the early Thirties had been much impressed with the beauty of the town as it was approached from the sea, declaring that it was "in many respects magnificent". Later on, of the town itself, he declared that in its buildings, commerce and shipping, "and indeed in everything, it far surpasses all I ever saw or expect to see in America".

In the Eighteen Forties, ships came to Charleston from the ends of the earth, but mostly from the West Indies, and bananas, cocoanuts, coffee bags, cotton bales and bags of rice, especially bags of rice—the staple product of the immediate hinterland—were everywhere. And in and out of it all, through the warp and the weft of the harlequin pattern, is the slave, not at all the despairing, downtrodden person the word conjures up. "The negroes," declared an amazed traveller from the North about this time, "notwithstanding their degraded condition, looked bright and happy."

In the matter of slaves, as in almost everything else, the Charleston of the Eighteen Forties was at its best. Abolitionism, as urged in Boston, reached the Carolinas as a disturbing echo, but it is doubtful if the sound of it ever reached the stable or the kitchen or the field with any very telling effect. "The institution of the South" was working with ever greater smoothness. Slaves were well cared for and, especially with the wealthy planters or merchants, each generation had found the family bond connecting master and servant stronger and less galling. The slaves, particularly the house servants, the grooms and the inevitable jockeys, took a tremendous pride in their "famblies", while as to the "famblies", "my servants next to my children" was the creed of the master and mistress; anything less would have been impossible.

It was a fascinating community, the like of which had never appeared before, or since. Unlike New England, which was largely colonized by yeomen, the Carolinas drew their first settlers from the upper classes.

The Lords Proprietors, who obtained their amazing charter to a new empire from Charles II, reckoned among their numbers Lord Clarendon, the historian; the Duke of Albemarle, who as General Monk had brought back the king—Charles II—from exile "to enjoy his own again"; Sir Anthony Ashley Cooper, Lord Ashley afterwards Earl of Shaftesbury; Lord Craven, Lord Berkeley, Sir George Carteret, Sir John Colleton and Sir William Berkeley, all cavaliers of the most worthy standing; and Charles, with, it is to be imagined, no little relief, took this way of rewarding their services. He was, moreover, as he declares in his patent, more especially moved to do so by reason of the fact that the Lords Proprietors "were incited by a laudable and pious design of propagating the Christian religion".

By their charter from the king, which granted them all the territory now comprised in North and South Carolina and Georgia, with an unlimited western expansion "to the South Seas", whatever that might mean, they were *enjoined* to establish the Church of England but *permitted* to grant liberty of conscience. They might make laws, but only with the consent of the "greater part" of the people—a most unusual provision in those days—and they were required to establish a nobility but not to give its members English titles. The new territory and its people were forever to remain "of His Majesty's allegiance".

The provision as to the founding of a nobility was what gave the Carolinas, and indeed the old South generally, that distinctive quality which at every turn in its history has marked it off abruptly from the foundationally democratic North. For although the new nobility was little more than plutocracy depending upon the amount of land owned by a man, the titles passed by descent as well as by purchase and gave to the holder a standing distinctly above his fellows. The owner of twelve thousand acres was a baron; of twenty-four thousand acres, a cassique; and of forty-eight thousand acres, a landgrave. For some reason, while no one was ever called "baron" or "cassique", the title Landgrave survived, and Landgrave Morton and Landgrave Smith are among the outstanding figures in Charleston history. It might be difficult to define the exact status of this untitled class of landed gentry, but it was perfectly well understood and accepted during the colonial period, survived the Revolution curiously enough with even added distinction, and was perhaps the most influential element in Charleston society down to the Civil War.

The rule of this little oligarchy of rice and cotton planters, in the Eighteen Forties, was undisputed. That was their unquestioned privilege. The large trade of the town was left almost entirely to foreigners. Englishmen and Scotsmen especially came there, engaged in trade and accumulated great wealth, and the landed gentry were content that it should be so, so long as they and their traditions represented Charleston before the world.

The picture presented was an extraordinarily gracious one, at least on the surface. The planters ruled well and generously. They were men of culture and refinement. Most of them had been educated in England. They were travellers, readers, and often scholars, and they had a standard of "honour" so high as to keep the plain man in a state of breathless expectancy. A man's word must be better than his bond because it had no guarantee. A woman's name and a promise however foolish were sacred. If one man wronged another, he must be willing if necessary to give his life in expiation, and he must always be ready to fight for his State or his lady.

It was into this new world, so strange and unaccustomed to the New England concept of almost everything, that George Glover introduced his young wife when they stepped off the packet at Charleston. It was all familiar enough to George. Charleston was famous for its hospitality to strangers, especially strangers from the North if they came well accredited, and George had evidently done well and made good use of his opportunities in the five years he had been there. He had been given an honorary position on the staff of the governor of the State, enjoyed the title of Major and was generally called Colonel. To be sure, colonels in South Carolina were almost as frequently met with as they were in Kentucky; nevertheless, when a man attained to the title, whether he had a right to it or not, it showed quite definitely that he had been accepted. To be on the Governor's staff, even in an honorary capacity, was to be in the midst of everything. Governors at that time in South Carolina almost had to be Landgraves, in other words, landowners on a very large scale, and so leaders in the class that ruled Charleston and prided itself in its culture.

Colonel Glover, moreover, was a Mason, and the Masonic order in Charleston comprised some of Charleston's most prominent men.

The fact that the young couple arrived in the Queen City in the New Year was a fortunate thing—for Mary, certainly—for it gave her time to find herself a little before the rush of the "season" began. Charleston was quite regular in this regard. As soon as the first frost had fallen in November—it was supposed to kill the malaria—the family departed for the country, and from November to the end of January everyone who was anyone was on the plantation. By the end of January the "gay season" brought the young people back to town and the round of concerts, dances, races and theatre goings was soon in full swing. The old Theatre on Meeting Street was the scene of many grand assemblies. The stock companies were uniformly good and stars came frequently. Fanny Ellsler danced there, Jenny Lind sang and Rachel acted Adrienne Lecouvreur, while a little further down the street in the large hall of the Apprentices' Library Thackeray lectured on literature, Agassiz on zoology and Macready read *Hamlet* to an enthralled audience. While over and above and beyond it all were the race meetings with their exuberant negro jockeys in their exuberant jackets, their gay crowds and the long procession of round-bodied coaches, all resplendent with hammer cloth and bands. On the box, a coachman radiating grandeur, behind a footman radiating alertness, and within and alongside on horseback, all the beauty and gallantry of the ages.

It is difficult to imagine a greater contrast than that presented by Sanbornton Bridge and Charleston, but Mary seems to have grasped it all quickly enough. Very little is known of their story during the scant six months they lived in Charleston or in Wilmington, North Carolina, where Colonel Glover often went on business. That they were very happy, blissfully happy at times, is clear enough from such allusions as Mrs. Eddy made to those times in later life and from some of her earlier poems.

But no record, as to where exactly they lived and how, what was the manner of their household and how Mary passed her time while her husband was away or at work, is preserved.

From such material, however, as is available, not a little can be gathered. Thus it was not long before Mary was appearing in print and in such a way as to show that she and her young husband were taking a keen interest in politics, always a grand question in Charleston. The bitter campaign between the Democrat, Martin Van Buren, and the Whig or Republican, Henry Clay, for the Presidency, had already begun, and Mary, true to the Democratic principles of her father and Albert and Franklin Pierce, was eager in her support of Van Buren and her opposition to Clay. Her few weeks in Charleston, as will be seen, had greatly intensified her native horror of slavery, but with her at that time, as with all but whole-hearted abolitionists, the question was one of states' rights against federal rights. Slavery should be abolished, but it should be abolished in such a way as to preserve unimpaired the right of each state to self-government, on the terms provided for in the Constitution. Van Buren was the champion of the old Democratic principle of States' Rights, Clay was all for increasing the power of the Federal Government. Mary had been born and bred a Democrat, and so she sided with Van Buren against Clay.

> *If I e'er consent to be married,*
> *(And I am not quite sure that I may)*
> *The lad that I give my fair hand to*
> *Must stand by the patriot, Clay.*
>
> *He must toil in the great undertaking,*
> *Be instant by night and by day;*
> *Contend with the Demon of Party,*
> *And vote for the Patriot, Clay.*

So did a Clay partisan burst into print in Wilmington towards the end of March, 1843. To which Mary promptly replied:

65

> *O! plight not your troth to be married,*
> *And don't the bridal array;*
> *For your lad's at a banner frolic,*
> *If he stands by the Demagogue Clay.*
>
> *If he tug in a blind undertaking,*
> *To stand by your side soon as may;*
> *Be content to live single! my fair one,*
> *He'll "stand by" the Demagogue Clay.*

There were many more verses to both original and parody than are here given, and deprived of an atmosphere impossible to recapture, both seem sorry stuff, but they leave no doubt as to the writers' views and show clearly enough that Mary was at least keeping abreast of the times.

On the larger issue of slavery, Mary's attitude was much more important. In her support of Van Buren and her opposition to Clay, her point of view was typically inherited. Gilbert's wisdom fitted her case exactly.

> *Every little boy or gal*
> *Born into this world alive*
> *Is either a little Liber-al*
> *Or a little Conserva-tive.*

In her attitude on slavery, she not only ran counter to her family traditions but also to the burning convictions of practically all her friends in her new home. Abolitionism in South Carolina, when Mary Glover was there, was not only political heresy but something very like treason.

There can be no question as to Mary's feelings in the matter, but it says much either for her own clear judgement or for Colonel Glover's wise influence that she did not launch out into some indiscretion in the way of an open attack on the "institution". Such an attack would, of course, have been worse than useless, and would have endangered her husband's position, if not ruined it. That she did raise the question in print under an assumed name seems certain, but she was careful not to disclose her identity.

In her own home she was quite definite about it. She had heard a lot about slaves, but actually to see them and talk to them and, worse still, have them wait on her was a new and almost incredible experience. She apparently lost no time in trying to persuade George to set such slaves as he had, at liberty.

He may from time to time have had quite a number, as they were constantly offered in payment of debts, and were in fact conventionally legal tender. George had to explain as best he could that, under the laws of South Carolina, there was no way by which a slave could be legally freed, and that just to turn them out would be like turning out a dog or a horse and leaving them to fend for themselves. They would simply be homeless, and that would be all.

It was a hard problem, but, meanwhile, there were many things to do. Above all, there was her husband's work. The cathedral in Haiti was an ambitious undertaking, perhaps too ambitious, but to a young girl of Mary's temperament it was full of wonderful possibilities, not the least of which was the prospect of a trip to the West Indies. That Colonel Glover at one time seriously thought that such a trip might be necessary is made clear by one of Mary's poems still preserved entitled, "When expecting to leave for the West Indies." It is no more than the usual fond farewells to her family, to her father and mother, her brother and sisters, but it draws aside the curtain on many discussions between the two on how the great enterprise was faring and what it might be necessary for them to do.

Then there was for Mary the wonder of the Southern spring. All things unfolding fresh and green and the air fragrant with jessamine and dogwood and magnolia. Mary revelled in it, as is shown in perhaps the happiest of these early verses of hers, a poem, "Written at the Sound in Wilmington," in which she tells how much she loves it all and how eagerly she is looking forward to yet other unfoldments of rapture.

As a background to the picture were her letters, those she wrote and those she received. Of those she wrote, practically none has been preserved, but her mother in one of her letters already quoted from speaks of how much she rejoices "to hear from you so often". Mary was always a good correspondent, and some of the news she sent home may be gathered from references to it in the replies she received. Thus Mrs. Eddy, in later life, used to tell of how Colonel Glover at one time had a quarrel with a quick-tempered Southerner over the question of slavery. The quarrel resulted in a challenge to a duel, and Glover as the challenged party had the choice of weapons. He chose "toe to toe and muzzle in the mouth". As such terms placed the "indomitable courage" of both parties beyond question, a reconciliation was quickly effected and honour was satisfied. It is probably to this incident that Mrs. Baker refers in one of her letters to Mary when she says: ". . . Please give much love to your dear George and tell him from his affectionate mother that to err is human, to forgive divine and I know his own goodness tells him it is better to forgive an injury than revenge it."

Mark, too, wrote at least once, the same Mark, only worse. Mary had evidently written home about the unhealthiness of the climate in the approaching summer, and Mark under date of February 6th, 1844, takes up a foreboding pen to expatiate on reward and penalty, on duty and esteem, softening enough before closing to say concernedly: "If it should be, quit that unhealthy clime and come to a better, it would be pleasing to me."

One more letter and then this back and forth picture, now of the old home at Sanbornton and now of Mary radiantly looking forward to the future in her new home in the South, is complete. It is from Mahala Sanborn, the local blacksmith's daughter, who had been a kind of upper servant in the Baker household for many years, a complacent gossipy letter such as Mary would no doubt rejoice to receive. To "dear, dear Mary," Mahala writes:

"Shall I this pleasant morning devote a few moments in conversing with my dear and old friend M and how do you do would that I could shake hands with you and kiss your cheek this morning."

And then she goes on to tell how she had just spent three weeks nursing at "Mrs. Holems", how Mrs. Ack is very sick and how sad it will be for the children, "left in a cold hearted world alone," if she should not recover, adding that Mary knows well "how to pity them. . . . Your mother and I have been very busy this spring a cleaning house and quilting. . . . We go into the clock room together and exclame O that the Girles were here today what a good time we would have . . . my love to Mr. G. and a kiss for yourself goodbye farewell do write soon wont you Mary from your true friend, M Sanb."

So it went, through the spring and on into the summer. And then suddenly it all came to an end. Summer in those days in the lowlands of the South was considered almost deadly for white people, and as soon as the streams and the ponds began to look green and filmy, the women folk were hurried off the plantations to the coast and the men followed as quickly as the work would permit. The clearing of the forests and the embanking of the rivers and the flooding of the lowlands had added greatly to "the fever of the country", as malaria was called, and the exodus from the plantation in the summer often began early in May.

In was early in June that George and Mary set out from Charleston on what was to be their last trip together. The material for the cathedral in Haiti which had taken so many trips hither and yon to collect was at last being assembled on the dockside at Wilmington, and George had to go there to attend to the final loadings. A day or two after their arrival, George was stricken with a fever and twelve days later he died.

Mary was carrying a seven-months child but, as she was to write her brother George Sullivan later, "day and night I watched alone by the couch of death."[1] She could only wait and pray. She prayed very hard, so hard that the good doctor was almost sure she was availing and told her so. George died, but if the testimony of the Reverend Albert Case who was with him in his last moments is to be accepted, Mary's prayers availed at least to the extent of making his passage easy and peaceful. "Conscious that the time of his departure was at hand," wrote Mr. Case in the *Masonic Magazine*, "he calmly arranged his business—prepared for the removal of her he loved to the home of her youth, and consoled her

[1] Letter to George Sullivan Baker, January 22, 1848.

69

with the thought that they would meet again in heaven. Said he, 'I have a precious hope in the merits of my Saviour.'"

Behind the stilted language of a rather stilted age, the good intent is clear enough.

George Glover was buried at Wilmington with full Masonic honours, the local Lodge sending out a general invitation to the funeral:

"The Citizens of Wilmington are respectfully invited to attend the funeral of Major George W. Glover, decd. at 6 o'clock p.m. from Hanover House to the usual place of interment. June 28."

The funeral was attended by the Governor of the State and his staff, who walked in the procession with other citizens and friends from the Masonic Lodge to Hanover House and thence to the churchyard of St. John's Church. There he was buried, and Mary turned over the page on to another chapter of her long life—a chapter opening not too auspiciously, for despite her late husband's sometime prosperity, his passing found him "in indigent circumstances," as the Masonic record of St. John's Lodge No. 1, in Charleston, establishes. It is said on fairly reliable authority that his earnings had gone for lumber to be used in the projected cathedral at Haiti and that during his illness this was stolen from the docks. One of lesser character than Mary Baker would have been crushed for all time, but this frail woman in a day of frail womanhood was to rise again and again, triumphantly, above what surely appeared to be malevolent circumstances under which men would reel.

The Return to Sanbornton

IN THE WILMINGTON *Chronicle* for August 21st, 1844, appeared the following letter:

"SIR: Through the columns of your paper, will you permit me, in behalf of the relatives and friends of the late Maj. George W. Glover, of Wilmington, and his bereaved lady, to return our thanks and express the feeling of gratitude we owe and cherish towards those friends of the deceased, who so kindly attended him during his last sickness, and who still extend their care and sympathy to the lone, feeble and bereaved widow, after his decease. Much has often been said of the high feeling of honour, and noble generosity of heart which characterizes the people of the South, yet when we listen to Mrs. Glover (my sister) whilst recounting the kind attentions paid to the deceased during his last illness, the sympathy extended to her after his death, and the assistance volunteered to restore her to her friends, at a distance of more than a thousand miles, the power of language would be but beggared by any attempt at expressing the feelings of the swelling bosom. The silent gush of grateful tears alone can tell the emotions of the thankful heart. Words are indeed but a meagre tribute for so noble an effort in behalf of the unfortunate, yet it is all we can award; Will our friends at Wilmington accept it the tribute of grateful hearts.

"Many thanks are due to Mr. Cooke, who engaged to accompany her only to New York but did not desert her, or remit his kind attentions until he saw her in the fond embrace of her friends.

"Your friend and obedient servant

GEORGE S. BAKER"

"Sanbornton Bridge, N.H.
August 12 1844"

So the story is told in the grandiose language of the day. It is supplemented by a diary kept by Mary herself of her sad journey and still preserved, a simple weary record to modern thought of almost incredible laboriousness. The thousand miles must have seemed interminable. By rail from Wilmington to Portsmouth, Virginia, with a change of cars at Weldon, North Carolina; thence by boat to Baltimore and on by another boat to Frenchton. From Frenchton the two travelled across the state of Delaware by rail to Newcastle, whence they took a boat to Philadelphia; they took another boat to Bristol, Pennsylvania, and then on by rail to Jersey City and by ferry to New York. And so on by stage and train to Concord, New Hampshire, and Sanbornton.

We must imagine the actual home-coming, of the meeting of Abigail with her widowed daughter, of the one by one hesitant approach of old friends, of the messages which must have come from far and near, of the letters from Augusta and many others and the visits of the old minister, with all the time Mark in the background, a monumental struggle between Calvinism and the Sermon on the Mount.

It is not difficult to picture it all, interwoven as it must have been with the ever-present pathetic looking forward to the event that was now so near.

It was on September 11, 1844, that the child, a son, was born. He was called George after his father and immediately sent away to the care of a woman nearby, a Mrs. Amos Morrison, wife of a mechanic, who had recently had a child of her own.

For Mary was very low. The death of her husband, the long and weary journey home, followed by a difficult confinement, had left her so utterly exhausted that for weeks her life was despaired of. Characteristically enough, the whole situation seems to have reacted on Mark more hardly than on anyone else. The same sudden revulsion of feeling which had caused him, years before, to rouse himself from the foreboding part in which he always cast himself and drive frantically down the hill from Bow to fetch the doctor, crying to a neighbour, "Mary is dying," now caused him to do everything in his power to protect his sick daughter from the slightest disturbing noise. He strewed tan-bark on the road outside her window, so the story goes, and seemed possessed by a desire to make some kind of reparation, however clumsy, for past hardness.

Very slowly, Mary got better, but weeks had passed into months before a really decided improvement could be observed, and even then it became evident that more than one chronic disability would have to be contended with. The spinal weakness, which she had had from early girlhood and to which her mother alludes in one of her letters, was very much accentuated and at times she suffered great pain. Abigail and the faithful Mahala were devoted in their care, and in the end Mary struggled back to life.

It was months before she could see her little son, and the months had almost run into years before she had him around with her as much as a normal mother would want. Thus, from the very first, was established that severance in association, so much stronger in effect upon the child than the mother, which, in years to come, was to result in their complete separation. Mahala Sanborn was the one that looked after the little boy. It was to her he had recourse in his first troubles and with her he shared his first exuberant excesses. For little George took after his father. From the first, he was a sturdy, restless youngster, and even before he learned anything else, he learned, with the inevitable intuition of the young animal, that it was Mahala who did not care how much noise he made, while with his mother his excesses had to be abated, if not by her by somebody else.

Very slowly Mary began to pick up the threads of her new old life. It was rather a sad business at first. She was more beautiful than ever, and, always possessed of a strangely compelling charm, it was not long before first this one and then that one among the young men in her circle were with no little diffidence offering their humble respects again. But her brief excursion into happiness, with its tragic ending, remained a poignant memory, and, although outwardly entering more and more into the life of those around her, nothing was the same as it had been before. One little poem still preserved written about this time reveals her attitude of mind with a curiously pathetic beauty which crept into her verse-making only when she was really deeply moved. It is entitled, "Wind of the South," and its last two verses are nearer real poetry than anything Mary had written up to this time.[1]

> *Yes, balmy breeze, when evening glows*
> *O, pitying come and kiss my cheek—*
> *But no, thy sighing would disclose—*
> *Thee hither from the grave I seek.*
>
> *O say do worms dare revel round*
> *The casket where no gems can rust?*
> *Hath loveliness a level found,*
> *Beneath the cold and common dust?*

But once again, youth and time, combined with an indomitably optimistic religious sense, won the victory. She took up writing again and, this time, she made use of every medium. Fiction, poetry, essay writing.

According to the reminiscences of Sarah Clement Kimball, village tongues were set wagging by the eager attentions paid the young widow, hard upon her return to Sanbornton, by a young clergyman, the Reverend Richard S. Rust, who became principal of a Methodist Academy, called the New Hampshire Conference Seminary, which was opened in Sanbornton early in 1845. The two had much in common, and it was not long before he had offered Mary a position as substitute teacher in the

[1] Published in the *Ladies' Home Journal*, June, 1911.

Academy. Mr. Rust was also editor of a fraternal magazine called the *Covenant*, and he welcomed Mary's writings to its columns. She made good use of her opportunity, as the files of the magazine clearly show, and if the quality of her output obviously suffers from a lack of that discipline involved in an acceptance on merit only and not on favour, it shows that she was making a serious effort to support herself with the only means she had. *Emma Clinton, A Tale of the Frontier,* a novelette in four chapters; *The Test of Love,* a short story; *Erin the Smile and the Tear in thine Eyes,* an essay advocating Irish freedom, and quite a number of short poems, "The Emigrant's Farewell," "The Moon," "The Old Man of the Mountain," and so on. There is nothing distinguished about it all. Most of it is hack writing in the remorselessly pedantic style of the day. It is interesting, however, as a revelation of the fact, to become so evident later on, that Mary writing for effect and Mary writing on something about which she really cared, were almost unrecognizably different.

"Can a feeling pervade the benevolent bosom in any one of Eve's fair daughters, opposed to the best interests of her sex—the extension of benevolent institutions—simply because they are of secret origin? Even with such, if indeed there are any, we trust the avenues to reason and sentiment though chilled, are not quite frozen in the icy fetters of speculative views, or the colder icebergs of popular surmise closing them effectually from the genial sunshine of truth—reason's twin sister. Rather would we spare this immortal boon, heaven's best gift to mortals, so sad a libel on its power of research, as to suppose any subject not first fully understood, would be condemned. But if reason is not suffered to act, slumbering on an unwary sentinel at her post, truth is her foe, ignorance her friend; yea unwarrantable ignorance, whose legitimate offspring are prejudice and blind error; and what enlightened female of this century would not blush to acknowledge herself the dupe of some misguidings?"

Thus an extract from an essay on "Odd Fellowship" in the *Covenant*. The sentiment is good enough, even characteristically sound, but compared with the simple power of her later prose, the style is incredibly bad.

It is only so by comparison, however. It was largely the newspaper, and to a very considerable extent, the literary style of the day, and, however indifferent, it laid the foundation, in Mary's case, for something of real excellence.

Anyway, it more than passed muster with the Reverend Richard Rust. For the young widow began to have no lack of admirers and the Reverend Richard was a frequent visitor in the Baker household, so frequent that those whose business it was to do so were already beginning to speculate as to the significance and probable outcome of it all. It quickly became apparent, however, that Richard was not the only one. There were John M. Burt and Luther Bean and James Smith and a boy who finds a record only under his nickname "Sleeper", and several others, all of whom were duly speculated upon in their turn.

As to Mary, although she entered into it all as would any other young girl—she was no more—she got very tired of it at times. In a letter to her friend Martha Rand, who was later to marry her brother Sullivan, she indulges herself in a mild outburst of annoyance over the gossip about herself and John Burt. "John M. Burt", she writes, "has paid an annual visit to the homestead (not I) recently, and spoke of Miss Rand very kindly—wished me to send a little love to her. He now intends to go to Wisconsin after he graduates in August. I hope then people will mind their business about us, as I am getting a little mad at their lies, for such they are."

This letter to "Mathy", as Mary calls her friend, gives an interesting picture of Mary about this time—the spring of 1847. In many ways it is reminiscent of the letter she wrote from Bow to her brother Sullivan, "the second letter I ever wrote," so many years before. It is again a sleepy afternoon and again with the family away, this time "all at church", and again the solitude and the silence are "well calculated to influence memory to bring up the light of other days". It is the same kind of cloud and sunshine letter. At one moment, "so weary of solitude I have half determined this very moment to throw aside my pen and wait to weep," and the next rallying herself to a more cheerful outlook and entertaining her friend with some excellent gossip about their mutual friends and their doings in Sanbornton. The "Sem. ladies" are getting up "a fare (not fair)" to defray the expenses of building operations, such as fitting up an assembly room. Miss Lane is the directress. Prof. Sanborn is leaving the town with his wife and children, and so on. And then she comes back to Mathy and how she wishes they could be together somehow during the coming summer, "get a school together or in some way manage it". She begs Mathy to be careful of her health, "the greatest earthly blessing, without which little else can be enjoyed," and bids her not to be anxious about the future but to rely on God.

"Please excuse this hasty scrawl. George has been constantly at my elbow which must account for the execution. Let me hear from you very soon and all I could wish. And now adieu—Believe me truly thine.

MARY M. GLOVER"

The picture seems to be complete enough. Mary making the best of it. Her little boy constantly at her elbow. She is interested, tremendously so at times, in all that goes on around her, but there is evident through it all a deep-seated discontent which every now and again sinks out of sight and sound, but is never completely eliminated. "Is it not so?" she writes to Mathy, "Does not the heart find utterance in disappointment?"

Of all the suitors who thronged Mary about this time, there was just one who seems to have won some place in her affections, John M. Bartlett, a young lawyer, who, after a brilliant record in the Harvard Law School, went out to Sacramento, California, to engage in law practice and died there within a few short weeks of his arrival. He had known Mary for some years and, before leaving for California, spent the summer in Sanbornton. Mary by that time had no doubt achieved a certain measure of freedom, so that her future was not, as it was at first, so much a matter of speculation. At any rate, although the two were together quite often, it seems to have attracted very little attention and probably nothing would have been known of the understanding which existed between them if it had not been for a pathetically prim notation in Mrs. Eddy's handwriting under Bartlett's obituary notice which she had cut out and put in her scrapbook. It runs, "He was engaged to marry Mrs. Glover when he left N.H."

Many years afterwards, Mrs. Eddy was to write in her book *Retrospection and Introspection*: "Early had I learned that whatever is loved materially, as mere corporeal personality, is eventually lost."[1] It is not difficult to believe that she had reference to these days, for the loss of her husband was only the beginning of a long series of bereavements and separations which in the course of a few years were to leave her alone.

When she said good-bye to young Bartlett, as he set out for the then almost mythical California, she was already within the shadow of another loss, perhaps the most bitter of her life—her mother. Abigail Baker had fought a good fight. She had worked hard all her life, not only in the great task of peacemaker and moderator in a household which but for her would often have been hard pressed by the grimness of her husband's religious views. She had been ailing for some time and eager at first from a sense of duty to recover. Her youngest son, George Sullivan, was soon to marry Martha Rand, and she held up until then, but, after she had seen them married and wave their last farewells as they set out for their new home in Baltimore, she realized that she was very worn and tired. "Let me go to my home of eternal rest," she said. That was on November 4, 1849. She died on the 21st.

Mary was desolate and there was no one to whom she could turn. As so often happens in such cases, she never seems to have thought of her father apart from her mother, and now that her mother was gone, her father was almost a stranger to her. Mark in the aura of her mother's plea to "think kindly" of her father, and of her assurance that he loved her as much as any of his children, was one thing, but Mark deprived of this benediction was quite another. It was much the same with Mark. He never seems to have thought of Mary apart from Abigail. Only thus can be explained the change which seems to have come over them both after Abigail died.

But that was to come afterwards. Meanwhile, Mary writes to George at Baltimore:

[1] *Retrospection and Introspection*, p. 32.

78

"Oh George, what is left of earth to me. But oh, my mother! She has suffered long with me; Let me be willing she should now rejoice, and I bear on till I follow her. I cannot write more. My grief overpowers me."

Her mother had been buried only a few weeks when news came to her that John Bartlett had died in Sacramento.

All her life, Mary was at her best in a crisis, and at this crisis when her long struggle against ill-health would seem inevitably to presage complete collapse under the added burden, a traditional sense of duty, so common in New England in those days, came to her rescue. She was the only one left at home and she was needed. Mark Baker had prospered. Some shrewd railroad investments had proved very profitable, and the year before Abigail's death he had built a handsome house in the Colonial style just off the main street of Sanbornton and next door to the home of his eldest daughter Abigail Tilton, and moved his family there. He could well have afforded to employ a housekeeper, but Mary was now the natural head of the house from the woman's standpoint, and she bravely rose to the occasion. She kept house for him loyally through the winter, bore, as best she could, with his uncertain temper and his growing dislike of her little boy, and sought to make a home out of the wreckage left by Abigail's passing.

The task was one of increasing difficulty and it ended abruptly in what for Mary was another tragedy.

Mark Baker was 64. All his life he had been used to having a woman around his home, who—as far as he could see—had no doubt as to her place or his, who cared for her part of the great enterprise efficiently and well and left him undisturbed in the satisfying assurance that he was the head of the household and the final arbiter in all matters of importance, religious or profane. First it was his mother, the wise, placid Ann Moor McNeill, then it was Abigail. Left alone with Mary, in whom he had found, all too often, his own dogged obstinacy confronting him in the form of quiet convictions which made him feel defeat before he had begun to argue, it is no wonder that he sought a quick way out of his difficulty. He decided to marry again, and his choice fell upon Mrs. Elizabeth

Patterson Duncan, a widow of Candia, New Hampshire. She was a woman of good family, sister of George W. Patterson, sometime Lieutenant-Governor of New York, an ample, placid-looking woman, judging from her picture, who probably fitted exactly into the place in his home that Mark Baker had designed for her.

The prospect filled Mary with dismay, for it quickly became evident that it would not only mean that she would have to leave home, but that she would be separated from her boy. Her sister, Abigail, next door, offered her a home, but she had a son of her own, a delicate ailing child of four, and Mary's six-year-old George who always had given promise of outdoing his father in energy would not be welcome. It was one of those unhappy circumstances which was probably nobody's fault. Abigail had always been kind to Mary, but she was becoming a wealthy woman. She had grown used to comfort, and the prospect of having George about the house all day and every day did not appeal to her from any angle. Moreover, there was as she saw it an easy way of solving the problem. George had always regarded Mahala Sanborn, the old Baker servant, as his staple recourse. Mahala was devoted to him and he to Mahala. What more natural than that George should be sent to live with Mahala, who, now happily married to one Russell Cheney, had settled in the little village of North Groton some forty miles away.

And so it was arranged. Mary, delicate and without resources—the final winding up of her husband's affairs had left her practically nothing —could not have much voice in the matter. George was sent away and Mary moved into Abigail's home. "The night before my child was taken from me," she wrote years afterwards in *Retrospection and Introspection*, "I knelt by his side throughout the dark hours, hoping for a vision of relief from this trial."[1] Outwardly when he had gone she made the best of it, but thenceforward her every thought was motivated by one desire, to find the vision to bring about a reunion between herself and her son, she always maintained.

The first need, as she rightly saw it, was to make herself self-supporting. She had tried writing with a certain measure of success, but it was too

[1] *Retrospection and Introspection*, p. 20.

uncertain when it came to the question of actually supporting herself and her child. So she conferred with her old friend Richard Rust, and he, a long way ahead of his time, having had experience of Mary's ability as a teacher in his own academy, urged her to open an infant school in the little town.

It was a novelty, of course, but Mary took up the idea with enthusiasm. She secured a small building behind her sister's home which had formerly been used as a shoemaker's shop, and there she opened her school. She had painted it red, as a school house should be, and fitted it out with little desks and chairs all complete.

There is not much evidence as to how she fared or how long the novel experiment carried on. Only one of her pupils in later life left any recollections of the little school and its teacher. That was one Sarah Clement, daughter of Zenas Clement, a friend and neighbour of Mark Baker at Sanbornton, and she only remembered isolated incidents such as would fasten themselves on the memory of a small child of six or seven. One incident, however, which she recalled very vividly, is worth recording. It appears that Sarah was not being at all well behaved in class, indeed she was behaving very badly. And so, after repeated admonitions, Mrs. Glover sent her out into the garden to get a switch with which she was to be "whipped". When Sarah returned with the smallest twig she could find, Mrs. Glover, regardless of all the claims of dignity or discipline, burst out laughing, openly forgave her, and sent her back to her seat unpunished.

Sarah seems to have been devoted to her young teacher. She loved her, she says, for her "kindness and cheerfulness", and the picture she has left of how on summer evenings she would run across the road, climb up on the gate of the Tilton home and watch Mrs. Glover as she worked in the garden, the two talking comfortably back and forth, is welcome enough, if only for the measure of peace it suggests.

But Mary was just making the best of it. In her heart all the time was the thought of the little boy in Groton, and then there was Abigail, meaning to be kind, but more masterful than ever. No "vision of relief" had so far been seen.

81

Daniel Patterson

ABOUT THREE MILES from Sanbornton Bridge to the west, at the point
where the Pemigewasset and the Winnepesaukee rivers unite to form the
Merrimac, is the little town of Franklin, even in the middle of last century famous or infamous, according to the political views held, as the
birthplace of Daniel Webster. It was in those days, as it still is to a very
large extent, the shopping centre for all the district round about. Sanbornton Bridge drove down the Winnepesaukee river, and Webster and such
like places drove down the Pemigewasset to do their shopping in Franklin. It was a thriving mill town with unlimited water power in the hills
just at hand and right in its very midst. All that Sanbornton had, Franklin had, only, in addition to its industries, it had its merchants and its
craftsmen, its doctors and its lawyers who cared for the needs of the
countryside.

Among the doctors of Franklin, in the days when Mary Glover was living in her sister Abigail's house at Sanbornton, was one Daniel Patterson.
He was primarily a dentist, but, like so many dentists in those days, he
had made some study of the then rebel art of homeopathy and practised

it on the side. His headquarters were at Franklin, but his practice extended much further afield, and, sometimes for a week or more at a time, he would take the road on horseback, and, having previously advertised his coming, would move from one little town to another, take a room, generally provided for such purposes in the local hotel, and attend to such patients as came to him. It was quite a common practice in New England in the middle of last century.

Daniel Patterson was a good dentist, and within a short time of his settling in Franklin was apparently much in demand. He was a distant relative of the new Mrs. Mark Baker of Sanbornton, and it was probably because of this connection that Mary Glover came to know him. The acquaintance was, at first, purely professional. The art of filling teeth was rapidly improving and was being resorted to increasingly in preference to the time-honoured method of tooth-pulling, and Mary, who was evidently having trouble with her teeth, had gone to him for professional service.

On December 12, 1852, she writes to him very formally, "Mr. Patterson Dear Sir," and asks him if he thinks that the teeth he had examined should be filled at once. She is evidently anxious that this should be done, as she adds half-humorously, "I would like to retain as long as possible all I have *left*. Never knowing before the loss of teeth I was ignorant of all the difficulties I find attend it."

The tone of the letter, in spite of its formal opening, suggests that the two already knew each other quite well and it is, of course, probable that, through his relationship with Mrs. Baker, Doctor Patterson had been a visitor in the Baker and Tilton households at Sanbornton. He was a personable man, tall and broad-shouldered, with excellent features and full flowing black beard. He was, moreover, something of a dandy, dressed in broadcloth with "varnished boots", and affected at all times the formal fashion of the day, a silk top hat.

He seems from the first to have been determined to marry the young widow at Sanbornton, and the stars in their courses aided him. Quite apart from the separation from her boy, Mary's position in her sister's house was one particularly galling to a woman of her temperament. Abigail Tilton was coming to be a great lady, and, in those acutely political days, her home at Sanbornton was naturally the headquarters for vigorous political discussion of all kinds, generally centring round the ever-inflammable question of slavery. The Tiltons were good northern Democrats. They did not like slavery, and would not have tolerated it in any circumstances in their own state or home, but they believed profoundly in "States' Rights", and any act or manner of speech which savoured of a willingness to invade these rights for any reason whatsoever was regarded by them as something very like treason.

Mary also was a good Democrat, but she had been brought in contact with slavery in the South, and had been torn ever since between her heartfelt horror of the whole system and her loyalty to the old Democratic viewpoint. Generally, she seems to have managed to avoid any expression of opinion at the gatherings in her sister's house, but on one occasion she was directly challenged. The debate had turned to the question of Slavery, and what would be the effect of the election of Franklin Pierce— a strong Democrat—to the presidency. One of the guests asked Mrs. Glover her views. She might have passed it by, but for some reason she determined to make a clean breast of it. Franklin Pierce was her friend, and not only her friend but her childhood's hero; nevertheless she did not hesitate. She believed, she said, that not only the North but the South suffered from the continuance of slavery and its spread to other states; that the election of Franklin Pierce would tend to inflame the situation, and she did not think that his election would benefit the country as a whole. Abigail Tilton was aghast, but when she asked Mary how she dared make such a statement in her house, Mary replied quite firmly that she dared say what she believed in any house.

Such was the situation as far as Mary was concerned in the early part of 1853 when Daniel Patterson was pressing his suit. He had formally proposed in March, but had been refused. Romance entered into the average New England marriage in those days only on a level with many other considerations. Marriages were contracted, especially second marriages, with deliberation, and considerations of expediency were given much weight. Mary had an unhappy home. She was entirely dependent on her sister. She was separated from her child, and she was wretchedly ill most of the time. Daniel Patterson, the breezy optimist, told Mary, and Abigail and Mark as well, that homeopathy was just the thing to cure her of her ills, that in the case of anyone so finely strung as Mary the "highest attenuations" would work miracles, and that if she would marry him, he would treat her and she would get well.

There is no reason to doubt that he believed all he said. The effect his marriage to the beautiful daughter of Mark Baker might have upon his practice may have had something to do with it. It would not have been New England in the middle of last century if it had not. But there seems to be no doubt that Mary attracted him enormously, and with his usual optimism he evidently felt sure that all the rest would follow. Their not inconsiderable correspondence shows that Mary was not immune to his charms, either.

He almost failed, however. Early in April, Mary refused what was evidently another petition. Some differences as to religion had arisen between them, for Mary writes that she cannot yield her religion to his. "I could not," she adds, "other things compared to this are but a grain to the universe."

But by the end of the month she had given in and accepted him. No doubt Abigail had something to do with it. Mary's marriage would quite clearly solve many problems for her. Although there had always been a strong bond of sympathy between them, Mary's unorthodox political views and the constant reproach presented by Mary's separation from her son, rendered the proposed change a most desirable one, from Abigail's point of view. Mary happily married, reunited to her son and living at the convenient distance of Franklin, was, she must have thought, just as it should be. Mark Baker was not so sure. He would naturally desire the marriage for much the same reasons as would Abigail, but Daniel Patterson was not the kind of man to appeal to Mark Baker. He might have forgiven the varnished boots and the Prince Albert coat, but he was not quite sure of Daniel's religious views. In Mary's vigorous doubts which almost brought disaster at one point, it seems reasonable to detect a strong parental pressure. There is no doubt that her father did at one time very much disapprove of the match on the grounds of Daniel's religion or lack of it. He also seems to have entertained grave uncertainties as to the entire excellence of the doctor's character. Patterson's farewell letter to Mary when she refused his second petition on some grounds of religious difference shows this very clearly: "I thought," he writes from Franklin on "Monday morn Apl. 11, 1853", "I would at first vindicate my moral character, and prepared a letter for your father's perusal—but on more mature deliberation, and knowing that you had become dissatisfied with my Disposition and wished—yes had already irrevocably dismissed me, I concluded to withhold all I had written."

However, he did not destroy the letter of vindication which seemed so good on Sunday night but so doubtful on Monday morning, for after Mary had relented, he showed it to her. It is still preserved, dated Franklin, April 10, 1853. Daniel is clearly very much hurt. Instead of "Dear Mary", it is "Mary M. Glover", and he plunges at once into the midst of things:

"Much to my surprise, I learn that your family object to our union on grounds new and strange to me—

"You say they have heard 'Dark things'."

And then in the sonorous and almost melodramatic style of the day, with a heavy interlarding of biblical and poetical metaphors, he says he cannot guess what these dark things are with which his name is besmirched but that he is sure of their source in "some low cess-pool of Slanderous Suspicion—down which Lucifer plunged his hydra head and dividing hoof." Why even if the Arch Angel issued forth from the very throne of God, he would not be spared the whiplash of innuendo and falsehood.

There is more to the same purpose and amazing as it sounds to modern ears it must perhaps be regarded as sincere enough. At any rate, when he finally reaches his "Vindication", Daniel is nothing if not wholly without reserve.

He offers to take her father around to all the places where he has stayed to check on the nature of his irreproachable conduct. He will take him to his native town to meet clergymen and business men and social leaders "who have long known and dealt with me," who have known him from infancy upwards, in fact, some of them being members of the Congregational Church, to which the Bakers subscribed, and not blood relations of his, either. "If he will take the trouble to go, I will bear his expenses or I will give him any number of reliable names whom he may address in the matter."

It certainly seems full enough to satisfy Mark Baker, for in the end he seems to have approved the match heartily and with the aid of the new Mrs. Baker, who had a real affection for Mary, prepared for the wedding to be held from the Baker homestead.

They were married on June 21, 1853, and after some delay went to live in Franklin.

Doctor Patterson's Micawber-like optimism carried all before it at first. He bought a little house in Franklin, furnished it—mainly with things Mary brought with her from Sanbornton—and engaged a housekeeper. But he quickly revealed the defects of his superficially attractive virtues. His claims were always ahead of his achievements. His varnished boots, Prince Albert coat and silk hat were always really in the world of his dreams. He could see Daniel Patterson clothed in them in a thousand different engaging situations, but his dreams often had rude awakenings and he was in the dust until he could dream again.

Squire Baker of Sanbornton was by this time a quite important figure throughout the countryside, and Doctor Patterson's marriage to his daughter certainly would give him, Daniel, added prestige. He apparently made much of it, but only socially. He gave up his journeyings abroad in search of business, sold his horse and settled down to living all the time in Franklin. He had not enough work, however,—the good people of Franklin soon reached the limits of their modest dental demands and his practice steadily dwindled.

Meanwhile, Mary did not get any better, and within a few weeks of her marriage suffered her first cruel disappointment. Daniel Patterson was unwilling that her little son should come to live with them, we are told by Mrs. Eddy, in her book *Retrospection and Introspection*. "My dominant thought", she writes, "in marrying again was to get back my child, but after our marriage his stepfather was not willing he should have a home with me."

Mary, however, never lost hope. She did her best to make a home for Daniel Patterson, and, for a time, the outlook was not so bad. Mary had again a home of her own, and all her life she had a faculty for making much out of very little in the matter of her surroundings. The townspeople called upon her and she returned their calls, but for her the whole atmosphere of those days must have been one of disappointment. She was sick. Before they were married, Patterson had held out hope of recovery under his care that amounted almost to a promise.

The months that followed, stretching out into years, were dreary enough. Doctor Patterson was not doing well, and it is hard not to read into the falling off, an effect which supervened upon his marriage, a disappointment that his wife's rich relations had done nothing for them.

It would be a mistake, however, to assume that the situation was entirely unrelieved. Daniel Patterson may have had many faults, but deliberate unkindness was not one of them. It took very little to raise his spirits, for the moment at least, and when thus raised the whole world rose with him, and in his breezy boisterous way he could carry conviction as to the new heaven and the new earth to those around him. It was undoubtedly this characteristic which constituted his chief attraction in the eyes of the sorely tried and unsatisfied woman he had made his wife. He had, moreover, a great love of natural beauty. "There was one time in my ride to this place," he wrote to her on one of his journeys—from Wolfborough on Lake Winnepesaukee—"when I said to myself—'now I wish Mary was with me'—it was on attaining the summit of a hill, the first view of the lake burst upon my vision with its smooth face scarified and lacerated by numerous islets and points, and yet it was beautiful, then I really wished you by my side."

But when all has been said in his favour that can be said, the picture still remains much the same. Daniel Patterson was a man of many fair weather friends and no enemies save himself, and during the three years that he and Mary lived in Franklin more and more of his friends tended to pass by on the other side, while the one enemy entrenched himself more firmly than ever as the man in possession.

Meanwhile, it does not seem likely that Mark Baker or Abigail Tilton sat idly by and let things drift without any effort to change their course into a better direction. Abigail could not but feel a certain amount of responsibility in the matter, and from the way in which she—more than once—came to the rescue later on, it is natural to assume that she did what she could. Indeed it was probably due to Abigail that a plan was ultimately consummated which gave promise to Mary of the fulfillment of her great desire to have her boy with her, or in any case, close at hand.

In the hill town of North Groton where little George was living with Mahala Cheney and her husband, the Tiltons owned a small property, a good house and land on the outskirts of the town. Through the land ran a little trout stream with an excellent fall and on the stream was a saw-mill.

There was a small mortgage on the property, and the plan that was finally worked out was that the equity in the property was transferred to the Pattersons, who, on taking it over, assumed responsibility for the mortgage.

The proposition evidently appeared very attractive to Doctor Patterson. For him it solved more than one problem. His wife would be near her son. The interest on the mortgage was nominal when considered as rent, and a saw-mill properly worked would provide a welcome addition to the uncertain income derived from his practice.

Mary was, of course, overjoyed at the prospect, and so in the spring of 1855, as soon as the roads were passable and the accustomed sudden mildness of coming summer was everywhere, they loaded their household effects onto a wagon and took the road into the hills. It was a climb most of the way, for the town near the entrance of the Franconia Range of the White Mountains lies at an elevation of over one thousand feet.

In the middle of last century North Groton was a thriving community, much smaller than Sanbornton but considerably larger than Bow. It had a good school, a large general store which catered to the needs of a wide countryside, and it even had a small public library. The Pattersons' new home was not far from the main road, along which the slow-moving ox teams made their way down the hill to the little town of Rumney on the then newly constructed railroad and back again. It was not isolated even in winter, and Mary who could make a home out of almost anything had very soon transformed the little unpainted house into a very attractive place in which to live. Years afterwards, she used to declare that she was "impatient of a speck of dust", and the few records of her life at North Groton show that somehow in spite of her burden of continued illness she managed to secure "perfect housekeeping".

The records are indeed very scanty, affording only occasional glimpses of the passage of the months running on into years. There is no word of her first meeting with her son, of the visits of Mahala, his foster mother and her own devoted nurse, of the goings and comings of Patterson, or of the letters which must have passed back and forth between her and Abigail. Such few records as are preserved are, however, strangely revealing, one especially.

Shortly after they arrived and settled in—no doubt with the help of Mahala—Doctor Patterson secured a housekeeper. She was efficient enough, but evidently the type of woman who imperatively demanded that things should be run her way, and it was not long before the matter of authority came to an issue. One day a blind girl came to the house seeking work and Mrs. Patterson, immediately interested, after talking to her for some time, decided to take her in and see what she could do. In spite of her blindness she seems to have been remarkably capable and quick to learn, but the housekeeper from the first was profoundly disapproving. Finally, she told Mrs. Patterson, perfectly straightly, that the blind girl would have to go or else she would. Mrs. Patterson did not hesitate a moment. She let the housekeeper go and she and the blind girl went on together.

The blind girl's name was Myra—Myra Smith. She stayed with Mrs. Patterson all the time she was in Groton, and many years afterwards her sister, then a very aged woman, recalled how she used to go to the Pattersons' home some two or three times each week to visit Myra, and how Mrs. Patterson "was ill nearly all the time". She recalls how the sick woman was always reading, but that whenever she came to her bedside she would lay aside her book and pat her on the head and say, "Oh you dear little girl. You are worth your weight in gold. I wish you were mine." She also recalled how "one of the greatest pleasures of the children was to carry in the earliest berries and wild flowers to the 'poor sick lady'."

Such recollections, scanty as they are, draw aside the curtain a little. As to George and his visits, Myra Smith herself recalled when a very old woman how the boy would come to his mother to be helped with his lessons, how his mother loved to have him there, and how he seemed to be always happy with her. Doctor Patterson, however, disapproved these visits, and one day when he returned home and found the boy with his wife after he had forbidden him to come, he sent him back to the Cheneys with the injunction not to return. It is not known whether the Doctor disliked the child or if, as he has been quoted as saying, he felt the presence of the husky youngster taxed Mary's already overtaxed strength.

It is only possible to piece together a surmise as to the meaning of it all, but the generally accepted theory that Doctor Patterson, annoyed by the boy's presence, found it easy to persuade himself that his wife was always worse after he had been there and therefore forbade him the house, is plausible. There seems, however, to have been quite definitely another reason. It was Mahala. She was well over forty and had no children of her own, and had had George with her almost continually since he was a baby. It was more than possible that the prospect of losing him as she saw the boy becoming more and more attached to his mother was more than she could bear to contemplate. Only indeed on some such assumption can be explained what quickly followed Doctor Patterson's drastic action. Mrs. Eddy in *Retrospection and Introspection* says her husband was unwilling her son should have a home with her, and adds: "A plot was consummated for keeping us apart. The family to whose care he was committed very soon removed to what was then regarded as the Far West. . . . We never met again until he had reached the age of thirty-four."[1]

She does not say how she bore up or went down under this latest blow, but it was soon after the departure of the Cheneys—they went to Minnesota—that an incident occurred which, in view of what was to follow in Mary's life, has a significance all its own. In the long days and often nights she spent reading, she devoted herself to just two subjects, religion and medicine. She read the Bible as she had always done for long hours together, but now she also studied any book she could get on homeopathy. Daniel Patterson, as has been seen, practised homeopathy to a certain extent, and from the first its study seems to have had a peculiar fascination for Mary. This was no doubt partly due to the fact that she hoped by studying the system herself to discover some cure for her own troubles, such as her husband had not been able to find, but also because in its early days homeopathy frankly presented a mental and even a spiritual element calculated to make strong appeal to a woman of Mary's mentality and background.

In his monumental work on the subject (*Der Organon der rationellen Heilkunde*), in which he expounded his system, Friedrich Hahnemann was quite definite on this point. The *Organon* was first translated into English about 1825, a few years after the study of homeopathy had first been introduced into the United States by a Danish doctor, one Hans Busch Gram. The system, although bitterly opposed by the orthodox medical profession, gained ground rapidly. Curiously enough, the date of its formal introduction to each state is on record, and the spread is remarkable, running from New York in 1825 to Iowa in 1871. Homeopathy reached New Hampshire as a serious study about 1840, and at the time Mary Patterson was passing through such deep waters in the little house at North Groton, some fifteen years later, it was definitely coming into favour as a remedial agent. The *Organon* had reached

[1] *Retrospection and Introspection*, pp. 20-21.

several editions. Hahnemann had by that time been dead many years and two bitterly opposed schools of thought had arisen in the practice of his system, the Hahnemannians and the Rationals. Hahnemann had definitely laid it down in his *Organon* that, although drugs might be the medium, the actual healing agent was purely mental and spiritual.

"It is only", he wrote, "by means of the spiritual influence of a morbific agent that our spiritual power can be diseased, and in like manner only by the spiritual operation of medicine can health be restored."

The Hahnemannians accepted this teaching implicitly, regarded the *Organon* as their Bible and insisted, as they still insist, that "the doctrine of the spiritual dynamization acquired by trituration and succession as indubitable". The Rationals on the other hand maintained that the spiritual side of the remedy if it existed at all was only part of the cure and that they were free to use "all adjuvants known to science".

Mary Patterson was absorbingly interested in the whole subject, as is shown by her many allusions to the matter in the course of her writings, and especially by one case of cure in which she herself was the practitioner. This she describes in detail. No date is given, but it is more than possible that it was one of her experiences while at North Groton, as it is known that while there, although she did not seem to be able to help herself, she tried to help others through homeopathy. The case she describes is one of dropsy:

"We prescribed for her the fourth attenuation of *Argentum nitricum*, with occasional doses of a high attenuation of *Sulphuris*. She improved perceptibly. . . . It then occurred to us to give her unmedicated pellets for a while, and watch the result. We did so, and she continued to gain as before, and finally said she would give up her medicine,. . . . but the third day she suffered, and was relieved by taking it. She went on in this way, taking the unmedicated globules, with occasional visits from us, employing no other means, and was cured."[1] (This was written in 1881, but the episode is retained in the present version of *Science and Health*, p. 156.)

[1] *Science and Health*, Third Edition, p. 158.

93

What actual effect this or other similar experiences had upon Mrs. Patterson at the time, it is difficult to say. Everyone is inclined to read into the past the convictions of the present, and these later accounts by Mrs. Eddy of her earlier experiences are generally designed to enforce an argument which was quite admittedly a later attainment. One cannot be sure that she even caught a glimpse at the time of that which later on she saw so clearly. The fact, however, that when writing of her discovery of Christian Science she declared that for twenty years before that event she had been "trying to trace all physical effects to a mental cause."[1] would seem to indicate that this was at least a highlight in her study of homeopathy.

Mrs. Eddy leaves no doubt in her later writings that this study helped her, was indeed a definite step onwards, but that it failed even to help her at North Groton is made clear by the rather pathetic story of how one day she consoled her little blind maid who had dropped and broken a bottle of very highly considered homeopathic medicine by saying that it was "no good anyway". The woman with the dropsy might be cured by the faith begotten of a kindly deception. But Mary Patterson could not deceive herself, and so the remedy was no good.

She was, however, before she left North Groton, to receive another glimpse of the power of faith, this time in herself, so vivid as to leave upon her mind an impression which remained through the years and reappeared as a witness later on.

Not far from her home in North Groton there lived a retired minister, a devout old man, well over ninety. He was known as Father Merrill, and day after day he would walk over to the Patterson home to visit Mrs. Patterson, who, after her son was gone, was bed-ridden most of the time, and the two would read the Bible and pray together.

One day as he turned in at the gate from the road, to his complete surprise he looked up and saw Mary all smiles and with arms outstretched coming down the path to meet him. With Father Merrill there was no doubt as to what had happened. He cried out at once with joy, "Praise

[1] *Retrospection and Introspection,* p. 24.

God, He has answered our prayer." Mary for the time was equally joyous and equally sure that it was an answer to prayer. But that she was unsatisfied, restlessly insistent on knowing the why and how of it all, is made clear from her later experience. She could not hold on. The blind faith of the old minister could not be hers any more than could the faith of the woman sick of the dropsy. And so she sank back again.

And now things went from bad to worse. Patterson was away most of the time, but he earned less and less until even the interest on the mortgage was a long way in arrears.

Abigail could, of course, have saved the situation, and was no doubt appealed to, but to her practical mind it had long since become apparent that the enterprise in North Groton was a failure, that Mary was drifting into a state of chronic invalidism, and that the best thing for all concerned was to let the holder of the mortgage foreclose. Under date of September 29, 1859, Mrs. Patterson recorded in her note-book:

"On this day my sister sells our homestead"—for the holder of the mortgage was none other than Martha Pillsbury.

Abigail's intentions were no doubt good, but she left Mary to wring from the situation the last drop of humiliation and suffering. It was not until the actual day of the foreclosure that she came over in her carriage from Sanbornton to take her sister away.

Nor was this all that Mary was to bear helplessly. When one Joseph Wheet, with whom Doctor Patterson had quarreled, heard about this, he gleefully dispatched his son Charles to toll the church bell mockingly until the tormented Mary was well beyond reach of its clangour.

As they drove slowly down the mountain road towards Rumney, the little blind servant trudged some way behind. She would not ride or come too near the carriage. She could not bear to hear the low sobbing of her mistress as she leaned wretchedly on Abigail's shoulder.

CHAPTER 10

A New Hope

IT WAS TOWARD the end of March, 1860, that Mary Patterson left North Groton. She got no further than Rumney Station at the foot of the mountain road. There Abigail found a temporary home for her and her husband at a boarding house kept by a Mr. and Mrs. John Herbert. Patterson does not appear to have been with her when the actual move was made, but evidently the plan worked out by the all too efficient Abigail was that, in return for what she was doing in the way of financial rehabilitation, Patterson should make a serious effort to reform his ways and make a home for his wife.

Daniel apparently accepted the proposition with alacrity. He was never hesitant about accepting any chance to begin again. A new prospect fascinated him, for in his mind's eye, he could always see a new unfolding prosperity.

When next there is any record of him he is a gracious exemplary presence in the Herbert home at Rumney Station. He carries his invalid wife downstairs to all her meals, and carries her back again, and earns much approval for his devotion, while his Prince Albert coat and varnished boots and silk hat begin to attract attention and to inspire confidence in the minds of the patients who resort in increasing numbers to the office he had taken close by. For Daniel Patterson could always get work, and no man could be more suave and gracious and even, it is to be imagined, lovable at times. He was just the kind of character that would be forgiven, not until seven times but until seventy times seven.

His position, it must be admitted, was at no time an easy one. The contrast between the satisfying picture of married life as he had visioned it and as it really was, must have been harsh enough. Daniel Patterson married to the brilliant young widow, daughter of Squire Baker of Sanbornton, bringing her back to health and happiness through his care and skill and winning the gratitude and admiration of the Bakers and the Tiltons and the envy of a good half-dozen of his wife's former suitors, firmly established in his practice with a host of new patients—such a picture and one even brighter still must always have made the reality dreary indeed. To win happiness from the situation, as it was, would call for a love and patience and an abiding satisfaction in unseen things which Daniel Patterson did not possess, apparently.

He had a way, however, of pouncing on anything in the passing stream which fitted in with his mood and making the most of it while it lasted. At such times, he was at his best, and it was, no doubt, the constant renewal of these periods which made it possible for the two to stay together, even as long as they did.

The first few months at Rumney seem to have been just such a period for Daniel. It was not long before he had secured a little house where Mary could settle down to home-making once again, and get the full advantage of the coming spring and summer. The house was situated at Rumney village back in the hills about a mile from Rumney Station. It had a splendid view of the foothills and the mountains beyond, and, with the blind girl, Myra Smith, once again her devoted servant and companion, and Daniel still all attention, Mary began to get better.

So it was through the summer and winter, and then in the April of the following year, 1861, the whole face of things was changed by the outbreak of the Civil War. The war brought into the life of Mary Patterson a new if tragic interest. Always intensely patriotic, the fact that the whole struggle, at first, hinged on the question of secession and on that question only, caused her to throw her devotion without any mental reserve on the side of the North. Whatever other right a State might have under the Constitution, there could be no doubt of the fact, it had not the right to secede from the Union. Even on her sick bed she could do something to help. She could knit socks and make lint. She could throw open her little home for meetings of the sewing circles. She could write for the press, and she could defend and explain the stand of the North in all its phases to her friends and neighbours. She seems to have done all of these things, and to have been, of course, all the better for it. It was only a temporary stimulus, it is true, but it made life more tolerable, opening up to the sick woman an opportunity for service which all her life was literally a fundamental demand of her being.

The effect of the war upon Daniel was to afford him the most reasonable excuse that had ever come his way for "making a change". It is not sure he was consumed with patriotism. He was well over forty and never particularly attracted by the prospect of high adventure, but he loved to be where things were happening, where he could meet with and talk to people who were doing things about which he in turn could talk, and the papers every day were full of such matters. And so, within a few months of the outbreak of the war, he was hard at work exploring every means of getting into the main stream of events, as an army doctor, if nothing better offered, but preferably on some special commission such as would bring him more varied opportunities. In the end, probably through the Tiltons, he received a commission from Governor Barry of New Hampshire to carry to Washington funds which had been collected in the state to aid Northern sympathizers in the South, and attend to their distribution.

It was exactly what Daniel wanted. He could see in his coming sojourn in Washington a most satisfying social round which he would undoubtedly have opportunities for extending to an almost unlimited extent. In

Washington, a Prince Albert coat, varnished boots and a silk hat would be necessities.

And so in March of 1862, leaving Mary alone with the little blind girl, he set out for—the front.

A few months before he left, a strange new hope had come into Mary's life.

The second quarter of last century was a period of mental upheaval throughout the world, but especially in New England. The willingness to try anything once, which in later years became so characteristic of the Far West, was typical of New England at that time. It was an era of dynamic change. Railways were spreading themselves everywhere; newspapers, turned out by machines, were starting up overnight in every town and village. The electric telegraph was on the way. Emerson and Longfellow, Whittier and Lowell and a host of disciples were preaching new freedom and inevitably opening the way for the excesses of their virtues, while, in the realm of the occult, mesmerism and spiritualism were among the stock subjects of conversation and eager inquiry.

This was specially true of mesmerism. Since its first promulgation by Friedrich Anton Mesmer in 1766 in his book *De Planetarum Influxu,* mesmerism had swept into and out of popular interest several times. Its amazing domination of Paris just before the Revolution had been followed by complete discredit, and for fifty years or more its practice was regarded as simple charlatanism. In the early twenties of last century, however, it began to creep back into serious notice, and, in 1831, a committee of the Academy of Medicine of Paris reported favourably on "magnetism" as a therapeutic agent. Ten years later, James Braid, a surgeon of Manchester, England, in an able work on the subject, definitely brought the whole question back into the fold of scientific research. He renamed the phenomenon, Hypnotism, and the possibilities of "magnetic sleep" in the practice of surgery began to attract wide attention.

At that time hypnotism seemed to be in a fair way to becoming orthodox, but, a few years later, the discovery of chloroform on the practical side, and the sudden rise of spiritualism in the realm of mental phenomena, tended to make mesmerism once more an outcast.

The inevitable result of this "neglect" was to consign the practice once again to the hands of the charlatan, using the term in its broadest sense. The mesmerists who toured the towns and countrysides of New England so frequently in the second and third quarters of last century were often men of exceptional ability in their doubtful practice, but they were first of all showmen, with apparently one objective, to make as much money out of it as possible. The papers of the day were full of their advertisements, and if one were to judge from the claims those advertisements advanced, their powers were stupendous. They were, however, overshadowed in the mind of the public by the rapidly rising tide of Spiritualism. In the middle of last century, spiritualism was spreading over the eastern United States like an epidemic, mainly on the strength of its appeal as the possible beginning of a new revelation. "Spirit Circles" sprang up everywhere and Andrew Jackson Davis' book *The Principles of Nature, Her Divine Revelation*, which he declared had been dictated in clairvoyant trance, quickly attained the status of a textbook.

Mary Patterson must have read all about both spiritualism and mesmerism; indeed, this is evident from her later discussions. To one who was attracted as she was, almost to the point of fascination, by the mental and even the spiritual side of homeopathy, their possibilities would almost necessarily appeal very strongly at first. All her life, however, Mary's great standby had been her Bible, and no doctrine survived in the end for her which was not, in its final analysis, justified by the Bible. Her search, as she herself was wont to point out in later years, was for Spirit not spirits.

During the latter part of her stay in North Groton, there began to appear in the papers which came to her bedside stories of amazing works of healing that were being done by one Phineas P. Quimby, a doctor in Portland, Maine. He was, it was clear at once from the various reports, no ordinary doctor. Indeed, he departed entirely from the ordinary paths of medicine, discarded drugs and relied for his cures upon a new power which he designated *Wisdom*.

Mary Patterson must have read the early accounts of it with eagerness.

It must have seemed to her to fit in exactly with the dim conclusions that had been forced upon her by her study of homeopathy. As she put it to herself later, "Less and less medicine until there is no medicine."

Thus in the Lebanon, New Hampshire, *Free Press* of December 3, 1860, appeared a long article on this new form of healing. It was copied widely by other New England papers, and either the original issue in the *Free Press*—Lebanon is only some twenty miles from Rumney Station —or a copy of it must almost certainly have been seen and read by Mary Patterson, who was always an eager reader of newspapers.

The opening paragraph of the article could hardly fail to rivet her attention, for it tells of the healing of a woman whose trouble must have seemed to be almost exactly her own.

"Just at the present time," the article opens, "there is a good deal said about Dr. Quimby of Portland, and it may not be considered amiss to mention the case of a young lady of this town who has been greatly bene-fited by him.

"For nearly three years she has been an invalid—a great part of the time confined to her bed, and never left the room unless carried out by her friends. A few weeks since she heard of Dr. Quimby and resolved to visit him. She did so, and after remaining under his care four days she returned home free from all pain and disease, and is now rapidly re-gaining health and strength."

The papers of the day were, of course, full of such cures achieved in the most amazing and unaccustomed ways. Professor De Grath's Original Electric Oil and the *Celestial Telegraph* vied with spirits and all manner of manipulations to produce instantaneous cures for all and sundry ills. But this way was different. In the first place, the article in the Lebanon newspaper was not a paid advertisement. Neither was it written by Quimby himself but by the editor of the paper or one of his staff, who evidently regarded the subject of sufficient importance to rank as news. The writer continues—and it is not difficult to imagine Mary Patterson's growing interest—

"The reputation of Dr. Quimby as a man who cures disease has ex-

101

tended without the narrow limits of his own state and the sick from various parts have learned to avail themselves of his services. The increasing respect and confidence of the public in his success, suggests the day of miracles and brings up a question as absurd as that of two thousand years ago, 'Can any good come out of Nazareth?' Can actual disease be cured by a humbug? Dr. Quimby effects his cures without the aid of medicine or outward applications, and his practice embraces cases like the above, where all ordinary treatment has failed to relieve. These facts at first, place him in the rank of the mysteries of a superstitious world, but there are few of his patients after a second interview who do not think the mystery is in them and not in him. . . . It is here that Dr. Quimby stands, his explanations and his cures go hand in hand. While his senses are penetrating the dark mystery of the sick, he is in complete possession of his consciousness as a man. Not fearing to investigate the operation of the mind, he penetrates the region where nothing but magicians, sorcerers, witchcraft and spiritualists have ventured, and going far beyond them in his experiments, he arrives at the principle regulating happiness."

An article such as this—and there were many like it—would be sufficient to account for the interest that Doctor Quimby aroused in the mind of Mary Patterson.

And she was immensely interested, so much so that in the October of 1861, on a rumour that Quimby was coming to Concord, she persuaded Patterson to write to him in Portland and state her case. It must have seemed to her almost a last chance and she was determined to take it. And so Daniel wrote from Rumney on October 14, offering to bring Mrs. Patterson up to Concord if he would exercise his "wonderful power" in her behalf whilst visiting that section "for the benefit of the suffering portion of our race."[1]

Within a few days, a reply came from Quimby to the effect that he had not then any plans to visit Concord, but enclosing a printed circular which he was apparently in the habit of sending out in response to inquiries. It is a long and tortuous document and very possibly explains

[1] *The Quimby Manuscripts*, First Edition, p. 146.

why the sick woman in Rumney waited another nine months, as she did, before she wrote to Quimby again.

The circular is a very businesslike one, wherein "Dr. P. P. Quimby would respectfully announce to the citizens of............................ and vicinity, that he will be at the............................ where he will attend to those wishing to consult him in regard to their health."

He then goes on to say that he gives no medicine and makes no outward applications, "but simply sits down by the patients, tells them their feelings and what they think is their disease." If the patients admit that he is right, then the explanation he gives them is the cure, "and if he succeeds in correcting their error, he changes the fluids of the system and establishes the truth or health."

After several paragraphs, devoted to severe strictures on orthodox medical practice, he concludes with a note as to fees. Referring again to his method, he says, "This can only be explained to patients, for which explanation his charge is............................ dollars. If necessary to see them more than once,............................ dollars."[1]

What effect this circular, combined with all she had read about him, had upon Mary Patterson, is not known. That she did not at that time follow her inquiries further is clear from her subsequent letters. The probability is that the stimulus of the war all around her, together with the preparations for her husband's departure for Washington, diverted her thought sufficiently to give her temporary relief. It was about this time, too, that she received a letter from her son, the first direct news she had from him since he was taken away from her some eight years previously. This brought the great struggle more nearly home to her, for the letter told Mary that her son had enlisted in the army two years before and how tremendously—with all the enthusiasm of a lad of eighteen—he was looking forward to going to the front.

Mary wept over the letter and kissed it. Her hopes had been broken so often where her boy was concerned that she seems through these years to have had no heart to make further effort. She simply took what little

[1] *The Quimby Manuscripts*, First Edition, pp. 144-5.

comfort she could get—when it came. She wrote to him, of course, and there is some evidence that he wrote to her more than once, but the war made any thought of their seeing each other again more improbable than ever. Meanwhile, Doctor Patterson had gone to Washington, and Mary settled down with her blind servant to make the best of things, and to watch eagerly and anxiously, as did so many mothers and wives in those days, for letters.

She did not have to wait long, for about the middle of April she received one morning a letter from Abigail, enclosing a letter from Washington addressed to her husband, Hamilton Tilton. It was not from Patterson, but from one of his friends, and it told the absurdly pathetic story of how Daniel, all eager to see and hear all there was to be seen and heard, had driven out from Washington in a sulky with a party of friends to view the battlefield of Bull Run, how going off on his own he had strayed too near the Confederate lines and had been picked up by Stewart's cavalry and carried off, possibly on the suspicion of being a spy.

No doubt Abigail in her covering letter did her best to soften the shock, but it must have been severe enough in any case. The fate of a spy was summary, and the suspense might have gone hardly with Mary. But fortunately within a day or two she received a letter from Patterson himself from Libby prison, a cheerful, incorrigible letter, the letter of a boy who has got himself into a scrape but is secretly enjoying every moment of it. Due deference is paid to the solemnity and seriousness of the occasion, but it is impossible to escape the impression that Daniel is having a good time. He writes:

"DEAR WIFE,

You will be amazed to learn that I am in prison in the Confederate States prison, but it is so, I was taken one week ago today." He tells her not to be uneasy as he is safe and that his fellow prisoners are friendly gentlemen. The letter is nothing if not tender, but an incongruous yet characteristic note is struck when he says, "I left my travelling bag and a new pair of boots at 381 Pennsylvania Avenue, Washington, at Mrs. C. W. Heydon's." He asks her to communicate with their representative in Congress, gives directions for reaching him in prison by letter, re-asserts his concern for her welfare and signs, "Your affectionate Husband."

Mary rose to the occasion as she always did. She wrote at once to T. M. Edwards, and he took the matter up with the Secretary of War. Nothing, however, could be done, as no prisoners were being exchanged. An appeal to her old friend Franklin Pierce was equally fruitless. There was nothing to do but wait, and when the stimulus of the new demands had passed, the old wretchedness descended upon her worse than ever before.

In her extremity, she remembered Quimby. She wrote to him begging him to come to Rumney and help her, as she could not go to him. It is a fear-wracked, despairing letter, dated Rumney, May 29, '62.[1]

The shock of her husband's capture, she writes, brought on a relapse just when she was getting well from a chronic disease which completely incapacitated her for a year at a time. Writing from bed, she begs him to visit her immediately, explaining, "I have entire confidence in your philosophy as read in the circular sent my husband Dr. Patterson."

But Doctor Quimby was unable to come to her, and Mary turned to her sister Abigail for help. She now had one purpose and one purpose only in mind, to get to Doctor Quimby, for it seems certain from subsequent events that she had already begun that process—so evident later on —of reading into Quimby's philosophy what she most desired to find there. Throughout her long years, Mrs. Eddy's great source, at once of strength and vulnerability, lay in just this facility with which she endowed those associated with her with the qualities she most desired to find in them. As she herself put it some twenty-four years later after many bitter experiences, "It has always been my misfortune to think people bigger and better than they really are."[2]

This accounts, in a measure perhaps, for the amazing sudden ruptures of friendships with which her life and career are punctuated. The friend of yesterday would suddenly appear before her for what indeed he had

---

[1] *The Quimby Manuscripts*, First Edition, p. 147.
[2] *Christian Science Journal*, June, 1887.

always been, while the "spiritual genius" would be seen for what he always was, just another human being of common clay.

Doctor Quimby was the first and perhaps the most notable example of this tendency. When she wrote to him in her despair from Rumney, she had quite evidently worked through to an estimate of him far ahead of desert and one she did not have when her husband had written some nine months previously.

Abigail's response to her appeal was instant, as it always was, and when she drove over from Sanbornton to Rumney, she insisted that Mary go back with her there until Doctor Patterson should be released. Mary readily acceded to the proposal. She was determined somehow to get to Portland to see the man who she was convinced could help her, and Abigail she felt sure would make it possible. This decision gave her new strength. Instead of having to be carried to the carriage, as Abigail had evidently expected she would have to be, she rose and dressed herself and the two set out together on the long drive back to Sanbornton.

On the way, Mary told her sister of her great desire. Abigail was utterly shocked. Quimby was nothing but a charlatan or worse still a mesmerist. She would not think of helping any sister of hers to go to him.

Nothing is known for certain of Mary's impressions on returning to Sanbornton after an absence of nearly ten years, or of the wretchedness of her own thoughts as she contemplated the burden of making yet another effort at a fresh beginning.

She did make the effort, of course. Within a few weeks Abigail had arranged a new plan, down to the last detail, as she had arranged so many other things in the past. Mary was to go to Doctor Vail's Water Cure Sanatorium at Hill, New Hampshire. Abigail provided her with a suitable companion and nurse, a young woman named Susan Ward, made all the provisions for a comfortable journey, supplied her with the necessary funds, saw her on her way and felt sure that all would be well.

Mary agreed to everything, without protest. Hill was nearer to Portland than was Sanbornton, and Mary was determined somehow or other to get to Portland.

Phineas P. Quimby

PHINEAS PARKHURST QUIMBY was a native of Lebanon, New Hampshire, where he was born, on February 16, 1802, to Jonathan Quimby, a blacksmith, and his wife Susannah. When he was two years old, his father and mother moved to Belfast, Maine, and when he was thirteen or thereabouts, being small of stature and not overly strong, his father decided that the calling of a blacksmith would be too hard for him and apprenticed him to a clockmaker.

It was not a hit-or-miss choice on his father's part. From his earliest childhood, the little Phineas was fascinated by anything that "worked", and in order to get things to "work" exactly his patience was inexhaustible. Clockmaking was almost an obvious choice. It was, moreover, a trade in which a man could quickly make a name for himself if he was an honest and skilled craftsman. People demanded good clocks, and bad clocks quickly revealed their deficiencies. Seth Thomas, the elder, of Plymouth Hollow, Connecticut, was already turning out clocks which attained a standard only exceeded by that of his son, and to make a clock as good as one turned out by Seth Thomas was, in all probability, the dizzy height set for himself by young Phineas Quimby when he entered on his apprenticeship in Belfast, Maine. If it was, he reached his objective, for "Quimby clocks" are still to be found in Maine, and they long enjoyed a reputation for accuracy and good workmanship.

However, young Quimby was not only interested in the workings of clocks, but in the workings of anything. He was a natural inventor, and never was so happy as when he had some new contraption with which to amaze his friends. Moreover, boy and young man, he was eager in debate and mercilessly Socratic in argument. Quick to recognize faults or inaccuracies in almost anything where others would pass them by, he had a way in an argument of compelling his opponent to toe the line which quickly earned him a reputation at the general store or where not as a champion debater.

Belfast, Maine, in those days, was a busy little town devoted to ship-building, and, lying as it does at the head of Penobscot Bay, it was considered of sufficient importance to be invested by the British towards the close of the War of 1812. Like many other coast towns, moreover, Belfast enjoyed an intercourse with the outside world and the great coastal cities like Boston, New York and Baltimore, denied in the days before the railways to the inland towns, and was, as a consequence, sure sooner or later of a visitation from any "rage" or person much in the public eye.

And so, one day, in the late thirties, there arrived in Belfast, a certain Frenchman named Charles Poyen, who advertised a course of lectures in the town hall on the then much discussed question of Mesmerism. Belfast flocked to hear him, and among those eagerly present was Phineas Quimby. Charles Poyen found a sympathetic and attentive audience, and all went excellently well until he came to giving practical demonstrations of mesmeric influence. Immediately he found himself in difficulties. Things did not work as they should, and the task which he claimed he usually found so simple was laboured and exhausting. At last, he spoke to his audience about it. Someone, consciously or unconsciously, was working against him, was his explanation. He would be glad if the person responsible for it would remain after the meeting and have a talk with him, as he felt sure he must be a mesmerist of considerable promise.

Whether Phineas Quimby thought himself the man or not, he was evidently determined to make the claim. Such an opportunity was too good to let pass by, and so as the audience filed out, he remained, and very soon he and M. Poyen were in close conference. That Poyen succeeded in convincing Quimby of his mesmeric powers, is evident, for within a few days Phineas is giving free exhibitions in the general store, and much to the satisfaction of the proprietor, "willing" people to come in off the street and buy of his wares.

Phineas Quimby took the matter seriously, as he always did. He read everything he could get on the subject, among others, no doubt, Poyen's own book, *Progress of Animal Magnetism in New England*. He also seems to have followed Poyen for a time from town to town, until at last, quite convinced of his own powers, he began to practice on any of his friends who were willing to become subjects. His success in inducing "magnetic sleep" was immediate and uniform, and from that he went on to "willing away" minor ailments. Once satisfied that he could do that, the matter was settled as far as he was concerned. Here was something infinitely more engaging than clockmaking or inventing. If minor ailments could be healed, more serious ones could be healed. He tried and was apparently successful. People began to talk about him and to come to him for help in increasing numbers.

So matters went until some time in 1842, when Quimby made a new discovery. Among the many subjects who had come under his influence was a youth named Lucius Burkmar. He was a boy that, according to the neighbours, had always been "queer". But under Quimby's influence he exhibited the most surprising powers. When thrown into a mesmeric trance, so some said, he could describe people and places he had never seen, tell the location of ships at sea and report happenings of the moment in distant places which were subsequently verified. Most amazing of all, he also appeared to have the power of "looking into people" and diagnosing disease and prescribing remedies which in many cases healed them instantly. So goes the story.

Quimby was astounded and enthusiastic. He determined to give up clockmaking and go on a lecture tour with Burkmar. This he did for a time with great success. Quimby, however, was an intelligent man, indeed he had unquestionable gifts as a scientific research student. He never had been satisfied with just seeing things work, he demanded to know how they worked. At first he had been satisfied that his "power" flowed from himself, but an experience he had with Burkmar raised in his mind serious doubt on the subject. It appears that, in course of their association, Burkmar left Quimby for a time and was engaged to diagnose cases for another mesmerist named John Bovee Dods—later a man of considerable repute and author of a book entitled *The Philosophy of Electrical Psychology*. Dods had a wealthy clientele compared with that of Quimby, and when Burkmar came back to him again, as he eventually did, Quimby found that the remedies he had been prescribing while working for Dods were much too costly for his, Quimby's, patients. The two conferred on the subject. Burkmar agreed to prescribe cheaper remedies, and the patients got well just the same, we are told!

As the result of this and other experiences, it gradually began to dawn on Quimby that the healing agent was faith in the drugs and not the drugs themselves. Here he would seem to have arrived at much the same point as had Mary Patterson from her experiments with homeopathy. Their fundamental divergence thence onwards lay in the fact that Quimby sought his solution along the lines of a philosophy; Mary Patterson sought hers along the lines of revealed religion, in the broadest sense of that term. But that is, of course, to anticipate the record.

When Mary Patterson wrote to him from Rumney in the early summer of 1862, Doctor Quimby had a commodious suite in the International Hotel in Portland and was treating as many as five hundred patients a year. His remarkable cures were talked of everywhere, and the nearer one got to Portland the more detailed was the picture. When Mary reached Doctor Vail's Sanatorium, she found that Doctor Quimby of Portland and his work were one of the main subjects of conversation. The whole Sanatorium seemed to be in a state of vague unrest and expectancy. Several of the patients had actually been to Portland and seen Quimby. One

Julius Dresser—afterwards to figure so prominently in Mary Patterson's life and story—returned to the Sanatorium from such a visit shortly after Mary got there. He was much improved in health and quite enthusiastic about Quimby's work and methods.

Mary was more than ever satisfied that she must get to Portland at all costs. She was, however, entirely without funds of her own, and there was apparently no one upon whom she could call. Abigail would not think of sending her money for such a purpose. She did, however, send her little extra sums from time to time, and these Mary saved carefully, denying herself the small comforts for which the money was intended. She grew worse rather than better, and at last she wrote to Quimby again almost in despair. She wants to come to him. Apparently she has at last the where-withal to pay her way, but now the question arises, has she the strength to make the journey? After saying how clearly she now sees the mistake she made in not trying to reach him when she had more strength, she continues by explaining that her stay for two or three months at this water-cure place has been anything but helpful. Her ability to walk several miles has diminished until she can only sit up in bed occasionally and now doubts whether she has the strength to reach him or, having that, whether any foundation or reserve would be left for him to build on. "I would rather die with my friends at Sanbornton hence I shall go to you to *live* or them to *die* very soon. Please answer this yourself."[1]

Quimby answered at once with that kindly consideration which seems to have been characteristic of the man, encouraging Mrs. Patterson to come to him, and assuring her she would be able to make the journey. And so, a few weeks later, Mary Patterson set out for Portland, and on October 10th, 1862, presented herself at Quimby's office at the International Hotel. She was so weak and exhausted that she had to be assisted up the steps to his room.

Quimby came out to see her almost at once, and as she looked up she would have seen advancing towards her a small kindly man with broad forehead and white silken hair and beard, one who managed somehow to

[1] *The Quimby Manuscripts*, First Edition, pp. 147-8.

establish for himself at once an atmosphere of sympathy and understanding. It was just what she had longed for, and when he sat down beside her, as was his custom, and maintained quietly that he would "explain" her trouble to her and that that explanation would be the cure, she felt herself roused to a sense of expectancy almost reaching exaltation. Anyway, what followed would suggest some such process, for as he told her that she was "held in bondage by the opinions of her family and physicians", and that "her animal spirit was reflecting its grief upon her body and calling itself spinal disease", that "she could be cured, and would be cured", a sense of peace and new strength came over her, and, next moment, she was standing before him—healed, no less. She was quite sure of it.

Within a few days, with enthusiasm, she was writing about it to the Portland *Courier*:

"Three weeks since I quitted my nurse and sick room en route for Portland. The belief of my recovery had died out of the heart of those who were most anxious for it. With this mental and physical depression I first visited P. P. Quimby, and in less than one week from that time I ascended by a stairway of one hundred and eighty-two steps to the dome of the City Hall, and am improving ad infinitum."

And so her great hope was fulfilled. She was healed. There could be no question of it in her mind.

She must, however, learn the way of it. She had no doubt whatever that the method of Quimby's work was one that could be elucidated and learned by anyone who applied himself to the study. Quimby himself does not seem to have been so sure. He is reported frequently to have declared that he did not know how it was done. But even as early as her letter to the Portland *Courier*, Mary Patterson seems to have had no doubt at all on the subject. Quimby had rediscovered the healing method of Jesus. She had to go through deep waters indeed before she was reluctantly satisfied that this was not so.

Meanwhile, she began at once with the eager devotion of a convinced disciple to take of the things of Quimby and set them up as way marks along her own spiritual journey. She spent every moment she could in his suite at the International Hotel talking to him, asking him questions, reading any notes or longer manuscripts he had to give her, and building up her own concept of the new teaching at a rate which must, at times, have kept the kindly little doctor running breathlessly behind, if indeed he was able to follow her at all.

Quimby, however, seems to have appreciated it all immensely. He was in many ways a remarkably selfless man. At the time Mary Patterson came to him, his work and teaching were his very life. He cared little or nothing for the money his practice brought him. Many times his letters to patients—a great number of which letters are still preserved—show him returning money that had been sent him, on the ground that for some reason or other he did not feel that he had earned it. He was, moreover, always eager to learn more of his own doctrine, and he must have regarded with interest if not assent Mrs. Patterson's confident interpretation of everything he taught in the light of religious faith.

Mary Patterson was probably happier in these few weeks than ever before in her troubled life. At first, she seems to have enjoyed perfect health. No doubt intervened at any point to give her pause, and life must have seemed opening out to her with a promise such as she had never ventured even to outline before.

And then, right in the midst of it all, a strange thing happened, one that must have seemed to her in her overflowing gratitude yet another instance of the "power" of her new-found faith. One day a message was brought to her in her room at the International Hotel that a gentleman was below who desired to speak to her. And when she went down, there stood Daniel, very thin and worn, sadly unkempt and very chastened. He had escaped from the Confederate prison, and after many bitter hardships had found his way first to Sanbornton and then as quickly as he could on to Portland to his wife. In spite of all their strange incompatibility, it must have been a happy reunion. Patterson would be at his best in such circumstances, and the appeal of his chastened self and condition to Mary would have carried all before it.

113

It was all so utterly unexpected. Some months previously Mary had had a letter from him, not from Libby, but from Salisbury, North Carolina, whither fortunately for him he had been removed shortly after his capture. It was dated May 19, 1862, and after telling his wife how McLellan's "eternal tardiness" had blasted their hope of liberty, he added how they felt now they were "fixed for the war beyond a possibility of earlier release". He went on to dilate on the comfort of his surroundings. North Carolina in May has much to commend it and Daniel, it is evident from his letter, was settling down to enjoy it all.

"The air", he writes, "is clear and balmy and I am allowed to breathe as much as I please through the window. My bed is just by the window. I believe all will end right so be of good cheer. God is over all and does all things well. Give yourself no uneasiness on my account."

Mary would have received the letter about the time she was leaving Rumney with Abigail for Sanbornton, and so it must have set her mind at rest about her husband, at least for the moment.

Whether Daniel meant to convey to Mary any hint that he might be planning escape, by his innocent mention of the fact that his bed was just by the window, it is not possible to say, but as a matter of fact the position of his bed evidently did help. For, some four months later, on the night of September 20, taking advantage of a heavy rainstorm, Daniel and two companions let themselves down from this window by means of a rope improvised from sheets and blankets and made good their escape into the adjoining woods. There they wandered for several days, fearful of coming out into the open, and subsisting on what they could get by means of night raids on the gardens, orchards and chicken roosts of such farms as they came to in the clearings. At last, after two months of great hardships, during which they were time and again near recapture, they succeeded in reaching the headquarters of General Milroy of West Virginia. There they were provided with means for their journey to Washington, where Patterson arrived about the first week in November, continuing on almost immediately to Sanbornton and Portland.

On November 26, 1862, the New Hampshire *Patriot* reported the

114

story in full under the heading "Escape of Dr. Patterson", and a few weeks later, Daniel, fully restored to health and, it may be hoped, to his usual dress, is lecturing on his experiences in the Mechanics' Hall, Portland, no doubt to a large and interested audience, who had paid fifteen cents each for the privilege.

By January 12, 1863, the Pattersons are back again in Sanbornton Bridge, and from Mary's first letter to Quimby—which bears this date—it is clear that her remarkable recovery has greatly impressed her family and friends. Five or six of these friends, she tells Quimby, are going to visit him, while Abigail is anxious he should see her son Albert, and plans shortly even to see him herself. Lying as it does amid a desert of so much suffering, the letter is like a small oasis of joy: "I eat drink and am merry; have no laws to fetter my spirit now, though I am quite as much an escaped prisoner as my dear husband was." Her husband, she sighs, yearns to join the army and she is trying to acquiesce.[1]

However, Daniel seems to have suppressed his yearning and to have refrained from doing anything impetuous. After his many and sore trials, the comfortable home of the Tiltons, combined, at first, with the interest of his friends in his experiences, must have made life seem very pleasant to him. After all, there was plenty of time, and in describing—as few could so well—the horrors of a Confederate prison, he was doing something to arouse proper feeling and raise the general morale.

Mary is not so sure that all is well. Her next letter written from Sanbornton under date of January 21, 1863, to Quimby, shows that the situation is worrying her. She longs for a place of her own, while her faith is unimpaired, she fears the onset of old troubles.

"You know", she writes rather plaintively, "I am less than one year from the thirty-nine of supposed disease, and the habit is yet so strong upon me that I need your *occasional* aid." Enclosing a remittance for the last treatment, or "sitting," she requests another.[2]

Some time in February, Abigail made a trip to Portland to see Quimby, taking her son Albert along with her. The boy, never robust, had con-

[1] Ibid., p. 148.
[2] Ibid., p. 149.

tracted habits which were causing his family much anxiety. He smoked to excess and drank considerably, and Mary's complete faith in Quimby evidently aroused in Abigail a genuine hope that he might be able to help and even cure her son. She was, moreover, herself suffering from an abdominal rupture and Mary was equally insistent that that, too, could be healed. And so Abigail went to Portland, full of a hope which rested, however uneasily, on a fundamental scepticism.

For Abigail Tilton had none of Mary's faith. A capable woman with a remarkable executive capacity, she never had had a thought—where Mary had had so many—of questioning the established order. Once, many years before, during a revival at Sanbornton she had "felt the change"—Mary had written joyfully to her friend Augusta Holmes about it—but it was not long before she had settled easily back into that routine which made of her religion a habit rather than a faith. Mary, however, had unquestionably been healed. She, Abigail, did not understand it and did not much like it, but if it could help her son, she was willing to try it. And so she went.

Mary's next letter to Quimby, written on March 10, tells the further development of the matter. Abigail and her son had been back at Sanbornton just a week, and already the boy is slipping. She begs Quimby, in behalf of his mother and herself, to "renew" his "influence" in order to "hold him back from his easy besetting sins".

"His parents are truly grateful and somewhat encouraged at the success thus far."[1]

"Somewhat encouraged" must indeed have seemed to her in sorry contrast with her own unqualified rejoicing when she had returned to Sanbornton some two months earlier; "I eat drink and am merry; have no laws to fetter my spirit now."

But Abigail was not Mary; neither was Albert. Where Quimby succeeded easily with the woman full of faith, he failed completely—as subsequent letters show—with the woman full of doubts and her son. For Mary Patterson had full faith in Quimby. She not only fitted him

[1] Ibid., pp. 149-50.

at once at their first meeting into her ideal, but continued to carry him along with her in the months and years to come through her every spiritual experience. It is not without significance in this connection that a few days before she wrote this last letter to Quimby she had written a letter to a friend in Portland, evidently one of Quimby's patients, which would seem to indicate that she was already attempting to put into readable form her own interpretation of Quimby's teaching. "I will try", she writes, "to send my philosophy by Mrs. Tilton when she accompanies her son to the International."

But Mary herself is beginning to be full of trouble once again. She is "suffering somewhat from old habits, pain in the back and stomach, a cold just now and bilious."[1] So she wrote to Quimby. And then she has been trying to help Albert, and won't the doctor laugh when she tells him that she is suffering from "a constant desire to smoke". But adds, pleadingly, "Do pray rid me of this feeling."

It was part of Quimby's theory at that time that he took his patients' "griefs" upon himself and then "threw them off" by his own superior wisdom. Mary evidently feared her wisdom was not strong enough.

Then there was always Daniel. He had at last bestirred himself, it is true, had gone to Lynn, then as now a busy manufacturing town some twelve miles north of Boston, and resumed his dental practice in partnership with two other dentists. Mary followed him, but whether Daniel succeeded so well that they could afford to go off on a holiday, or, as is more likely, so ill that there was not much else to do, in any event, the following September found them in Saco, Maine. Saco was Daniel's native town. He had a brother still living there, and so, as they had never been there together before, it is possible that the trip was just one of those little romantic contrivances with which Mary often tried to hold the queer restless man to whom she was married.

Saco, on the Saco river, some fifteen miles west-south-west of Portland, was at that time a thriving town with the inevitable grist, cotton and lumber mills climbing up the river, which at this point drops some forty

[1] Ibid., p. 150.

feet on its way to the sea a few miles away. It was a cultured place, too, with a fine library and an old established academy. The grand stretches of Old Orchard Beach were close by.

The proximity of the little town to Portland was no doubt a great attraction in Mary's eyes. From the one letter of hers to Quimby written from there that has been preserved, it may reasonably be inferred that she saw him frequently, as may the fact that she sought his help and advice on the perennial problem which Daniel presented. Growing worse instead of better, he gradually drifted from mild semi-professional flirtations to more serious and more sordid associations. He would go off and leave his wife for days and weeks at a time. Mary evidently had great hopes of reformation from their visit to Saco, and it is possibly due to the failure of these hopes that she is alluding when she writes to Quimby: "But I have conquered my first disappointment."[1]

The letter also contains another appeal for help—they are pathetically frequent from now on—"I would like to have you in your *Omnipresence* visit me at eight o'clock this eve, if convenient. But consult your own time. Only come once a day until I am better."

The bitterness of hope deferred was evidently still to be her experience.

[1] Ibid., p. 150.

The Lecture at Warren

MARY PATTERSON WAS a born teacher. To be a successful teacher it is necessary to love teaching, and Mary, all her life, had loved teaching. Her "discursive talking", which Albert recalls so interestedly in one of his letters, her little school at Sanbornton, her writings regarding slavery and other political issues, and now her eager advocacy of Quimby's teaching or her own interpretation of it, all reveal that urge to teach which later on was to be put to such tremendous purpose.

When she first conceived the idea of teaching and healing along the lines laid down by Quimby, it is impossible to say, but it seems reasonable to suppose that her failure to make a permanent home for her husband turned her thought definitely in this direction. She was almost tragically in need of an objective in life, and this course seemed to offer her one.

Be that as it may, the early winter found her back again in Portland studying eagerly. Writing of these times, George Quimby, Doctor Quimby's son, who acted as his father's secretary, recalls the persistence with which Mrs. Patterson sought to grasp what his father was teaching. "She learned from him," he writes, "not as a student receiving a regular course

. . . but by sitting in his room, talking with him, reading his manuscripts, copying some of them, writing some herself and reading them to him for criticism. . . . I have heard him talk hours and hours, week in and week out when she was present, listening and asking questions."[1]

And so in the spring of 1864, she set out on what was to be—whether she intended it or not—her first missionary journey. It came about in this way. Among Quimby's patients who were staying at the International Hotel in Portland at the time Mary was there, were two women, Miss Mary Ann Jarvis of Warren, Maine, and Mrs. Sarah Crosby of Albion. The three women became close friends. Miss Jarvis suffered from asthma and was threatened with tuberculosis, while Mrs. Crosby was recovering from some kind of nervous disorder. All three were earnest students of Quimby's methods, and Mrs. Crosby and Miss Jarvis began to look more and more to Mrs. Patterson for further enlightenment. "He (Quimby) told me many times", Mrs. Crosby declared years afterwards, "that I was not so quick to perceive the truth as Mrs. Patterson."

Mrs. Crosby and Miss Jarvis seem to have left Portland for their homes early in the new year, both greatly improved in health, but, in March, Miss Jarvis had a relapse and wrote to Mary begging her to fulfill at once a promise she had evidently made to both her and Mrs. Crosby to visit them in the near future. She had great faith in Mrs. Patterson's understanding of Quimby's teaching and felt sure she could help her if she would only come at once. It was a definite call for help and Mary, after doubtless talking it over with Quimby, decided to answer it and go to Warren.

Her next letter to Quimby is written from there under date of March 31, 1864. It opens in a happy, engaging way, telling of her arrival at Warren after a hectic trip involving an all-night stop-over. "Next morning at ten o'clock got into a villainous old vehicle and felt a sensation of being in a hen coop on the top of a churn dash for about six hours! when the symptoms began to subside, and so did the old cart."[2]

And then she goes on to tell of her friend, how warm was her welcome

[1] *The Quimby Manuscripts*, First Edition, p. 438.
[2] Ibid., pp. 150-1.

and how anxiously she had been awaited, her hostess having expected her a day or two before.

But she has good news. Miss Jarvis is better already, and it seems possible to detect in her account of the matter a strange new expectancy as of one who tries something for the first time, and, half doubt, all hope, begins to realize that perhaps, after all, she can do it. After telling Quimby that the Saturday before Miss Jarvis had had "a paroxysm of what she called 'difficulty of breathing on account of the easterly wind'," she continues:

"I sat down by her, took her hands and explained in my poor way what it was, instead of what is was not as she had understood it. In a little her breath became natural, and to my surprise even, she raised phlegm easily and has scarcely coughed since, till today. So I have laughed at her about the wind veering according to P. P. Quimby. I say to her, 'why even the winds and the waves obey him'."[1]

There is a word about Mrs. Crosby at Albion, and how she looks forward to seeing her soon, quite a little about her own struggles "to keep the faith," a plea to the little doctor to continue helping her, and then, in the end, what would seem to be an allusion, pervaded with an unconscious pathos, to Daniel. "If I could have my husband with me and be at home, I would like it there; but! but! but . . ."[2]

But if she could heal she ought to be preaching and teaching, and very soon she began to be convinced that she could heal. "Miss Jarvis is doing well," she writes to Quimby on April 5, "and I shall not stop here longer than is necessary to make her happy." On April 10, "a lame back and some other ailments have all gone." And then on April 24 comes the final triumph. "When I came here she could not do but a little housework. . . . In three weeks she did her *washing*! a thing she told me she had not thought of being able to do ever again. . . . She never knows which way the wind blows now, east or contrawise."

It was clearly her business to preach and teach the word wherever and however she could. And so in due time there appeared in the Post Office

[1] Ibid., p. 151.
[2] Ibid., p. 151.

and other "marts" in Warren this notice: "Mrs. M. M. Patterson will lecture at the Town Hall one week from next Wednesday on P. P. Quimby's spiritual Science healing disease—as opposed to Deism or Rochester-Rapping spiritualism."[1]

The story of the lecture is contained in two letters to Quimby, one written on April 10[2] and the other on the 24th.[3] It was "thinly attended", but the "precious few" there were described by "a lady present (the manufacturer's wife)" as the "uppertendam", while Mr. Hodgeman, "a man of sixty years old, said it was the nearest *right* of anything he ever heard in Warren." "I had no poetry at the close, 'twas all *truth*. Will read it to you if you like when next I see you. . . . I have changed it to suit the occasion"—she was planning to deliver it again—"This seems to me a spiritual need of this people." The hearts of Warren folks she finds very respectful and kind.

The lectures were not barren in results, for within a few days "Mrs. Fuller (the woollen-manufacturer's wife)" is writing to Mary telling her she is sick and asking Mary to help her. Only Mary hesitated. "I returned a note", she writes, "that I was not done with my pupilage yet, and recommended her to visit you."

Meanwhile, she is evidently writing and thinking constantly and longing to be able to write and think more. "I long to be strong," she writes Quimby, "and then would I not be happy saying just what I wish to do and letting people read it."

"Dr.," she continues, "I have a strange feeling of late that I ought to be *perfect* after the command of science, in order to know and do the right. So much as I need to attain before that, makes the job look difficult, but I shall try. When men and above all women revile me to forgive and pity. When I am misjudged because misunderstood to feel: Wisdom forgive them for they know not what they do. . . . All things shall work together for good to them who love wisdom. . . . If I could use my pen as I long to do, and not sink under it, I would work after this model till it should appear 'a thing of beauty which is a joy for ever'."[4]

[1] Ibid., p. 155.
[2] Ibid., pp. 152-4.
[3] Ibid., pp. 152-4.
[4] Ibid., p. 155.

This last sentence, in view of all that was to follow, is perhaps significant enough.

Meanwhile, the road continued up hill for her all the way. The light and shade in her letters to Quimby are almost crudely vivid in contrast. The joy of being able to help others is overcast perpetually by the fear that she would not be able to "throw off" the "griefs" that she took upon herself in effecting a cure under Quimby's strange healing process, Albert's smoking, Miss Jarvis' asthma, threatened tuberculosis and other troubles.

"When Miss Jarvis would come to my bed it would invariably set me to coughing. And before I was sick she had lost . . . the least approach to a cough; now she is coughing a little, but she can't get back for I have borne her sins and you have saved me."[1] This strange doctrine of transference was to cling stubbornly throughout many years to come.

It was indeed all too evident a hard path that Mary Patterson was trying to follow, but her faith remained unshaken, and some time in the latter part of May, 1864, she returned to Portland, and for a month or more resumed her former day by day association with Quimby. It seems likely that one of their subjects of conference was Daniel, but whether the kindly doctor had anything to do with it or not, it was not long before Mary had determined to make yet another effort to bring about a better understanding with her husband.

Daniel himself seems to have enjoyed at this time one of those splendid visions of a new heaven and a new earth which rose periodically above the horizon of his life. This time, his vision was surely the greatest yet, for, now, his appeal was not to be to the few or even to the many, but to all the world. And so in the Lynn *Weekly Reporter* for June 11, 1864, appeared the following advertisement:

Dental Notice
Dr. D. Patterson

"Would respectfully announce to the public that he has returned to Lynn and opened office in B. F. & G. N. Spinney's new building, on Union Street between the Central Depot and Sagamore Hotel, where he

[1] Ibid., p. 157.

123

will be happy to meet the friends and patrons secured last year while in the office of Drs. Davis and Trow, and now he hopes to secure the patronage of 'all the rest of mankind', by the exhibition of that skill which close study and many years of first class and widely extended practice enable him to bring to the aid of the suffering. He is aware that he has to compete with able practitioners, but yet offers his services fearlessly, knowing that competition is the real stimulus to success, and trusting in his ability to please all who need Teeth filled, extracted or new sets. He was the first to introduce LAUGHING GAS in Lynn for Dental purposes and has had excellent success with it. Terms lower than anywhere else for the same quality of work."

It was all no doubt a part of a mutual effort of the two to live together again. Mary must have read the advertisement with some misgivings, but she evidently determined to make the attempt and early in July returned to Lynn.

It was all to no purpose, however, Daniel's periodic reformations were of briefer duration as the years passed, and Mary had hardly settled in their new home before she realized that her husband was just as he had always been, only worse. Previously, his obvious contrition for his failings had won from Mary forgiveness again and again, but now he did not bother to be contrite. The bad boy had become a rather down at heel Don Juan, and each time it took a larger dose of ill-doing to find a reaction in repentance. He was no longer an itinerant dentist, but he went away just the same for days and weeks at a time. Mary stood it as long as she could. But at last when proof was brought to her of a particularly sordid intrigue on the part of the doctor with one of her friends—proof in the form of letters written by him (still preserved) which are unprintable in the warmth of their expression—she packed up her few things and once more sought refuge with Sarah Crosby in Albion, Maine. That Mary did not drive him to infidelity is shown by an affidavit in 1902 by his boarding-house keeper, R. D. Rounsevel of Littleton, quoting him as saying he could have had as pleasant and happy a home as anyone could want if he had only done as he ought by Mary.

Many years afterwards, Mrs. Crosby recalled how Mary arrived at her home in Albion—a small farmhouse on the outskirts of the town—almost destitute, without money or proper clothing, "her only assets being her indomitable will and active mind". But the two women were genuinely devoted to each other and Mrs. Crosby received Mary gladly. To Mary, the little farmhouse at Albion must have seemed a veritable haven of refuge, for not only was she cut off from her husband but from her family as well. There is very little information on the point, but it would seem clear that Mary's devotion to Quimby and his teaching had by this time—the fall of 1864—led to a complete breach between her and Abigail. Her father, now an old man over eighty, was also estranged from Mary for some reason as is shown by the fact that when he died, as he did the following year, he left Mary nothing out of a very considerable estate.

The cause of Abigail's estrangement was of course Quimby. The doctor's failure to help her or her son had convinced her at last that he was what she had always thought he was, just a mesmerist, and that "Mary was healed by her own faith". Mary would have none of such heresy, and so they parted. During the next five years of her life, Mary Patterson was often in the direst poverty, but she never asked Abigail for help again, and Abigail never offered to help her. They were, after all, Bakers, both of them.

Mary remained with Sarah Crosby at Albion for several months, and it was during her stay there that an incident or series of incidents occurred, apparently so alien to the general trend of Mary Patterson's thought about this time as to be quite baffling until explanation is sought quite outside the realm of any philosophic unfoldment.

As has been seen, Spiritualism at this period was one of the great subjects of talk and experiment throughout New England. The "Spirit Circles" of the fifties were still in eager existence, and the very fact that it demanded no equipment for its practice made it specially popular and available in out-of-the-way places and amidst out-of-the-way people.

Mary Patterson at times was vigorous in her repudiation of Spiritualism in any form. She made its denunciation the central point in her lectures at Warren, and in many of her letters to the papers on the teachings of Quimby she is careful to point out that Spiritualism has nothing in common with Quimby's doctrine.

And yet one day, as she and Sarah were sitting together in the parlour of the little farm at Albion, a strange thing happened. They had been talking as they often did by the hour about Quimby's teaching and about Spiritualism, in which Mrs. Crosby was more than a little inclined to believe, when suddenly Mary stopped talking. She leaned backward and began speaking in a low sepulchral voice. As the fascinated Sarah sat listening with all her ears, the voice explained after the orthodox fashion that "he" was Albert Baker, Mrs. Patterson's brother, and that he had been trying for some time past to get control of his sister in order to warn Mrs. Crosby against her. He told her that he was Mrs. Crosby's "guardian spirit", and in spite of his great love for his sister, he felt he ought to tell her (Mrs. Crosby) that, while Mary loved her as much as she was capable of loving anyone, life had been a severe experiment with her and she might use Mrs. Crosby's "sacred confidences" to further any ambitious purposes of her own.

The explanation of the incident usually put forward, is that Mary, having failed to bring her friend round to her own strongly adverse views of Spiritualism and all that went with it, took this way of proving to her how easily its manifestations could be faked. If this was so, she either badly underestimated her own powers of acting a part or Mrs. Crosby's credulity, for Mrs. Crosby was convinced that the manifestation was genuine, and, some forty years later, wrote a vivid account of the incident and subsequent happenings, insisting emphatically that the communications were beyond question.

However this may be, Mary followed up her first success with other "appearances". She even told Sarah—or Albert did through her—that if she would look in certain places she would find letters from him. Sarah looked, and, sure enough, there were the letters. The writing, it is true, was strangely like Mary's—the letters are still preserved—but that might be accounted for by a family resemblance. At any rate, such an explanation evidently more than satisfied Mrs. Crosby. Indeed, by the time the letters began to come, she was far beyond a touch of doubt. In her story, years afterwards, she declared that she believed implicitly in Albert's care and guardianship over her, that she derived constant strength and comfort from it, and that this spirit friendship was "one of the most real" she had ever known.

Perhaps the main importance of the matter, at least to the present purpose, is the indication it affords of the confusion which pervaded Mary Patterson's thinking at this time. In many ways, the next two years, the two years that immediately preceded the incident which was to change her whole life, are the most difficult of all to appraise. They are years wherein there is no outward sign of development, in any direction. After some months spent with Mrs. Crosby at Albion, she returns to Lynn; tries, once again, valiantly to make a home for her husband; is physically better. She writes for the papers—poetry, news items, gossipy reports of local happenings. She enters vigorously into temperance work, joins the Good Templars, is raised to the position of presiding officer, writes for them and speaks for them and becomes popular and sought after.

There is more than a hint, however, from her own writings that, in spite of all the outward show of great happiness, there was a desolation in the heart of this woman at that time such as she had never known before. Hope deferred and deferred again has made the heart sick. She has tried so many things and so many things have failed her. She tries them over again with ever lessening hope. She plays with Spiritualism, now as a medium and now as a clairvoyant letter writer; but even in her "spirit letters" she has her brother begging her friend to "love and care" for his sister because "a great suffering lies before her". She can fool Sarah Crosby into well-being with a fake spiritualism, just as years before she had fooled the woman sick of dropsy into health with her unmedicated pellets. But she cannot fool herself into anything now, any more than she could then.

In the bleak days of January, 1866, came the final blow, the death of Quimby. For the last few years of his life, he had been struggling manfully against an internal ailment (abdominal tumor), always declaring that, if his wisdom was not strong enough to heal him it was yet strong enough to hold the disease in check. But he gave himself ungrudgingly to his work, too ungrudgingly, and at last his wife and children, who had never shared his views, seeing him failing every day, prevailed upon him to give up and take a much needed rest. And so in the summer of 1865 he closed his office in Portland and retired to his boyhood's home in Belfast.

But the end came swiftly. He failed a little each day, and at last acknowledged that the task was beyond him. When his wife begged him to have a doctor, he consented, did everything the doctor told him to do, but only, as he put it, because he hoped thereby to "comfort his family". He never thought that the doctor could help him, but calmly waited for the end. "I do not dread the change," he said to his son George, who was at his bedside during his last hours, "any more than if I were going on a trip to Philadelphia."

He died on the morning of January 16, 1866. A few days later there appeared in the Lynn *Advertiser* a little poem written by Mary Patterson, "On the Death of P. P. Quimby, Who Healed with the Truth that Christ Taught". It is not great poetry, but the sincerity of its sorrow brings it almost within the light of the golden circle.

> *Can we forget the power that gave us life?*
> *Shall we forget the wisdom of its way?*
> *Then ask me not amid this mortal strife—*
> *This keenest pang of animated clay—*
> *To mourn him less . . . .*

And so her friend was gone. His "kindness and humanity", which she was to remember and acknowledge all her life, Mary Patterson could enjoy no longer. His "influence" and "power" and "Omnipresence" had passed from her life.

In her book *Retrospection and Introspection* Mrs. Eddy raises the curtain for a moment on the bitterness of these years. "The trend of human life", she writes, "was too eventful to leave me undisturbed in the illusion that this so-called life could be a real and abiding rest. All things earthly must ultimately yield to the irony of fate, or else be merged into the one infinite Love."[1]

And then she goes on to tell how that as these lessons became clearer they grew sterner; how that, up to then, the clouds that surrounded her had always seemed to have a silver lining, but that now they were not even "fringed with light". "The world was dark. The oncoming hours were indicated by no floral dial. The senses could not prophesy sunrise or starlight."

So it was, she says, when the moment arrived "of the heart's bridal to more spiritual existence". And then, looking back on it all through the perspective of the years, she could add simply: "When the door opened, I was waiting and watching; and, lo, the bridegroom came!"[2]

[1] *Retrospection and Introspection*, p. 23.
[2] Ibid., p. 23.

The Turning Point

IN THE LYNN *Reporter* of Saturday morning, February 3rd, 1866, there appeared this paragraph.

"Mrs. Mary Patterson of Swampscott[1] fell upon the ice near the corner of Market and Oxford Streets on Thursday evening and was severely injured. She was taken up in an insensible condition and carried into the residence of S. M. Bubier, Esq. nearby, where she was kindly cared for during the night. Dr. Cushing who was called, found her injuries to be internal and of a severe nature, inducing spasms and internal suffering. She was removed to her home in Swampscott yesterday afternoon, though in a very critical condition."

There can be no doubt that Mary Patterson was badly hurt. Dr. Alvin M. Cushing, then one of the leading physicians in Lynn, when called upon to testify some forty years later, declared from his notes taken at the time that when he reached the Bubiers' house he found Mrs. Patterson "partially unconscious, semi-hysterical and complaining by word and action of severe pain in the back of her head and neck". He attended her through the night, and next morning against his better judgement but in response to Mrs. Patterson's earnest pleas, he arranged for her to be taken

---

[1] A suburb of Lynn.

home. "As soon as I could", the account concludes, "I procured a long sleigh with robes and blankets, and two men from a nearby stable. . . . We placed her in the sleigh and carried her to her home in Swampscott."

What Mary Patterson called home at that time was a little two-room apartment which she and her husband had rented some time previously in the home of Mr. A. C. Newhall at 23 Paradise Court, Swampscott. The apartment was on the second floor, and from the bedroom window there was a welcome view over the tree tops towards the sea. To this bedroom Mary was carried.

Daniel was away, but Mary's active association with the Good Templars had won her many friends, and two of these friends, a Mrs. Carrie Miller and a Mrs. Mary Wheeler, came to her aid and took turns in watching by her bedside. They watched with her through Friday and Saturday. She apparently rallied in some measure and regained consciousness, but Sunday morning found her still practically helpless and in a condition generally which evidently caused those around her much misgiving. Doctor Cushing came and went, and then Mary asked for her Bible and that she might be left alone. We have no account of what followed except that which she has given us. Writing many years afterwards in an article entitled "One Cause and Effect", she says, referring to this incident: "I called for my Bible and opened it at Matt. IX.2. As I read, the healing Truth dawned upon my sense; and the result was that I rose, dressed myself, and ever after was in better health than I had before enjoyed."[1]

This was the third time in her life that Mary had passed through a similar experience, once at North Groton when after weeks and months of invalidism she one day surprised old Father Merrill on his way to visit her by running down the garden path with arms outstretched to meet him; once in Portland when Doctor Quimby told her she could be made well and would be made well; and now in Swampscott as she read the account of Jesus healing the man sick of the palsy.

Neither in North Groton nor in Portland had she been able to hold

[1] *Miscellaneous Writings*, p. 24.

131

for long the new ground she had won. As she drove down the mountain road from North Groton to Rumney with her sister Abigail, she was a wretchedly sick woman, and within a few weeks of her healing in Portland she was writing to Quimby begging him to come to her and "remove this pain".

It is not surprising, therefore, to find that the question whether this latest healing would not result as did the other two was the fear now that most sorely tried her faith. She was surrounded by doubt. "My friends were frightened", she has written in her *Miscellaneous Writings,* "at beholding me restored to health. A dear old lady asked me, 'How is it that you are restored to us? Has Christ come again on earth?'" Mary answered bravely enough, "Christ never left. Christ is Truth, and Truth is always here."[1] But then she goes on to tell how another person, "more material", met her and how she shuddered at her approach.

And so within a few days she is writing to Julius Dresser and begging him to come to her aid. Quimby is dead. Julius Dresser was one of his earliest students, the man in fact whose healing had finally decided Mary to go to Portland at all cost; he could surely help her if he would. She writes to him from Lynn, under date of February 15, 1866, and after telling him how constantly she is wishing he would step forward into the place vacated by Doctor Quimby and how confident she is that he is more capable of occupying his place "than any other I know of", she continues: "Two weeks ago I fell on the side walk, and struck my back on the ice, and was taken up for dead, came to consciousness amid a storm of vapors from cologne, chloroform, ether, camphor &c., but to find myself the helpless cripple I was before I saw Dr. Quimby. The physician attending said I had taken the last step I ever should, but in two days I got out of my bed *alone* and *will* walk; but yet I confess I am frightened, and out of that nervous heat, my friends are forming, spite of me, the terrible spinal affection from which I have suffered so long and hopelessly."[2]

She is evidently very much afraid, and as so often happens, the more

[1] Ibid., p. 180.
[2] *McClure's Magazine,* vol. xxviii, p. 510.

she wrote about it the worse her fear became until her cry for help is like that of a drowning man:

" . . . Can't you help me? I believe you can. I write this with this feeling: I think I could help another in my condition if they had not placed their intelligence in matter. This I have not done, and yet I am slowly failing. Won't you write me if you will undertake for me if I can get to you?"[1]

Julius Dresser, lately married, was at that time engaged in newspaper work in Portland and had apparently given up all thought—if he ever had any—of actively pursuing Quimby's teaching. He replied to Mary's appeal for help with a few well-chosen platitudes, but made it quite clear to her that she could, in his opinion, do much more for herself than he could do for her, which was probably true.

As to Mary's suggestion that he come forward as Doctor Quimby's successor, Julius Dresser is quite emphatic in his dissent. He expresses himself well, but it is difficult to avoid the thought that the cautious nature of his approach, combined with the character of his comment, may have had a profound impression upon Mary and unwittingly opened the way towards her own future. Whatever may have been her concept of the teaching of Quimby at that time, it is certain from all subsequent developments that she was continuing steadily that process of interpreting it in her own way and still unquestioningly calling it his, which she had begun almost at their first meeting. If a homely illustration may be forgiven, she took the Quimby shoes, and within a very short time she had soled them with soles of her own fashioning, and not long afterwards she had remade the uppers.

At this period, however, her whole thought was to find some means for carrying on Quimby's work. She had not yet in all probability had the faintest glimpse of the fact that the work she was destined to carry on would not be Quimby's. Julius Dresser's letter on the subject could hardly fail to make her think:

"As to turning doctor myself," Julius wrote, "and undertaking to fill

[1] Ibid., p. 511.

133

Dr. Quimby's place and carry on his work, it is not to be thought of for a minute. Can an infant do a strong man's work? Nor would I if I could. Dr. Quimby gave himself away to his patients. To be sure he did a great work, but what will it avail in fifty years from now, if his theory does not come out, and if he and his theories pass among the things that were to be forgotten? He did work some changes in the minds of the people, which will grow with the development and progress in the world. He helped to make them progress. They will progress faster for his having lived and done his work. So with Jesus. He had an effect that was lasting and still exists. He did not succeed nor has Dr. Quimby succeeded in establishing the science he aimed to do. The true way to establish it is, as I look at it, to lecture and by a paper and make that the means rather more than the curing, to introduce the truth. To be sure faith without works is dead, but Dr. Quimby's work killed him, whereas if he had spared himself from curing, and given himself partly and as considerately, to getting out his theory, he would then have at least come nearer success in this great aim than he did."[1]

Whether Julius Dresser's letter really had anything to do with it, it was clear about this time that Mary first began to feel that the task of carrying on and developing further the work of mental and spiritual healing might devolve upon her. To turn away from any labour because of its difficulty or the hardship it involved was something quite foreign to her nature and to every instinct of her heritage. The Bakers always had been faithful alike to their virtues and their failings. It was up to her to succeed where Quimby had failed. If teaching and writing were demanded as well as healing, she would do all three. Certainly her future shows that at some time or other she reached some such decision.

In her book *Science and Health* Mrs. Eddy puts the matter simply enough. Dating, as she always did, her discovery of Christian Science from this experience in Lynn, she writes that for three years thereafter, she lived a secluded life, so as to give herself entirely to the finding of a positive rule of practice. The quest, she says, "was sweet, calm, and buoy-

[1] Julius Dresser to Mrs. Patterson, March 2, 1866.

134

ant with hope." Conceding the basis of "all harmonious Mind-action to be God, and that cures were produced in primitive Christian healing by holy, uplifting faith," she felt driven to establish the Science of it all. She declares she did achieve "absolute conclusions through divine revelation, reason, and demonstration."[1]

Her statement that the "search was sweet, calm and buoyant with hope" must in itself be accounted a tribute to the efficacy of her faith, for it is hard to imagine three years into which more harassment could be crowded. Quite literally she often had nowhere to lay her head, and much of the time endured a poverty on the borderline of destitution.

History does not tell whether she ever renewed her plea to Dresser for help. Indeed it would seem clear that, thrown back at last entirely on herself, she somehow met the demand. Within a few weeks, she is writing an article for the Lynn *Reporter* on the amenities of Swampscott in general and of 23 Paradise Court in particular. Mr. Newhall wants to sell his house and Mary is doing her best to help him.

But before the article appeared in print, Mary had set out on her three years of wandering. Daniel had somehow reappeared on the scene and the two took rooms in Lynn, in a house owned by a Mr. Russell at the corner of Pearl and High Streets. It was Mary's last effort to make her home with Patterson. He finally deserted her here and, although for some years he made her a small allowance of two hundred dollars per annum, paid in irregular instalments, after their separation in Lynn he more or less completely passed out of her life. Seven years later she secured a divorce from him, and some twenty years later still, after wandering from place to place, sinking each time a little lower in the scale, he found his way back to Saco, Maine, where he was born. There, for a few years longer, he lived the life of a hermit. When Mrs. Eddy, then a wealthy woman, heard from his brother, like a voice out of the past, that he was in sore need, she sent him money but she never saw him again. He died in 1896 in the poor house, his last resting place the potter's field.

To what extent, if at all, Mary realized that the separation was final

[1] *Science and Health*, p. 109.

when he left her in Lynn, it is impossible to say, but whatever her feelings, her actions from now on are the actions of an independent woman with a single purpose.

At first the Russells had received her gladly, especially Mrs. Russell. She thought her a wonderful woman, but, by degrees, as was to come about in Mary's experience so often in the future, the strangeness of her teaching—when curiosity had been satisfied and it became apparent that real demands were to be made on life and conduct—began to arouse at first a mild resentment, but, later, positive offence.

Moreover, Mr. Russell's father was a retired Baptist minister with very decided views, and it was not long before Mary realized that she would have to move again.

She took a room in a boarding house on Sumner Street kept by a Mr. and Mrs. George D. Clark, and it is here that a clearer view of Mary Patterson is to be had than has been possible for some time. Years afterwards, George Clark, Jr., who was then a young man, wrote his recollections of Mrs. Patterson, which are full of welcome detail, even to providing a diagram showing where each of the guests sat at table. As to Mary Patterson's appearance, she was now forty-five, but George Clark recalls her as "a beautiful woman with the complexion of a young girl". He remembers that she usually wore black, but "occasionally violet or pale rose in some arrangement of her dress". He remembers especially "a dove coloured gown trimmed with black velvet that she wore in the summer". But what he remembers best about her is her way of talking and a little gesture she had with her right hand as though she were "giving a thought from her heart". Describing her fellow-guests, he says: "We were rather a mixed household and were fourteen at table. There were several shoe operatives from the factories, a salesman or two, and a man who has since become a well-known bootmaker. . . . The wives of several of the men were also guests at the table, and conversation was usually lively, often theological." He also adds that "everyone liked her".

But Mary had among her friends at Lynn at that time quite a number of people more in her own circle, whom she knew through her family or through her association with the Good Templars. There were the Phillipses, a Quaker family, who lived near the Clarks on Buffum Street; their married daughter Susan, Mrs. George Oliver, who lived close by; and Mr. and Mrs. Winslow, people of considerable means, who had a beautiful house on Ocean Street. Both the Phillipses and the Olivers were well off, Thomas Phillips and George Oliver being prominent men in the shoe business, for which the Civil War had made Lynn famous throughout the country.

It was in these three families during the summer of 1866 that Mary Patterson first apparently demonstrated to her own satisfaction her ability to "heal the sick"—for so she always thereafter spoke of it. During the time she was boarding at the Clarks, the Phillipses were her great resort. Mr. and Mrs. Phillips made her welcome at any time, and she came to call them "Uncle Thomas" and "Aunt Hannah". She was particularly devoted to Mrs. Phillips, who somehow reminded her of her own mother, and as if to make the recollection of her early childhood's home complete, there was a Grandmother Phillips, a devout old Quaker well over ninety, whose name, too, like that of Grandmother Baker, was Mary. They had long talks together, especially about healing, and Mr. Phillips would refer to them jokingly as "the two saints". It was the healing of Dorr Phillips, the Phillipses' youngest son, a lad of about fifteen, that Mary Patterson seems to have regarded as her first definite "case". She had had instances of healing, of course, before that—there was the apparently clear-cut case of Miss Jarvis at Warren—but there seems to have been, in Mary's mind, some doubt as to whether such healings might not be, in some way, due to the "master influence" of Quimby. "I have healed her and you have saved me," she wrote to him from Warren.

But now Quimby was gone, and if she was to be saved from the dire effects of healing anyone, she would have to save herself. It is possible, of course, that she was already freeing herself—as she did ultimately, completely—from this "penalty doctrine" of Quimby's method, but, however that might be, the school boy Dorr Phillips presented a clear objective.

There could be no question here of "nerves" or imagination. The lad

137

was suffering from a badly infected finger, was in great pain, and had been for several days. There was apparently little that could be done to afford him immediate relief. Mary asked the boy if she might help him and Dorr readily agreed. He had, no doubt, often heard Mrs. Patterson talk; and, mixed up with his eagerness to get better, was surely a tremendous boy-like curiosity to see if this strange thing about which he had heard so much would work. Mary seems to have had a good idea of the "psychology" involved. She made a bargain with Dorr, and put him on his honour to keep his side of it. He was not to look at his finger again or let anyone else look at it, until she told him he might, and he was to be a man and try not to bother about it any more.

That evening Dorr went over to his sister Mrs. Oliver's house to stay the night. His finger had not pained him all day, but when Susan Oliver wanted to see it, he firmly refused. He told his sister of his promise and how he was determined to keep it. When he came down to breakfast next morning, he had evidently forgotten all about his trouble, for the bandage was off, and when his sister drew his attention to the fact and they both looked at the finger, they found it was perfectly well. Years afterwards, Susan Oliver became a Christian Scientist, and eventually made her testimony as to the details of this case.

After this, other instances of healing followed quickly. A young man from Boston who was staying with the Olivers was healed almost instantly of a fever which had reached the point of delirium, and Mrs. Winslow, who had been going about in an invalid chair for sixteen years, was so far cured as to be able to walk unaided around her garden and even venture as far as the beach. So runs the testimony.

The effect of all this was interesting. While it did not arouse resentment as it had done in the case of Abigail, it did arouse what is perhaps best described as a sense of uneasiness. The Winslows thought it was wonderful, but begged Mary not to talk about it or attempt to go into it further. The attitude of the Phillipses and the Olivers was much the same. So long as it was all just an interesting phenomenon, they were glad to talk about it, but when it was put before them, as Mary was evidently beginning to do, as a new explanation of life and religion which might have disturbing effects upon their accustomed convictions, they very definitely began to draw away from it.

To Mary, now, such a course was impossible. She did not break with her friends, but she began to look in other directions for an audience. She found it in the strangely mixed assembly at the Clark boarding house. Among the boarders interested in hearing Mrs. Patterson and taking part in the arguments on Spiritualism and other kindred subjects, which provided a nightly feature at the dinner table and afterwards, was one Hiram S. Crafts and his wife. Hiram Crafts was an expert heel finisher whose home was in Stoughton, Massachusetts, a small town some thirty miles south-west of Boston, and having come to Lynn for the winter to do some special work in one of the shoe factories, he had found his way to the Clark boarding house. His place was next to Mary's at the dinner table, and although an enthusiastic Spiritualist he began from the first to listen eagerly to what Mary Patterson had to say. He had, of course, heard of Quimby, and it was still as an exponent of Quimby's teaching that Mary was seeking to make herself heard.

And so from taking part in the arguments at the dinner table young Crafts sought more detailed knowledge, and after dinner each night he and Mary would sit together talking for long hours. Mary evidently saw in him, or thought she saw in him, an apt pupil, one who would at last go all the way with her, and she was unsparing in her efforts to help him. She not only talked to him for hours each day, but she began about this time to fashion from the mass of writing she had done during her association with Quimby some kind of systematized exposition of his teaching. This manuscript or a copy of it she handed in instalments to Crafts for his instruction and guidance, thus beginning a practice which she seems to have followed generously for years, with ultimately bitter results to herself.

Writing of these early manuscripts years afterwards in the preface to her book *Science and Health* Mrs. Eddy says that they "show her comparative ignorance of the stupendous Life-problem up to that time, and

139

the degrees by which she came at length to its solution". She values them, she says, "as a parent may treasure the memorials of a child's growth, and she would not have them changed".[1] The trouble was, however, that the student not unnaturally took these manuscripts as the final word, and went off on his own to teach and preach a doctrine which his teacher was leaving rapidly behind. It took Mary Patterson many years to free herself entirely from the essentials of Quimby's teaching, and every manuscript of her own which seemed to perpetuate them came up in later years to cause bitter trouble for herself or some of her followers. But that is once again to anticipate the record.

For the time being all was well, and when Hiram Crafts left Lynn early in 1867 it was with the intention of giving up his work in the shoe trade and devoting himself to the further study of what he had learned from Mrs. Patterson and to the healing work which it entailed. He felt, however, that he was still in need of instruction, and he and his wife asked Mary to come to Stoughton also and make her home with them.

Mary agreed. Many years afterwards, Hiram Crafts gave the details of the agreement reached between them. Mrs. Patterson was to have a room and board free in return for instructing Mr. Crafts, and Mrs. Crafts as her share of the work was to do the housekeeping for the three. Mrs. Crafts was apparently as earnest as her husband in her efforts to understand "the new faith", and after spending the remainder of the winter in study the little family moved to Taunton, another small town a few miles from Stoughton. There they took a house. Mrs. Patterson furnished her bedroom and the front parlour with her own things, and the Crafts cared for the rest of the house and the garden. Most important of all, Hiram Crafts took an office, and having, with the gracious simplicity of those days, endowed himself with the proper designation, announced himself on the door as Dr. Hiram S. Crafts. At the same time he inserted an advertisement in the local newspaper. It runs:

> *To the Sick*
> *Dr. H. S. Crafts*

[1] *Science and Health*, Preface.

"Would say unhesitatingly, *I can cure you,* and I have never failed to cure Consumption, Catarrh, Scrofula, Dyspepsia and Rheumatism with many other forms of disease and weakness, in which I am especially successful. If you give me a fair trial and are not helped, I will refund your money."

Viewed in the light of today, such an advertisement makes strange reading, but announcements of the kind, even by regular practitioners, were then quite common. Moreover, Hiram seems to have been successful, at least to the extent that one grateful patient allowed her name and address, with a description of her cure, to appear in a later issue of Hiram Crafts' announcement. In a small place like Taunton, such testimony could, of course, have been easily verified.

And so all was well. Mary Patterson was absorbed in her writing, and it begins to be a matter of comment among those who come in contact with her at this time that she always carries with her a heavy roll of papers, steadily growing in bulk, which somehow, they gather, she regards as her most treasured possession.

Sanbornton Revisited
—and Afterwards

EARLY IN 1866, when Patterson deserted Mary in Lynn, Abigail made one last effort to solve the problem which her sister presented and to solve it in the way she desired. She wrote Mary a letter in which she promised to do anything and everything for her on one condition, namely, that she should give up her "queer ideas", and return to the orthodox religious views of her family.

Abigail was a typical New Englander of her period, wherein nothing was dreaded so much as "queerness", and queerness was, of course, appraised on the universal basis of numbers. Spiritualism at that time had long ceased to be queer. It had too many adherents. In any event, it claimed to be no more than an adjunct to orthodox faith, and some of the "best people" quite unfearfully admitted an interest in it. If Mary had professed a devotion to Spiritualism, the probabilities are that Abigail, far from being embarrassed by it, would have felt nothing but approval, even though she could not follow along with her. But this strange new teaching to which her sister was devoting herself so earnestly, with its outlandish claims of spiritual healing, moral regeneration and what not, was "queer" in the fullest sense of the word. No wonder people like the Phillipses and the Olivers and the Winslows of Lynn had been trying to dissuade Mary from having anything to do with it.

That this, or something very like it, was Abigail's line of reasoning is clear from her letter, in which she offers to build her sister a house right next door, in which she can live her own life unmolested and pursue her writing undisturbed. But there is a string attached to this tempting offer. "There is only one thing I ask of you, Mary, that you give up these ideas which have lately occupied you, that you attend our church and give over your theory of divine healing."

In all the years that Mary had been suffering from sickness and want and loneliness, Abigail had never offered to do so much. True, she had helped her again and again, but her aid was always characterized by a sound New England caution, which is quite absent from this offer.

It is hard to say to what extent it constituted any temptation to Mary. Her reply to Abigail's letter has not been preserved, but the facts speak sufficiently for themselves. Mary did not accept the offer, and shortly afterwards, as has been seen, left Lynn to join the Crafts at Stoughton.

But Mary Patterson loved Sanbornton. Like Bow and Concord, it was essential New Hampshire, and all her long life, the hills and valleys of her native state, its ruggedness and grandeur, had place in her heart which only became more simple and more secure as the years went by. And so in the summer of 1867, when everything seemed to be moving well with her and the Crafts in their new home at Taunton, with Hiram Crafts well established in his office and apparently on the way to success, Mary's thoughts turned towards Sanbornton. She had not been there since her brief visit in 1861 when she stopped with Abigail for a few days on her way from the misery of Rumney to the still greater misery of Doctor Vail's Sanatorium at Hill, and then she was too ill to care much about anything. But now her health was better—from now on sickness enters steadily less and less into the record of her life—and she is eager to see Sanbornton and her friends and family once again. So much may perhaps be justly inferred from the simple course of things, but in any event, the

August of 1867 found her in Sanbornton staying with her sister Martha.

Time had wrought many changes. Martha, it will be remembered, had married Luther Pillsbury, a young lawyer of Concord, and now Luther was dead and Martha had come back to Sanbornton with her daughter Ellen, a girl of twenty-one, to make her home there. Mark Baker had been gone a year or more, and in the big house off the main street, which Mark had built for himself next to the Tiltons, Mary's brother George—the much loved "Sullivan" of her earliest letters—lay dying.

It was in many ways a sad home-coming. George, who had long managed a branch of the Tilton Mills at Baltimore, had been struggling against failing sight for several years. It preyed upon him sadly, until at last, totally blind, and broken in mind and body, he returned to his old home at Sanbornton, to die.

Next door was Abigail, now far and away the first lady of the first family in Sanbornton. Hamilton Tilton had prospered greatly, and Abigail was more and more developing that remarkable ability, which, on her husband's death some ten years later, enabled her to take entire charge of his business and build up a fortune which at the time of her death was one of the most considerable in the state.

The local records show that in 1882, when Abigail took over the business, the mill property embraced seventy-five acres, extended a third of a mile down the river and controlled "an immense water power". There were "thirty-two looms and 1700 spindles"; the mill employed seventy-five hands, and had a monthly product "in tweeds and meltons" of 30,000 yards.

Abigail was a great lady, and she was so in much more than a merely ironic sense. She was so often right in business that she had come to expect as a matter of course that obedience which real ability so often secures. Her mistake was the common one of expecting a similar obedience in other fields. Mary's determination to think for herself had always irritated her, and this, her latest exhibition of free thinking, seemed to Abigail the last straw. As Mrs. Eddy put it many years afterwards in an article replying to one of her critics, "My oldest sister dearly loved me, but I wounded her pride when I adopted Christian Science, and to a Baker that was a sorry offence."[1]

There is no record of Mary's meeting with Abigail on this occasion, but from a pathetic little poem found among her papers and written about this time it might reasonably be inferred that she saw Abigail and saw her often, that Abigail strove with a high hand to have her way, and, when she failed, determined that the breach between them should be final and told Mary so.

But before the final break took place, Mary had done other things to cause Abigail offence. She had done the worst thing she could do, she had put her queer ideas into practice almost in Abigail's presence, and, perhaps most unforgivable of all, had been successful.

It was towards the end of Mary's stay that it happened. Ellen Pillsbury, her sister Martha's daughter, developed an abscess which failed to yield to ordinary methods of treatment, until the girl became seriously ill. Mary was eager to help, but hesitated. On this point the whole family was as one against her. There is some evidence that she had tried to induce George to allow her to help him, but had been rebuffed. Ellen, however, was not so prejudiced—Mary was to find this true of young people frequently in the future—and when her aunt with the queer views asked the girl if she might help her, she readily assented.

Mary appears to have gone into her niece's room just before the family sat down to supper, for it was while they were still sitting around the table that the door opened and she and Ellen entered together. There was silence for a moment as the little company looked from one to another in amazement. And then before anyone could speak, Ellen told them calmly that she was quite well and wanted to sit down and have supper with them. There was instant protest from everyone present. To them it was the most dangerous bravado. But Ellen was determined, and in an atmosphere which changed kaleidoscopically from resentment to acquiescence and thence to sullen surrender, she made a good supper, using her hand as before, with no trace of her trouble. Next day found her completely recovered.

[1] *Miscellany*, p. 313.

145

As subsequent events proved, far from being impressed by this exhibition of a power they did not understand, the family was more outraged than ever. Ellen, however, was for the time being completely won over, and when Mary, realizing that no spark of welcome remained for her anywhere, determined to return to Taunton, Ellen insisted on going with her.

And so they set out together. There is no picture of the leave-taking of Mary with her family as she left Sanbornton for the last time. It is, however, a fact that friendly relations were never restored, and that not even letters ever again passed between her and her sisters. "I loved Mary best of all my sisters and brothers," Abigail was wont to say, "but it is all gone now."

It must have been with strangely mixed feelings that Mary made the long journey—over a hundred miles by stage and train—from Sanbornton to Taunton. She was estranged finally from her family, and she had parted from Abigail in such a way as to make it certain that she could never ask her aid or counsel again. But there were compensations. Her niece Ellen was apparently devoted to her, and Mary can hardly have failed to hope that this love might prove a healing link between her and her people. Then, too, she was going back to her work at Taunton. Hiram Crafts, as far as she knew, was still doing well, and no one could tell what Ellen might not do.

This dream of better things was destined to be rudely shattered soon after she got back to Taunton. For instead of the serenity and promise which was all around when she left, she came back to find Mrs. Crafts dead set against the renewed monopolizing of her husband by this Mrs. Patterson's all-absorbing teaching, and Hiram Crafts a man more than half inclined to see the matter through his wife's eyes and agree that he could get on as well without Mrs. Patterson as with her, perhaps better. Neither was that all, for within a few days, in a sudden revulsion of feeling, Ellen rounded upon her, insisting that her mother and Aunt Abigail were right about her and her queer ideas and common associates and that she was going back to Sanbornton.

And so Ellen went. A few days afterwards on August 13, 1867, Mary sat down and wrote the little poem already alluded to which, some forty years later, was found among her papers. It is called "Alone".[1]

> I've sought the home my childhood gave—
> A moment's shelter from the wave—
> Then those when sick, whose pain I bore,
> A Sister drove me from the door.
> O weary heart, O tired sigh,
> So wronged to live—alone I'd die.

There are five stanzas in all. The first three are occupied with these thoughts of her aloneness and with frailty of all human ties. As always, with Mary, it is not great poetry, but in the last two stanzas, wherein she rises to a sense of joy in contemplating the compensations of the spiritual vision, the woman attains to those simple devotional heights which were to make her one of the most effective hymn-writers of her time.

> To bless mankind with word and deed—
> Thy life a great and noble creed.
> O glorious hope, my faith renew,
> O mortal joys, adieu! adieu!

Mary set out once again in search of a resting place. Her writing occupied her time and thought more and more,[2] and her first desire when she left the Crafts at Taunton would naturally be to find some place where she could pursue her purpose in this direction in peace and quiet. But she did not know where to turn, and so she went back to Lynn and sought the advice of her old friends, the Winslows. It was the Winslows, it will be remembered, who in spite of the fact that Mrs. Winslow, through Mary's ministrations, had been released from a wheel chair in which she had spent

---

[1] Published in *The Ladies' Home Journal*, June, 1911.

[2] A clear glimpse of her daily routine at this period is afforded in the record of one Fred Ellis, a master at a boy's school in Boston. He lived with his mother, Mary Ellis, at Elm Cottage, Swampscott, and Mary Patterson apparently had found a refuge there for a few weeks between leaving the Clarks and joining the Crafts in Stoughton. It was for Mary a brief interlude of comparative peace, and Fred Ellis later recalled how Mrs. Patterson would spend the greater part of each day in her room writing, and how, in the evening, she often would join him and his mother downstairs and read them what she had written during the day. Quimby was at that time uppermost in her thoughts, but Fred Ellis recalls significantly how she was developing his teaching along her own lines.

the previous sixteen years, had earnestly begged her not to pursue her studies further, and, above all, not to talk about them to anyone. Mr. Winslow was a retired Unitarian minister, and the position of Unitarianism at that time is perhaps sufficient explanation of his fundamental disquiet over anything savouring so strongly of mysticism as he conceived "Mary's healings" to do. Unitarianism in America had recently gone through deep waters in this direction, and it was only a few years previously that the National Unitarian Conference, viewing with grave concern a wayward tendency in their body towards "German idealism, rationalism and mysticism", had adopted a definitely Christian platform, affirming that its members were "disciples of the Lord Jesus Christ". The fact, however, that a large minority had refused any such acknowledgement and had gone out and formed the "Free Religious Association", could only render the orthodox Unitarian more distrustful than ever of anything so unorthodox as spiritual healing.

The Winslows seem, however, to have been sincerely devoted to Mary, and when she explained to them, as she must have done, that all she wanted was quiet to think and write, they bethought them of a friend they had in Amesbury, a little town some forty miles to the north near the New Hampshire border, who might take her in and give her what she needed. Amesbury was an ideal place for the purpose. It was the home of the poet Whittier, who was then at the height of his career, and while Whittier was a Quaker and a rebel in many respects, the Winslows evidently had no doubt as to his fundamental orthodoxy.

And so Mary set out. It was late fall, and it was evening when she arrived in Amesbury. In all probability she carried with her a letter of introduction to Mrs. Mary Esther Carter, the friend of the Winslows already mentioned. At any rate, this was her first house of call. Mrs. Carter, as it turned out, could not take her in, but advised her to go down the street to the home of a Mrs. Nathaniel Webster, who had a large house and was always glad to welcome strangers.

So Mary set out once more. It must have been quite dark, by this time, but as she made her way down Merrimac Street towards the river, it would not be long before the lights of Mrs. Webster's big three-storey house could be seen through the trees. There could be no mistaking it—Mrs. Carter had told her that it comprised fifteen rooms at least—and in a moment or two Mary had passed through the gate in the picket fence, under the two giant elms on each side of the porch and was knocking at the big front door.

It was opened by Mrs. Nathaniel Webster herself, a large woman with a broad kindly face, clearly justifying her reputation for hospitality, and to her, in the dim light, Mary told her story. She must have been very tired, but she evidently wanted Mrs. Webster to know the facts, and, when she had finished she added simply that she knew she had been led to come to her. Mother Webster had apparently no doubt about it, and standing aside to let Mary enter, she exclaimed, "Glory to God! Come right in!"

CHAPTER 15

Amesbury

MOTHER WEBSTER—FOR so she was generally known—was a queer woman. She was a Spiritualist of the type then called a "drawing medium". She would produce strange drawings which in turn she interpreted into messages from the departed. Captain Nathaniel Webster, her husband, was a retired sea captain, who held a good position in Manchester as superintendent of a cotton mill and visited Amesbury only about twice a month, coming up on a Sunday just for the day.

As a consequence, Mother Webster was left a good deal alone, and partly to relieve the loneliness of her life, and partly out of the generosity of her heart, opened her house to almost anyone in need, but especially to anyone interested in Spiritualism or what she would regard as kindred subjects. When Mary told her, as she seems to have done the first evening, that she was interested in something "far in advance of Spiritualism", that was more than enough for Mother Webster.

A vivid picture of the woman herself and of her strange household is afforded in an account written for *McClure's Magazine*, some forty years later, by her granddaughter, a Mrs. Mary Ellis Bartlett. According to her, there was apparently no limit to Mother Webster's charity. "Invalids, cripples, and other unfortunate persons", the account runs, "were made welcome, and my grandmother took care of them when they were ill and lodged and boarded them free of charge."

In such circumstances, the guests could hardly refuse to take part in the spiritistic seances which were evidently among Mother Webster's happiest relaxations. She had a room specially fitted up for the purpose "in the rear of the front parlour". It was decorated in blue, as this was regarded as a colour unusually pleasing to spirits. The room was furnished much as other rooms, with good sturdy New England tables and chairs, but Mother Webster always alluded to this equipment as "spiritual furniture". Moreover, she had in the room a "spiritual couch", upon which she took her daytime naps and to which she even resorted occasionally at night if she was restless, being convinced that she could sleep there when she could not sleep anywhere else.

To complete the furnishings there was at the head of the table a large arm chair which had belonged to Captain Webster's mother. It was alluded to as the "spiritual chair", and Mother Webster always occupied this chair at her seances or when she was engaged on her spirit drawing. Above the "spiritual room" was a bedroom, a bright sunny room with a view over the river, and this room, much to her satisfaction as it must have been, Mother Webster turned over to her new guest. Mary was used to Spiritualism and to Spiritualists. Later in life she used to say that in those days she found them more ready to listen to her than were most people, and in many cases quick to abandon their views in favour of what she had to give them. And so Mother Webster's "spiritual room" and its "spiritual furniture" had no terrors for Mary. She was far too grateful for Mrs. Webster's kindness, and it was not long before the two women became close friends.

Mrs. Bartlett declares that Mrs. Patterson attended many of her grandmother's seances in the "spiritual room", and it is more than likely that she did. Spiritistic seances in those days were like silver in the days of Solomon—nothing accounted of. It is, however, significant that, as the winter wears on, Mary is found established in the "spiritual room", using it as her study, seated in Mother Webster's "spiritual chair", with the "spiritual table" strewn with her papers and books.

The exact significance of this recorded fact may not be clear, but it seems reasonable to suppose that in securing the use of the "spiritual room" with its equipment for her study, Mary had at least persuaded Mother Webster that the room could thus be used without impairing in any way its spiritual value. Mother Webster, moreover, was much interested in Mary's writing. She seems to have grasped little of what it was about, but that it impressed her is shown by the fact that she dwelt in wonder to her granddaughter on how Mrs. Patterson, after she had written for hours, "would gather up all the pages she had filled with writing and tear them up, because she could not make them read as she wished."

Of the other guests in the house at the time Mary was there, there is no record save in the case of two, a Mrs. Richardson and a young man—destined later on to figure prominently in her story—named Richard Kennedy. Kennedy was a bright, energetic lad—he was no more—who, left alone in the world, had at the age of eighteen established himself in a little box business which already employed several extra hands. From the first, he was tremendously interested in what Mrs. Patterson had to teach, and was eager to learn as much as he could about it. The same was probably true, in a measure, of many of the guests who came and went. Mrs. Bartlett does not mention it, but it seems likely that some of them were helped and even healed by Mary, for at the turn of the year it began to be whispered about in the little town that in Mother Webster's house was a woman who "worked miracles". Such stories would lose nothing in the telling, and by the time the spring came round and Mary and Mother Webster would be going for a walk in the evening along the river bank, the curious would sometimes walk after them at a distance to see if by any chance Mrs. Patterson would "walk on the water".

Mary shrank from such notoriety, and was apparently beginning to wonder whether she ought not to move again, when the matter was suddenly settled for her in a way which must have made her feel that she had surely reached the depths of humiliation.

It appears that almost from the first, when Captain Webster returned home on his bi-monthly visits, he had objected to Mary's presence. Whether he resented the assurance implied in her occupancy of the "spiritual room" and his wife's "spiritual chair", or thought she had too much influence over her, in any case, according to Mrs. Bartlett, he insisted to his wife that Mrs. Patterson should not be allowed to remain. Mother Webster, however—she had a will of her own—indignantly refused, and no more would probably have been heard of the matter if it had not been for the arrival in the early summer of Mother Webster's son-in-law, William Ellis, from New York.

William Ellis, to judge from his photograph, was a man of determination. Even in moments of relaxation—the photographer has discovered him seated at a desk clad in a flowered dressing gown and shod with embroidered slippers—his straight mouth flanked by side whiskers is firm and set of purpose. His wife had died a few years previously, leaving him with three young children, and it had been his custom to have the children spend the summer in Amesbury with their grandparents. It was a satisfactory arrangement for him in every way, but he strongly objected to Mother Webster's penchant for hospitality, and trading, no doubt, on her desire to have her grandchildren with her through the summer, he insisted on the departure of all his mother-in-law's guests or such of them, at any rate, as he did not approve of, before the children arrived. His daughter, Mrs. Bartlett (one of the children), has left a vigorous picture of her father's method of procedure. "When it was time for us to leave New York," she writes, "my father always went to Amesbury in advance of the rest of us, in order to clear my grandmother's house of broken down Spiritualists and sick persons, so that we might have enough room in the house and because he thought the atmosphere of so much sickness and Spiritualism was unwholesome for young children."

One Saturday evening early in June, 1868, William Ellis arrived in Amesbury on his annual visitation. Mrs. Bartlett does not mention his attitude towards any of the other guests, but in regard to Mary Patterson he was decisive from the first moment. She would have to go and at once. Mother Webster emphatically refused and at first seems to have stood her ground, but faced with the usual alternative and also, it would seem, with the possibility of violence, at last tearfully consented to ask Mrs. Patterson to go. It was just the kind of tyranny to arouse in Mary an indignation and determination to resist which had the whole Baker tradition behind it. She took one look at Mother Webster's tear-stained face and another at Mother Webster's son-in-law, and then quietly but firmly refused to move.

She had, however, to deal with something cruder and more brutal than had ever previously come into her experience. The day had been hot and sultry and towards evening a storm had broken, one of those semi-tropical thunderstorms which sweep occasionally over New England at night in high summer, with rain pouring down at times in unbelievable deluge, and the sullen roar of one crash of thunder rolling in on the echo of the last, each flash of lightning the while only rendering more impenetrable the following darkness. Storm or no storm, however, Mr. Ellis was determined Mrs. Patterson should go.

The rest of the story is perhaps best told in Mrs. Bartlett's own words: "My father", she says, "commanded Mrs. Patterson to leave, and when she steadfastly refused to go, he had her trunk dragged from her room and set it outside the door, insisted on her also going out the door, and when she was outside he closed the door and locked it. . . . It was dark at the time and a heavy rain was falling."

Very fortunately the front door of the house was protected by a small entrance porch, and, there, on the narrow stoop, Mary sat down and waited, not knowing what to do or where to go.

It is easy and perhaps not altogether idle to speculate as to the thoughts that passed through her mind as she sat there listening to the echoing peals of thunder and the swirl of the rain as it swept by. One thought almost surely would have been there, the recollection of Abigail's offer, "We will build a house for you next to our own and settle an income upon you . . . we can be together very much, and you can pursue your writing. There is only one thing I ask of you, Mary . . . ."

Mary knew Abigail well enough to know that the offer was still open. The harder the battle, the more frequent the apparent defeats, the more would Abigail love to win in the end. But the one thing that Abigail asked was the one thing that Mary would never give, and so if the thought ever came at all, it only came to be dismissed.

How long she waited there is not known, but, after a time, she heard the door being unlocked, and, next moment, she saw Richard Kennedy and Mrs. Richardson standing in the doorway. As the door was shut and locked behind them, Mrs. Richardson told Mary that she and Dick had decided that if she (Mary) was to be turned out, they would go too, that she knew a kindly woman living nearby, one Sarah Bagley, who would certainly take them in for the night, and possibly they could make arrangements to stay there permanently. Dick would carry their baggage over, and they might as well go at once.

After waiting no doubt for a lull in the storm, Mary and her friends set out, and a few minutes later were drying themselves around the hospitable fire in Sarah Bagley's kitchen, telling their story and finding a full measure of that kindness and compassion which Mrs. Richardson had anticipated. One door had closed, but another had opened. Next day Mrs. Richardson and Richard Kennedy seem to have gone elsewhere, but Mary arranged to stay. Sarah Bagley had evidently heard all about her, if she did not know her personally, and the agreement reached between them was that in addition to a small sum which Mary would pay for board she should teach Miss Bagley what she could of the doctrine she was evolving.

In Miss Bagley, Mary found a woman much more in her own tradition than any she had associated with at all intimately for some time. A spinster living alone, she was the last survivor of a well-known New England family. Her father, Squire Bagley, was a man of much the same type as Squire Baker or Squire Pierce. His journal, which is one of the literary landmarks of New England, is a delightful haphazard mosaic of great names, shrewd comment, humorous aphorisms, and household expenses. The Bagleys had once been very well off, but the Civil War and changing times had reduced the family fortune until Sarah, the sole survivor, was left with the old house on Merrimac Street and little besides. She supplemented that little by working as a dressmaker, and "managed" somehow.

Old Squire Bagley had been a Universalist and so was Sarah, but of late years she, like many others, had turned to Spiritualism. She had an open mind, however, and from the first displayed an eagerness to understand the new teaching, which to the much-enduring Mary Patterson must have been strangely refreshing. Richard Kennedy had secured a room close by and would come in and join them in the evenings. He, too, was eager to learn, and gradually as the days and weeks passed, a great change came over Sarah Bagley. She had been a very lonely, stalemated woman. She kept her head up in proper New England style, changed her gown and tidied up for company every afternoon, and sat in the front parlour on Sundays, but the glory of it all had departed, and the coming of Mary Patterson into her life seems to have brought some of it back again.

Georgine Milmine when collecting material for her articles in *McClure's Magazine* interviewed a number of people who had known Mary in those days. Some of them had come to be strongly opposed to her and her teaching, but one and all they "loved to talk of her and were glad to have known her". As Miss Milmine sums it up, "There was something about her according to these people that continually excited and stimulated, and she gave people the feeling that a great deal was happening." In a household like that of Sarah Bagley's, where nothing ever happened, this must indeed have been as a wind from the south.

To Mary it would all have an unaccustomed sweetness, for the small circle in which Sarah moved was very different to the strange medley which surrounded Mother Webster. Whittier was one of her closest friends. When Squire Bagley died, leaving Sarah and her sister little beyond the old family house, Whittier was one of the first to come to the rescue, and when Sarah in order to eke out their income sought to teach school, Whittier did all he could to help her and was one of her committee men. Then, it was of Captain Valentine Bagley, Sarah's uncle, that Whittier wrote his poem "The Captain's Well", which tells of how the Captain being wrecked on the coast of Arabia and almost dying of thirst, vowed a vow that if ever he got back to Amesbury he would dig a well by the wayside so that the wayfaring man and the wayfaring beast that passed by might always have the means to slake their thirst. The Captain did return to Amesbury and digged his well by the wayside near to where Sarah lived. And so the Bagley home was a home of gracious tradition and the little town itself a place of peace and quiet.

> *The belfry and steeple on meeting house hill,*
> *The brook with its dam and the grey grist mill.*

Mary always retained a deep affection for Amesbury. It is not certain that she met Whittier at this time, but she did meet him later, on a return visit, and in circumstances which both must long have remembered.

Meanwhile, happy as conditions were, and busy as she was writing and teaching, Mary was ever ready to make a move which promised wider opportunity and greater independence. After she had been with Miss Bagley about six months, such an opportunity presented itself in the form of an invitation from a friend in Stoughton, a Mrs. Sally Wentworth, to visit her.

Mary had met Mrs. Wentworth when she was living with the Crafts at Stoughton. Mrs. Wentworth had brought her daughter Lucy, who was suffering from tuberculosis, to Hiram Crafts to see if he could help her, and as the child quite definitely improved under his care, her mother became very interested in what Mrs. Patterson was teaching, and eagerly desired to learn more of it. She was herself a practical nurse, with strong leanings towards Spiritualism, and her story affords an interesting view of the quasi-magical healing methods which were so common in New England in the years immediately following the Civil War. Mrs. Wentworth was herself a "gifted rubber", and combining forces as she did at times with "Old Asa Holbrook", a Spiritualist and clairvoyant "doctor" who appears to have had a considerable reputation and following, she undoubtedly thought that a knowledge of Mrs. Patterson's "method" would still further enhance her own and Old Asa Holbrook's powers.

And so Mary came back to Stoughton. Her arrangement with Mrs. Wentworth, as it was finally worked out, was that Mrs. Wentworth was to pay three hundred dollars for a complete course of instruction, but that this payment was to be received not in cash but in board and lodging over a considerable time.

At first, the arrangement seems to have worked out very well for all concerned. The daughter Lucy, now apparently fully restored to health, became devoted to Mary, as did her older brother Charles. They were fifteen and seventeen respectively, and many years afterwards, in an interview with Sibyl Wilbur, Lucy Wentworth described how eagerly the two looked forward each day to the time when Mary would have finished her writing for the day and would "unlock her door"—she evidently had to keep it locked against them—and let them in. "I loved her," Lucy Wentworth declared in this interview, "because she made me love her. She was beautiful and had a good influence over me. I used to be with her every minute that she was not writing or otherwise engaged."

And then she went on to tell how they would read and talk together and, perhaps most interesting of all, take "long walks in the country". Whatever it was that Mary was writing and thinking at that time, she was evidently steadily working out the problem of her own health. She was, moreover, working out or perhaps it would be more true to say, beginning to be aware of another problem which was to present itself to her in many different forms repeatedly in the future, the problem of family relations in connection with what she was trying to do. It was, of course, the age-old problem of Martha and Mary. In every family with which she was brought in intimate contact, this problem inevitably presented itself—the Russells at Lynn, the Crafts at Taunton, the Websters at Amesbury, her own people at Sanbornton, and now the same thing was apparently to happen with the Wentworths.

Mary, however, this time, seems to have been dimly aware of what was coming and to have done her best to prevent it. The devotion of Lucy Wentworth was clearly the kind to arouse something very like resentment with other members of the family. She would not tolerate the smallest criticism of Mrs. Patterson, and when her eldest brother Horatio, who was married and lived close by, or her cousin Kate Clapp, much given to mimicry, would, as they often did, speak jokingly of something they had heard of Mrs. Patterson's teaching or their mother's interpretation of it, Lucy would spring to the defence in such a way as to ensure a renewal of the "attack" on still more generous lines. It was probably for this reason more than any other that Mary tried to restrain Lucy Wentworth's devotion. That she was in a large measure successful is shown by the fact that she remained with the Wentworths the better part of a year before the inevitable break took place.

The exact cause of the break is not quite clear. Mary's life at this point is rapidly moving into that atmosphere of bitter controversy and clashing opinion which was to surround her in ever widening range right through to the end. Thenceforward, apparently, there could be no such thing as neutrality and very little of moderation in the average estimate of men and women regarding her. On the one side in this simple matter of record is Horatio Wentworth's lurid story of how Mrs. Patterson was finally ejected from his father's house because, when his father was ill, she retired to her room which was over Mr. Wentworth's and having locked herself in deliberately hammered on the floor, keeping it up "with short intermissions . . . for a long time", in order to prevent the sick man from sleeping. Then, as if this were not enough, he adds that when they finally did get her out of the house, they found on entering her room the carpets "slashed up through the middle", the feather bed "all cut to pieces", and an obvious attempt to "set the house on fire".

Side by side with this shameful and shameless picture may be placed that provided in Lucy Wentworth's account of the matter. It lacks the vigour and resource of Horatio's narrative, but what it lacks in vigour, it would seem to gain in probability. "A coolness", she says, "grew up in the family toward our guest. I don't know how it came about. My father thought she absorbed my mother too much and that she was weaning me away from them. . . . I never missed anyone as I missed her."

And so Mary packed up her few things once more and moved on. But her years of wandering and obscurity were almost over. She had used, to the uttermost, the days of small things. She had preached her gospel to anyone who would listen. She had taught now a shoemaker, now a seamstress, now a boy in a box factory; and everywhere she had gone, she had been writing. The pile of papers, "tied up with a string", had grown bulkier and bulkier, and the more it grew, so much the more a great deal did she treasure it. As the sharp-tongued Catherine Clapp has left record, "she called it her Bible". As a matter of fact, the manuscript which she was now working on—and it is still preserved—was the beginning of a monumental work to be called "The Bible and its Spiritual Meaning," for the Bible-minded Mary Baker must now reconcile what she saw, or thought she saw, in Quimbyism with what she had always accepted as eternally sacred.

A Small Beginning

WHEN MARY DECIDED to leave the Wentworths at Stoughton, her thoughts naturally turned to Amesbury and Sarah Bagley. In the old Bagley homestead, with Sarah as an eager student, she had known a peace and understanding to which she had long been a stranger, and the two women had corresponded frequently while Mary was away. Sarah evidently wrote that she was more interested than ever in Mary's teaching, and that she and young Richard Kennedy spent much time in studying the manuscripts which Mary had left with them. None of the correspondence has been preserved, but it would seem more than likely that as Mary recounted to Sarah the growing difficulties of her position in the Wentworth household, Sarah would urge her to return to Amesbury, assuring her of a warm welcome in her home.

At any rate, Mary did not hesitate. She went straight from Stoughton to Amesbury, arriving there in the early fall of 1869. To her it was something more of a homecoming than she had known for many years. She had been a welcome guest in many households through her long period of wandering, but, in coming back to Sarah Bagley, she could feel that she was not only welcomed but needed, that she had a real opportunity for service and for furthering the great purpose, which, about this time, was beginning to take definite shape in her thought.

For it would seem clear from what follows that it was while she was at Amesbury on this second visit that Mary Patterson began definitely to emerge from the borderland of half light, in which she had lived for so long, into a mental realm where more confident advance was possible. While she was at the Wentworths she had completed a manuscript which she entitled *The Science of Man,* and had allowed Mrs. Wentworth to make a copy of it. This copy is still preserved, and, apart from its contents, reveals two points of special interest. She still loyally attributes the teaching it presents to Quimby, and yet so unceasing is the development of her own concept that she cannot even leave Mrs. Wentworth's manuscript alone after she has copied it, but must needs change it to bring it into line with her own changing thought. There is no mistaking Mary's character-istic handwriting as seen in the corrections and interlineations.[1]

Writing of these days many years afterwards in her book *Science and Health* Mrs. Eddy tells how when Christian Science was "a fresh revela-tion to the author, she had to impart, while teaching its grand facts, the hue of spiritual ideas from her own spiritual condition, and she had to do this orally through the meagre channel afforded by language and by her manuscript circulated among the students."[2] And then, she adds—and this illustrates the point in question—that as former beliefs were gradu-ally expelled from her thought, the teaching became clearer, "until finally the shadow of old errors was no longer cast upon divine Science".[3]

Any comparison of this Wentworth manuscript with the Quimby manuscripts, which were eventually published in 1921, shows that while the language is often much the same, there is clearly here emerging that fundamental doctrine of Christian Science which differentiates it from all other interpretations, namely, the unreality of matter from the stand-

[1] The Board of Directors of The Mother Church state, in their letter to the author under date of September 8, 1941, that they have this manuscript in Sally Wentworth's hand and that it contains a dozen words in Mrs. Eddy's unmistakable and authenticated penmanship.

[2] *Science and Health*, p. 460.

[3] Ibid.

point of Spirit. This is a doctrine Quimby never affirmed and one that Julius Dresser and others of his immediate followers always repudiated. It is this teaching and its involvements which must, of course, enter more and more into the warp and weft of the story from now on. It will be found before long challenging thought in all directions and, whatever the view of it may be, transforming the lives and the outlook of many people.

The moment this demand, the unreality of matter and consequently the unreality of all matter's manifestations, including disease and death, is imported into the teaching of Quimby, thence onwards the only relation between the old and new theories is the relation between the Ptolemaic and the Copernican theories of the universe. Copernicus did not and, of course, could not disregard the Ptolemaic literature of the heavens, but he could render it all obsolete by the simple demonstration that the earth moved around the sun and not the sun around the earth. Quimby declared that mind was stronger than matter, and that, through certain strange and devious methods, this could be practically demonstrated. Mary Patterson in the manuscript she gave to Mrs. Wentworth is rapidly reaching the point where she sees that Mind can overcome matter and all materiality in the human consciousness, not because Mind is stronger than matter and all materiality, but because Mind is the only reality, and matter and all materiality are in the realms of illusion. As she often put it in effect later on, "Matter, like twice two is five, is not, but seemeth to be."

All of which is, of course, to run ahead of the record, but some such digression is perhaps necessary to render intelligible the almost cyclonic movements which are to take place in the near future.

Meanwhile, Mary Patterson, like a passenger on board a boat crossing the horizon as seen from the shore, is quite unaware of anything out of the ordinary happening. She comes back to Sarah Bagley with her familiar bundle of papers—now much bulkier than when she had left Amesbury some two years before—and gets down to work at once.

The fall and winter which followed seem to have been for Mary one of the few oases of peace and tranquillity in her long life. It was the calm

163

before another storm, more tempestuous than any before, but while the quiet lasted it must have been strangely welcome. Miss Bagley, like the good New England spinster that she was, was essentially a home-maker. She had a place for everything and everything was in its place. In this, she and Mary were very profoundly in agreement. Years afterwards, in the great house on Chestnut Hill, careful servants on cleaning days would put thumb tacks in the carpets so that they might return each piece of furniture to its exact position in Mrs. Eddy's study.

Then, Sarah Bagley had a new interest in life. In the evenings when young Richard Kennedy came round and the three would sit and talk and read together, Sarah no longer watched the clock so as to be ready to move on her way upstairs the moment it pointed to a quarter of ten. Already both she and Dick, as she always called him, had had some success in helping sick people, and they were eager to learn more of the means by which it could be done. Mary, too, was more sure of herself. The one thing that had always troubled her about Quimby's healing, or rather Quimby's attitude towards it, was his often expressed uncertainty as to how it was done. From the first she was confident that if it was done at all there must be a discoverable way by which it was done. Quimby, however, as has already been noted, was not so sure and was at times inclined to believe that the "power" was in him and might "perish" with him.

Every day was now affording Mary proof that even if she had not discovered Quimby's way of healing the sick, she had none the less discovered a way and that she could pass on the knowledge as to how it was done to others.

So the winter passed happily and profitably, and as the spring came on, the question as to what should be the next move seems to have come up for discussion among the three. By this time, Richard Kennedy, who was a distant relative of Miss Bagley by marriage, had moved over to the Bagley house, and so eager and interested was he in his new studies that it began to be a question with him whether he should not give up his work of making boxes and devote himself instead to the work of healing. He was only twenty-one, but in those days everyone started out on their life's work earlier than they do today, and to be a full-fledged doctor in practice at twenty-one was not at all uncommon.

Mary Patterson seems to have been rightly doubtful about the move, but as spring merged into summer the idea took more definite shape until at last it was decided that Mary and Dick should move to Lynn, that Dick should set up as a doctor, take an office and keep regular hours, while Mary devoted herself to teaching—much the same as the arrangement followed with the Crafts at Taunton.

Before the actual move was made, Mary had an interesting experience which must have gone a long way towards confirming her and her two faithful friends in the feasibility of the plans they were working out. One very hot day in early summer, Sarah came to Mary and asked her if she would not go with her to visit her old friend Whittier, who had lately suffered the loss of a much-loved sister and was himself far from well. Mary readily agreed and it was not long before the two women reached the large gabled house under the elms which Whittier had built for himself some thirty years before. They found the poet sitting before a large fire, with flushed cheeks and coughing painfully. He greeted his visitors with what graciousness he could muster, but when Sarah asked him what on earth he wanted with a fire on such a hot day, he answered irritably, with the liberty of an old friend, that he had the fire because he was cold and that if Jesus Christ lived in Amesbury he would need brass-lined lungs to survive. This was all that Mary needed. She sailed right in. There is unfortunately no record of what she said, but as Whittier listened to her with growing interest, Sarah noticed that he stopped coughing and that the flush left his cheek and that he moved away from the fire. Within a little while all his gloom was gone, and when his visitors rose to go, he took both of Mary's hands in his and said eagerly, "I thank thee, Mary, for thy call. It has done me much good. Come again." Whether she ever did go again is not recorded, but "professionally" it was not necessary, for next day Whittier was out and about, completely recovered.

It was not long after this incident that Mary and Richard Kennedy set out for Lynn. Sarah must have been sad to see them go, but she herself was rapidly making new friends with her healing work. She kept it up with profit to herself and varying success until she died some twenty years later, but she was one of the first of a long succession of students of this new teaching who never advanced in thought beyond the point at which they entered. When Mary Patterson taught Sarah what she knew at that date, her teaching was still mixed up with the mesmerism and manipulation of Quimby's doctrine. She herself was to leave it entirely behind, but Sarah Bagley never did.

It was early in the summer of 1870 when Mary and Richard Kennedy arrived in Lynn. They went first of all to the house of a Mrs. Clarkson Oliver, a friend who had formerly lived in Amesbury. She received them gladly, and next day Richard went in search of suitable quarters wherein to set out on the new adventure. It was some time before he could find just what he wanted, but, finally, towards evening at the corner of Shepherd and South Common Streets he came upon a large three-storey house, standing a little back from the street. In front of it was displayed a notice to the effect that there was established a private school for young children, that the Principal was Miss Susie Magoun, and that the second floor, which comprised five rooms, was for rent to a suitable tenant. It seemed to Richard just what he was looking for, and within a few minutes he was talking to Miss Susie Magoun herself, explaining his mission. He was seeking offices for a physician, with sleeping quarters adjoining, and had seen the notice that the second floor was to let and thought it might be suitable. Miss Magoun, contemplating the boyish figure before her, not unnaturally assumed that the physician in question was his father, but none the less readily acquiesced when Richard somewhat diffidently explained that he was the physician and that he wanted the rooms for himself and "an elderly woman who was writing a book". Miss Magoun had, it transpired, only recently opened the school, and she was eager to have her second floor rented as she herself occupied the third.

Within a few days, all the necessary agreements as to rent and notice having been arranged, Mary Patterson and Richard Kennedy moved into their new quarters, and next morning, on a tree outside the front door, appeared a sign bearing the simple legend, "Dr. Kennedy".

The reasons for success are often difficult of discovery and still more difficult of just appraisal. But in the case of Richard Kennedy the cause of his success—for he was from the first extraordinarily successful—is simple enough. He did what he said he would do. He healed the sick. The sign on the tree, outside Miss Magoun's school, brought in one or two curious people almost the first day. They may have gone in idle curiosity, but they came out enthusiastic, self-appointed publicity agents for the new doctor and his new theory of medicine. One grateful patient passed on the good news to another, and it was not long before Richard had a large and thriving practice.

Then, quite a number of his patients desired to know and to learn more of the theory, and it was here that Mary Patterson took up the work. At first she talked to each one separately, as she had been doing now for a number of years, but after a time she came to see that if she was to carry on the work to the best advantage and make her just contribution to the partnership which existed between her and young Richard, she would have to work out some way of teaching more than just one person at a time. Richard could charge a regular fee for a definite service rendered, but there seemed to Mary no way in which half an hour's talk could be evaluated, and she apparently shrank from making the attempt.

If, however, she were to form a class, give people an outline of what they might expect to learn, fix the number of lessons to be given and charge a certain definite fee, it would place the whole enterprise on an intelligible basis and open the way for sound development. She decided upon this course.

The great problem was one of fees. Limited as her experience so far had been, Mary Patterson had evidently learned the lesson that the human mind never values highly what it secures easily and cheaply. She must already have been familiar with the type of mind that came to her on the basis that it would cost nothing, could do no harm and might do some good, and she must often have seen the sorry results of such an attitude.

And so she took what was to prove a momentous decision. She was dealing for the most part with working people, almost all of them connected in varying capacities with the shoe industry. Their average wage would probably have been considerably less than $1,000 a year, and yet she decided on a fee of $300 for a course of twelve lessons. This fee was never changed. Years afterwards, when she had secured a charter for a college of her own, carrying with it the right to confer diplomas and degrees, the fee for instruction—$300—remained the same. Writing of it in her book *Retrospection and Introspection* Mrs. Eddy says:

"I could think of no financial equivalent for an impartation of a knowledge of that divine power which heals; but I was led to name three hundred dollars as the price for each pupil in one course of lessons at my College,—a startling sum for tuition lasting barely three weeks."[1]

She often, as will be seen, received students for nothing, often remitted part of the fees, but in the final settlement she always gave them a receipt in full. The fee was $300. To those who desired to pay but could not, she was notable in her consideration and forbearance, but to those who had taken what she had to give, who could pay and would not, she was unremitting in her demands that the obligation be met.

And so the work got under way, and the first class was formed. It was a strangely mixed and strangely troubled gathering. Perhaps the best view of it is obtained from the account preserved by one of its members, Samuel Putnam Bancroft, who in 1920 published his recollections of those early days of the Christian Science movement, together with some interesting original documents, in a book entitled *Mrs. Eddy as I Knew Her in 1870*.

Putney Bancroft, as he was known to his friends, was a young shoe operative, a foreman in the factory of Bancroft & Purington in Lynn, and he recounts how one evening in the fall of 1870 he received an unexpected call from a young man under his supervision in the factory named Daniel H. Spofford and his wife. They seemed very full of something and after the usual greetings Mrs. Spofford plunged at once into the subject, telling him of a remarkable woman, a Mrs. Patterson, lately come to Lynn who

[1] *Retrospection and Introspection*, p. 50.

was teaching "a new method" of healing the sick and that this woman had a young man with her, a Dr. Richard Kennedy, who was treating patients with great success; that Mrs. Spofford had been treated by him and had been greatly benefited and had now enrolled herself in a class just being formed by Mrs. Patterson for the purpose of giving instruction in her method so convincingly demonstrated by the young doctor. Mrs. Spofford urged Putney Bancroft to join, and after some further discussion Bancroft was so impressed that he asked Mrs. Spofford to arrange an interview for him with Mrs. Patterson. They met soon afterwards and Bancroft found everything as Mrs. Spofford had said. "I was greatly pleased with the lady," he writes, "and favourably impressed with her proposition to the extent that I decided to accept it."

Among the other members of the class, some of whom were to figure prominently in the events which were to follow, were George W. Barry, a foreman in a workshop; Miss Dorcas Rawson, also a shoe worker; Mrs. Frances Pinney, who had a small specialty workshop for women's shoes; George H. Allen, a worker in his father's box factory; George H. Tuttle, a young sailor; Mrs. Miranda Rice, a sister of Miss Rawson; Charles Stanley; Wallace W. Wright and Mrs. Otis Vickery.

The class was held in Mrs. Patterson's rooms over Miss Magoun's school, and in spite of the many difficulties which seem to have attended its every session lasted through the full twelve lessons. In word and deed it illustrated Mrs. Eddy's later contentions that her early teaching was a groping in the dark, and that while the fundamental principle was the same from the beginning it was so overlaid with the irrelevancies she inherited from Quimby or her own more orthodox convictions as to be almost unrecognizable when placed side by side with what she ultimately evolved. Bancroft's brief description and comment present the complete picture.

"Before studying", he writes, "we were treated by Dr. Kennedy, in order to render us receptive and to acquaint us with the physical methods used, after which Mrs. Patterson was to teach us the spiritual methods."

"Dr. Kennedy's treatment consisted of manipulation of the head and solar plexus. The theory as we understood it, was, that these were considered the most sensitive portions of the body. Mrs. Eddy taught us, however, that there was no sensation in matter. To some of us this seemed a paradox. This paradox, or seeming contradiction of theory, led to many serious complications and brought sorrows to Mrs. Eddy and reproach on her teaching. This she did not realize for some time. As soon as she did, her students were instructed to modify the physical methods and finally to abandon them altogether."

In this first class, Doctor Kennedy's energetic preparatory exercises were accepted as a matter of course, but as the class progressed, the argument waxed so vigorous at times that at last Charles Stanley, who seems to have passed all bounds in the matter of criticism, was asked to withdraw, Mary not unreasonably insisting that he came there to learn not to teach; in other words, that he might at least hear "the whole story" before he began to criticize it. She was, however, eager for questions and discussions, and when Wallace M. Wright presented her with a series of written questions, she answered them fully and carefully in writing.

Wallace Wright was perhaps the best educated member of the class. He was the son of a Universalist clergyman and brother of Carroll D. Wright, later United States Commissioner of Labour. The questions he submitted are not of sufficient importance to warrant detailed consideration here. They are concerned for the most part with side issues, and any points of principle involved must be dealt with later on. Wallace Wright's last question is, however, particularly apposite at this juncture as showing how loyally, even at this late date, Mary was still attributing her teaching to Quimby. It would not be long before she was to learn from bitter experience the difficulties this would create for her. But for the moment when Wright asked her, "Has this theory ever been advertised or practiced before you introduced it, or by any other individual?" she answered faithfully: "Never advertised, and practiced by only one individual who healed me, Dr. Quimby of Portland, Me., an old gentleman who made it a research for twenty-five years, starting from the standpoint of magnetism thence going forward and leaving that behind. I discovered the art in a moment's time, and he acknowledged it to me; he died shortly after and since then, eight years, I have been founding and demonstrating the science."

How little the good doctor, Quimby, had really "left magnetism behind" in his teaching, Mary was to learn through much tribulation within a few short months of making this statement.

Meanwhile, the class laboured along. Mary had made elaborate preparation for it. Not only did she give to each of its members a manuscript copy of *The Science of Man*, the manuscript which she had permitted Mrs. Wentworth to copy, but she also wrote specially for this class two other pamphlets, *The Soul's Inquiry of Man* and *Spiritualism and Individuality*. All are published by Bancroft in his book from his original manuscript, and taken together they provide an excellent summary of Mrs. Eddy's teaching in 1870 some five years before the publication of *Science and Health*.

Mary Patterson was, as Bancroft affirms, "a faithful teacher". Although the course consisted nominally of twelve lessons, she taught any student who seemed to need it "between lessons" and continued to instruct them afterwards. "We were never really graduated," he wrote. "Every meeting with her was a lesson; every letter received from her. This continued for years."

Mesmerism

DICK WAS A great success. He had a way with him and with everybody. Miss Magoun may have had some misgivings, at first, when she saw the rigid economy exercised by Mary in the furnishing of the apartment on the second floor; only the most necessary articles of furniture, "paper" oil cloth on the floors and the cheapest shades at the windows. But, as the patients arrived in ever increasing numbers, she began, rather incredulously at first no doubt, to take heart of grace. By the end of the month when the rent was paid promptly and fully, she was completely won over.

Moreover, Dr. Kennedy was a most agreeable person. He had a pleasant word for everyone, and, within a few weeks, had secured the devotion of the children in the school. Busy as he was, he would somehow manage to run downstairs about the time the pupils were being dismissed for the day and help Miss Magoun with the task of getting the younger children into their wraps and overshoes. Then naturally when the patients were so numerous as to overtax the waiting accommodation on the second floor, Miss Magoun would cheerfully place her parlour on the third at the young doctor's disposal. She always had a good word for him among her friends and with the parents of her pupils, and as her school was in good standing, success for Dick succeeded as only success can. "Go to Doctor Kennedy. He can't hurt you, even if he doesn't help you," became a common admonition from their friends to discouraged invalids, and they seem to have taken the advice in ever larger numbers.

Many of those who came to Richard for treatment went on to Mrs. Patterson for teaching, and so, outwardly at least, their plan was succeeding even beyond their most sanguine expectations. Richard Kennedy undoubtedly thought so and with every reason, but Mary seems to have been more than doubtful. She was learning very rapidly and the troubled passage of the first class had taught her much. Some things almost baffled her. The practice of manipulation which she had inherited from Quimby, and to which, up to now, she had loyally adhered, troubled her most of all. As practised by Quimby in connection with the explanation of his "Wisdom", it had never seemed to create any difficulty. The presentation had moved forward as one consistent whole, but the inconsistency between what she was teaching about the allness of Mind and the nothingness of matter and the apparent re-enthronement of matter involved in manipulation, seemed to her to become more glaring every day. Putney Bancroft probably put it mildly when he said that to some of them it seemed a paradox.

It was a puzzling situation. The physical manipulation was supposed to make the students "more receptive". Yet Mary Patterson found, much to her bewilderment, that far from this being the case, she had to labour as she had never laboured before in order to lift the thought of her students into a mental atmosphere of sufficient calmness and spirituality to apprehend anything of what she was trying to teach. The downward tendency of manipulation was quite definite, and with many members of the class the mental wrench involved in passing from physical practice to spiritual teaching was so violent as to cause them to become confused and resentful. But the solution this crisis demanded brought her teaching quickly into a freer atmosphere.

When Mary finally did see this, she was immediate and thorough in her action. She required her students to score from the manuscripts she had given them all references to manipulation, insisted that it was pure mesmerism, and banished it forever from her class and teaching. In her first edition of *Science and Health,* published a few years later, her repudiation of the practice is final and emphatic: "Sooner suffer a doctor infected with small-pox to be about you", she wrote, "than come under the treatment of one that manipulates his patients' heads and is a traitor to science."[1]

Mary Patterson's conviction on this point was not, as may well be imagined, at all welcome to Richard Kennedy. Manipulation was an established feature of his method, which had become known beyond the circle of his regular patients. He had become an expert in its use, and experience had proved to him that far from minimizing its importance, the more he could make of it, the better. He found it especially efficacious with women patients. The very ceremony of taking down the hair before "treatment", and drying and putting it up again afterwards, suggested to them that something important was being done in their behalf, and they responded most favourably. In fact, he never did attempt to do anything more than this, it is said. He did not pretend to teach. He left that to his partner.

Years afterwards, when called upon to testify in court as to his practice about this time, he made his position quite clear: "I went to Lynn to practise with Mrs. Eddy. Our partnership was only in the practice, not in her teaching. I practised healing the sick by physical manipulation. The mode was operating upon the head giving vigorous rubbing."

He then went on to relate how Mrs. Eddy had tried to teach him "the science of healing by soul-power", but that he "never had been able to understand it". This, of course, was after the lapse of years when the recollection of his long and eager discussions with Miss Bagley and Mary Patterson at Amesbury and the early vision of their great undertaking had become blurred, but it shows clearly his position.

When, therefore, Mary came to her young disciple, Richard, after her

[1] *Science and Health,* first edition. p. 193.

174

first class and told him of her decision, she found herself confronted with a problem which, in varying forms, was to present itself to her at every turn in the future, the problem of the student who would not or could not advance with her, who entered her teaching at a certain point and out of what he found or thought he found, at that point, evolved something of his own. Richard Kennedy refused to give up manipulation. He was the first of several. As Bancroft puts it: "Some of her pupils refused to comply. Dr. Kennedy was one of them, and after labouring with him for some time she was obliged to sever the partnership which existed between them."

The conviction that manipulation in general and Richard Kennedy's practise of it in particular was pure mesmerism did not come to Mary in any sudden "revelaton". It is, indeed, clear from Bancroft's account of it that, at first, she was inclined to think it was the character and amount of manipulation that was at fault, and she sought to get over the difficulties bound up with its use by suggesting modifications. Water was, first of all, eliminated from the head-rubbing process, and the process itself considerably shortened. Later on, under pressure of a growing conviction, the whole preliminary exercise was greatly reduced.

That Kennedy viewed these developments with increasing disfavour cannot be doubted, and for the next twelve months the relationship between the two must have been characterized by that process of disagreement and compromise which can only have one outcome.

Meanwhile, the arrangement was profitable to both parties. In a little notebook of Mrs. Eddy's still preserved are careful records of her receipts and expenditures at this period. These show that from June, 1870, to May, 1871, Mrs. Patterson's share of the receipts was $1,742. As the division was made after the deduction of all expenses, rent, living costs and so on, it is clear that, from a financial point of view, the partnership was a complete success.

It was, however, for Mary, a hard and rugged road. The tumult of her first class did not come to an end at the close of the final session. There were long lulls in the storm, but, for years afterwards, the flotsam and

175

jetsam of its wreckage would be cast up on the shore. The first great outburst occurred more than a year after its close. The central figure was
Wallace W. Wright, the man whose written questions at the time of the
class Mrs. Patterson had answered so fully. Mary's answers had apparently more than satisfied him, and he left the class full of enthusiasm for
the new teaching. He seems to have practised in Lynn for some time,
evidently profiting by Mrs. Patterson's ever readiness to help and further
instruct, which Bancroft mentions, and then early in the summer of 1871
he set out for Knoxville, Tennessee, where he had connections, planning
to enter into the practice of spiritual healing there with another of Mrs.
Patterson's students.

At first he seems to have had considerable success, but, later on, for
some reason that he could not understand, he began to "lose his power",
and as more and more cases came his way which "utterly refused to yield
to treatment", he began to have "doubts". From doubts he went on to
convictions, and the conviction he finally reached was that what he had
learned and had been practising was mesmerism and nothing else.

As soon as he was satisfied on this point, he wrote to Mary in Lynn,
demanding that she refund the fees he had paid her and telling her just
what he thought of her and her teaching. If it had been a simple case of
inability to demonstrate what he had learned, Mary would not, in all
probability, have hesitated to return the money. She had shown herself
more than generous in this regard, but, in this case, to return the money
would have been virtually to admit that Wright's charge was true and that
her teaching was mesmerism. Coming as it did at the time when her sus-
picions as to Kennedy's part in it were reaching the point of conviction,
this was the last thing Mary would admit. She absolutely refused to do
as Wright demanded.

A few months later, Wright himself was back in Lynn. He called on
Mary and renewed his demand, and when Mary again refused, he decided
to thrash the whole matter out in the public press. It was a particularly
cruel form of attack, but one to which Mary was to become accustomed in
the future.

The first broadside came in the Lynn *Transcript*, January 13, 1872. Beginning at the beginning, Mr. Wright says: "The 9th of last June found me in Knoxville, Tennessee, as assistant to a former student. We met with good success in a majority of our cases, but some of them utterly refused to yield to treatment. Soon after settling in Knoxville I began to question the propriety of calling this treatment, 'Moral Science' instead of mesmerism. Away from the influence of argument which the teacher of this so-called science knows how to bring to bear upon students with such force as to outweigh any attempts they may make at the time to oppose it, I commenced to think more independently, and to argue with myself as to the truth of the positions we were called upon to take. The result of this course was to convince me that I had studied the science of mesmerism."

This was more than enough for Mary. The following week she replied fully to Wright. She did not attempt to deal with his charges of teaching mesmerism, but she did indicate what Wright's real purposes were, namely, simple extortion and revenge. She said he had demanded from her not only the return of his tuition fee, but $200 "damages" extra, and threatened that if she did not comply, he would see to it that she should never hold another class in Lynn. The controversy was taken up with less wisdom than zeal by several of Mary's students who rushed to her defence. Wright was in his element, and finally, after much writing back and forth, he issued a challenge to Mrs. Patterson to give a public demonstration of the practical value of her teaching by "methods" he would "enumerate".

In return, he promised that if she was successful he would retract all his charges, "asking forgiveness publicly for the course he had taken". He added that refusal to comply, "by silence or otherwise", should be considered "a failure of her cause". The methods of proof he proposed were as follows:

1st: To restore the dead to life again.
2nd: To walk upon the water without the aid of artificial means.

3rd: To live 24 hours without air, or 24 days without nourishment of any kind without its having effect upon her.

4th: To restore sight when the optic nerve has been destroyed.

5th: To set and heal a broken bone without the aid of artificial means.

Mary Patterson very naturally ignored this challenge, but some of her followers, not so wise, joined issue with vigour, repudiating Wright's charges and bearing testimony to the high character of their teacher and the true spirituality of her teaching.

Mr. Wright was exultant. Mrs. Patterson, he declared, had, as he knew she would, utterly failed to meet his demands, and that it must be clear to everyone that both she and her Science were "practically dead and buried", which after all was a singularly unfortunate excursion into the realm of prophecy.

The whole incident served to bring into focus for Mary, as nothing else perhaps could have done, the dangerous tendency of all students to stop at a particular point instead of going along with the evolving doctrine as it necessarily progressed with advancing discernment. This was, of course, highlighted by the controversy over Kennedy's manipulations, and it was soon afterwards that she and Richard came to the parting of the ways. She was evidently very much attached to him at one time, entertaining high hopes for his future, and the break-up of their partnership would mean for her a complete realignment of her plans. The arrangement they had agreed upon in Amesbury had worked out well. The more successful Richard was in demonstrating the value and practicality of her teaching, the more eager were those thus helped to learn more about it from her. But now she could not be certain that what Richard was doing was really a demonstration of spirituality. And as the days and weeks passed and she saw more and more of the character of his work, she gradually concluded that it was not.

It was, of course, all new to her, as it was to Kennedy, but it must have been with grave misgivings that she saw the large and increasing number of people, mostly women, who came to Richard for treatment again and again, "because they could not stay away", and Richard's apparent satisfaction that this should be so.

It is quite evident from Richard Kennedy's testimony, already quoted, that he had from the first—no doubt, unconsciously—regarded Mary Patterson's teaching merely as an addendum to manipulation, and that the more successful he was, the more certain he became that for him, at any rate, manipulation was the only thing that mattered.

And so the partnership was dissolved—in the spring of 1872. It had lasted less than two years, yet, when the final accounting was made, Mary Patterson's share of the funds accumulated amounted to some $6,000. She remained for the time being in the apartment over Miss Magoun's school. Richard took offices further down town.

Richard Kennedy enters into the story of Mary Patterson's life for several years after this, and in many ways profoundly affected the course of her development, not so much, or at all, for what he was as for what, in her view, he stood for. He was, to her by this time, the arch mesmerist, and in order to appreciate the importance of the part he played in this record, it is necessary to appreciate the extraordinary part which mesmerism played in popular thought in the last quarter of last century.

As has already been noted, Spiritualism, especially in the years immediately succeeding the Civil War, had overshadowed mesmerism as a popular excursion into the unseen. Mesmerism had had its day, and, in that day, had held out the promise of many possibilities. There had been at first nothing sinister in what the world was led to expect from it. It had been advocated as a healing agent, and many men like Phineas Quimby had practised it successfully in this connection. When it lost favour as a means of healing, it continued to maintain itself as an interesting exhibition, and few forms of entertainment were more common in the middle of last century than an exhibition of mesmerism or hypnotism by some well-publicised exponent.

Up to this time, however, mesmerism, as far as the general public was aware of it, had been practised only on willing subjects, with the mesmerist personally present. Later on, as was inevitable, the possibility

179

of mesmerizing people at a distance without their knowledge, much less their consent, began to be discussed as though possibly a demonstrable fact. The question was debated everywhere; short story writers and long story writers began to develop it as a theme. Bram Stoker wrote his *Dracula* as did—later on—Du Maurier his *Trilby.* But what placed mesmerism as a sinister agent in human affairs most forcibly before the public was Henry Irving's play, *The Bells,* with its tale of horror, centring round the mesmerized murderer of the Polish Jew. *The Bells* was first produced in London in 1872, and immediately the possibilities of mesmerism as a means for compelling criminals to confess was discussed in all its aspects in newspapers and magazines throughout the world. From this particular use, discussion ranged over every other kind of use or misuse, until nothing was thought impossible.

Upon one point there was complete agreement, namely, that either ignorance or acquiescence was really necessary to successful hypnosis. This, however, was far from removing the fear of it. Acquiescence could be withheld, but who could guard against an attack of which he was ignorant?

The whole subject is still one about which very little is popularly known. The possibility of the most extravagant claims as to the power of mesmerism, in certain circumstances, is still to be proved, but the effect of suggestion—itself a form of mesmerism—on individuals or on large masses of people is today recognized and traded on to an ever increasing extent.

In 1872, it was still almost a virgin field, and to a man of Richard Kennedy's temperament and parts it offered unlimited scope for experiment. It has been charged that, after he severed his connection with Mary Patterson, it was this experimental study that claimed and absorbed his interest and practice. To him it had all the fascination of laboratory research. His one absorbing interest was to see the thing work. He had accepted from Mary Patterson the supremacy of Mind. He was now proving it, as he thought, every day. He failed to realize the distinction which Mary Patterson was beginning to draw between the divine Mind and what she called its counterfeit, the human mind.

But the partnership had been dissolved and thus, for the moment, all was quiet. Richard Kennedy went his way, and Mary, saddened and troubled but not dismayed, went back to her rooms over Miss Magoun's school, more determined than ever to go forward. A few weeks previously, in defending herself against the attacks of Wallace Wright in the Lynn *Transcript,* she had declared simply that what remained to her of life would be devoted to the cause she had espoused, "Well knowing as I do", she added, "that God hath bidden me."

CHAPTER 18

Three Years

LYNN, MASSACHUSETTS, IS one of the oldest towns in New England. It was first settled in 1629, less than a year after John Endicott landed at Salem as the first Governor of the Colony of Massachusetts Bay and a full year before John Winthrop's company reached Charleston and selected the windswept and tideswept Trimountaine peninsula as the site for the future city of Boston.

In those days, Lynn was known by the Indian name, Saugus, but in or about the year 1637, there came to Saugus a refugee Puritan minister from England, one Samuel Whiting. He was a native of King's Lynn, the old town on the Wash in Norfolk, and not being a Separatist with his "Farewell Babylon, Farewell Rome", but having a love for "dear England" deep in his heart, he, with the consent of his fellow-colonists, changed the name of the little settlement from Saugus to Lynn. And so it is to this day.

Lynn is one of those places which through all its changing history has always managed to be important. It has no golden age to look back upon, unless it be the years of the Civil War when its factories were working night and day to turn out shoes and saddles and harness for the Federal forces. Only ten miles from its big neighbour, Boston, it has maintained its identity through the years and is today one of the great manufacturing cities of New England.

Seventy years ago, Lynn stood well back from the sea. A few houses had crept out towards the rough unwalled beach, but where the broad plaza, the sea wall and promenade are today were only cow paths, winding in and out between the boulders down to the shore.

Well out from this shore, but easily reached, save at high tide, was a great mass of rock. It is still there, of course, and known today, as seventy years ago, as the Red Rock. It rises some twenty feet above the water in a series of ledges, and anyone finding his way to the eastern side of it would have nothing between him and the old world but the ocean, with the new world shut off behind him by a wall primeval. As far as nature could provide a symbol, the Red Rock at Lynn was certainly a "No Man's Land" between the old and the new. Today it is visited by many people from all over the world, but, seventy years ago, it was just another rock on a rocky coast.

Through the summer of 1872, on into the fall, and for nearly three years off and on when the weather was fair, a lone woman might have been seen of an afternoon making her way along the cow paths towards the shore, carrying a book and a roll of papers. She would cross the shingle towards the Red Rock and disappear round its southern wall. A couple of hours later she would reappear again and make her way towards Lynn.

This woman was Mary Patterson. Her bitter experience with her first class, the breach with Richard Kennedy, the controversy with Wallace Wright and other similar experiences had convinced her that her teaching would never be safe from misrepresentation until she had embodied it, not as heretofore in a written manuscript but in a printed book. Soon after her break with Richard Kennedy, she seems to have become convinced that she should give up teaching, give up everything, and devote herself to this one thing of writing a book. She wrote or worked out a good deal of it as she sat thinking and dreaming on the Red Rock at Lynn.

183

Quite apart from the mental labour demanded, the writing of this book *Science and Health*, as she later called it, must have involved a tremendous physical task. The first edition amounted to some 150,000 words. It had, of course, all to be written in long hand, and, after tireless correction, emendation or complete rewriting, a fair copy of the final recension had to be made. At first, Mary attempted to do all this herself, but, later on, she had the help of George Barry, a student in the first class.

It is only possible to get occasional glimpses of the work as it progresses, but from what few records there are one may detect in the unfolding story a growing sense of expectation among Mary's small number of loyal followers that something really portentous was in the making. Putney Bancroft, in his *Memoirs*, draws aside the curtain for a moment on the little group struggling along after the defection of Doctor Kennedy, meeting each Sunday in Mary's rooms for a kind of informal service and discussion and listening to any new interpretation their teacher had to offer. It was a very small band, indeed, Samuel Bancroft, George Barry, Dorcas Rawson, Mrs. Miranda Rice, her sister, and a few others.

"Those of you who call yourselves Christian Scientists," wrote Bancroft half a century later, looking backwards, "those who attend the beautiful churches which have been erected . . . can hardly realize the situation in which Mrs. Eddy and her loyal students were placed, or the sentiments with which they were regarded at that time. We were considered much the same as the 'Holy Rollers' or the 'Howling Dervishes' are today." But he adds, "We were a happy company, notwithstanding our loss of numbers and the ridicule and contempt with which we were sometimes regarded." [1]

These Sunday gatherings in Mrs. Patterson's rooms were very informal in character. "Mrs. Eddy read the Scriptures to us," Bancroft writes, "and gave us an extemporaneous explanation of them." [2] That they had music and singing is clear from a letter of Mary's to Bancroft written one Friday morning and reminding him of the meeting to be held on the following Sunday. "We have an instrument in the parlour again," she writes. "The Berry family will be here and we shall have music from you all." [3]

[1] *Mrs. Eddy As I Knew Her in 1870*, by Samuel Putnam Bancroft.
[2] Ibid.
[3] Ibid.

But perhaps the most important thing that arises out of these informal gatherings or Bancroft's account of them, is the first clear glimpse they afford of Mary Patterson's teaching, especially in her interpretation of the Lord's Prayer which Bancroft gives in full. All her life Mrs. Eddy evidently had a devoted regard for this prayer, and it is no doubt significant of the way in which the principle of her teaching was becoming fixed that although the actual wording of the interpretation, as given by Bancroft, differs greatly from that finally embodied in *Science and Health,* the meaning is essentially the same. Bancroft's rendition follows:

Teacher: After this manner, therefore, pray ye:
Student: Our Father which art in heaven,
Teacher: Harmonious and eternal Principle of man,
Student: Hallowed be Thy name.
Teacher: Nameless and adorable intelligence.
Student: Thy will be done on earth as it is in heaven.
Teacher: Control the discords of matter with the harmony of spirit.
Student: Give us this day our daily bread.
Teacher: Give us the understanding of God.
Student: And forgive us our debts, as we forgive our debtors.
Teacher: And Truth will destroy sickness, sin and death, as it destroys the belief of intelligent matter.
Student: And lead us not into temptation but deliver us from evil.
Teacher: And lead man into Soul, and deliver him from personal sense.
Student: For thine is the kingdom, and the power, and the glory, for ever.
Teacher: For God is Truth, Life and Love for ever.[1]

Mary remained in the apartment over Miss Magoun's school for about six months after her break with Kennedy, and then she went to stay for a time with Miss Dorcas Rawson, who was rapidly becoming a very successful practitioner. Mary was better off than she had been for many years,

[1] *Mrs. Eddy As I Knew Her in 1870,* by Samuel Putnam Bancroft.

185

but she needed to conserve her resources. She had no source of income, her allowance from Doctor Patterson, of $200 a year, had long ceased, and she had given up her teaching in order to devote all her time to writing. She was, moreover, it is to be imagined, looking ahead to the time that she might need money to publish her book, and, meanwhile, she had to pay for such help as she needed on it. Dorcas Rawson no doubt urged her to make the change and come to live with her for a time. Mary was glad to do so, but the break-up of her little home in Miss Magoun's schoolhouse ushered in for her three more years of wandering from place to place, from friend to friend, or from one boarding house to another.

Doubtless Mary Patterson was at this time, as she had often been in the past and was often to be in the future, a very difficult person to live with. More and more was she utterly absorbed in what she was doing, and more inclined to subordinate everything and everybody to her work. Those who could go along with her, who could share something of her vision and consequently enjoy something of its rewards, far from being irritated over the demands she made upon them, either directly or through her teaching, rejoiced to meet them. But time and again in a student this devotion would wane, displaced or overshadowed often by seemingly the most trivial circumstances. In a long succession of cases, some of which have already been noted, devotion would be transformed overnight to hatred. But it is an interesting fact that in after years, not infrequently after a breach lasting the better part of half a century, these same men and women would bear eloquent testimony to the fact that they still looked back upon the days of their association with Mary Patterson as the *anni mirabili* of their lives.

It was possibly for this reason that Mary, after a last bitter experience with the Wentworths at Stoughton, never attempted to stay very long with friends, even when they were as faithful and devoted as was Dorcas Rawson. As she put it very cogently years afterwards, "Human reason becomes tired and calls for rest. It has a relapse into the common hope."[1] Dorcas Rawson remained faithful through the years to come, but it is

[1] *Miscellany*, p. 165.

doubtful if even she could have borne for long the tremendous pace of Mary Patterson, in those days. Once satisfied that the next step demanded of her was to write this book, she literally worked at it day and night.

And so, after a few weeks with Dorcas Rawson, Mary took rooms again in the boarding house on Sumner Street kept by Mr. and Mrs. George Clark where she had stayed for a time after Doctor Patterson had left some four years previously. It was George Clark, Jr., it will be recalled, who years afterwards, gave such a vivid description of Mrs. Patterson as he remembered her when she was living with his parents in the summer of 1866. George Clark was now six years older, and in his leisure from the inevitable shoe business had been devoting some time to writing—tales of adventure for boys. Mary took an immediate interest in his work, and in his recollections he tells of an incident, interesting for its own sake but specially so for the light it throws on one of Mary's most lovable characteristics, her ability to rejoice utterly in another's success.

It would seem that, at the time she was staying with the Clarks, she began definitely to seek a publisher for the book she was writing. George Clark had finished a book of his own, and, probably due to Mary's encouragement, determined to get a publisher for it. And so the two joined forces and George Clark with his finished copy and Mary with a prospectus of her book went up to Boston from Lynn to see a publisher they had decided upon, namely, Adams & Company, whose headquarters were on Bromfield Street. George's book, a boy's story of seagoing life, was accepted at once. Mary's prospectus was rejected with equal promptness. The publishers were confident, they said, that Mr. Clark's book would sell well, but they could see prospects of nothing but loss in a book such as Mrs. Patterson was outlining.

With all the enthusiasm engendered by a first acceptance George was jubilant, and Mary was so full of rejoicing, too, and so cheerful in her encouragement and confident expectations for his future that it was not until after they had reached Lynn on the homeward journey that the young author realized how different must be the feelings of his companion. When he did realize it, he recalled thirty years afterwards how contrite he felt over his own apparent selfishness and how he could almost have found it in his heart to wish that the situation had been reversed. Whether he said anything about it to Mary at the time, he does not relate, but he does say that as they were walking up from the station towards Sumner Street, Mary suddenly caught his arm as they were passing a church and said quietly, "I shall have a church of my own some day." She was never long cast down by apparent defeat.

Moreover, her life was an almost constant demonstration of a fact insisted upon in her later teaching, namely, that opportunity is always at hand and that to the individual who recognizes this, the closing of one door is but the signal that another is opening. Frequently what she found as she passed through the new door was only a very temporary "salvation", doomed to further denial, but it made for that eternal renewing of hope which, especially in these early days, was Mary's sheet anchor. Kennedy had hardly gone his way before Putney Bancroft was at hand.

Putney was a very different man. Richard had been brilliant in his way. Putney Bancroft was far from that, but he had a certain quality of patient consideration which was just what Mary most needed. He had lately married, and after Mary had been with the Clarks for some time he and his wife asked her to come stay with them. They had just purchased a house in Swampscott and had a good room they could place at her disposal. Mary accepted the invitation gladly, and all went well for a while. She was once again in an atmosphere of understanding, free from the necessity of meeting people whose interests were quite divergent from her own, and she settled down to work with renewed vigour. Bancroft speaks of how earnest she was and how unremitting in her application.

It was not long, however, before the great question of finances began to loom large once more. Mary had paid liberally for the quiet she needed and so much treasured, and funds were running low. The necessity for earning again became urgent. Fortunately, she now had the means always at hand. She could teach, and among her growing band of followers there were always a number eager to learn more of the teaching set forth in the little Sunday gatherings which Mary Patterson continued to hold in the homes of her friends.

She hesitated about adventuring upon another formal class—the difficulties and perversities of her first effort in this direction were still all too fresh in her memory. But she decided to take just a few at a time. Bancroft says "one or two," but the fact that she left the Bancrofts about this time in order to secure more accommodation for teaching seems to indicate that she contemplated a larger gathering.

She left the Bancrofts with regret, not only because she was fond of them and they had been loyal to her, but because she seems to have felt that the loss of what she could give them for her board and lodging might straiten the young couple unduly. Bancroft, however, makes it clear that she was oversensitive on this score, and in quoting a letter from her on the subject remarks how it shows "her loving kindness and thought for others, particularly her pupils."

Certainly the letter reveals the difficulties under which Mary Patterson was working.

She trusts her hosts will not be wounded by her moving elsewhere, but sees no alternative. "I have one student engaged and expect others," she writes, and it would be awkward trying to teach in so small a place. And there are other handicaps. Every word she would say could be heard in the adjoining parlour, students would have to come through the parlour to enter and, anyway, Annie's wanting to practice on the piano would make the whole situation untenable.

And then, in the same letter, she goes on to speak of her book, the first clear statement that is available. She is within sight of the end. Three months more will see the first draft completed, but even then there will still be a great deal to do. It still has to be "compiled" and after that "written out for the last time".

It was exacting, toilsome work, and Bancroft makes it clear that Mary about this time had moments when she yearned for some sign of human friendship and encouragement. He reproduces a letter from her written on "Thanksgiving Day", prefacing it with the remark that "knowing her

189

loneliness so well", he cannot "read it or think of it without emotion". To him, it is "a cry of distress and suffering as of one lost in the wilderness". Written to "Friend Bancroft", the letter is pitiful enough. "They tell me this day is set apart for festivities and rejoicing; but I have no evidence of this except the proclamation and gathering together of those who love one another. I am alone today. . . . Family ties are broken never to be reunited in this world with me. . . . My spirit calls today, but who of all my students hears it."

There is little word of it, but, from a few poignant sentences like the above which appear in her letters during the next year or so, it would seem that these months of intense mental and spiritual labour were among the most lonely of her life. Formerly, in times of deep trial she had a last recourse in her family. She could write to Abigail, and, even if Abigail did not understand, she could catch again the strange homesick comfort which flows from ties which had once been happy and joyous even when they are but pale ghosts of their former selves. But now, even this poor comfort is denied her. "Family ties are broken never to be reunited in this world for me."

Only one word appears to have reached Mary in these years from her family, and it comes from a most unexpected quarter, from her step-mother, Mark Baker's widow. It is a loving, complacent note, the very placidity of which may well have thrown into still more bitter relief the lone struggle of Mary's life. Calling Mary her "own dear daughter," Mrs. Baker expresses a yearning for more frequent word and sends tenderest loving greetings "to yourself and all who are kind to you." [1]

But the loneliness of the lonely Thanksgiving Day passed and in the next picture that Bancroft supplies, Mary and he are busily engaged in working out a new plan full of promise for both of them. Mary had decided that the best answer to the suggestion of failure or stagnation was a definite expansive forward movement. Richard Kennedy had failed her. Wallace Wright had pilloried her in the public press, and she cries out in one of her letters to Bancroft against the bitterness of it all: "Oh

[1] *Historical Files of the Mother Church.*

190

how I have worked, pondered and constantly imparted my discoveries to this wicked boy that I shall not name and all for what? God grant me patience. Mrs. Susie Oliver told me once that Richard said he thought I had suffered so much from bad students if he did not well it would kill me, but it won't." [1]

All the Baker in her surged to the surface at such moments. Not only was she not going to succumb to the malice of her enemies, she was going to show herself stronger than ever.

And so it was arranged that Putney should go to Cambridge, open an office there, and that Mary would follow as soon as she could find a suitable place to live. Owing to the death of Bancroft's uncle, the firm of Purington & Bancroft had been dissolved, and Putney had to decide upon a new move in any case. In his account of the matter he says that the decision was taken only "after much deliberation and investigation", and that Cambridge was chosen because it was "the seat of learning", that "men and women of cultured and developed minds were to be found there", and that "some of them would gladly welcome her and the Truth she would bring them". [2]

Mary seems to have canvassed all the little group before finally deciding on Putney, as is shown in his engaging prim record: "Dorcas Rawson had her own little coterie. Mrs. Rice could not desert husband and child. George Barry was employed in copying her manuscripts, and was expected to take an active part in promoting the sale of her book. George Allen had his box factory. Who was available? It was the old story, 'one had taken a wife, another at the plough,' etc. etc." [3]

And so the lot fell upon Putney. He set out for Cambridge, carrying with him some newly printed cards and a sign which read:

S. P. Bancroft
Scientific Physician
Gives no Medicine

[1] *Mrs. Eddy As I Knew Her in 1870*, by Samuel Putnam Bancroft.
[2] Ibid.
[3] Ibid.

191

How seriously he took his mission may be gathered from his diary, in which he records under date, December 7, 1874: "Today I took another step, and one which I take with fear and trembling, but in which I feel that I am obeying the call of wisdom which call I dare not disobey. I have today come before the world as a demonstrator of the Science of healing the sick by the power of the Soul over matter, as taught by Mary M. B. Glover, and which I believe to be the true Science of Man." [1]

Poor Putney! Both he and Mary were doomed to another disappointment. They did everything they could. Mary wrote letters to the Boston and Cambridge Press, but the papers inevitably refused to print the letters save as advertisements. Putney sent out letters to "prominent divines and men of learning", but received answers to none of them. "Our efforts to obtain recognition were futile," he writes, "and continued to be of no avail." [2]

Yet, all the time, healing work was going on and the fame of it was somehow getting abroad. Mary Patterson in her letters of encouragement to Putney refers to several cases and Putney in his diary speaks of his work and of the advice that Mary gives him from time to time. One item of news in one of Mary's letters is of special significance as showing how far afield word of her work had travelled. "Miss Sweetland of California", she writes, "has written to me to take her case there."

[1] *Mrs. Eddy As I Knew Her in 1870*, by Samuel Putnam Bancroft.
[2] Ibid.

Completing the Book

THE REGISTRY OF DEEDS for Essex County in the State of Massachusetts shows that on March 31, 1875, Frances E. Besse, in consideration of the sum of $5,650,[1] deeded to "Mary M. B. Glover, a widow woman of Lynn", the property at Number 8 Broad Street.

The house is still there—carefully preserved—a small two and a half storey building surrounded by a narrow strip of lawn with a large shade tree at one corner. Its purchase was a great adventure for Mary Patterson and an act of faith of no small order, but it solved for her the wearing problem of a place to live and write. After her plan to move to Cambridge and help Bancroft with his work failed to mature, she took rooms in a boarding house in Lynn at Number 9 Broad Street, and looking out of her window one morning she saw a new sign on the house opposite, to the effect that it was for sale. The thought came to her that if she could only manage to buy that house, reserve the best room on the ground floor as a class room, a small room for herself as a bedroom and study, and rent out the rest, it might afford her that quiet and sense of settlement for

[1] She assumed a $2,850 mortgage and paid $2,800 cash.

which she craved as her book neared completion. Once she had made up her mind, Mary always acted promptly, and it was not long before the deed was signed and the house was hers.

However viewed, this act of Mary Patterson's in buying the house at Number 8 Broad Street marks quite definitely her emergence "out of tradition into history". Up to now, the story of her life could have presented to the onlooker no unmistakable trend or purpose. There was no focal point towards which the rays of her effort could gather. She may have known, and her followers may have suspected, that the movement—if so it may be called—for which she stood was already much wider than any outward and visible sign would lead one to expect. If bad news travels fast, good news often travels faster, and already, as has been seen, requests for help and teaching were reaching Mary from as far afield as California. Nevertheless, concrete evidence of establishment and growth was largely lacking. Word of it all had gone out through so many devious ways that two neighbours might quite well be interested without either knowing of the other's interest.

As soon as Mary Patterson bought her house and put up, as she did, her blue and gold sign bearing the legend, "Christian Scientists' Home", the movement, as a movement, was born. It was not long before Lynn was talking about it and news items appeared in the press about Mary Patterson and her teaching.

Georgine Milmine, in preparing her articles for *McClure's Magazine*, made exhaustive enquiries about these early days from a number of people in Lynn then alive who could remember them, and she stresses the growing sense of wonder which these people recalled over the devotion of Mary Patterson's followers and the reports of healing work. Whatever trouble and disappointment she had with individual students, their number from now on constantly increased, and, as Milmine has it, "for every deserter there were several new adherents".

Perhaps most remarkable of all, is the vivid recollection of these people, even of those who afterwards were completely alienated from her, of the power of her teaching. Their common testimony was that "what they got from her was beyond equivalent in gold or silver."

194

"They speak", Georgine Milmine writes, "of a certain spiritual or emotional exaltation which she was able to impart in her class room; a feeling so strong, that, it was like the birth of a new understanding, and seemed to open to them a new heaven and a new earth . . . They came out of her class room to find that for them the world had changed. They lived in a new set of values. . . . One of the students who was closest to her at that time says that to him the world outside her little circle seemed like a mad house where each inmate was given over to his delusion of love, or gain, or ambition, and the problem which confronted him was how to awaken them from the absurdity of their pursuits."[1]

Meanwhile, in spite of her rapid attainment in other directions, Mary had but one care and one labour, the completion of her book. Besides the large class room on the ground floor she retained for her own use only one small room, a little attic on the third floor, lighted by a skylight in the roof which could be pushed outwards and upwards to secure ventilation. Here she completed her manuscript and made her final corrections. This combined study and bedroom was furnished austerely enough, and was unheated save for a small kerosene stove. On the walls—the sole adornment—a framed text from the Bible which ran, "Thou shalt have no other Gods before Me."

It was, however, for Mary, a home at last. The vacant rooms were quickly filled for the most part by those who were eager to have her teaching, and there—and then—seems to have been born that devoted service on the part of certain individuals which Mary needed so much and which, in varying degrees, she was to enjoy for the rest of her life.

At first, this position of service was never filled for long by one individual, but when one fell out there was always another to take his place. It was George Barry and Miss Dorcas Rawson who arranged all the details of the purchase of Number 8 Broad Street. George Barry, it will be remembered, had been a member of the much-discussed first class. When he met Mrs. Patterson he was suffering from tuberculosis in a serious form, and his healing was one of the most striking that there had

[1] *McClure's Magazine*, vol. xix, p. 109.

195

been up to that time. His devotion to Mary was deep and sincere, and, in addition to copying out her manuscripts, he sought to relieve her as much as possible of all lesser cares. He arranged all the details of moving and furnishing, attended to all the business matters, ran errands and wrote letters, and in every way showed himself most helpful.

And yet, although in the fullest sense of the word a disciple, he was not an apostle of the new faith. No one could have been more devoted or efficient in the matter of carrying out instructions than was George Barry, but he had none of those qualities of initiative and independent action which Richard Kennedy had possessed in such a marked degree. George Barry was an excellent orderly, but he had none of the qualities of a sergeant-major. Mary Patterson had need of someone with these qualities, someone upon whom her other students could depend, who could be trusted to speak for her intelligently and authoritatively when she was not present to speak for herself. Such a man Richard Kennedy, at his best, had been, and up to now his place had never been filled by another.

It was not, however, to remain vacant much longer. As will be remembered, Putney Bancroft was first introduced to Mrs. Patterson by a man in his department at the shoe factory, one Daniel Spofford. Mrs. Spofford, who had been greatly benefited in health by Richard Kennedy, was planning to enter a class to be held by Mrs. Patterson, and together they urged Putney Bancroft to join. This, as has been seen, he did. Mrs. Spofford also joined, and although her husband for some reason did not, he was apparently very much interested in the whole subject and studied his wife's manuscript eagerly at night. The two left Lynn shortly after the close of this class for the far west, where Daniel planned to take up farming or some employment which would give him outdoor work. They carried copies of Mrs. Patterson's manuscripts with them, and the more Daniel studied them, the more convinced he became of their verity. He gradually evolved from them a system of healing which he thought was more or less his own, and after some four years in the west, during which he found himself devoting less and less time to farming and more and more to the practice of healing, he decided to return to Lynn and devote all his time to the work.

196

Whether or not he had heard from his friends there—as indeed would seem very likely—of the rapid development of Mrs. Patterson's teaching is not clear, but when Mary was organizing the first class to be held in her new home—which she did early in April—having heard of Daniel Spofford's return to Lynn, she sent him a letter inviting him to join as a guest student. "Mr. Spofford," she wrote, "I tender you a cordial invitation to join my next class and receive my instructions in healing the sick without medicine, without money and without price." He accepted immediately.

Daniel Harrison Spofford was, in many ways, one of the most interesting of Mary Patterson's early followers. He was a great contrast to Richard Kennedy. Born at Temple, New Hampshire, he was early left an orphan, and at the age of ten came with his elder brother and widowed mother to eastern Massachusetts. There, when little more than a child, he went to work on a farm, and although rather a frail boy managed to do a man's work. Thoughtful and reflective by nature, he was an earnest student of the Bible, and even when a chore boy around the farm would often worry over the problems which a strong Calvinistic theology presented. Then, when he was twenty, came the Civil War. He fought through it all, some twenty engagements, among them Gettysburg and the second battle of Bull Run, and was finally mustered out in 1864. Thereafter he worked in a shoe factory in Lynn, as a farmer in the far west, and now back again in Lynn as a practitioner and student of mental healing.

It was no doubt because she recognized in him some qualities above the average that Mary Patterson invited Daniel to her class and gave him a receipt in full for the three hundred dollars which he otherwise would have had to pay. But whether she did or not, he quickly showed himself an exceptional student, and in less than a month after he entered the class he had opened an office in Lynn and put out his sign, "Dr. Spofford, Scientific Physician".

His success was immediate and even more pronounced than that of Richard Kennedy. And yet he had none of the qualities which were

197

apparently the main cause of Richard's popularity. Richard was hail-fellow-well-met with everybody, had a remarkable capacity for friendship and a warm enjoyment of everything. Daniel, on the other hand, was an idealist and something of a dreamer, gentle in manner as he was somewhat frail in build. He carried about with him an atmosphere of aloofness contrasting strangely with Richard's breezy intimacy. His success, like Kennedy's, lay in his healing works.

People came to him in increasing numbers for healing, and Mary got into the way of turning over her students to him for further instruction.

The little group was growing rapidly now, so much so that the Sunday morning gatherings were taxing severely the capacity of the front room at Number 8 Broad Street. It quickly became evident indeed that something would have to be done about it, and so on June 1st a meeting of students was held at the Broad Street house for the purpose of considering the advisability of renting a hall in which to hold public meetings.

The resolution adopted at this meeting, which has, of course, a special historic interest, was as follows:

"Whereas in times not long past, the Science of Healing, new to the age, and far in advance of all other modes, was introduced into the city of Lynn by its discoverer, a certain lady, Mary Baker Glover,

"And, whereas, many friends spread the good tidings throughout the place, and bore aloft the standard of life and truth which had declared freedom to many manacled with the bonds of disease or error,

"And, whereas, by the willful and wicked disobedience of an individual, who has no name in Love, Wisdom or Truth, the light was obscured by clouds of misinterpretation and mists of mystery, so that God's work was hidden from the world and derided in the streets,

"Now, therefore we, students and advocates of this moral science called the Science of Life . . . have arranged with the said Mary Baker Glover, to preach to us or direct our meetings on the Sabbath of each week, and hereby covenant with one another, and by these presents do publish and proclaim, that we have agreed and do each and all agree to pay weekly, for one year beginning with the sixth day of June, A.D. 1875, to a treas-

198

urer chosen by at least seven students the amount set opposite our names, provided nevertheless, the moneys paid by us shall be expended for no other purpose or purposes than the maintenance of said Mary Baker Glover as teacher or instructor, than the renting of a suitable hall and other necessary incidental expenses, and our signatures shall be a full and sufficient guarantee of our faithful performance of this contract.

(Signed)

"Elizabeth M. Newhall - - - $1.50
Daniel H. Spofford - - - - $2.00
George H. Allen - - - - $2.00
Dorcas B. Rawson - - - - $1.00
Asa T. N. Macdonald - - - .50
George W. Barry - - - - $2.00
S. P. Bancroft - - - - - .50
Miranda R. Rice - - - - .50"

This made a total of ten dollars a week. Five dollars were to be paid to Mrs. Patterson, the other five being used to defray the cost of renting a hall and "other incidental expenses".

These Sunday sessions—which were more in the nature of lecture gatherings than church services—provided a rallying point for her following, a sounding board for her crusade and a satisfying compromise with her childhood Congregationalism.

On the following Sunday, June 6th, the first public Christian Science meeting was held in the Templar's Hall. Putney Bancroft came over from Swampscott to lead the singing, while his wife played the melodeon. The congregation numbered between sixty and seventy. The weekly meeting seemed fair to becoming a Sunday service.

This first meeting appears to have been in every way a success, and no doubt Mary and her faithful band looked forward to a peaceful development of their plan, increasing numbers and expanding usefulness. They were, however, quickly to learn that whatever things the future had in store for them, peace, as far as the outside world was concerned, was not to be one of them. Word of the meetings soon got abroad and the merely

199

curious came in ever larger numbers. With them also came the covertly and openly antagonistic. Mary Patterson's well-known condemnation of Spiritualism brought many Spiritualists to her Sunday services, and in the time reserved for questions they sought in every way to trap her in her speech and involve her in argument. She struggled on valiantly for a time, but at length became convinced that no matter how successfully she might defend her teaching, the atmosphere of argument and contention was not what she and her followers were in search of. After the fifth meeting, the public Sunday services were abandoned.

It must have been a disappointment, but it was not the first of many, and, after all, Mary Patterson's great work was the book, and that was now rapidly nearing completion. It was a hard task, but she was happy in it. Bancroft in his memoirs makes mention of this. "I consider", he says, "the summer of 1875 the most harmonious period of the twelve years from 1870 to 1882, during which, Mrs. Eddy had continued to reside in Lynn. I never knew her so continuously happy in her work."[1]

And yet she could never have been able to see very far ahead. No publisher could be found who would even consider her book, and all her available funds had gone into the purchase of the Broad Street house. She would need some $1,500 to $2,000 if she was to publish it herself, and she had little or nothing. It was George Barry and Elizabeth Newhall who finally solved the problem. They decided to advance the money and publish the book themselves. And so, as far as the book was concerned, they disappeared as George Barry and Elizabeth Newhall and reappeared within a few days as "The Christian Science Publishing Company".

They went to work with a will, but their troubles were far from over. Even with the money guaranteed and with a considerable sum paid in advance, the printer proved dilatory beyond all reason in carrying on the work. This very dilatoriness, however, in the end, resulted in a development of considerable importance and in an incident which evidently made a deep impression on Mary at the time and was often recalled by her afterwards.

[1] *Mrs. Eddy As I Knew Her in 1870*, by Samuel Putnam Bancroft.

It appears that ever since she parted from Richard Kennedy she had steadily become more and more convinced as to the dangers of mesmerism in any system of mental healing. She began to reason, first, that Quimby's teaching, consciously or unconsciously, had been based on mesmerism; and, secondly, that wherever her own interpretation became involved in any way with Quimby's, it became obscured to that extent. She herself felt sure that she had carried through, without any suggestion of mesmerism in her own practice, but developments seemed to indicate that certain people seized upon any mesmeric possibilities she allowed to remain, as Kennedy had done, and quickly developed them, until, as far as she could see, such doctrine crowded out all else. Mary Patterson was to encounter this again and again in the years that were to follow. Elements of Quimby's teaching, which she loyally but mistakenly associated with her own for so long, were to dog her steps right up to the end of her long life.

In the spring and summer of 1875 the practice of Richard Kennedy was considered to be a kind of opposition camp in Lynn. He had a large clientele, but Mary Patterson decided that the effect of his work in a number of cases was like that of a habit-forming drug—the patient came more and more under his influence. She also became convinced of a growing enmity in the most unexpected quarters, and suspected, with almost a sense of horror, that when any of her students came under the influence of Kennedy the most fantastic things were likely to happen. It was all new to her, but, in the end, she seems to have reached the conviction that Kennedy was a mesmerist of the first water, that his one purpose was to see how far he could go, while the one consuming interest of his life was the exercise of his new-found power in any and every direction. At least, this was how she saw it, so she said.

Her trying experiences of this period, interpreted in the light that all is mental, began to bring into sharp focus the heretofore nebulous doctrine of malicious mental malpractice—the teaching that one may be injured or destroyed through the secret, silent machinations of an enemy who has eaten of the tree of knowledge of good and evil. So thoroughly did

201

this view take hold that we find Mary Patterson working diligently and rallying her closest followers to work diligently with mental declarations designed to offset the enemy's attack and to render him impotent in his perfidy. It was considered possible that his directed malice might even return upon him, to his own undoing, in a sort of law of compensation. Notes to her students to "take up" the culprit are still in the historical files, and they stand as milestones in the advancement of Christian Science doctrine ever more out of the personal sense of the attack-and-defense, the affirmation-and-denial, in "treatment."

With this conviction as to Kennedy and his purposes, apparently came another conviction, namely, that the basis of Kennedy's seeming power was the general ignorance of what was going on. She herself was satisfied that just in proportion as she realized the intent of mesmerism, to that extent it was powerless, and out of all this grew the final conviction that she ought to embody something on the subject in her book. She was very late in doing this, and it is probable that if it had not been for the dilatoriness of the printer in Boston she would not have done it, at any rate, not at that time. In her account of the matter in *Retrospection and Introspection* she tells how, as the weeks and even months passed during which the printer was holding up the work, she at last yielded to the constant conviction that she should insert in the last chapter of her book "a partial history of what (she) had already observed of mental malpractice".[1]

Thence onward, the work went through without further delay, and, in the fall of 1875, the Christian Science Publishing Company had completed its task. The book was published under the title of *Science and Health*, and put on the market in an edition of one thousand copies, at a price of $2.50 a copy. It was well printed on good paper in a substantial cloth binding of green, blue, grey and brown.

Daniel Spofford was placed in charge of sales and commenced his task by sending out copies for review to the most important New England newspapers, with the rather unfortunate request not to mention the book

[1] *Retrospection and Introspection*, p. 38.

at all unless it could be reviewed favourably. Later on, Mary was to learn —if indeed she knew of Spofford's request—the wisdom of Mrs. Stevenson's dictum, "Speak for my son or agen my son but aye be speakin' about my son."

Most of the papers took the course of not mentioning the book at all, but those that did, some of them, like the Springfield *Republican* of excellent standing, received it with surprising cordiality.

CHAPTER 20

Science and Health

IT HAS BEEN well said that anyone who commences to read the Bible as if it were any other book will quickly find that it is like no other book. The same is true, in a measure, of *Science and Health*. It is like no other book. There are no standards, either of literature, form, or content, by which it can be appraised. Perhaps the most revealing statement that ever was made in regard to it is Mrs. Eddy's own in the preface to the last edition, issued in 1908, where she says that "until June 10, 1907", she had never "read this book throughout consecutively".

Between the appearance of the first edition in 1875 and the last in 1908, *Science and Health* ran through 382 editions. In many of these, changes of considerable importance were made, especially in the early editions. In the sixteenth edition, issued in 1885, the book was completely rearranged and to a large extent rewritten, and yet the author never read it through consecutively until it had been out more than three decades.

Anyone, therefore, who expects to find in *Science and Health* the progressive unfoldment of a thesis in what he would regard as orderly advance from step to step will quite certainly be disappointed. The chapter on Prayer with which the book now commences, was, until 1902, one of the later chapters of the book, while only three chapter headings appearing in the first edition are retained in the last.

For these reasons a review of *Science and Health* in the accepted meaning of the term must be impossible, whether in its first or last edition. It is, however, possible, and very readily possible, to grasp its purpose; and when this purpose is grasped, each chapter, practically each page, becomes a treatise on the fundamental issue, almost complete in itself.

Mrs. Eddy, in her teaching, laid stress on the proposition that Christian Science differed from orthodox Christianity in nothing save that it was "a step more spiritual". In other words, she places all the Christian virtues in the forefront of doctrine. Paul's famous summary, in his epistle to the Galatians, finds an honoured place in *Science and Health*. Her purpose is to "advance from the rudiments laid down". Her faith was that in the light of the great revolutionary dictum as to the allness of Spirit and the consequent nothingness of matter, every Christian virtue would be revised outward and upward, until, as she puts it, "joy is no longer a trembler, nor is hope a cheat".[1]

While not nearly so outspoken as the first edition, the last revision of Mrs. Eddy's book reduces most of her basic propositions from page-long dissertations down to brief paragraphs and even, in some instances, to short sentences. Here is a typical passage from the first edition:

"We learn from science mind is universal, the first and only cause of all that really is; also, that the real and unreal constitute what is, and what is not; that the real is Spirit, which is immortality, and the unreal matter, or mortality. The real is Truth, Life, Love and Intelligence, all of which are Spirit, and Spirit is God, and God, Soul, the Principle of the universe and man. Spirit is the only immortal basis. Matter is mortality; it has no Principle, but is change and decay, embracing what we term sickness, sin, and death. God is not the author of these, hence Spirit is not the author of matter; discords are the unreal that make up the opposite to harmony, or the real that emanates Truth and not error. Spirit

[1] *Science and Health*, p. 298.

never requires matter to aid it, or through which to act; no partnership or fellowship exists between them; matter cannot co-operate with Spirit, the mortal and unreal with the real and eternal, the mutable and imperfect with the immutable and perfect, the inharmonious and self-destroying with the harmonious and undying. Spirit is Truth, matter its opposite; viz., error; and these two forces control man and the universe, and are the tares and wheat that never mingle, but grow side by side until the harvest, until matter is self-destroyed; for not until then do we learn ourselves Spirit, and yield up the ghost of error, that would make substance, Life and Intelligence, matter. God and His idea are all that is real primitively; all is mind, and mind produces mind only, nature, reason and revelation decide, that like produces like; matter does not produce mind, nor, *vice versa*. We name matter, error, it being a false claim to Life and Intelligence, that returns to dust ignored by Spirit, that is supreme over all, and knows nothing of matter."[1]

This thought is, in the final version (from 1908 on) embodied in one compact paragraph on page 468, which has become famous as "the scientific statement of being." Beginning, "There is no life, truth, intelligence, nor substance in matter," it declares Mind all and immortal, with matter or error unreal and temporal, concluding that "man is not material; he is spiritual."

Science and Health is simply the iteration and reiteration of these statements in many different forms. No matter what the subject under consideration, whether it be Creation, Marriage, Spiritualism, Atonement, Healing the Sick, or what not, sooner or later it will be found to lead up to a new view of the original thesis, the allness of God and the nothingness of matter.

Science and Health has been subjected to criticism from every point of view—few books more so. Sometimes, as in the case of Mark Twain's memorable onslaught, the discussion was carried to the limits of the English-speaking world and beyond. Any attempt to traverse anew the field of these discussions, casting them into one comprehensive review,

[1] *Science and Health*, First Edition, pp. 10-11.

would be as profitless as it would be tedious. It is a fact, however, that any biography of Mrs. Eddy must, as it moves from point to point, cover incidentally most phases of the long controversy, linked as they so often are to momentous passages in her life. Mrs. Eddy's life, after the publication of *Science and Health,* was inextricably interwoven with her teaching. It would be impossible, therefore, to present any just picture of her life without at the same time discussing her teaching; and a discussion of her teaching, in whatever phase, involves her book *Science and Health.*

It has been often said that the movement came not out of the book, but that the book thrived because of the movement. In any event, the book of 1875 was almost stillborn. No one seemed to want it outside of its author's immediate circle. Members of this circle, however, certainly did everything in their power to get the book into circulation. Dorcas Rawson and George Barry made excursions into neighbouring towns, literally hawking it from door to door, and talking of the teaching it contained wherever they could find anyone willing to listen. Advertisements were inserted in local papers, accompanied by testimonies of healing, and copies were sent to libraries, universities, and many prominent and well-known people in various parts of the world. At first there seemed to be little response, but after a time the clouds began to break. Dorcas Rawson's and George Barry's vigorous frontal attack seems to have been more or less successful. Quite a number of copies of the book were sold and read by an ever-widening circle, with the result that, almost from the first, the number of people seeking Mrs. Patterson's help and counsel increased greatly.

The outside world, however, had been almost silent, and then one day Mary received a letter, the first of several, from no less a person than Bronson Alcott, the philosopher of Concord, the father of *Little Women* and friend of Emerson and Longfellow. It was not just a simple acknowledgement, as some few had been. He had not only received the book, but had read it through chapter by chapter, right to the end, and with growing enthusiasm. It must have been a wonderful letter for Mary to receive: "The profound truths which you announce, sustained by facts of the immortal life, give to your work the seal of inspiration—reaffirm in modern phrase the Christian revelation. In times like these, so sunk in sensualism, I hail with joy your voice, speaking an assured word for God and immortality, and my joy is heightened that these words are woman's divinings."

He then goes on to say that reading her book has awakened an earnest desire to know "more of yourself personally". And, he adds, "May I then enquire if you would deem a visit from me an impertinence? If not, and agreeable to you, will you name the day when I may expect the pleasure of fuller interchange of views on these absorbing themes." That letter was written on January 17, 1876, and, a few days later the two met in Lynn.

Bronson Alcott was one of those men whose place in the history of philosophy and letters seems to grow in importance as the years pass. In his day, although standing out vividly enough by himself—too vividly at times—his theories and methods were so utterly revolutionary as to carry them often, in the popular estimate, into the realm of fantasy. And so, although he was listened to eagerly wherever he went and could hold audiences large or small enthralled by his marvellous conversational powers on an extraordinary variety of subjects mostly transcendental in character, the effect on his auditors was again and again vitiated by the reckless way in which he forged ahead and left them to follow as best they could. He had no school of philosophy and never made any attempt to found one. As a consequence, his audience never quite knew what to expect. They could understand him, and applaud or condemn according to their individual predilections, when he launched out on his favourite topics, the primitive greatness of the child mind or superior spiritual promise of the woman's. But they could not always follow him when he dwelt upon the "illumination of mind and soul by direct communion with the Creative Spirit", or insisted on the "all but audible spiritual counsel and monitions of external nature", or the "invaluable benefits which must flow to man from serenity and simplicity".

And yet Emerson could and did take the same ideas—catching from

Alcott the inspiration behind them—and so present them as to make them intelligible and instantly acceptable to great multitudes. If there is such a thing, Alcott was and is a philosopher's philosopher and, as such, is being steadily discovered.

The teaching of Mary Patterson was just the kind to attract such a mind. The position she took up and claimed to prove as to the allness and consequent ever-presence of God, Spirit, only went a step further than his own theory of "direct communion", and so, after he had read *Science and Health,* he was eager to meet its author.

We have no description of their first meeting in Lynn, but that Bronson Alcott was far from being disappointed is evidenced by his next letter to Mary. It is written from Concord and dated January 30th. It shows that he lost no time after his return in seeing Emerson and his circle and telling them all about it.

Recalling his visit with pleasure, he speaks of her grace and charm and of his desire "for more intimate fellowship" with her and her "devoted circle." At a gathering in Emerson's home that week, he had spoken of her and her teaching. "Mr. Emerson had heard of your book, it appeared, and the company listened to what I had to tell without disloyal criticism." After this manner he hopes to advertise Mrs. Glover and her work and feels she can trust his commendations anywhere. Perhaps the subject can be introduced next week when he is to meet the Divinity Students at Cambridge "for conversation on Divine Ideas and methods."

Meanwhile, Daniel Spofford and George Barry went forward with renewed hope in their efforts to develop the sale of *Science and Health.* Spofford was building up a very considerable practice. Besides his office in Lynn, he had opened offices also in Haverhill, Newburyport and Boston, and, as one of the main objectives of his work was to lead his patients on through their own healing to a further study of the new teaching, he found a ready sale for *Science and Health,* which even at that early date was beginning to be regarded and spoken of as "the textbook."

Then some more or less favourable reviews were beginning to come in.

The Springfield *Republican* had described the doctrines of the book as "high and pure" and "wholly free from those vile theories about love and marriage which have been so prevalent among the spiritualists". The *Christian Advocate* of Buffalo, New York, declared that the book was "certainly original . . . not influenced by superstition, or pride, but striking out boldly and alone . . . full of philanthropy, self-sacrifice and love toward God and man." While the Boston *Investigator* summarized its view comprehensively enough, by saying: "We shall watch with keen interest the results of *Science and Health*. The work shows how the body can be cured and how a better state of Christianity can be introduced, which is certainly very desirable. It has likewise a hard thrust at Spiritualism, and taken altogether is a very rare book."

Such notices, combined with the favour of a man like Bronson Alcott, while Emerson and his "pleasant circle" at Concord listened "without disloyal criticism", must have been more than welcome to Mary and her little band. As Bancroft puts it, "Such notices as these made us all very happy, and we gathered around our leader with renewed confidence in her and hope in the future of Christian Science."[1]

Meanwhile, the leader herself also seems to have enjoyed about this time one of those brief periods filled with the satisfaction of hope realized, which she enjoyed, or rather allowed herself to enjoy, so seldom. It is indeed a significant fact in Mrs. Eddy's whole life, but especially from now on, that although so many contemporary records comment on her cheerfulness, she never seems to have had much use for a cheerfulness which was begotten from what the world would call success. Later on when she had become one of the world's best-known women, she wrote of herself: "I rejoice with those who rejoice, and am too apt to weep with those who weep, but over and above it all are eternal sunshine and joy unspeakable."[2] She always gives the impression of one seeking this "eternal sunshine", and the fact that she apparently found it again and again, even in the most difficult circumstances, is the only possible ex-

[1] *Mrs. Eddy As I Knew Her in 1870*, by Samuel Putnam Bancroft.
[2] *Miscellaneous Writings*, p. 279.

planation for her serenity, which, to an increasing extent was wont to amaze her friends and confound her enemies.

To this ability may also perhaps be attributed the impression of extraordinary beauty which she gave at times and to which both her friends and her enemies alike bear testimony. She never seems to change very much. Almost the same words are used in describing her at sixty as at sixteen. "Slim, alert, graceful . . . big grey eyes deep set and overhung with dark lashes . . . her skin clear, red and white," so testified an old neighbour at Bow in 1836. Putney Bancroft, in 1876, in his prim, formal style, presents much the same picture. He, too, speaks of her regular and finely moulded features, of her eyes, "deep set, dark blue and piercing, sad, very sad at times, yet kind and tender," of her splendid carriage, her slim, "yet well-rounded figure". Ten years later still, a student speaks of her as "exquisitely beautiful, even to critical eyes", and twenty years after that, when Mrs. Eddy was in her eighty-seventh year, the matter-of-fact Arthur Brisbane finds this word "beautiful" the only word by which to describe her.

But in these Lynn days especially, what seems to have made the most profound impression on her followers, was Mary Patterson's self-sacrifice and devotion to her purpose. As Bancroft puts it, "In all the years during which I knew her, Mrs. Eddy's life and her activities were dominated by this one idea, the promulgation of her theories. She was undoubtedly sincere in thinking that to be of more importance to the world than all else she had to offer."[1]

It was, on the other hand, just this devotion to purpose which betrayed Mary at this time into doing and saying many things and resorting to methods which time and experience, often most bitter experience, caused her, later on, to abandon. The conservatism and modesty; the obligation to respect the opinions of others; the policy of discretion—not to push forward aggressively but to await alertly the appeal for help; the wisdom of restraint and the paramount value of charity which characterized her later teaching and actions, find little place in these early days. If the sick

[1] *Mrs. Eddy As I Knew Her in 1870*, by Samuel Putnam Bancroft.

did not come to be healed, then let the practitioner of Christian Science go out and find the sick and heal them, in spite of themselves. If any man reviled you or failed to appreciate your teaching in the public press, then a certain amount of judicious reviling in return was quite in order. If the practitioners of Materia Medica advertised themselves and the benefits of what they had to offer, then the practitioners of Christian Science should not hesitate to do the same and more also.

Thus, when Bancroft wrote to Mary from Cambridge, complaining of his lack of patients and the apparent failure of his work, she told him sharply, in so many words, to stop growling and get to work. "Do not stand still," she wrote. "Make a stir. Go to the sick and heal them if they do not send for you."

When an unfavourable review of *Science and Health* appeared in the Boston *Globe,* she did not hesitate to write to the paper, characterizing the review as "stupid"; the comments of the reviewer as "of no value whatsoever"; and the reviewer himself as one prevented by his own sensualism from a "clearer perception of supersensual truths". All of which was possibly true, but in marked contrast with the restraint of her later years.

Most startling of all, however, were some of the methods used to promote the sale of *Science and Health*. It is, of course, entirely possible that Mary Patterson, labouring under the ever-increasing burdens of a new movement, every step forward in which was into new country, had no knowledge of many of those means and methods until after they were an accomplished fact—although it is to be admitted there is no record that she ever objected to such things. Anyway, in those days, characterized, as has been already noted, by the most extravagant claims from all manner of "doctors" and "healers", they would not be nearly so offensive as they would be today. And yet, one of Spofford's efforts is startling enough. He got out a circular describing the book in the most extravagant terms, and also a hand bill which reads like nothing so much as the advertisement for a patent medicine. It commenced:

A HOLIDAY PRESENT
SOMETHING THAT WILL DO GOOD
SCIENCE AND HEALTH
Hundreds of invalids have been cured by reading it

Thereafter, follow a series of some ten or twelve testimonials from doctors and others testifying to the benefits they have received and the names of booksellers in Boston from whom the book might be procured.

Mary Patterson's bitter complaint to Putney Bancroft about this time, "My students . . . disgrace my recommendation," would seem to have been often more than justified. Help, however, was near at hand, and from an unexpected quarter.

Asa Gilbert Eddy

SOME THREE YEARS before that "obdurate Separatist", John Baker, left his native village of Lyminge in Kent, in 1634, and set out for the New World, two young men, John and Samuel Eddye, sons of the Reverend William Eddye, Vicar of Cranbrook, another Kentish village not far from Lyminge, had made the same journey. John Baker, it will be remembered, ultimately built himself a grist mill on the outskirts of Boston and prospered greatly. John and Samuel Eddye took up land not far from Salem and devoted themselves to farming. Whether the three ever met, it is impossible to say. The colony was still a small one, and they came from neighbouring villages in England. They may have met. In any case, the Eddyes, too, seem to have prospered, John especially, and in the 1830's, Asa Eddye, the son of Abel, the son of Ebenezer, the son of Samuel, the son of Samuel, the son of John, still a farmer, was living in Londonderry, Vermont. He and his wife, Betsy, had several children, of whom Asa Gilbert was the next to the youngest.

Farming in Vermont in the early part of last century was very much the same as farming in New Hampshire at that time, a constant struggle, late and early, with the inexorable demand everywhere upon everyone to do his share. In the case of the Eddyes, the situation was rendered somewhat different by reason of the fact that Betsy Eddye, far from yielding to custom in this respect, had the most original ideas as to her status and obligations. She had a passion for driving, and as soon as the children were old enough to go to school she would, after seeing them safely delivered at the school house, set out with her horse and buggy and drive all day long around the countryside.

There is no record that Asa Senior ever protested. He was less inclined to do so, perhaps, because in the evenings Betsy would train her children, boys and girls alike, in all the arts of housekeeping. They were taught, not only to cook and sew, wash and iron, but to spin their own wool, weave their own cloth, and make their own clothes. The more successful she was as a teacher, the more she was relieved of household cares and the more time she could take off to indulge her "ruling passion".

At first, she was influenced to a certain extent by weather conditions, remaining at home if the day was wet or stormy; but later, finding such restraint irksome, she fashioned for herself a kind of helmet on the "diver" principle. It was made of thick cloth, was attached more or less rigidly to her shoulders, and had a nine by ten-inch pane of window glass inserted in an opening opposite her face. The contrivance served, of course, as a perfect windshield, and with this protection she could venture out in all weathers in complete comfort.

Then, Betsy had unusual ideas about doctors. When she or any of the children was ill, her unfailing recourse was one "Sleeping Lucy". "Sleeping Lucy", whose right name was Lucy Cook, had a remarkable "gift of nature". When summoned professionally to aid the sick, she just naturally went into a trance and, while thus conditioned, diagnosed the trouble and prescribed the remedy, apparently in very much the same way as the boy Burkmar, it will be remembered, was doing for Quimby about the same time, away at the other side of the mountains in Maine. Betsy, moreover, had a great love for fine clothes and, what was still more unusual in a New England housewife of a hundred years ago and a cause of still greater perplexity to her neighbours, she was credited with having a "fine library".

The boy, Asa Gilbert Eddy, who had taken up weaving as a trade, in the end inherited the farm. It was deeded to him in 1859 by his parents on condition that he agreed to support them for the rest of their lives. They did not survive long. Betsy died in 1860 and the elder Asa three years later. Asa Gilbert continued to manage the farm for a time, but his heart was really not in farming, and before long he leased it and returned to his trade as a weaver.

Asa Gilbert Eddy was a man of somewhat unequal parts and unusual traits. As a boy at school he moved ahead steadily enough, and ultimately achieved a good common school education, but he was outstanding in nothing save in the art of penmanship. In this, even at a time when penmanship had many amazing exponents, he was apparently regarded as exceptional, and all his life he delighted in its exercise. A rather small, mild-mannered man, he was just a little bit different in everything he did or affected. He designed his own clothes and the cloth from which they were made, and he secured the impression of added height by wearing his luxuriant hair in the highest possible pompadour style. He loved to play the violin and to draw animal pictures for little children. He was genial and candid and just naturally kind, and he had two other qualities which, later on, as they found occasion for exercise, were to overshadow all others, self-sacrifice and tenacity of purpose.

When he first enters this record, about 1876, he is living in East Boston working as an agent for a sewing machine company. Among his friends were a Mr. and Mrs. Godfrey, who lived in the little township of Chelsea, close by. Being a bachelor living alone, he was often asked to their home, and one day early in 1876, on going to visit them, he was conscious at once that something unusual had happened. Mrs. Godfrey did not leave him long in doubt. She had, it appears, for some weeks previously, been suffering from a badly infected finger caused by a broken needle and complicated by poison from some coloured thread. It was so serious that the doctor had advised amputation. Gilbert Eddy evidently knew all about it, and, as the Godfreys had been away in Lynn for a few days, had come round on their return to see how Mrs. Godfrey was. When she showed him her finger, perfectly healed, he was naturally overjoyed, and eager to hear the story they were evidently more than eager to tell. And so they told him of how they had been invited by some friends, who lived in Lynn and who knew of Mrs. Godfrey's trouble, to visit them; how these friends had rooms in the house of a Mrs. Mary Patterson at Number 8 Broad Street; how they persuaded Mrs. Godfrey to ask Mrs. Patterson for help; how Mrs. Patterson had agreed to do what she could; and how when she, Mrs. Godfrey, got up next morning, her finger was perfectly well.

Gilbert Eddy was immediately interested and, suffering from some minor ailment himself, was anxious to try the effect of the new treatment. The Godfreys had met Spofford at Lynn and, probably at their insistence, Gilbert went to consult him at his office in Boston. The result was all he could have wished. He recovered, if not instantly at any rate so quickly and thoroughly as to make him eager to learn all he could as soon as he could about the new teaching. Spofford had no difficulty in persuading him to come with him to Lynn and meet Mrs. Patterson. The result of their meeting seems to have been an instant appreciation on both sides, and within a few days Gilbert Eddy had enrolled himself in a class that Mary was then forming.

Asa Gilbert Eddy was one of the most satisfactory of all Mrs. Patterson's students up to that time. He never seems to have hesitated a moment at any point. He accepted as truth what he was taught the first time Spofford explained it to him. Mrs. Patterson admitted him as a student as soon as she saw him. He entered a class she was forming, studied the usual three weeks, and at the end of that time assumed at once, with the usual ease, the title of "doctor" and set to work, being the first of Mrs. Patterson's students to announce himself as a "Christian Science practitioner".

It was a clear-cut example of orderly development which might have occasioned in the hearts of the little band nothing but satisfaction and rejoicing. On the surface all was calm. The calm, however, was very much of the kind that precedes a storm. Gilbert rose rapidly. He had a certain quiet capacity for getting things done and a sense of order, which to Mary, burdened at every turn by ever-increasing calls upon her time and attention, was an indescribable relief. She tended to lean upon him more and more and to act, either actually or apparently, on his advice, often with all too drastic thoroughness.

The slowness of the sale of *Science and Health* was perhaps what troubled her most. Already, she was hard at work revising it and planning for a second edition. She could not, however, issue a second edition before the first had been sold and some of the necessary funds for the second edition thus made available. It was probably on the advice of Gilbert Eddy that she decided to take vigorous action. She asked Spofford to come to Lynn and go into the whole question with her. As a result it was decided that Spofford should turn over part of his practice to Gilbert Eddy and devote all his available time to promoting the sale of *Science and Health*.

In ordinary circumstances, such a plan might have worked very well. Spofford had built up quite a large connection and had had charge of the sale of the book since its publication. He was resourceful, and if his methods were sometimes somewhat crude, even for those days, he was enthusiastic and anxious to do the best he could. The circumstances were, however, far from ordinary. The rapid rise of Gilbert Eddy was being viewed by some of the older members of the group with steadily increasing disfavour. The advent of this eleventh hour worker, at a wage not only equal to but obviously greater than their own, was the cause, at first, of much secret heart burning and, later on, open rebellion, and the weeks and months which followed were to present as unlovely a picture of the results of petty jealousy as is possible to imagine.

The first to reach the breaking point was George Barry. So long as he occupied the position of head man, his devotion knew no limits. He may have felt that the more indispensable he made himself, the higher must he be in the estimate not only of his teacher but of his fellow-students. He enjoyed this sunshine to the uttermost, apparently, and evidently had no idea of sharing the position with any newcomer like Gilbert Eddy. Mary tried to reassure him, but it was all to no purpose, and when she completed the new arrangement with Spofford and Gilbert Eddy for managing the sale of *Science and Health*, he went off in high dudgeon and refused to return.

Spofford himself was hardly less disaffected. He appeared to acquiesce in the new plan wholeheartedly, but it became evident before very long that discontent over Gilbert Eddy was colouring his interpretation of every move that was made from Lynn. He went about his work without complaint, but without any enthusiasm or accomplishment, and Mary seems to have felt it all intensely.

Indeed, there began to develop anew about this time with Mary Patterson and her followers a phase of thought which, although ultimately seen by Mary herself for what it was and definitely overcome, was to remain for many years a possible source of ever-recurring wrong development. It was a phase of the old Quimby belief that, in the process of healing, the healer took upon himself the "griefs" of his patient, and then proceeded to cast them out of his own thought and experience. The cruder phases of this theory had long been abandoned, but there remained the conviction that the healer was open to the mental demands of his patients and to the burden which his emotions, whether of anger, hatred, and resentment and so forth, would impose, if he were personally present.

Apart from this, there can be no doubt that in addition to the cares of a young movement, Mary Patterson was subject day and night to calls from her students for healing for themselves and advice in the healing of others. She had not yet reached the heights of her later teaching when she could affirm calmly, "Evil thoughts and aims reach no farther and do no more harm than one's belief permits. Evil thoughts, lusts, and malicious purposes cannot go forth, like wandering pollen, from one human mind to another, finding unsuspected lodgement, if virtue and truth build a strong defence."[1] She was conscious in these months of a steadily growing burden and, with her feet still uncertainly planted in the new way,

[1] *Science and Health*, pp. 234-35.

219

she was often fearful and anxious. Sometimes, she reached a point almost of despair, as is clear from a long letter to Daniel Spofford written towards the close of 1876. Spofford had been complaining, insisting that he was being driven away from her, and in every way showing clearly that he was constantly mulling the whole thing over in a spirit of dissatisfaction and hurt. Mary is well nigh desperate.

"Now, Dr. Spofford," she writes, "won't you exercise *reason* and let me live or will you *kill* me? Your mind is just what has brought on my relapse and I shall never recover if you do not govern yourself and turn your thoughts wholly away from me. Do, for God's sake and the work I have before me, let me go out of this suffering I never was worse than last night and you say you wish to do me good and I do not doubt it. Then won't you quit thinking of me. I shall write no more to a male student and never more trust one to live with. It is a hidden foe that is at work. Read *Science and Health* page 193, 1st paragraph.[1]

"No student nor mortal has tried to have you leave me that I know of. Dr. Eddy has tried to have you stay. You are in mistake. It is God not man that has separated us and for the reason I begin to learn. Do not think of returning to me again, I shall never again trust a man. They know not what manner of temptations assail. God produces the separation and I submit to it, so must you. There is no cloud between us, but the way you set me up for a Dagon is wrong, and now I implore you to return forever from this error of *personality* and go alone to God as I have taught you.

"It is mesmerism I feel and it is killing me. It is mortal mind only that can make me suffer. Now stop thinking of me or you will cut me off soon from the face of the earth."

It is the letter of a sorely tried and fear-filled woman, and is chiefly significant for the contrast it presents to the calmness and serenity per-

---

[1] The passage from *Science and Health* (First Ed.), page 193, runs: "Evil thoughts reach farther, and do more harm than individual crimes, for they impregnate other minds and fashion your body. The atmosphere of impure desires, like the atmosphere of earth, is restless, ever in motion, and calling on some object; this atmosphere is laden with mental poison, and contaminates all it touches. When malicious purposes, evil thoughts, or lusts, go forth from one mind, they seek others and will lodge in them unless repelled by virtue and a higher motive for being." The contrast with the same passage from the last edition of *Science and Health* (page 234), is interesting.

vading her later dealings with much more difficult situations. In these early days, there is abundant evidence that Mary Patterson was, at times, fearfully conscious that she was advancing into a realm of thought hitherto unexplored, that she was leaving old landmarks behind her, and that there was no human being of whom she could inquire the way or even take counsel as to its probable direction. The spirit was willing, and not only willing but inflexibly determined. Nothing, apparently, could turn her aside. All through these years of struggle and disappointment, she must have been aware that she could free herself and return, almost at will, to a life of ease and comfort with her people at Tilton. From the one bitter letter she was to receive from Abigail, some ten years later, it was clear enough that, so deeply did her sister feel the talk and criticism that Mary's actions had brought upon her, she would have welcomed any prospect of their being abandoned with all her heart and at almost any cost.

But if the spirit was willing and inflexible, the flesh was often weak, and this letter to Spofford reveals Mary Patterson down in one of those deeps, plumbed at times by every prophet, great or small, whether without the walls of Ur of the Chaldees or Jerusalem. It was an experience she was often to have in the future. As she puts it, looking back over the years, in her book *Retrospection and Introspection*: "A realization of the shifting scenes of human happiness, and of the frailty of mortal anticipations, —such as first led me to the feet of Christian Science,—seems to be requisite at every stage of advancement. Though our first lessons are changed, modified, broadened, yet their core is constantly renewed; as the law of the chord remains unchanged, whether we are dealing with a simple Latour exercise or with the vast Wagner Trilogy."

In the midst of it all a strange thing happened. Gilbert Eddy asked her to marry him. It might be assumed she had no thought of it and that marriage held little attraction for Mary Patterson. The tragedy of her first marriage, followed by the long drawn out misery and disappointment of her second, left little in the prospect that anyone should desire it. She was fifty-six years old, and Gilbert was some ten years younger. Moreover, she had now in life just one great, all-absorbing purpose. She could not think of it, and so she refused him.

But that night she had a dream, a very common incoherency begotten of the troubles of the day, in which she found herself wandering in a wheat field surrounded by "swinish forms", fearful and alone and quite at a loss as to what to do. Then, suddenly, she was conscious of a very simple, honest presence close at hand, and next moment she heard a voice saying to her, "Come on, Mary, I will help you."

It was Gilbert Eddy, of course. They were married next day, New Year's Day, 1877, with a suddenness confounding to Spofford, coming hard upon her renunciatory letter of two days before!

That they entertained a real affection for each other which only deepened as the years passed, seems clear enough, but Mrs. Eddy, as she indicated later on in one of her books, had at this time and always afterwards, one dominant preoccupation. Gilbert Eddy, as will be seen, shared this ambition and this joy with amazing faithfulness and loyalty, and because she recognized these qualities Mary Patterson found the promise of security and encouragement in him.

No doubt they hoped, too, that by their marriage they would put an end to the petty jealousies which had made their useful co-operation so difficult, and their hopes in this direction were to a certain extent justified, at any rate, as far as the rank and file were concerned. To George Barry and Daniel Spofford, as will be seen, it was the last straw; but the rest of the little group, after they had recovered from the first surprise, rallied round their teacher with renewed affection and loyalty. Indeed it quickly became clear that, coming as it did at a time when a vague sense of uneasiness as to the ultimate demands of the new teaching was beginning to make itself felt, the very simple human act of this marriage had a wholesomely clarifying effect.

There is something very homely and accustomed about the Lynn *Reporter's* account of the celebration of the event which was held at the Broad Street house a few weeks later. Under the caption "Christian Scientists' Festival", and under date February 10, 1877, the account runs:

"A very pleasant occasion of congratulations and bridal gifts passed off at the residence of the bride and bridegroom Dr. and Mrs. Eddy, at No. 8 Broad Street, on the evening of the 31st ult. The arrival of a large number of unexpected guests at length brought about the discovery that it was a sort of semi-surprise party, and thus it proved, and a very agreeable surprise at that. It afterwards appeared that the visitors had silently assembled in the lower parlour, and laden the table with bridal gifts, when the door was suddenly thrown open and some of the family invited in to find the room well packed with friendly faces; all of which was the quiet work of that mistress of all good management, Mrs. Bixby.

"One of the most elaborate gifts in silver was a cake basket. A bouquet of crystallized geranium leaves of rare varieties encased in glass was charming, but the presents were too fine to permit a selection. Mr. S. P. Bancroft gave an opening address—a very kind and graceful speech, which was replied to by Mrs. Glover Eddy with evident satisfaction, when alluding to the unbroken friendship for their teacher, the fidelity to Truth and the noble purpose cherished by a number of her students and the amount of good compared to others of which they were capable. The happy evening was closed with reading the Bible, remarks on the Scripture &c. Wedding cake and lemonade were served, and those from out of town took the cars for home."

Little imagination is needed to describe the scene when the last guest had gone, Mary always ready to hope for the best, happy in the evidence of so much affection and peace restored, and Gilbert methodical and almost woman-like in his care of things—"he could do up a shirt as well as any woman," as his sister-in-law once said of him—happy because she was happy, moving quietly about tidying the room, putting chairs back in their places, stacking up the plates and carrying them to the pantry and putting the remains of the wedding cake back in the cake box.

The Second Edition

IT WOULD BE a mistake to suppose that all the days of these years of Mrs. Eddy's life or indeed any years of her life were characterized by gloom and anxiety. From the good and often amazing results later achieved, it is clear that, in these early days, a great deal of confident and satisfying work was being done, and that the compensation of such successes, small or great, must have gone a long way to relieve the pressure of apparent failure elsewhere. Bronson Alcott had followed up his first interest with several kindly acts. He received both George Barry and Daniel Spofford in his home at Concord, visited Mary several times in Lynn, on one occasion at least stopping overnight in order to remain to the close of a session with her students. At another time, when some specially violent attack on *Science and Health* had come to his notice, he set out for Lynn and characteristically announced himself to Mary when he arrived with the words, "I have come to comfort you." Years afterwards, Mrs. Eddy recalled the incident, adding how his conversation, "with a beauty all its own," reassured her.

At another time Bronson Alcott wrote to her from Concord, telling her how Mrs. Emerson had expressed a wish to meet her, and how he had commended herself and her book "to respectful consideration . . . to some of our best people", adding with remarkable insight, "I judge your worst opponents will be found among professing saints and worthless men." All of which must have been a great help and encouragement.

Nevertheless, the road was rough enough. The lull in the storm which followed her marriage with Gilbert Eddy was hardly more than momentary. George Barry was completely irreconcilable, and within a few weeks he had brought suit against Mrs. Eddy to recover the sum of $2,700 which he said was due to him "for services rendered over a period of five years". His bill of particulars went into the smallest detail; even the errands which he had shown himself so willing to run and the small services he had apparently been glad to render were all charged for. He put a price on his judgement in selecting carpets and furniture, and on his time in going to the bank for money or in paying the house rent, these together with the more reasonable demands for compensation in the work of copying out manuscripts. The monetary consideration, although serious enough, was small compared with the anxiety and disappointment which the whole episode occasioned Mrs. Eddy at a time of great stress and uncertainty. She was working hard on the second edition of her book and seeking at the same time to straighten out the ever more entangled problem of Spofford's dealing with the first.

At length she could apparently stand the strain no longer, and decided to put an end to it by going away for a time and leaving no address behind her. And so, one day early in March, she and Gilbert set out together and, without disclosing their plans to anyone, took train for Fairhaven in Connecticut on a visit to Gilbert Eddy's brother, Washington Eddy, who was married and had a home there.

On the eve of her departure she wrote to Spofford, but carried the letter with her to Fairhaven and did not mail it until some time after her arrival. Like several other letters written about this time, it is pervaded by a sense of strain and fear. Quimby's doctrine of penalty died hard, and she had still the most incredible depths of suffering to plumb before she could reach the point she did later when she realized, as she put it, that "the belief and the believer are one", that no belief can go further "than thought permits". Even as early as 1881 she could write, looking back on these days: "In years past we suffered greatly for the sick when healing them . . . that is all over now, and we cannot suffer for them."

But in 1877 she was suffering for them, and not only for the sick but for many other misconceptions from which she was later to shake herself free. Her letter to Spofford when she was leaving Lynn is almost pathetic in its burden: "The book lies waiting, but those who call on me mentally in suffering are in belief killing me, stopping my work that none but me can do . . . the book must stop. I can do no more now if ever. They lay upon me suffering inconceivable."

Later on, she wrote in another letter that whenever she tried to concentrate on her work of writing she felt the demand of those who needed healing "as sensibly as a hand", and towards the end of the letter declared wretchedly that if it were not for her husband she would gladly "yield up the ghost of this terrible earth plane and join those nearer my Life".

But whenever Mary Baker or Mary Patterson or Mary Baker Eddy reached such depths it was invariably the signal for a tremendous rebound. Neither was this reaction any ordinary reaction. It almost always meant for her the attainment of a new height. As she was to put it years afterwards in one of her articles: "First purify thought, then put thought into words, and words into deeds; and after much slipping and clambering, you will go up the scale of Science."[1]

She slipped and clambered more than enough in these early days and she never hesitated to admit it, but the general trend was always upwards.

Moreover, she never stayed long in the deeps. Thus in this case, a few days after she had written to Spofford in terms of despair, telling him that the book must stop and that she can do no more "now if ever", she is writing to him at length about it, planning in detail for the second edition. It is a long letter in which eager interest in her work and careful considera-

[1] *Miscellaneous Writings*, p. 341.

tion of business details alternate with doubt and fear and a feeling, not
untouched with bitterness, over the actions of some of her students.
Writing under date, Fairhaven, April 19, 1877, she says:

"My dear Student,

"I will consider the arrangements for embellishing the book. I had
fixed on the picture of Jesus and a sick man—the hand of the former
outstretched to him as in rebuke of the disease; or waves and an ark.
The last will cost less I conclude and do as well. No rainbow can be
made to look right except in colours and that cannot be conveniently
arranged in gilt. Now for the printing—would 480 pages include the
Key to Scriptures and the entire work as it now is? The book entitled
Science and Health is to embrace the chapter on Physiology all the same
as if this chapter was not compiled in a separate volume; perhaps you so
understand it. If the cost is what you stated, I advise you to accept the
terms for I am confident in the sale of two editions more there can be a
net income over and above it all. If I get my health again I can make a
large demand for the book for I shall lecture and this will sell one edition
of a thousand copies (if I can stand it). I am better, some. One circum-
stance I will name. The night before I left, and before I wrote you those
fragments, Miss Brown went into convulsions from a chemical, and was
not expected to live, but came out of it saying she felt perfectly well and
as well as before the injury supposed to have been received. I thought at
that time if she was not 'born again' the Mother would die in her labours.
O, how little my students *can* know what it all costs me. Now, I thank
you for relieving me a little in the other case, please see her twice a week;
in healing you are benefiting yourself, in teaching you are benefiting
others. I would not advise you to change business at present the rolling
stone gathers no moss; persevere in *one line* and you can do much more
than to continually scatter your fire. Try to get students into the field
as practitioners and thus healing will sell the book and introduce the
science more than aught but my lecturing can do. Send the name of any
you can get to study for the purpose of practicing and in six months or

227

thereabouts we will have them in the field helping you. If you have ears to hear you will understand. Send all letters to Boston. T. O. Gilbert will forward them to me at present.

"Now for the writings you named. I will make an agreement with you to publish the book the three years from the time you took it and have twenty-five per cent royalty paid me; at the end of this period, we will make other arrangements or continue those we have made just as the Spirit shall direct me. I feel this is the best thing for the present to decide upon. During these years we shall have a treasurer such as we shall agree upon and the funds deposited in his or her hands and drawn for specified purposes, at the end of these three years if we dissolve partnership the surplus amount shall be equally divided between us; and this is the best I can do. All the years I have expended on that book, the labour I am still performing, and all I have done for students and the cause gratuitously, entitle me to *some income* now that I am unable to work. But as it is I have none and instead am sued for $2,700! for what? for just this, I have allowed my students to think I have no rights, and they can not wrong me!

"May God open their eyes at length!

"If you conclude not to carry the work forward on the terms named, it will have to go out of edition as I can do no more of it, and I believe this hour is to try my students who think they have the cause at heart and see if it be so. My husband is giving all his time and means to help me up from the depths in which these students plunge me and this is all he can do at present. Please write soon.

"As ever,

MARY"

The letter is typical, and presents a picture, clear enough, of the problems which confronted Mrs. Eddy at this time, and of the way in which their burden was added to by doubts and fears, both her own and those of her students, which a fuller insight was at length to dissipate. The letter also shadows forth a difficulty which was to present itself at every turn

228

in the future, a difficulty with which the leader in almost any cause is apt to be confronted, that of finding disciples with the capacity to grasp a vision and with sufficient faithfulness to follow a leader without demand for a place either at his right hand or his left.

Spofford, though, had a mind of his own. Already fundamentally alienated by the blow to his feelings involved in Mary's marriage, he probably was none too sympathetic or co-operative.

His reply to the letter just quoted was to the effect that he saw no favourable prospect at all for the second edition, that the royalty she asked for was excessive, and that he could not possibly undertake the work on those terms.

At first glance, it might appear that he was in a large measure justified in his contention as to the royalty. In ordinary circumstances twenty-five per cent would be high royalty and one seldom enjoyed, but the circumstances were not ordinary. Practically all Spofford's sales were and would be at the full published price. In other words, he would not have to meet the thirty or forty per cent discount to the bookseller such as a publisher usually has to write off, in addition to the author's royalty and cost of production, before he can begin to reckon his own profit. Thus even after paying the twenty-five per cent royalty which Mrs. Eddy asked for, he would still stand to make at least a twenty per cent higher profit than a regular publisher could have expected.

In answer to his complaint, Mrs. Eddy wrote that she thought what she asked for was just; that over against the capital he was investing, she had given three years and more of work. Spofford's reply to this was to close out the remaining copies of the first edition at what he could get for them and turn over the proceeds, approximately $600, to George Barry and Elizabeth Newhall, the two students who, it will be recalled, advanced the money (over $2,000) for the publishing of the book and had not yet been reimbursed. (Spofford, too, had contributed about $500 to the project.) This left Mrs. Eddy without any copies of her book and no funds with which to secure even a reprint. Much disturbed she returned immediately to Lynn, and when Spofford called upon her at her request

229

to talk the whole matter over, neither minced words, if we are to judge by their letters to each other (still extant) and the results which followed, for their partnership was rudely terminated.

It was a bitter blow, not so much because of its effect upon her book—that she must have seen could be remedied—but because of the further evidence it seemed to supply of the malignity of this strange power that was able to turn her friends into enemies. First, Richard Kennedy, and now Daniel Spofford. If they had just gone out from her, it would have been bad enough, but she and her little band were positive that both Kennedy and Spofford were now actively engaged in a mental opposition, the results of which might well prove disastrous.

Mrs. Eddy determined to do what she could to offset the effects of the onslaught. She was beginning to perceive what is today so generally acknowledged, that mesmerism in all its forms, from the public exhibition of direct hypnosis to mass mesmerism as practised by the skilled propagandist, is effective in proportion to the ignorance of its subject. And so in the second edition of her book she determined to tackle the question thoroughly.

In many ways this second edition of *Science and Health,* which was published early in 1878 by "Dr. Asa G. Eddy", reflects the stress and confusion amid which it first saw the light of print. A slim book of 167 pages against the 456 of the first edition, it consists of five chapters against eight in the first edition. Of these five, the first and second entitled respectively "Imposition and Demonstration" and "Physiology", are Chapters II and VII in the first edition; while of the remaining three, all quite short, the first (Chapter III) is entitled "Mesmerism", the second (Chapter IV) "Metaphysics", and the last (Chapter V) "Reply to a Clergyman".

In its make-up the book follows the form suggested by Mrs. Eddy in her letter to Spofford, save that instead of a frontispiece representing Jesus healing a sick man is a line drawing, not too badly executed, of Jesus raising Jairus' daughter, while the outside cover is embellished with a floating ark done in gilt line. It is full of typographical errors—more than thirty are listed in the "errata" and there are many others. The numbers of the pages are sometimes repeated and the title of the book appears correctly only on the outside cover.

The probabilities are that the book was rushed into print in order to secure the earliest possible publication of Mrs. Eddy's statement on "Mesmerism", which, as already noted, appears in the second edition as Chapter III.

This statement, in view of the circumstances in which it was written, has an interest all its own. Today viewed strictly from a psychological standpoint, it may seem at times elementary, but as a product of sixty years ago, it reveals an insight into the processes of the human mind—then almost a virgin field for research—which must be accounted remarkable. The application of her findings to her teaching is, of course, her own and unique.

Her great desire was to forearm by forewarning. As she saw the matter, foreknowledge in the case of mesmerism was just as sure a protection against deception as the foreknowledge that twice two is four is an inevitable protection against the deception that twice two is anything else. But there still lingers the old bugaboo of malignant telepathic bombardment.

"The best mode of self-protection from this mental outlaw", she writes in the second edition, "is to understand Metaphysics, and get your eyes open to the fact of what he is attempting. Then you are safe; and his malevolent attempts, through a mental process, to harm you are futile. His mind cannot influence yours,—causing motives, resolutions, loves, and hates, purposes and acts, that you would never have known but for him,—when you know what he is about; and his attempt will be powerless, and fall before you a pitiful spectacle of defeated malice, that can no more affect you than the bullet that strikes against the armour of steel. . . . Ancient magic, sorcery, and whatever method employed by the demoniacal mind, were less barbarous in their codes and tendencies than the modern modes or secret impregnation of thought by the unscrupulous manipulator and subtle mesmerist."[1]

[1] *Science and Health*, (2nd Ed.), pp. 138-139, 143.

This doctrine, so strange today but so plausible then, of the mental transmission of evil, was to recede steadily as the years rolled thence onward.

While Mrs. Eddy was writing thus in the fall of 1877, the suit against her instituted by George Barry had come up at last for trial, and she found arrayed against her as witnesses in support of Barry, not only Daniel Spofford, but several others who had at one time been her devoted friends. Perhaps subpoenas left them no alternative, but it must have been none the less galling.

It was for her the first of many similar experiences. She had been really fond of Barry and he of her. He was the first of her students to call her mother and, in the days of his devotion, had written a little poem, not without merit, emphasizing his debt to her:

> O, Mother mine, God grant I ne'er forget
> Whatever be my grief or what my joy,
> The unmeasurable, inextinguishable debt,
> I owe to thee, but find my sweet employ
> Ever through thy remaining days to be
> To thee as faithful as thou wast to me.

However viewed, the suit was a sorry business and a strange commentary on human nature. By the time counsel had finished reading the plaintiff's bill of particulars, it was evident that Barry desired to take up the position that in all of the eight or nine years he had been associated with Mrs. Eddy, he had never received from her any value even such as could be made to offset the carrying up of a bucket of coals from the cellar, for which service he charged at the rather high rate of fifty cents a bucket. But then, as has been seen, practically everything was included, even walking out with her in the evening when they went house-hunting before the purchase of Number 8 Broad Street.

Mrs. Eddy went on to the stand and told of their relationship, saying she had taken him when he was a lad little more than eighteen, taught him practically everything he knew, even how to write properly; that she had remitted half his fees when he went through her first class; and that he had begged her to be allowed to copy her manuscripts in order that he might the better study them. Some of which Barry admitted under cross-examination by Mrs. Eddy's counsel. The jury was in a quandary. It was possible that the relationship existing between the two was, as Mrs. Eddy contended, one of reciprocal service, but to what extent it was difficult to decide. The verdict of $350 in Barry's favour ultimately tendered was a compromise and represented compensation only for the actual copying of portions of *Science and Health* for the printer.

Mrs. Eddy saw in it all simply the malign effects of mesmerism, as she called it. This is evident from her handling of the matter in the second edition of *Science and Health*. She reasoned soundly enough that there can be no such thing as a falsehood that has not an antecedent truth; but that the falsehood, like any other falsehood, would operate as truth until it was shown to be a falsehood. All of which was, of course, but a logical deduction from the admitted fact that the mesmerist is powerless in the presence of an understanding denial of his power.

And so when the second edition of *Science and Health* at last appeared in January of 1878, it was found to contain the vigorous denunciation of mesmerism and mesmerists already referred to. The result was an immediate and very sharp separation of the sheep from the goats. Spofford and Barry, for the time being at any rate, were classed with Kennedy, while those remaining were pronounced loyal.

The movement was growing—much more rapidly than appeared on the surface. But even on the surface it was presenting to an increasing extent tangible evidence of its existence. The little Christian Scientists' Home on Broad Street in Lynn, the Christian Science Publishing Company and the Christian Scientist Association which had been organized, chiefly through the efforts of Spofford, in the summer of 1876, were all evidence that a movement was afoot.

It was this last, the Christian Scientist Association, that now, with ironic justice or injustice, took action against Spofford. Under their Rules of Order, he was now declared expelled—for "immorality."

Notice to this effect was published in the Newburyport *Herald*. His retort was a letter to that paper, stating he could not be expelled from the Association as he had never been a member. To which Mrs. Eddy, always quick in response, contradicted his assertion and elaborated on the charges against him.

"Our Constitution requires," she wrote, "when a member is expelled for immorality, that it should be made public. The motive for this article in the Constitution was to prevent a member from going astray, or in case this could not be prevented, to forewarn the community, so ignorant of the evil that can be done by this student, of the secret agent for mischief that a mental malpractice becomes. . . . The time is not far off when the witnesses to the secret sins, yea, crimes, committed in the name of Science, and those who have been the unconscious victims of such abuses will be heard in our halls of state; and because a man heals in some instances (as all mesmerists do) and does incalculable evil in others, he will not blindly be upheld by the sick, and pin his wicked deeds on the better deed that the one may offset the other; or make *Science and Health* the pretence for such malpractice. May the direct line of duty from which I never swerve, be taken by those of our worthy students as we know it will be finally, and Truth will triumph over error."

There were more letters and statements and questions from George Barry and Elizabeth Newhall, with a vigorous rejoinder from Miranda Rice, but Spofford did not return to the attack. It was not long, however, before Mrs. Eddy was called upon to face even more difficult issues.

Edward J. Arens

NO BETTER EXAMPLE could be offered of Mary Baker Eddy's lifelong inclination towards endowing many of those who came to her aid with qualities they did not possess than that of Edward J. Arens. Arens was a Prussian who had come to Lynn as a young man, working at first as a carpenter, but later opening a cabinet-making shop of his own. A stocky, glowering man, to judge from his photograph, with shaven chin overhung with a fierce walrus moustache merging into luxuriant sideburns, which, in turn, run up and around into a veritable mane of dark hair. His whole face, his full lips and deep-set snapping eyes suggest pugnacity in a high degree and convey a strange impression of a mind hovering on the edge of unbalance.

In the years before he met Mrs. Eddy, he was frequently involved in litigation. Indeed, he seems to have been one of those people for whom going to law about anything and everything had an inevitable fascination. Instead of being a last resort with Arens, it was apparently a natural first resort and, as so often happens to such people, from claiming his rights under the law, he has been generally described as seeking much more than his rights. The line between this and plain fraud is not easy to draw.

On June 24, 1876, Edward J. Arens was arrested in Lynn in connection with a notorious series of swindles carried out by a group known as the Gremlaw-White gang, which operated in Lynn and Boston and further afield. Ultimately the charge against him was withdrawn—possibly because he knew how to "arrange" it—but the suspicion remained, and from subsequent amazing events which must be later described, the inference seems reasonable that he was intimately acquainted with the underworld of the New England seaboard towns.

Arens entered one of Mrs. Eddy's classes in the fall of 1877, just after her break with Spofford, and very quickly established himself in a position of influence, not only with Mrs. Eddy but with her husband. The source of this influence was in all probability his intimate knowledge of the intricacies of the law. Up to this time, Mrs. Eddy had never voluntarily resorted to court proceedings. Indeed, she seems to have had a very wholesome aversion to anything of the kind, and there can be little doubt that quite a number of her less scrupulous students had taken advantage of the fact, leaving their obligations unmet and, in some cases, failing to return money loaned to them for one purpose or another.

To a man like Arens, such a number of "unredeemed rights" would be little short of shocking, and it was not long before he was urging Mary and Gilbert Eddy to turn over the various unredeemed notes and promises to him, and let him bring suit against the delinquents for recovery. In the third edition of *Science and Health,* published in 1881, Mrs. Eddy is evidently alluding to the circumstances when she writes:

"In the interests of truth we ought to say that never a lawsuit has entered into our history voluntarily. We have suffered great losses and the direst injustice rather than go to law, for we always considered a lawsuit, of two evils, the greatest. About two years ago the persuasions of a student awakened our convictions that we might be doing wrong in permitting students to break their obligations with us . . . . The student who argued this point to us so convincingly offered to take the notes and collect them, without any participation of ours; we trusted him with the whole affair, doing only what he told us, for we were utterly ignorant of legal proceedings."

Be this as it may be, in the February of 1878, Arens, on her behalf, sued Richard Kennedy to recover $750 upon his promissory note of eight years before. In the following April he actually sued two members of the first class, namely, George H. Tuttle and Charles Stanley, for unpaid fees, and later still Spofford for breach of contract. All three actions were ultimately lost but, quite undeterred by such failure, Arens went on to consummate his masterpiece in the art of litigation, a suit against Daniel Spofford for witchcraft.

He did not so style it, of course, but from the first announcement of the suit in the Newburyport *Herald,* it was so styled in the press, and the case subsequently became famous in the legal annals of Massachusetts as the "Ipswich Witchcraft Case". Ostensibly this case was an appeal to the court by one Lucretia L. S. Brown of Ipswich to restrain one Daniel Spofford, who, the complainant affirmed, was a mesmerist, from practising his arts upon her and causing her "great suffering of body and mind and severe spinal pains".

Appropriately enough, the case ultimately came up for trial in the Supreme Judicial Court at Salem.

The strange story is soon told. In her letter to Spofford from Fairhaven, in which she went into some details about the second edition, Mrs. Eddy mentioned a Miss Brown whom she had restored to health evidently from invalidism of many years standing, the result of an injury. This Miss Brown is the Lucretia L. S. Brown in the case. Lucretia Brown was a spinster about fifty years of age, who lived with her mother and sister in an old house in Ipswich facing on School-House Green. It was a typical New England house and household, with an emphasis on neatness and order in itself and all its surroundings. Indeed, it used to be a saying in Ipswich in those days, that Essex was the cleanest county in Massachusetts, and Ipswich the cleanest town in Essex County, and the Browns were the cleanest people in Ipswich. Miss Lucretia had suffered all her life from spinal trouble caused by a fall when a child and, although not actually bedridden, she was often confined to her bed for weeks at a time and never could walk further than around the house or across the Green, or on her good days, to church. In spite of all her handicaps, she had built up with the aid of her sister a crocheting agency, taking orders for city dealers—it was the period when crocheted antimacassars were everywhere—and giving out piecework to "the ladies" in the village who desired to earn something in their spare time.

Miss Lucretia was noted for her system, from which she never deviated. At exactly two o'clock in the afternoon on certain days in the week, she gave out the crochet work. Those who arrived before that hour assembled in the parlour, and, exactly on the stroke of the hour, the door leading into Miss Lucretia's bedroom was opened and the ladies admitted, one by one, in the order of their arrival. She received them in bed, whereof the turned-down sheet, the counterpane and pillow were always so incredibly white and smooth as to arouse comment as to how it could possibly be done. Even when the last lady had taken her order and gone her way, after all the yarn had been handled and the directions given, the bed was still as unrumpled as ever and Miss Lucretia still as neat and prim.

Miss Lucretia had been healed by Mrs. Eddy. There was no doubt of it. She was able to be up and about the house all day, and on several occasions, to the amazement of her friends and neighbours, had walked distances of two or three miles to make an afternoon call on days when she was not "receiving". The healing of Miss Lucretia Brown was everywhere the talk of Ipswich and the neighbourhood.

Then, one day, she had a relapse and, when in great fear, she appealed to Mrs. Eddy. Mrs. Eddy sent her loyal friend, Miss Dorcas Rawson, to see her. Miss Rawson was usually very successful, but she could do nothing with Miss Lucretia, who, baffled but determined, took to her bed again. It was just at the time when the Spofford controversy was at its height and the alliance between him and Kennedy had been suspected. The fear of mesmerism, or malicious animal magnetism as it was called, was everywhere. Mrs. Eddy could insist that forewarning was a complete protection, but her followers were not at all so sure; and when one day shortly after Miss Lucretia's relapse, Daniel Spofford for no apparent reason at all called to see her, some of the students were in an uproar. No further explanation could satisfy them save that Daniel Spofford was a mesmerist and, in order to have his revenge on Mrs. Eddy and her loyal students, had brought about the relapse of Miss Lucretia Brown, whose healing was such an outstanding instance of the truth and effectiveness of Mrs. Eddy's teaching.

Mrs. Eddy herself had written in the Newburyport *Herald* that the time would come when the courts would take cognizance of the malpractice of the avowed mesmerist, and so nothing would do, in Arens's judgement, but that Spofford should be sued at once and enjoined by the court from further wrong-doing. To what extent Mrs. Eddy was consulted in the matter, if at all—until too late—is uncertain. She herself, in the third edition of *Science and Health,* declares that the case was brought into court "contrary to her advice and judgement". But in any event, the Bill of Complaint was duly drawn up and presented. It is a strange document and runs in part:

"Humbly complaining, the Plaintiff, Lucretia L. S. Brown, of Ipswich, in said County of Essex, showeth unto your Honors, that Daniel H. Spofford of Newburyport, in said County of Essex, the defendant in the above entitled action, is a mesmerist and practises the art of mesmerism and by his said art and the power of his mind influences and controls the minds and bodies of other persons, and uses his said power and art for the purpose of injuring the persons and property and social relations of others and does by said means so injure them.

"And the plaintiff further showeth that the said Daniel H. Spofford, has, at divers times and places, wrongfully and maliciously and with intent to injure the plaintiff caused the plaintiff, by means of his said power and art, great suffering of body and mind and severe spinal pains and neuralgia and a temporary suspension of mind, and still continues to cause the plaintiff the same. And the plaintiff says that the said injuries are great and of an irreparable nature and that she is wholly unable to escape from the control and influence he so exercises upon her and from the aforesaid effects of said control and influence."

239

The case attracted instant attention as soon as the Bill of Complaint was filed, and the Boston *Globe* sent a reporter down to Ipswich with instructions to interview Miss Brown. When he arrived, Lucretia was actually or ostensibly away from home, but he did succeed in seeing her sister, who was evidently most emphatic on the question of Spofford's delinquency.

"The lady informed the *Globe* reporter," the account ran, "that she and her family believed that there was no limit to the awful power of mesmerism, but she still had some faith in the power of the law, and thought that Dr. Spofford might be awed into abstaining from injuring her sister further. That he does so she believes there is no possibility of doubt. In answer to a query put by the reporter, she admitted that should Dr. Spofford prove so disposed even though he be incarcerated behind the stone walls of Charlestown, he could still use his mesmeric power against her sister."

In due course, the case came up before the Supreme Judicial Court of Massachusetts in Salem on May 14, 1878. Edward J. Arens appeared as counsel for the plaintiff, and as soon as Judge Horace Gray, who was to hear the case, had taken his seat on the bench, Arens arose and presented his petition for a hearing on the Bill of Complaint and made an exposition of the case to the judge. It was more or less of a routine. The judge ordered that a notice be served upon Mr. Spofford and appointed the following Friday, May 17th, for a hearing of the case.

On Friday morning, a great crowd thronged the Court House, and the newspapers were evidently prepared to make the most of it. They were all, however, to be disappointed. The proceedings were brief and colourless. Spofford did not appear, but his attorney appeared for him and filed a demurrer which Judge Gray immediately sustained, giving judgement that it was not within the power of the court to control Mr. Spofford's mind. Arens immediately appealed the case. The appeal was granted but was never prosecuted.

There seems to be little doubt that, from the first to last, the whole strange proceeding was arranged and promoted by Arens as part of his singularly ineffective campaign to secure Mrs. Eddy protection for her teaching by appeal to the law. Mrs. Eddy herself, before she realized where this policy was leading, left the matter, she says, entirely to Arens. It was the first and last attempt of the kind, and, on the whole, seems to have had a very clarifying effect on the infant movement. The statement in the Bill of Complaint, to the effect that the plaintiff had no power to protect herself against the real or imaginary attacks of mesmerism, was exactly contrary to everything Mrs. Eddy was trying to teach, and the net outcome of the case seems to have been to convince Lucretia Brown and her friends that, even if Spofford and his friends understood mesmerism and were using it or misusing it, they themselves had something better and stronger.

Anyway, Lucretia recovered completely and carried on her business as before, with the single difference that she now received her "ladies" in the parlour instead of, as formerly, in her bedroom. She remained a devoted follower of Mrs. Eddy until her death some five years later.

Meanwhile, although there is scant record of it, the new teaching was spreading rapidly and astonishingly far afield. Less than seven years after the "Ipswich Witchcraft Case", Mark Twain was to declare in something very like querulous amazement that he believed the "new religion" would "conquer half of Christendom in a hundred years".

Science and Health, in spite of its apparently limited circulation and chequered history, was being read by a great and increasing number of people. The book had a way of travelling from hand to hand, one copy often making long journeys, being read in its progress by many different people, many of whom were to find, often weeks and months later, that it had unconsciously changed the whole course of their lives. Numbers credited to it healing of physical troubles or infirmities of long standing. The story of its Odyssey, as it came to be pieced together in after years, is replete with testimonies of people who read the book, were helped by it, forgot even its title, who wrote it, or even who lent it to them, and then spent years in trying to find it again. But, in these early years, not much of all this appeared on the surface. It was like the coming of spring in an ice-bound country—the work was being done underneath. The transformation was to come almost overnight.

Mrs. Eddy in the second edition of *Science and Health* spoke of several cases of healing as the result of simply reading the book, while it was not long before letters to the same effect—still preserved—were coming in from practically every state in the Union and even from England and Ireland.

Years afterwards Mrs. Eddy was to place on record as one of her findings that students of her teaching who were thus thrown on their own resources, precluded by place and circumstances from any appeal to herself or others, seemed "stronger to resist temptation than some of those who have had line upon line and precept upon precept"; and she added, characteristically, "If they must learn by the things they suffer, the sooner this lesson is gained the better."[1]

When within a few years, Mrs. Eddy, her book and her teaching had emerged definitely into the light of national knowledge, these people were all more than ready to move forward and enter with enthusiasm upon the missionary field.

But meanwhile, in Lynn and Boston, the only record apparently unfolding is that of conspiracy and persecution, each one worse than the last. The Witchcraft Case was hardly out of the way before George Barry appears on the scene once more, this time in a role so entirely discreditable as to alienate from him any last vestige of sympathy. Possibly he hoped to regain by his action some of the influence and power he had once enjoyed, but, if so, he sadly misunderstood the woman with whom he was dealing. He wrote to Mrs. Eddy expressing regret for the course he had taken, offering to return the money that had been awarded him as the result of his suit against her, and proposing that she join with him in what was clearly no more than a disreputable plot to get rid of Richard Kennedy. Whether this letter had any connection with the amazing and inscrutable conspiracy which must next be related, it is impossible to say, but it certainly serves to reveal the character of George Barry as nothing else could.

[1] *Miscellaneous Writings*, p. 278.

"It is evident to me", he wrote, "that you desire Dr. Kennedy to leave the city, and I think also it would be for your interest to accomplish this end. The relations between he and I are probably of a different nature from what you suppose, as I owe him a debt on the past, which, if driving him from Lynn will accomplish, it can be done. He thinks I am your greatest enemy, and favour, if either, his side. Let him continue to think so; it will do no harm. For my part I rather a person would come out boldly and fearlessly as you and I did facing each other, than to sneak like a snake in the grass, spitting his poison venom into them he would slay. I have said I owe Dr. Kennedy an old score, and the interview I had with him last night has increased that debt, so that I am now determined, if it be your object also, as two heads are better than one, to drive him from Lynn. Why should we be enemies especially if we have one great enemy in common? Perhaps we can be united on this, and the result may be that this city will be finally rid of one of the greatest humbugs that have ever disgraced her fair face. All this can be accomplished; but as I said before, it is necessary to be very cautious and not let our communication together be known, as a friend in the enemy's camp is an advantage not to be overlooked."

In reply, Mrs. Eddy declined the proffered money, told Barry she would only help to do what was right and would always be ready to help him to do that, and, in the matter of his proposition regarding Richard Kennedy, recommended him to leave all such issues to God. Such a reply was certainly nothing if not restrained. That it was effective is evidenced by the fact that George Barry disappears now from the story and never returns.

In any event, he and his affairs would quickly have been overshadowed by what was to follow, the arrest of Gilbert Eddy on the charge of conspiracy to murder.

Conspiracy to Murder

TOWARDS THE END of October, 1878, a notice appeared in the Boston newspapers which greatly alarmed Daniel Spofford's many friends. Under the caption "Mysterious Absence", it ran as follows:

"Dr. D. H. Spofford, the Christian Scientist, has been missing since Tuesday, October 15, and much alarm for his safety is manifested. He had offices in Haverhill, Newburyport, and at Hotel Tremont, No. 297, Tremont Street, Boston, and was last seen at the latter place, in apparently good health and sound mind. The cause of his disappearance is beyond explanation. Dr. Spofford is about 35 years of age, has a light complexion and full beard, and wore dark clothes and black Kossuth hat. He was a member of the Grand Army in Newburyport and an Odd Fellow in Lynn. Any information regarding his whereabouts may be sent to the Boston police or to A. A. Spofford, No. 151, Essex Street, Lawrence."

Shortly afterwards, a news item appeared in the press to the effect that Spofford's body had been identified at the morgue, and there was little doubt but that he had been foully done to death. Within a few days,

Gilbert Eddy and Edward Arens were arrested in Lynn charged with having conspired to procure his murder, and bail was set at three thousand dollars.

Only a few weeks previously, Mrs. Eddy had written to Spofford—her first letter to him in seventeen months—a plea that he desist from, and a warning against the boomerang effects upon himself of, the malicious mental malpractice which she said she could detect him directing against her. He had not answered her letter, and now she found her husband charged with being accessory to his murder. With characteristic energy she rose to the occasion and tackled the question of bail. It was quite a problem. She herself did not have the money in cash and her house would not be accepted in surety, as a part of the original mortgage still remained undischarged. Bancroft was willing to come to her aid, but his house, too, had still a mortgage on it, and so he was not available. Finally, Miranda Rice was accepted as surety, and Gilbert Eddy and Arens were released on bail. They had hardly got back to Lynn from Boston before the news reached them that Spofford had reappeared, as suddenly and mysteriously as he had dropped out of sight three weeks previously, and had visited his brother Albert that morning in Lawrence.

The relief which must have followed the first amazement in the little household at Lynn was destined to be short-lived, for it quickly developed that Spofford had come back with a story which only made more definite the charges against Arens and Gilbert Eddy. The charge of conspiracy to murder still remained to be answered. Spofford's story, as pieced together from press interviews and subsequent court proceedings, was nothing if not lurid.

One morning early in October, according to his story, he was sitting in his office at No. 297 Tremont Street, when a knock came to the door, on opening which he was confronted by a heavy-set rather brutal-looking man, who said that he wanted to see the doctor. Spofford took one look at him, and deciding quickly that he was certainly not the type of man that would be looking for him, asked him if he was sure he was the kind of doctor he wanted to see. Whereupon the man produced one of Spofford's cards from his pocket, explaining that he had found it on the door of his (Spofford's) Newburyport office, and that if he was the man indicated on that card then he was the man he wanted to see, that his name was James L. Sargent, that he was a saloon keeper and that his business was very important.

Rather doubtful, Spofford asked him to come in to his consulting room, and when they were seated Sargent launched at once into his subject by asking Spofford if he knew two men named Miller and Libby. When Spofford replied he did not, Sargent remarked bluntly: "Well, they know you, and they want to get you out of the way. Miller, the young man, says you are going with the old man's daughter, and he wants to marry her himself."

He then went on to explain that these two men had offered him five hundred dollars to put Spofford out of the way, and had already paid him seventy-five in advance. He declared that while he was determined to get all the money or as much of it as he could, he had no intention of risking his neck by killing Spofford, and that if Spofford would be sensible and just disappear for a little while, the whole thing could be settled satisfactorily. He then went on to make the surprising statement that he had already notified State Detective Hollis C. Pinkham and had asked him to watch the case. He told Spofford to think it over and let him know.

As soon as he had gone, Spofford lost no time in going round to see Detective Pinkham and found that Sargent had told him the same story. Pinkham declared, however, that he had paid little attention to the matter as Sargent had a criminal record and he figured that he was only attempting to square himself with the police by appearing in the role of a conscientious informer. He said that he would certainly look into the matter further, and Spofford went away.

A few days later, Sargent appeared once again in Spofford's Tremont Street office, complaining that Libby and Miller were pressing him. He had, he said, tried to get some more money out of them by telling them the job was done and that he, Spofford, was already dead, but that they had sent a boy round to his office to investigate, and were now accusing him, Sargent, of playing them false. Something had to be done and at once. He urged Spofford, now thoroughly alarmed, to go with him to his (Sargent's) brother's house at Cambridgeport, and hide himself there until he could collect the balance of the five hundred dollars promised him. Once again, Spofford consulted Detective Pinkham, who evidently advised him to comply with Sargent's suggestion, for the two set out at once for Cambridgeport. Spofford left Boston on October 15, and for something more than two weeks kept in hiding in the house of Sargent's sister-in-law. Sargent had promised to come out, from time to time, to let him know how things were going, but he failed to do so, and at last Spofford took his courage in both hands and returned to Boston, going first to the home of his brother in Lawrence.

Meanwhile, Arens and Doctor Eddy—as he was now generally called —had been identified by Sargent as the Miller and Libby in the case, and although Spofford was alive and unharmed they still remained charged with the conspiracy to murder him. It was in vain that they both insisted that they had never seen the man Sargent before and repudiated the charge with the utmost vigour; they were held in bail of three thousand dollars for examination in the Municipal Court in Boston on November 7th.

When the case was finally called on the afternoon of November 7th, a motley array of witnesses confronted the judge, Judge May, a well-known jurist in the Municipal Court. James L. Sargent, the central figure in the case on the side of the State, was a bar-tender with a criminal record. His friend and star witness, George Collier, was at that time under bond waiting trial on some particularly unsavoury charges, while other witnesses for the prosecution were James Sargent's sister Laura, who kept a disorderly house, and several of her girls, who, as it subsequently appeared, were needed to confirm evidence given by Sargent and Collier. H. W. Chaplin appeared for the prosecution, and Russell H. Conwell appeared for the defendants.

Mr. Chaplin in opening the case for the Commonwealth contended that he would be able to prove directly that the defendants, Arens and Eddy, had conspired to take the life of Mr. Spofford, and that Sargent had been paid upwards of two hundred dollars toward the five hundred promised him for carrying out their commission. The evidence may be briefly summarized:

James L. Sargent testified that he had become acquainted with a man who called himself Miller, but whom he now recognized as the defendant Arens, some four months previously; that Miller or Arens was in the habit of coming to his saloon to tell fortunes, and that one day he told him that he knew of a good job where three or four hundred dollars could be made without much trouble; that he, Sargent, on inquiring what it amounted to, was told that, he, Arens, wanted a man "licked", and "he wanted him licked so that he wouldn't come to again", but he wanted to be sure that the man who did the job was to be depended on. Sargent declared that he reassured Arens on this point.

"I told him", he said, "that I was just the man for him, and Arens said the old man Libby or Dr. Eddy would not pay more than was absolutely necessary to get the job done, as he had already been beaten out of seventy-five dollars. I met Arens the following Saturday at the corner of Charles and Leverett Streets at five o'clock, and we walked down Charles Street into an alleyway. He said Libby was not satisfied and wanted to see me himself, and so we selected a spot in the freight yard where he and the old man Libby would meet me in half an hour.

"In the meantime, fearing that the affair might be a plot of some kind against myself, I borrowed a revolver of a friend and got another friend named Collier to go with me. Collier secreted himself in a freight car with the door partially open, so that he could overhear any conversation, and at the appointed time I met Arens and a man who was known to me as Libby, but whom I recognize as the defendant Eddy.

"Eddy asked me how much money I wanted to do the job, and I told him I ought to have one hundred dollars to start with. He asked if I would take seventy-five dollars at the outset, and I said I would. He wanted to know if I would be square and I told him, yes. He then said he had but thirty-five dollars with him that night which he would give me and would send the remaining thirty-five by Arens on Monday morning. I told him, no, I must have the whole at that time. Just then a man came walking down the freight yard and Arens told me in a quick tone to meet him on Monday morning. I did so and Arens passed me seventy-five dollars. A few days later I met Arens again, and he said he would bring me directions where to find Dr. Spofford at his office in Haverhill and Newburyport."

Sargent then went on to describe in detail how he delayed as long as possible getting into touch with Arens again, how he spent the money, and at last when Arens got difficult and clearly could not be put off any longer, he met him again.

"We went to the Tremont Hotel," Sargent continued, "and Arens gave me sixteen dollars, with which I went to the doctor's office in Newburyport. I did not see the doctor, but brought away one of his business cards; came back and called at Dr. Spofford's office and had a conversation with him. I afterwards met Arens on the Common by appointment and told him I had made arrangements to have the doctor go out of town. . . . In a few days he met me on the Common again. He said I was playing it on him and that the whole thing was a put up job, for Dr. Spofford was in his office. He had sent a boy to find out."

Sargent went on to tell how he met Arens several times, and that finally they agreed that Sargent should take Spofford into the country on the pretence that he had a sick child. Their plan, he said, was to take Spofford out on some lonely road and "knock him on the head with a billy", afterwards causing the horse to run away, first entangling the body with the harness, so it would appear that death was caused by accident. Sargent said he took the doctor to his brother in Cambridgeport and kept him there for about three weeks. As soon as the fact of his disappearance was published in the papers, Sargent said that he sought out Arens and told him that he had made away with the doctor, and that he had done it at half-past seven the evening before. Sargent said that Arens replied that he had known this, that he had felt it, and had a way of telling such things that other people knew nothing of.

He saw him several times afterwards, seeking to secure more money, and finally Arens agreed to do something more for him, met him at Lynn and paid him another twenty dollars.

Another witness was a woman named Jessie MacDonald, who said she had lived as housekeeper with Doctor and Mrs. Eddy for several months, that she had never seen Spofford, but that she had often heard Doctor Eddy speak of his persecution of Mrs. Eddy and had on one occasion heard Mrs. Eddy reading a chapter from the Bible which said that all wicked people should be destroyed.

Sargent's sister, the keeper of the house of ill-fame, supported by the testimony of some of her girls, declared that Sargent had a room in her house, that Arens had come there three or four times to see him, and that, on one occasion, Sargent had given her seventy-five dollars to keep for him, telling her that he was going away to her brother's house in Cambridgeport.

Sargent's sister was followed by the detective employed in the case, Hollis C. Pinkham. He told how Sargent had laid the case before him, how he did not attach much importance to it at first, but told Sargent to go ahead and find out what he could, how he had seen Sargent and Arens in conversation together on the Common, how he had followed Eddy to his home in Lynn, and how he had seen Sargent go towards the door of Eddy's house there, how he had subsequently asked Eddy if he had arranged to have Spofford put out of the way, how Eddy had denied the charge, denied that he had ever been in Sargent's saloon, and how Arens had likewise maintained when questioned, that he had never seen and did not know Sargent, and that he stuck to this even when he was confronted with Sargent himself.

Another detective on the case, one Chase Philbrick, testified to seeing Sargent at Eddy's house in Lynn; saw him try to get in, but fail to do so. He confirmed Detective Pinkham's testimony. Finally came George A. Collier, the man who hid in the freight car in order to overhear the conversation between Arens and Sargent. His testimony corroborated that of Sargent.

This closed the case for the Commonwealth. The defence—inasmuch as the case was one where only probable cause for suspicion was to be shown—offered no evidence. The Commonwealth, on the other hand, submitted no arguments, simply laying the "chain of circumstances" before the court, and asking the court to decide whether or not the evidence was sufficient to show that the parties should be held to appear before the Superior Court. Judge May remarked that the case was "a very anomalous one", but thought the evidence was sufficient to justify the parties being so held, and ordered accordingly, fixing the amount of bail at three thousand dollars each for the appearance of the defendants at the December term of the Superior Court.

The case was never called. Anomalous as it certainly was, its final resolution—if so it may be styled—was the most anomalous part of it. Without filing any memorandum of his reason for this action, the District Attorney decided simply to take no further action in the matter. The Superior Court record reads:

"This indictment was found and returned into Court by the Grand Jurors at the last December term, when the said Arens and Eddy were severally set at the bar, and, having said indictment read to them, they severally said thereof that they were not guilty.

"This indictment was thence continued to the present January term, and now the District Attorney, Oliver Stevens, Esquire, says he will prosecute this indictment no further, on payment of costs, which are thereupon paid. And said Arens and Eddy are thereupon discharged. January 31, 1879."

This decision on the part of the District Attorney not to prosecute further the charges against Doctor Eddy and Arens precluded all possibility of a public exoneration through an effective defence. Between the date of the preliminary hearing in November and the time of the District Attorney's *nolle prosse* in January, counsel for the defence, largely through the efforts of Mrs. Eddy herself, had secured a complete confession from the Commonwealth's chief witness, George Collier, that the charges against Eddy and Arens were entirely false and that there was not a word of truth in the story he had told on the stand.

251

Before a justice at Taunton, under date December 17, 1878, Collier declared under oath:

"I, George A. Collier, do on oath depose and say of my own free will, and in order to expose the man who has tried to injure Dr. Asa G. Eddy and Edward J. Arens, that Sargent did induce me by great persuasion to go with him to East Cambridge from Boston on or about the 7th day of November last, the day of the hearing in the Municipal Court in Boston in the case of Dr. Asa G. Eddy and E. J. Arens for attempting to hire said Sargent to kill one Daniel Spofford, and that he showed me the place and the cars that he was going to swear to, and told me what to say in court, and made me repeat the story until I knew it well, so that I could tell the same story that he would, and there was not one word of truth in it all. I never heard a conversation in East Cambridge between said Eddy and Arens and Sargent, or saw them pay or offer to pay Sargent any money.

(Signed)   Geo. A. Collier"

There were several other depositions and affidavits making for complete exoneration, and on February 10, 1879, Gilbert Eddy wrote a letter to the Boston *Traveller,* summarizing the case for the defence. It was published next day under the caption, "A Personal Vindication", and ran:

"The confession of Geo. A. Collier, one of the principal witnesses for Daniel H. Spofford and against Dr. Eddy and E. J. Arens last October, came out on the 6th instant. But Collier's confession is only part of the evidence of the defence. There are other and as direct testimony, a part of which is that a dozen witnesses are ready to testify they were with Dr. Eddy at Boston Highlands until ten minutes of six p.m. on the very day and afternoon that Sargent and Collier swore Dr. Eddy was with him at half-past five p.m. bargaining to kill Spofford.

"The ride in the horse car from the Highlands to East Cambridge would occupy an hour, and when the doctor reached his residence in Lynn there were company there who will testify they were waiting to see him to inquire about his class and he reached home about a quarter-past seven—having taken the half-past six train from Boston. Upon the lawyer pinning him down to a date, Sargent swore he knew it was the day and

252

hour that he stated because a seizure was made in a rum shop on that day and at the hour he claimed to meet Dr. Eddy and E. J. Arens. The records show that a seizure was made on the rum shop that he named, and at the hour he named, but that the aforesaid gentlemen were with him then and there is proven a lie. Mr. Arens can show an alibi by several witnesses who were in a doctor's office in Boston, where he was at the very time."

So the matter was closed. The whole case is still as complete a mystery as it was in that long-ago day. Every suggested solution is fraught with apparently inescapable objections. The possibility that it was a kind of double-crossing extortion plot on the part of Sargent to get money from Eddy and Arens as well as Spofford, is vitiated by the fact that he never attempted to get money from Spofford, and apparently never got any from Eddy and Arens, as the whole story of their meeting was denied by Collier. Moreover, even if this were shown to be still a possibility, there would remain to be explained Sargent's dealings with the detective Pinkham.

That this was a deep laid plot on the part of Spofford to have this revenge on Doctor Eddy cannot be seriously considered; while its *vice versa,* that it was a deep laid plot on the part of Gilbert Eddy to have his revenge on Spofford, is equally incredible. There is, of course, what seems to be the genesis of a clue in Aren's former reputed connection with the underworld, but it apparently leads nowhere. No attempt was made to extort money from Arens, and if the object had been to get him out of the way, the method chosen was so tortuous and uncertain as to place it outside the bounds of possibility.

Mrs. Eddy, in her view of the case, quite definitely attributed the whole incident to mental manipulation, claiming that it only presented on a somewhat larger scale the same incoherent features to be found in other ruptures that had taken place in the development of her work. Incoherence was indeed characteristic of the case from first to last. As one commentator well said of it, "The evidence reads like the testimony heard in the nightmare of some plethoric judge."

Malicious Animal Magnetism

SOONER OR LATER, in traversing the lives of those who, like Mary Baker Eddy, lay claim to original thought, it becomes necessary to turn aside long enough to make sure that we understand their definitions; in other words, to make sure that when they use an expression or group of expressions, such use means the same to them that it does to us and *vice versa*.

The field of research along the major roads and bypaths of the human mind has extended enormously since 1878. At that time, Freud and his school were still thirty years below the horizon. The word "behaviourism" had not been coined, the word "propaganda" still found no place outside the "Sacred Congregation" of the Vatican, and no one had thought of asking why we "behave as human beings". At that time, no one was heard to speak of "mass mesmerism", and although fashion, devotion, patriotism, every kind of human emotion then as now came and went, no one had ever thought of attributing such movements to anything but specific and most reasonable causes.

Even today, research has not attempted to go much beyond the bounds of analysis. The ways and means by which the new propaganda attains its ends have been thoroughly investigated and are pretty well known, but no effective general antidote has ever been found, if it has ever been sought. Today, books are written on the use of mesmerism or suggestion or personal magnetism in the art of salesmanship or of making friends. There is not a failing or foible of human nature which has not been analysed to the end that means might be discovered for its exploitation. Yet, in spite of all this, the average man is satisfied to believe that his thoughts originate with himself, that his likes and dislikes are his own, uninfluenced by anything but his own intelligence and reasoned judgement. The fashions of yesterday and his changed views in regard to them are always there to have him in derision, but his confidence in himself and in the sovereignty of his choice is never impaired.

That far back, Mrs. Eddy reached the conviction that all final power is mental or spiritual. She reasoned, logically enough, that, inasmuch as the power that moved the muscles of her hand to write, of her limbs to walk, was purely mental, then there was at least nothing incongruous in the assumption that the power which controlled all the actions and changes of matter, from the stars above to the earth beneath, might be mental also. From this point, she went on to see that if this proposition which she embodied in the statement, "All is infinite Mind and its infinite manifestation," [1] were true, then, like all truths, there could be an untruth told about it; in other words, a counterfeit or supposititious opposite, and that the higher anyone attained in the realm of Truth, the more obtrusive would be the untruth or the counterfeit which could be brought to light by the discovery.

This counterfeit of Truth, of the divine Mind, as she called it, in all its manifestations, she declared to be the human mind, and from that she went on to maintain that, first and last, this human mind was a state of mesmerism from which the mortal needed to be awakened. The moment, however, she had proved that this divine Mind could waken the mortal out of the mesmerism of pain and disease, anger, sorrow, or what not, that moment there arose in a more aggressive form than ever before the counterfeit contention of the opposite of truth, namely, that it could induce or reimpose these limitations.

[1] *Science and Health*, p. 468.

255

The whole of human belief has been always unconsciously insisting on just this, but the work, Mrs. Eddy maintained, became much more rapid and effective when it was done consciously. The normal action of human belief to maintain its own convictions and standards she called "animal magnetism", and the conscious attempt to make use of this power by the individual for injury of others, she called "malicious animal magnetism" or "malicious mental malpractice".

There is, of course, nothing in all this but what is a commonplace in the study of psychology today. Where Mrs. Eddy clearly differs from the psychologist is in her contention first, that this mental influence can operate directly and without physical implementation, and, second, that an understanding of the supposititious nature of this human mind and a realization of the reality and ever presence of the divine Mind are a complete protection against the mesmeric influence of the former and a demonstration of the actuality and presence of the latter.

In brief, Mrs. Eddy, instead of taking it for granted that the sudden inexplicable hatreds, disloyalties and subterfuges which were constantly coming to light among her followers were simply part of the changes and chances of human life, in the presence of which she was helpless, insisted that they were the result of directed effort on the part of an individual or individuals and of failure of the student to guard himself against such imposition.

In the Conspiracy to Murder case, she maintained that she had support enough for her thesis. If it is possible to imagine a group of people being separately expertly mesmerised, in the manner of the public exhibitions of that period, or in the manner of the more serious experiments of the modern clinic, and then "willed" to conduct a similar case, the result could hardly have been more fantastic than that which actually took place in Boston in the eighties. "The nightmare of some plethoric judge" is an apt enough description.

It seemed to Mrs. Eddy that there must be some reason for it all, other than what appeared on the surface. And so she began to formulate her theory, and two years later in the third edition of her book *Science and Health,* under the title "Demonology", she considers in some detail the various attacks that had been made upon her and her teaching and upon the movement that she was fostering, from the first open break with Richard Kennedy to the final defection of Spofford, culminating in the incoherent medley of the Conspiracy to Murder Trial.

She considers it all from the mental standpoint. The actual translation of the thought into a deed is to her of secondary importance. She dismisses the overt act with the same logical inconsequence as did Jesus when he declared, "Ye have heard it said of old time, Thou shalt not commit adultery, but I say unto you, whosoever looketh upon a woman to lust after her has already committed adultery with her in his heart."

The man who, taking life as he knows it in his stride, indulges his hatred, his anger, his meanness, his cruelty, his fear and what not, in simple ignorance, believing that these feelings and emotions are just his own and cannot injure, save insofar as they are translated by him into specific deeds, Mrs. Eddy regards simply as an ignorant mental malpractitioner. In other words, he is a man who is thinking wrongly through ignorance and not from malice aforethought. He is ignorant of the fact that the "atmosphere" of fear or hatred or cruelty he carries around with him is contagious, or in the words of the modern psychologist "stampeding", in its effect.

The man, on the other hand, who knows what he is doing, has confidence in the dynamic power of thought and deliberately uses his knowledge to produce the evil effect, Mrs. Eddy calls a malicious mental malpractitioner, and his practice malicious mental malpractice. He is a man who practises wrongly, not from ignorance but with malicious purpose.

It is a long chapter, this chapter on Demonology—some thirteen thousand words—and, in the light of all that is known today regarding the mass application of suggestion and the effect of skilfully imposed propaganda, makes strangely interesting reading.

"There is but one possible way", Mrs. Eddy writes, "of doing evil through a mental method of treating disease, and this is mesmerism, that controls the mind with error instead of Truth. Whoever has witnessed the exhibitions of mesmerism has seen it stiffen a joint, suspend thought, produce pain, and move the individual mind to whatever issues intended, proving beyond a doubt that by mortal mind alone the body can be affected injuriously. . . . Falsehoods uttered aloud can be met with rebutting testimony; but a silent mental process of impregnating into the mind, and thence into the body, suffering, disease, fear, hatred, sensuality, etc., is 'Satan let loose', the sin that 'standeth in holy places', more subtle than all other beasts of the field, a crime at which everyone should shudder either to become the victim or the perpetrator."

The essence of her contention, of course, is that the wider the field opened up by metaphysics in the realm of Mind, the wider must of necessity be the field opened up to its counterfeit. And so she writes again: "The individual who employs his developed mental powers, like an escaped felon, to commit atrocities according to opportunity, is safe at no period. God hath laid His hand upon him, justice is manacling him. . . . From physics to metaphysics is full many a league in the line of light, but from the use of inanimate drugs to pass to the misuse of mortal mind is to drop from the platform of manhood into the mire of folly and iniquity."

From first to last, the whole chapter is the negative view of her faith. It is, however, important that its purport should be grasped in some measure, because of the tremendous part this teaching, or its misapprehension, played in the immediately subsequent history of the movement. The third edition of *Science and Health* represents what may be called the high point in the negative presentation of Christian Science. In every later edition, a movement is made towards the positive side. "Mesmerism can make mortals believe a lie, but metaphysics can make them unbelieve it", is the keynote of the third edition. "Keep your minds so filled with Truth and Love, that sin, disease, and death cannot enter them," is the keynote of the last.[1]

In 1879 it was the teaching of the third edition that held the place of emphasis.

[1] *Miscellany*, p. 210.

The Church

ONCE AGAIN, THE dissensions which entered so largely into the chronicle of Mrs. Eddy's life in 1878, important as they are, tend to obscure far more important developments. In spite of all defections and disloyalties, unwise suits and amazing criminal charges, the foundations of a great movement were being laid. It is only in the perspective of the years that this can be clearly traced, for in those early days it seems to have been one of the characteristics of the Christian Science movement that it never presented the appearance of rapid growth. New adherents were constantly coming in, many of them actuated largely by curiosity. They stayed for a time, and then stayed away for a time, and then came back again. Others remained longer and went on and never turned back, or went out and never returned.

The movement was, however, steadily expanding. Even those who dropped out, whether they did so early or late, in friendship or in wrath, were still missionaries of the new teaching, at any rate, to the extent that they told others about it. And very often, as the subsequent history was to prove conclusively enough, an adverse criticism was even more effective in making a new disciple than a favourable one.

But the movement had no definite headquarters outside of the little front room at Number 8 Broad Street in Lynn. Several attempts had been made to secure such a focal point. On June 8, 1875, it will be remembered, eight of Mrs. Eddy's students had banded themselves together informally, calling themselves "The Christian Scientists" and pledging themselves to raise money enough to have Mrs. Eddy address them every Sunday. The meetings were continued for five successive Sundays and then, as already noted, were abandoned, owing to the rising tide of argument brought to the meetings by Spiritualists and others who dissented from Mary Patterson's teaching and resented her well-known disapproval of Spiritualism.

Thereafter, for about a year there was no definite move towards an organization of any kind, and then in the summer of 1876 came "The Christian Scientist Association". This second attempt at organization differed importantly from the first in that it made no direct effort to enlist the interest of the general public. It was devotional rather than missionary in its purpose, and designed to establish and develop those already interested rather than to make new converts. It held more or less regular weekly meetings, but always in the homes of different students, usually in Lynn, but sometimes also in Boston, Roxbury and Salem.

Mrs. Eddy seems to have approached the idea of organizing a church of her own with a considerable amount of hesitancy. Indeed, in the nine years which intervened between what has come to be regarded as the date of her discovery of Christian Science in 1866 and her publication of the first edition of *Science and Health* in 1875, she was evidently convinced that church organization was a hindrance rather than a help to the highest spiritual development.

"We have no need of creeds and church organizations", she wrote, "to sustain or explain a demonstrable platform, that defines itself in healing the sick, and casting out error. . . . The mistake the disciples of Jesus made to found religious organizations and church rites, if indeed they did this, was one the Master did not make. . . . Christ's church was Truth, 'I am Truth and Life', the temple for the worshippers of Truth is Spirit and not matter. . . . No time was lost by our Master in organizations, rites, and ceremonies, or in proselyting for certain forms of belief." [1]

But Mrs. Eddy in the attic room of Number 8 Broad Street in Lynn, writing *Science and Health,* with the weapons of her warfare still largely untried and the world still largely uncontacted, was one thing, and Mrs. Eddy definitely confronted with the problem of spreading her gospel was quite another. As she was to write some years afterwards in a later edition of her book: "Until the author of this book learned the vastness of Christian Science, the fixedness of mortal illusions, and the human hatred of Truth, she cherished sanguine hopes that Christian Science would meet with immediate and universal acceptance." [2]

It cannot have been long before she was compelled to abandon this hope, and the conviction that the world of her day would find it difficult if not impossible to accept her teaching save through the accustomed channel of a church must have followed soon afterwards. This was especially true in the world of New England to which she first addressed herself. As long as a man went to church, or at least was not opposed to churchgoing, he might believe what he liked and, however regrettable, it would not be out of order. But if he did not go to church, or, worse still, was opposed to churchgoing, he could not expect to be accepted as a religionist at all, much less get a hearing as an exponent of a new faith.

A great many of Mrs. Eddy's most useful and effective students in these early days had been active in church work before they came into Christian Science—Baptists, Methodists, Congregationalists, all strongly evangelical in purpose and organization. They wanted a church to work for, and were all too evidently at a loss when confronted with the prospect of working out their own salvation and that of others in any but the accustomed way.

Mrs. Eddy was quick to grasp the situation, and so in the summer of 1879 steps were taken to form a chartered church organization. In August, she and some of her students met together, elected officers and directors, chose a name, "The Church of Christ (Scientist)", and applied

[1] *Science and Health,* First Edition, pp. 166-167.
[2] *Science and Health,* p. 330.

261

to the state for a charter. The officers and directors were: Mary B. G. Eddy, president; Margaret J. Dunshee, treasurer; Edward A. Orne, Miss Dorcas B. Rawson, Arthur T. Buswell, James Ackland, Margaret J. Foley, Mrs. Mary Ruddock, Oren Carr, directors. On August 23rd, the charter was granted. The purpose of the corporation was "to carry on and transact the business necessary to the worship of God", and Boston was named as the place within which it was established. The charter members numbered twenty-six.

These apparently orderly developments might reasonably suggest for their central figure a period of greater quiet and freedom from harassment than had hitherto been her lot. Such, however, was very far from being the case. The lawsuits of 1878, culminating in the Conspiracy to Murder Trial, had drained Mrs. Eddy's financial resources to the limit. They had also left her burdened with a sense of fear over the machinations of her enemies which at times cast her into the depths. If her opponents could seize her husband and throw him into prison, arraign him before the courts on the charge of murder and carry them all through a maze of incoherencies like nothing so much as an evil dream, what could they not do?

True, she put up a stiff fight against it all, but she had not only her own fears to combat, but those of her students. They crowded around her like frightened children, wondering which of them would be the next victim. Indeed, there emerges definitely about this time a situation or condition which was to become almost characteristic of the movement in the future, and a just appraisal of this condition would seem to be essential to a just appreciation of Mrs. Eddy's own history, especially in its relation to the movement she founded.

Much more than most leaders, Mrs. Eddy seems to have been uniformly ahead of her followers. With one or two exceptions to be noted later, there never was anyone, especially in those early days, who could be said to have been able to keep pace with her even to the extent of being readily within hail. By the time they had caught up to a certain point, she had gone on ahead.

262

Too, it often happened with some of her followers that when they reached a certain point they were so interested in it or concerned about it that they literally camped around it, and what they ultimately did with it largely depended on the view taken of it by those who got there first after Mrs. Eddy had gone on. These early comers "preached" to those who came after with all the authority of senior students, and in this way it was brought about that many went off entirely on some tangent or other, or if they went on they did so with clouded vision hampered with burdens which their leader had long discarded.

On the other hand, among those who came afterwards would always be large numbers who had read her book sufficiently aright to see where mistakes were being made by others and not to be influenced by them. These pressed on and often a very young disciple would be found suddenly in the van.

In no circumstances was all this more true than in this matter of the fear of malicious mental malpractice. To many students it became an obsession. They accepted the idea of "danger" with both hands and there they stayed. The sure defence which Mrs. Eddy had proclaimed and to which she was ever seeking to have recourse—namely, an understanding of its unreality—meant to them little or nothing. The new idea of God was to them completely overshadowed by what was nothing more than a new idea of devil.

The Conspiracy to Murder charge against Doctor Eddy and Arens left the whole movement under a cloud of fear which culminated in an incident almost as bizarre as the charge itself and the trial which followed. So sorely depleted were Mrs. Eddy's resources as the result of legal proceedings that she and her husband decided to rent their house and move for a while to Boston. This they did in the early part of 1879, living very simply in a two-roomed apartment. Shortly before they made the move, Mrs. Eddy had heard again from that strange shadowy character, her son George Glover. He was now a man in the early thirties, and after being mustered out of the army at the close of the Civil War had like many others disappeared into the unknown as far as his relatives were concerned.

George Glover and his relations with his mother and *vice versa* seem at first to present something of an enigma until his restless character and the nature of his upbringing are given their full weight. Having all his father's love of change, circumstances made him from his earliest childhood much more the son of Mahala Sanborn, the blacksmith's daughter and upper servant in the Baker household, than of his own mother. It was to her he learned to look in those first years when his mother was able to have him with her seldom, and what was at first a necessity quickly became a preference. The kitchen and the blacksmith's shop constituted for him the real venue of his life. Then when Mahala married Russell Cheney and he went to live with them at North Groton he became to all intents and purposes their son. However, the ruling passion of his life was freedom from restraint of any kind. When the Cheneys went west he, as already noted, went with them, but he always seems to have been a round peg in a square hole, and it was to get away from Mahala and Russell Cheney that he enlisted in the army at the outbreak of the Civil War. When the war was over, he drifted from one place to another and from one employment to another, eventually becoming interested in mining as his major occupation. He wrote to his mother occasionally, but he had a way of disappearing for years at a time, leaving no address or means by which he could be reached.

Towards the close of 1878, Mrs. Eddy had evidently heard from him again, for early in 1879 she wrote to him from Boston telling him how much she wanted to see him. She and Doctor Eddy had some thought at that time of going to Cincinnati to settle, getting away from the growing turmoil of Lynn and Boston and making a fresh start. The idea was given up almost as soon at it was conceived, but it was no doubt this plan that decided Mrs. Eddy to write to George Glover, for when she wrote to him she suggested they should meet in Cincinnati.

The invitation was evidently timed exactly right, for George seems to have gone at once to Cincinnati, and when he did not find his mother there he came on to Boston.

His arrival, as may be imagined, created quite a stir among Mrs. Eddy's students. She was sincerely fond of him and no doubt had often spoken to her friends about him, and now they were to see him in the flesh. His short sojourn in Boston was a veritable March visitation. He came in like a lamb and went out like a lion. At first, the novelty of the situation appealed to him strongly. He was the centre of attention among quite a number of people, and when Mrs. Eddy, perhaps too ready to believe the best of people, urged him to stay with her and study Christian Science, insisting that she was sure he would make a wonderful student, he cheerfully and hopefully assented.

It was at the period that the fear of malpractice was at its height. Mrs. Eddy herself had by no means found her feet, and her followers could talk of nothing else. George was all agog. Here was something he could believe in, and it was not long before he was up in arms against all his mother's enemies, real or imaginary. Among these, Richard Kennedy was still quite evidently the ringleader. He determined to stop Richard Kennedy and, simple Westerner that he was, adopted what was to him the normal and natural way of effecting his purpose. He always carried a gun which bulged ominously beneath his coat, and he determined to get the drop on Richard Kennedy and then make him acquiesce in his demands. Some thirty years later, at the time when Joseph Pulitzer was using the great power of his paper to "expose" Mrs. Eddy and discredit her movement, George Glover told the whole story, or his version of it, to the New York *World*. It bears all the earmarks of having been astutely written up for the occasion, but it makes interesting reading.

"Within a week of my arrival in Boston I learned strange things. The strangest of these was that rebellious students were employing black arts to harass and destroy my mother.

"The longer I remained with mother, the clearer this became. Pursued by evil influences of the students, we moved from house to house, never at rest and always apprehensive. It was a maddening puzzle to me. We

265

would move to a new house and fellow lodgers would be all smiles and friendliness. Then, in an hour an inevitable change would come; the friendliness would vanish under the spell of black magic, and we would be ordered to go. But mother made it all very clear to me.

"It was Kennedy that mother talked of most. He was a master hand at the black arts, as mother pictured him to me, until at last I made up my mind to cut him short in his evil work. But I kept my plan to myself. One morning I slipped my revolver into my overcoat pocket and left our boarding house.

"I had never seen this man, but I knew where he had offices, and I walked straight there. He was doing business as a healer, and his name, lettered on a brass plate, was on the door of his office. Every detail of that visit is as clear in my mind today as if it took place only a week ago.

"The girl who admitted me asked me if I was a patient, and I answered, 'Yes'. She then led me straight to Kennedy's office, on the second floor of the house, opened the door, bowed me into the room, and hurried away. Kennedy was before me, seated at his desk.

"He looked up smilingly and asked, 'Are you in need of treatment?'

"Pulling out my revolver I walked up to him, pressed the cold muzzle against his head, and said, 'I have made up my mind that *you* are in need of treatment.'

"There, while he shook like a jelly-fish in terror, I gave him his one chance to live. I told him that my mother knew of his black art tricks to ruin her, and that I had made up my mind to stop him or kill him.

" 'You needn't tell me that you *aren't* working your game of hypnotism to rob her friends and drive mother into madness,' said I. 'My word to you is this: if we have to move to another boarding house I will search you out and shoot you like a dog.'

"I shall never forget how that man pleaded for his life at the end of my weapon, and swore that the black art accusation was false, and my mother had deceived me.

"But it did the business all right. We were not ordered out of another boarding house that winter."

Richard Kennedy, who was still living in Boston at the time the *World* published George Glover's statement, vigorously denied that he was ever thus intimidated, and in any event, inasmuch as the *World* at that time was trying to show that Mrs. Eddy was incompetent to manage her own affairs and had for years been insane, grave doubts attach to the whole story. It is interesting, however, as showing that the strongest impression which George Glover carried away with him was that produced by Mrs. Eddy's explanation of animal magnetism. Whatever he may or may not have been told, his thought ran readily into the old lines of superstition and emerged eventually in a belief in witchcraft and black magic.

But whether it was all imagination or worse on the part of Glover, assisted by the *World* reporter, or there was more than a grain of truth in it, it is a fact that as the winter of 1879 gave way to spring and spring to summer, the fear of attack from their enemies which had been so acute at the time of the Conspiracy to Murder Trial began to abate in the little circle at Lynn and in the other circles which were now forming themselves in other centres, notably in Boston and Salem. When the church was finally formed in August, everyone seems to have been in a much happier frame of mind. George Glover had gone home, Mrs. Eddy and Doctor Eddy were back again in Lynn, and the infant movement entered upon one of those brief periods wherein the smoke lifted and enabled Mrs. Eddy and her followers to see something of what they were winning.

No attempt was made at first to bring the new church more prominently before the public. While Mrs. Eddy was in Boston, she and her followers had been in the habit of meeting on Sunday afternoons in a room hired for the purpose in the Baptist Tabernacle on Shawmut Avenue, and although Mrs. Eddy's talks on these occasions were sometimes reported at considerable length in the Boston *Globe* the meetings were still devotional rather than evangelical in character.

The circle of her students, however, was quietly and steadily increasing. One of her most devoted followers about this time was a Mrs. Clara Elizabeth Choate, who had been healed, some years previously, while reading *Science and Health*. She and her husband, George D. Choate, lived at

Salem with their little son Warren, and so deeply were they attracted to the new teaching that in the summer of 1878 they moved to Lynn and took a house directly opposite Mrs. Eddy at the other side of Broad Street.

In her *Reminiscences,* written many years afterwards, Mrs. Choate gives an interesting picture of Mrs. Eddy about this time and the house in Broad Street as she remembered it. Notwithstanding all the turmoil of her life, there always seems to have been that about Mrs. Eddy and her surroundings which caused those who met her to forget all else but that they were experiencing something entirely new. Mrs. Choate, in describing their first meeting in the front room at Broad Street, emphasizes just this point:

"When the double doors leading into the back parlour were at last opened," she writes, "and I saw her standing there, I was seized with a sense of great gladness which seemed to be imparted by her radiant expression. . . . I cannot describe the exhilaration that rushed through my whole being. I was uplifted and felt a sense of buoyancy unspeakable. It was as though a consciousness of purity pervaded Mrs. Eddy and from her imparted itself to me, whereupon I felt as if treading on air to the rhythmic flow of music."

The house, as Mrs. Choate describes it, must have been typical of what was best in the simple New England home of the day, with its soft grey paper and lace curtains looped back over gilt arms, its crimson carpets and black walnut furniture, its flowers and its neatness. Mary, it will be remembered, from early girlhood had a knack of making a "home" out of very little.

As to Mary herself, perhaps the most grateful contribution Mrs. Choate makes to the picture of her at this time is the emphasis she lays upon her good cheer and the way she had of rallying her students, when they were inclined to be discouraged or fearful, with some humorous remark which broke the spell for herself and everyone.

Boston

BOSTON IN THE early eighties of last century was just beginning to demonstrate to a reluctant world that, in addition to its culture, it was, after all, what it had always been, a great commercial city. For the better part of half a century, the most frequently heard word from Boston had been the word of the man of letters, whether in the realm of philosophy, literature or religion, until the very name Boston had become synonymous with blue stocking. Half joke, whole earnest, there had been fashioned the legend of Beacon Hill and Beacon Street and their exclusive aristocracy of thought and estate, while men everywhere had heard of the Concord circle and other circles of less import, those of Prescott, Ticknor, Bancroft, Motley and Parkman in the realm of philosophy; Lowell, Longfellow, Holmes and Whittier in the realm of poetry. They were all contemporaries and friends, these men, bound together with many ties of sympathy and constituted a group of writers that had carried the name of Boston throughout the English speaking world and beyond its borders.

By the early eighties, this race of giants had passed or was rapidly passing away. Emerson died in the April of 1882. Longfellow had preceded him by little more than a month. Alcott, old and war-scarred, lingered peacefully on for another six years, and Whittier longer still, as did Holmes and Lowell, but, in the eighties, the twilight had definitely descended on the gods, and cultured Boston was resting on its laurels.

The great fire of 1872 had hastened the change. For two long-remembered days, November 9th and 10th, fire swept over the city south of the Common until nearly a thousand buildings, most of them in brick and stone, had gone up in smoke and, for the first time in nearly two hundred years, men as they passed along the old cow path of Washington Street could look back and see the shipping at the wharves away to the south. The devastated area was rebuilt in a surprisingly short space of time, but when a new and finer business district had arisen from the ashes of the old, a new Boston emerged with it. The love of culture and tireless inquiry which had earned for the city the title of the Athens of America remained, but it now shared place with trade and commerce.

As a great religious centre it was still pre-eminent, if not from the devotional certainly from the theological point of view. From the time of Increase and Cotton Mather, through Jonathan Edwards up to Ellery Channing and Theodore Parker, Boston had always been in the forefront of religious controversy, and the "Boston Craze" of today had a way of becoming a national concern of tomorrow.

The early eighties of last century found Boston still running very true to form, preoccupied with the question of Spiritualism in all its many schools, remodelling its Unitarianism, and giving no little attention to the teaching of Robert Ingersoll. Just ripe for something new and revolutionary, it found this quite definitely in Christian Science. It was a sure instinct that decided Mrs. Eddy to look more and more to Boston as the centre for the promulgation on a large scale of her teaching. The people who came in increasing numbers to her informal gatherings in the Baptist Tabernacle on Shawmut Avenue were a very different type from those who had heckled her so relentlessly at her first few meetings in the Templars' Hall at Lynn some four years previously. They asked questions and raised issues enough, but they did so for the most part in the spirit of genuine inquiry rather than of controversy. The headquarters of the movement were still in Lynn, but, from now on, Mrs. Eddy found more and more of her work centring in the great city to the south.

As 1879 drew to a close, she and her husband once again rented Number 8 Broad Street and moved to Boston, taking rooms at first on Newton Street near Tremont, but later moving with the Choates into a house on Shawmut Avenue, which they took together, Dr. and Mrs. Eddy occupying the second floor and the Choates the first and third. In the spring of 1880 the Eddys returned to Lynn, but Mrs. Eddy continued to pay her share of the rent and used the Shawmut Avenue house as her resting place when they came to town.

Meanwhile, the meetings of the little church each Sunday in the Baptist Tabernacle on Shawmut Avenue became more stabilized and the attendance steadily increased. Mrs. Eddy generally travelled to Boston from Lynn to conduct the services which necessarily became less informal as the numbers grew. The meeting would open with silent prayer, followed by the Lord's prayer with Mrs. Eddy's interpretation. Then one of the students appointed for the purpose would read from the Bible and another from *Science and Health,* after which there would be an address from Mrs. Eddy. Quite often—possibly when the room in the Baptist Tabernacle was not available—the Sunday services would be held in the house of one of the Boston students, generally in that of Mrs. Clara Choate on Shawmut Avenue. Meetings were also held at Lynn, sometimes at Number 8 Broad Street, but more often in the front parlour of Mrs. F. A. Damon's house on Jackson Street. It was a carefully organized gathering, the one at Lynn, with a treasurer and a secretary who kept minutes of each meeting, some of which have been preserved. These minutes show how small at first was the whole enterprise. Sometimes five, sometimes seven, sometimes as many as twenty were present, but seldom more. Thus the record of the meeting held on September 5, 1880, runs: "Meeting opened by Mrs. Damon in the usual way. Mrs. M. B. G. Eddy, having completed her summer vacation was present and delivered a discourse. Whole number in attendance twenty-two."

271

But all the time the movement was steadily growing. The Boston meetings, especially, brought in a succession of students to Mrs. Eddy's classes, some of whom were to figure prominently in the rapidly expanding days which lay ahead. Julia Bartlett, Ellen J. Clark, Arthur Buswell and James Ackland were so eager that they left their work and homes in Boston and came to Lynn so as to study with Mrs. Eddy and commence work as healers under her guidance. Of those who became interested about this time perhaps the most notable was Julia Bartlett. She was one of the few among the earliest students who remained faithful to their teacher through the years, and was still with her at the end. Born in East Windsor, Connecticut, and descended from Robert Bartlett, one of the first settlers in Hartford, she lost her father and mother when she was still a young girl at school, and found herself at the age of sixteen the eldest of a family of five. Fortunately they were all well provided for and Julia was able to finish her education, but her responsibilities, as she saw them, weighed heavily upon her. She grieved over her father's and mother's death, and turned to religion with a devotion and fervour which only an adolescent girl can show. She was a member of the Congregational Church, which, in those days, was almost the established church of New England, but its teachings failed to bring her the comfort and assurance she so sorely needed, and she looked in vain elsewhere for help. Finally, she became seriously ill and, in the ebb and flow of partial recovery, gradually lapsed into a condition of chronic invalidism. She first heard of Christian Science in the April of 1880, and never apparently doubted for a moment. As soon as possible she set out for Lynn and placed herself under the care of Doctor Eddy, with the result that she recovered completely. She then went through a class with Mrs. Eddy, and returned to East Windsor determined to make the practice of the new teaching her life work. Later on, she moved to Boston and opened an office there.

This growing band of students was at once a strength and a care to Mrs. Eddy, a strength because her one great desire was to have as many as possible put to work, and a care because so few were able to work by themselves. They were forever returning to her for help and guidance, very often when the problem that presented itself was one they could quite well have worked out for themselves. Mrs. Eddy's straight speaking on many occasions led to jealousy and offence, and she was called upon, all too often, to settle differences which brought upon her only the condemnation of both parties. She pushed forward, however, and, in the December of 1880, launched boldly upon an enterprise which was to bring her teaching at one bound into the very presence of Boston's higher criticism. She hired the Hawthorne Hall, Number 2 Park Street, for her Sunday afternoon services.

Almost in the shadow of Park Street Church, Hawthorne Hall, named after Nathaniel Hawthorne, had long been the scene of some of Boston's highest flights into the realm of science, philosophy and religion. Many great people had spoken and lectured there, and cultured Boston found its way to Hawthorne Hall as readily as it did to Park Street Church or King's Chapel. It was an intimate kind of place with a good platform, a gallery at one end and seats sufficiently generous to make for comfort.[1]

The services were held at three o'clock on Sunday afternoons, and they quickly became a subject of much discussion both in the press and at church meetings, public and private. Up to now it had all been rumour. Ministers and others had heard of the queer movement in Lynn with mingled feelings of curiosity and strong disapproval, and they had no doubt read about the "Conspiracy to Murder" Trial with the feeling that it was the final wind-up of a rather discreditable craze. The last thing they could have expected was that they would next hear of this strange teaching from the platform in Hawthorne Hall.

It was some time before the storm actually broke, and, meanwhile, Mrs. Eddy carried her plans for development a step further by making a move which was certainly not lacking in courage and imagination. Under a State Act which had been passed in 1874, she applied for and secured a charter for a college to teach her system of metaphysics, and on January

[1] It was pulled down many years ago to give place to a block of business buildings.

273

31, 1881, the charter was granted to the new institution under the title of the "Massachusetts Metaphysical College". The purpose of the college, according to its charter, was "To teach pathology, ontology, therapeutics, moral science, metaphysics and their application to the treatment of disease." It was empowered to confer degrees and give diplomas and transact all the business necessary to these ends. As the act of 1874 was repealed in 1883, and Mrs. Eddy's college was the only institution of its kind to be chartered under it, the Massachusetts Metaphysical College quickly attained a unique position. The founders, whose names appeared on the charter, were Mary B. G. Eddy, president; James C. Howard, treasurer; Charles J. Eastman, Edgar F. Woodbury, James Wiley, William F. Walker and Samuel P. Bancroft, directors. In Charles J. Eastman, Mrs. Eddy had a link with the past. He had been one of her pupils in the little infant school she had organized in the shoemaker's shop behind her sister Abigail's house in Tilton.

The founding of the college was characteristic of Mrs. Eddy's method of approach to every development of importance in the work she had set herself to do. What the thing was to be in the end, so it was to her in the beginning. She was always willing to work with the scantiest and most indifferent material, but the project from the first had the full outline of the finished plan. And so she took her charter back with her to Lynn, and, a few days later, she was writing letters on paper that bore the heading, "Massachusetts Metaphysical College, No. 8 Broad Street, Lynn". There was no outward and visible change. Students came and went, and she continued to teach as before, when and as she could. Those who paid and those who could not pay were given a receipt for the fees. But now they were enrolled for a regular college course, and, although the granting of degrees came later, the right to confer was there from the first.

It was a time of much activity. Early in the spring, the third edition of *Science and Health* was ready for the press. In it the deficiencies of the second edition were made good and the chapter entitled "Demonology" added, as already noted. But it had hardly gone to the printers before Mrs. Eddy was confronted with another problem which was to remain a problem for many years to come, the question of plagiarism.

On the conclusion of the "Conspiracy to Murder" Trial, Edward J. Arens came immediately to Boston, took an office at 32 Upton Street not far from Faneuil Hall and began a vigorous missionary work among the market men in this wholesale district of the city. From the first, he seems to have gone off more or less on his own, fashioning his own ideas and drifting further and further away from Mrs. Eddy and her steadily growing band of students. He occasionally even hired a hall and gave a lecture on Metaphysical Healing, charging an admission fee of ten cents.

There was no definite break; indeed, for some time after the trial, he appears to have been specially earnest and wholehearted in following Mrs. Eddy's leadership, but he gradually drifted away. Then, one day, Doctor Eddy received a pamphlet entitled *Theology, or the Understanding of God as Applied to Healing the Sick*. It was by Edward J. Arens, and was, for the most part, a verbatim transcript from *Science and Health*. The only suggestion of indebtedness was contained in a notation in the preface to the effect that the author had used "some thoughts contained in a work by Eddy".

The matter came up later in the Federal Courts, but for the time being Gilbert Eddy tackled the question with vigour. He seems to have felt it much more than Mrs. Eddy. It was Mrs. Eddy who, later on, steadily pursued a single course until her legal rights were recognized and established and the purity of her teaching as she conceived it, safeguarded, as far as she could safeguard it; but it was Gilbert Eddy who took immediate action. He wrote a new preface to the third edition of *Science and Health*, then in the press, in the course of which he denounced Arens's action tersely.

"If simply writing at the commencement of a work, 'I have made use of some thoughts contained in a work by Eddy,' walks over copyright, any fool can aspire to be wise, commence a book with the announcement that 'I have taken some thoughts from Ralph Waldo Emerson,' and then copy verbatim, without quotation marks, from thirty to three hundred pages of his works, and publish them as his own. . . . This may be convenient for an ignoramous or a villain, but a real expounder of 'The Understanding of Christianity or God' would scarcely be caught at it."

And then warming to his subject he continues: "It would require ages and God's mercy to make the ignorant hypocrite who published that pamphlet originate its contents. His pratings are coloured by his character, they cannot impart the hue of ethics, but leave his own impress on what he takes."

But there were other and more serious difficulties ahead. So long as the centre of the little community was in Lynn, progress, although difficult enough, was fairly united. Every additional follower added to the prestige of the original disciples, but with the steady rise in importance and numbers of the movement in Boston, the labourers in Lynn who reckoned they had borne the burden and heat of the day began very definitely to murmur. They did not like to find that the last recruit in the great city in the south was to receive "every man a penny a day".

From murmuring, they drifted towards open rebellion, until one evening late in October, at a meeting of the Christian Scientist Association being held at Number 8 Broad Street, one of the members, in behalf of himself and seven others, presented Mrs. Eddy with a memorial, signed by each of them, announcing their intention to withdraw from the Association. It was quite an unexpected blow, and it must have been with a strange mixture of feelings that Mrs. Eddy scanned the names attached to it, those of her old and trusted friends, Miranda Rice, Dorcas Rawson, Margaret Dunshee, James Howard and the others.

"We, the undersigned, while we acknowledge and appreciate the understanding of Truth imparted to us by our Teacher, Mrs. Mary B. G. Eddy, led by Divine Intelligence to perceive with sorrow that departure from the straight and narrow road (which alone leads to growth in Christ-like virtues) made manifest by frequent ebullitions of temper, love of money, and the appearance of hypocrisy, *cannot* longer submit to such Leadership; therefore without aught of hatred, revenge or petty spite in our hearts, from a sense of duty alone to her, the Cause, and ourselves, do most respectfully withdraw our names from the Christian Science Association and Church of Christ (Scientist).

(Signed)   S. Louise Durant,
Margaret J. Dunshee,
Dorcas B. Rawson,
Elizabeth G. Stuart,
Jane L. Shaw,
Anna B. Newman,
James C. Howard,

"October 21st, 1881"   Miranda R. Rice."

Piecing the scene together from such scanty records as there are, notably Clara Choate's memoirs, it was not lacking in drama or pathos. Mrs. Eddy received the memorial in silence, and the eight students who had signed it filed out of the room one by one without speaking, leaving Mrs. Eddy and Gilbert and two students who remained faithful to make what they could of it. Of these two students, one was most probably Julia Bartlett, although Clara Choate does not mention her name. The other was a new student, already devotedly attached to Mrs. Eddy and destined to become one of the best-known figures in the movement. His name was Calvin Frye.

All that night, as Calvin Frye afterwards recorded in his notes, the four sat together sorrowfully but bravely enough to find some reparation for what at that period must have seemed a major disaster indeed. Calvin Frye, in his notes, shows how they prayed over it, and how, towards morning, Mrs. Eddy suddenly began to speak like one who, thinking herself alone, spoke aloud. It must have made a deep impression on him, for he records her words, as well as he could remember them. They are just ecstatic, disjointed phrases, most of them quotations from the Bible, but through them is seen clearly enough the progress of a journey through the darkness towards the light.

"Is this humiliation, the humility the oppressor would heap upon me! O, the exaltation of Spirit!"

"I have made thee ruler over many things!"

277

"Height upon height! Holiness! Unquenchable light! Divine Being! The Womanhood of God!"

"Well done, good and faithful, enter thou into the joy of thy Lord."

"One woe is passed, and behold, another cometh quickly; and no sign shall be given thee. Sufficient unto the day is the evil thereof."

"Woe, woe unto my people! The furnace is heated, the dross will be destroyed."

"And the false prophet that is among you shall deceive if possible the very elect, and he shall lead them into forbidden paths. And their feet shall bleed upon the jagged rocks. And the briars shall tear the rags from them. For they are not clothed with a garment of righteousness."

"And I will give thee, daughter of Zion, a new heritage and a new people."

"Her ways are ways of pleasantness, and all her paths are peace."

For three days they remained together in the house, conferring as to the next step. The final decision lacked nothing certainly in faith, for, on November 9th, 1881, the remnant of Mrs. Eddy's students in Lynn met together and formally ordained their teacher, Mary Baker Eddy, as pastor of the Church of Christ (Scientist), and the decision was reached to move the headquarters of the church from Lynn to Boston.

And so, a few weeks later, Number 8 Broad Street was dismantled, and on the last evening before Mrs. Eddy and Gilbert were to leave for Boston a meeting of the Christian Scientist Association was held in the front room that had been the scene of so many meetings during the previous seven years. There was little business to transact, but Mrs. Eddy spoke to them for a while and finished by reading the seventeenth chapter of the Gospel according to St. John. As they bore in mind her interpretation of the Christ, the passage probably seemed to the little band singularly appropriate, especially the closing verses.

"O righteous Father, the world hath not known thee: but I have known thee, and these have known that thou hast sent me."

"And I have declared unto them thy name, and will declare it: that the love wherewith thou hast loved me may be in them, and I in them."

278

CHAPTER 28

The Death of Gilbert Eddy

BEHIND THE SILENCE and underneath the gentleness of Gilbert Eddy there lay a tenacity of purpose which only adversity and opposition could fully reveal. His love for Mrs. Eddy was deep and abiding, and reinforced as it was by the conviction that she was the revelator of a great truth, in the promulgation of which he was privileged to have an effective part, his love and affection became a great passion.

It is hard to say which aroused Gilbert to more effective action, an attack on Mrs. Eddy or an attack on her work, and whenever he started on a campaign to offset either, he stuck to it until he had accomplished his purpose. Thus his denunciation of Arens's plagiarism in the preface to the third edition of *Science and Health* was by no means the end of the matter. He determined that Arens should be arraigned for infringement of copyright and the circulation of his pamphlet stopped. Before he took action, however, he wanted to be sure of his position. And so, when he and Mrs. Eddy left Lynn for Boston, it was with the intention of going on almost immediately to Washington in order that Gilbert might make an exhaustive study of the copyright laws in the Library of Congress.

They arrived in the Capital early in the January of 1882, and, for three months, Gilbert devoted himself to the work, securing a knowledge of copyright law and embodying it in writing, such as in later years, long after he had passed away, was to prove of inestimable value to Mrs. Eddy and her movement.

While her husband was thus employed, Mrs. Eddy was by no means idle. She had left Clara Choate in charge of things in Boston, but it was to Julia Bartlett that she apparently looked more and more to "lead this people" in her absence. Thus, in one of her letters written to Julia shortly after her arrival in Washington, Mrs. Eddy tells her how deeply she feels that there ought to be a "substitute for me" in Boston and how sure she is that, of all those whom she left behind, Julia is the most fitted for the task.

Running through these letters is still the dread of attack, and many are the warnings to Julia and the other students to be on their guard. But it is quite evident, both from the tone of the letters and the remarkable activity they reveal, that Mrs. Eddy, during the three months she spent in Washington, freed as she was from the daily care and cares of those around her, developed unexpected powers of endurance.

She is enthusiastic about Washington. "There is not in America so handsome a city as this, I do believe," she writes to Mrs. Choate, going on to tell her of the comfort and beauty of her surroundings. They have rooms at 13 First Street, N.E., for which they pay $100 a month, "front and rear parlours with board". "My front parlour", she writes, "commands the most magnificent view, and at this hour of writing, I am sitting at a desk with only the width of a street between me and the grounds that surround the Capitol."

But her work came first, and Mrs. Eddy was soon in the thick of it. She got out a circular announcing that she had opened an office at Number 13 First Street, and was prepared for lectures and discussions on "Practical Metaphysics". Some knowledge of the new teaching must have preceded her, for it was not long before she was holding a class. On February 28 she wrote to Clara Choate that during the preceding two weeks she had lectured every evening:

"I have worked here harder than ever. Fourteen consecutive evenings I have lectured three hours every night besides what else I am about. Get to bed at twelve, rise at six, and work. I have a goodly number already enlisted. . . . "

It was in Washington, too, that she met again that old friend, Fanny McNeil, Franklin Pierce's niece. Franklin had long since passed away, and Fanny, now Mrs. Fanny McNeil Potter, was living in Washington. They were, it will be remembered, distantly related, and Mrs. Eddy recalls in her *Miscellany* how, during her stay in Washington at this time, they went together one day to visit the grave of Fanny's father, General John McNeil, in Arlington Cemetery.

Her letters from Washington are full of little intimacies, sending her love to this one and that, especially to Clara's little boy Warren, for whom she seems to have had a particular affection. "Love and a kiss to dear Warren. . . . Tell him I know who the little boy in Boston is."

On the other hand, her students in Boston were also active. Undismayed by the defections in Lynn, they had set to work to make sure that no permanent injury was done to the cause in which they had enlisted. Early in February the remaining members of the Christian Scientist Association met together and drew up a series of resolutions in which they censured the act of seceding members, declared their charges to be untrue, and reaffirmed their loyalty to Mrs. Eddy. The resolutions were published in the Lynn *Union* and throw much light on the situation, both in regard to Mrs. Eddy herself and the movement developing under her care.

After expressing "to our beloved teacher, and acknowledged leader, Mary B. Glover Eddy, . . . sincere and heartfelt thanks and gratitude for her earnest labours in behalf of this association", the resolutions continue:

"*Resolved*, That while she has had little or no help, except from God, in the introduction to this age of materiality of her book, *Science and Health*, and the carrying forward of the Christian principles it teaches and explains, she has been unremitting in her faithfulness to her God-appointed work, and we do understand her to be the chosen messenger of

God to bear His truth to the nations, and unless we hear 'Her Voice', we do not hear 'His Voice'.

"*Resolved,* That while many and continued attempts are made by the malpractice, as referred to in the book, *Science and Health,* to hinder and stop the advance of Christian Science, it has with her leadership attained a success that calls out the truest gratitude of her students, and when understood, by all humanity.

"*Resolved,* That the charges made to her in a letter, signed by J. C. Howard, M. R. Rice, D. B. Rawson, and five others, of hypocrisy, ebullitions of temper, and love of money, are utterly false, and the cowardice of the signers in refusing to meet her and sustain or explain said charges, be treated with the righteous indignation it justly deserves. That while we deplore such wickedness and abuse of her who has befriended them in their need, and when wrong, met them with honest, open rebuke, we look with admiration and reverence upon her Christ-like example of meekness and charity, and will, in future, more faithfully follow and obey her divine instructions, knowing that in so doing we offer the highest testimonial of our appreciation of her Christian leadership.

"*Resolved,* That a copy of these resolutions be presented to our teacher and leader, Mary B. Glover Eddy, and a copy be placed on the records of this Christian Scientist Association."

Thus, as far as the faithful remnant was concerned, the vindication was complete, and Mrs. Eddy, in a letter to Clara Choate, speaks of her happiness in receiving this evidence of loyalty. Indeed, it quickly became clear that the defection of the Lynn students, far from crippling the movement, had given it a new impetus. As far as Mrs. Eddy was concerned, it served for the inauguration of a policy, if so it may be called, which was to be typical of her work and method in the future. She always met apparent defeat as though it had been a victory. She insisted upon "putting a tax on calamity", as she afterwards expressed it in one of her writings.

And so, while she was teaching and speaking in Washington, and Gilbert Eddy was familiarizing himself with the intricacies of the copyright law, the little circle in Boston was growing rapidly. When the two returned to Boston, as they did early in April, it was to an outlook more hopeful and encouraging than had obtained for some time. Mrs. Choate arranged a reception for them in her house in Tremont Street, at which practically every Christian Scientist in Boston was present, and there was much evidence on all hands of greater cheer and more settled conditions.

There was, however, one disturbing element. The Choates were the first among Mrs. Eddy's students to have any particular social pretensions, and the reception that Mrs. Choate gave to Mrs. Eddy was made far too much of a social occasion not to fill this woman of simple, almost austere, taste with grave misgivings. Along with those interested in Christian Science who attended were many of Mrs. Choate's personal friends who were not at all interested, but were glad of the opportunity to meet a woman concerning whom so much had already been heard. Mrs. Eddy was taken by surprise. She made a brief address but stayed only a short time, from which it was inferred that she did not think the real purpose of her teaching could be forwarded by such methods.

Meanwhile, she had much to do. While she was in Washington she had, with the aid of the Choates, rented a house in Boston at 569 Columbus Avenue, not only as a residence for herself and some of her students, but as the future headquarters of the Metaphysical College. Columbus Avenue then was in a better part of town than it is today, and Number 569 was a roomy house, four storeys and a basement, a grey stone front and a flight of steps leading up to the front door. In the matter of furnishing, Mrs. Eddy stood out firmly against anything but the most simple. The class room of the college was established on the second floor. It was laid with oilcloth. In one corner was a small raised platform on which Mrs. Eddy had her table and chair, while the seats for the students were set diagonally across the floor. Several students, among them Julia Bartlett, came to the college to live. It was not long before a class was in progress, and in many ways the outlook seemed brighter than ever before.

The skies, however, were to be darkened once again, and this time it must have seemed as if the light would go out altogether. Gilbert Eddy fell sick. He had suffered much. Kind and gentle at all times, he was cut to the quick by the malice which seemed to pervade the attacks on his wife, and he viewed every onslaught on himself or upon any of the students as an attack upon her. Even when accused of conspiracy to murder, he never seems to have thought of himself in any other light save as the channel through which an attack was being made upon his wife.

Shortly after their return to Boston from Washington, he seemed to fail. He tried valiantly to help himself, insisting to Mrs. Eddy and the others that it was nothing but what he could well handle himself. But he grew steadily worse, and at last Mrs. Eddy decided to call in a doctor to diagnose the case. There had been much perplexity among her students, and a strong insistence that if the nature of the trouble were known it would be more readily met mentally. And so Dr. Rufus K. Noyes, a graduate of Dartmouth Medical School, who afterwards became a distinguished physician in Boston, was summoned. He diagnosed the case as valvular heart disease.

Mrs. Eddy, however, had her own views on the matter. Whatever the outward and visible *secondary* cause, the primary cause was the load of hatred, fear and worry which the patient Gilbert had had to bear through the brief years of their married life. Thirty years later her diagnosis was to be a commonplace, but in those days Professor Elmer Gates and a host of others, with their test tube experiments designed to show forth the chemical changes brought about in the human body through hatred and anger, fear and worry and other strong emotions, were still thirty years ahead. The theory that diseases are sometimes traceable to a nervous and so a mental origin had not been advanced in 1882 and would not be for many years afterwards. But Mrs. Eddy was quite sure of it, and once again, as in all times of crisis, she had to carry not only her own burden but that of her students also. As Gilbert sank from day to day, their anxiety mounted. To their fear of Kennedy and Spofford had now been added the new fear of Arens, and while Mrs. Eddy and Gilbert stood firm, the students seem to have faltered in dismay.

At daybreak on June 3, 1882, Gilbert Eddy died. Only the day before, he had felt so much better that he had ventured out for a ride on the street car. Julia Bartlett went with him, and all were no doubt much cheered by this evidence of better things, so much so that Mrs. Eddy was persuaded to retire early. But towards morning Gilbert passed away in his sleep, so quietly that those watching at his bedside were scarcely aware that any change had taken place. He was a gentle person even in death.

The passing of Gilbert Eddy may well be reckoned to mark the nadir of Mary's life. She had suffered much, especially in the days before she launched Christian Science. But always, up to now, there had been a great if ill-defined hope to which she could cling. In the long days and nights of invalidism at North Groton or Rumney or Hill she seems to have been roused again and again by a conviction that there was a way out and she would surely one day find it. But the passing of Gilbert Eddy not only deprived her of a strength and support she so sorely needed, but, what was far worse, it seemed to controvert the great claim she was making and upon which she and her followers had built so much. She never really doubted, apparently, but the demand upon her to justify her teaching was tremendous, and her first care was to meet it. Her own grief was nothing to her in the presence of the necessity of convincing herself and her followers, both those already with her and those to come, that nothing had happened that could or should shake their faith in any way. Gilbert Eddy was the victim of malicious mental malpractice, in her understanding of the term, and, if it was the last thing she did, she would make this clear to her followers and to the world. And so, at her request, the newspapers, the Boston *Herald,* the *Journal* and the *Post,* sent reporters to see her, and to them she told her story. The report of the interview which appeared in the *Post* on June 5th, 1882, is perhaps the most comprehensive of the three:

"My husband's death was caused by malicious mesmerism. Dr. C. J. Eastman, who attended the case after it had taken an alarming turn, declares the symptoms to be the same as those of arsenical poisoning. On the other hand, Dr. Rufus K. Noyes, late of the City Hospital, who held an autopsy over the body affirms that the corpse is free from all material poison, although Dr. Eastman still holds to his original belief. I know it was poison that killed him, not material poison, but mesmeric poison.

"My husband was in uniform health, and but seldom complained of any ailment. During his brief illness, just preceding his death, his continual cry was, 'Only relieve me of this continual suggestion, through the mind of poison, and I will recover.' It is well known that by constantly dwelling upon any subject in thought there finally comes the poison of belief through the whole system. . . .

"This is not the first case known of, where death has occurred from what appeared to be poison, and was so declared by the attending physicians, but in which the body, on being thoroughly examined by an autopsy was found to possess no signs of material poison. There was such a case in New York. Every one at first declared poison to have been the cause of death, as the symptoms were all there; but an autopsy contradicted the belief, and it was shown that the victim had no opportunity for procuring poison. . . .

"Circumstances debarred me from taking hold of my husband's case. He declared himself perfectly capable of carrying himself through, and I was so entirely absorbed in business that I permitted him to try, and when I awakened to the danger it was too late. . . . I do believe in God's supremacy over error, and this gives me peace."

Thus she held on and put up a bold front, until she had done what she could to safeguard the integrity of her great thesis and reassure her students. It was only when all had been done that she began to realize the full effect of the blow. The funeral services were held in the house on Columbus Avenue, after which the remains were taken by Mrs. George Choate to Sanbornton Bridge, by this time renamed Tilton, and interred in the Baker family lot in the old burying ground overlooking the Merrimac. But Mrs. Eddy was not able to go to the funeral. Neither did she go to the memorial service which was held in Hawthorne Hall on the following Sunday afternoon.

She almost sank under the load. Her students rallied as well as they could, but they were badly shaken, and only the most faithful really stood by her in her hour of trial. One of these was Arthur Buswell, a student who had gone through class with her in Lynn the previous year. He had moved to Cincinnati, and now, in response to an urgent telegram from Mrs. Eddy, hurried to Boston to do what he could to help. It was he who took charge of things and brought some semblance of order and calmness out of the chaos which followed Mrs. Eddy's enforced withdrawal. He saw, at once, that the first thing to do was to get her away from it all as completely as possible. He finally persuaded her to accept an invitation for herself and a companion, Miss Alice Sibley, to spend the next few weeks or months at his old homestead in the small country town of Barton, Vermont.

And so they set out, leaving the faithful Julia Bartlett and Mrs. Abbie Whiting to care for what was left to care for in the big house on Columbus Avenue.

The road back was a long one and the way dark enough: "O, I have nothing left me of earth or on it to love, as I do love, satisfied to have solitude and toil if only I had one to call my own!" "I cannot feel much interested in anything of earth. Long after I shall smile and appear happy shall I have to struggle alone with my great grief." So she wrote to two of her students in Boston.

But it was a fight to the finish, and she never really gave in for a moment. As Mary Beecher Longyear puts it in her records derived from Arthur Buswell, "After a night of agony, she would emerge from her struggle with a radiant face and luminous eyes, and they would hesitate to speak to her for fear of disturbing the peace which enveloped her."

It was her last great struggle with threatened failure and defeat before turning into the road which was to lead on to continuous success. In the summer of 1882, she descended into the depths, but before the summer was over she had planted her feet firmly on the ascending path. From there and then on, she moved in only one direction and that was, upward

Calvin Frye

CALVIN A. FRYE was born on August 24, 1845, in Frye village, Massachusetts. Frye village is now a part of Andover, and had originally been known as Frye's Mills because it first appeared as a settlement around the saw-mill and grist-mill of Enoch Frye II, who was Calvin's grandfather. The Fryes were an old New England family with worthy records in the war of the Revolution and that of 1812. Enoch Frye III, Calvin's father, was born at the turn of the century, and as his father Enoch II was prospering and he himself early developed "a desire for learning", he was sent, first of all, to Phillips Academy at Andover and, later, to Harvard, whence he graduated in 1821. At Harvard, he was in distinguished company, for his class was the class of Ralph Waldo Emerson, Samuel Hatch, Edward Loring and Francis Cabot, and before their graduation they all agreed to hold a reunion every year for fifty years. Enoch Frye III remained faithful to the agreement. He was present at the fiftieth and last reunion of his class at Cambridge, in 1871.

He had not, however, been able to fulfill his early promise, for he had hardly left college and started on a career of teaching which might have led to still better things, when he was stricken down with a serious illness which left him incurably lame and not too strong, and so he returned to Andover where he subsequently opened a small grocery store. Meanwhile, he had married one Lydia Barnard. They had four children, of whom Calvin was the third.

Small grocery stores in small towns were no more remunerative one hundred years ago than they are today, and Calvin and his brother Oscar had to go early to work; and so, after attending public school in Andover, Calvin was apprenticed as a machinist, and worked in Davis & Furber's machine shops in East Andover. Early in the sixties the family moved to Lawrence, a manufacturing town close by, and shortly afterwards, when he was twenty-six, Calvin married Miss Ada E. Brush of Lowell. She lived but one year, and after her death Calvin went back to his father's house in Lawrence.

It was a sad household. While the children were still young the mother had become insane, and although she had lucid intervals she had to be sent away periodically to an institution. The father was a cripple and a semi-invalid, and Calvin's sister, Lydia Roaf, who lived with them, had been early widowed. After the loss of his young wife, Calvin would not find much in his father's house to put him in better heart. But the Fryes were essentially of that New England temperament that takes trouble with a kind of placid resignation not to be found elsewhere. They were all members of the Congregational Church, and attended services regularly, but their religion was to them, not so much a comfort, as one of the unquestioned necessities of life, wherein the only real stimulus was derived from the avoidance of backsliding.

To a thought such as this, Christian Science, if it could be accepted at all, would come almost as a bewildering light. And so it literally did to Calvin Frye. He and his sister Lydia first heard of it from their sister-in-law, Mrs. Oscar Frye. The Oscar Fryes lived in Boston and had become interested in the new teaching to the extent of attending some of the Sunday afternoon meetings in Hawthorne Hall. Mrs. Frye's thoughts, as she heard the testimonies of healing, naturally turned to the insane mother in Lawrence, and at last she talked to Clara Choate about it, with the result that Mrs. Choate consented to take the case and do what she could to help. Within a very short time, to the utter amazement of Lydia and Calvin, their mother was completely restored. In a lucid interval, after her second commitment to an asylum, she had begged the family not to send her away from home again in any circumstances, and for years before she was restored through Christian Science, Lydia had done little else but care for her. And now her mother was well.

Neither Lydia nor Calvin hesitated a moment. They would learn all they could about the teaching which had done such wonderful things. And so Calvin went off at once to Lynn to see Mrs. Eddy, and joined a class she was then holding. It was hardly over when the pitiful little tragedy of the defection of the students in Lynn occurred, and Calvin Frye, it will be remembered, was one of the two students who remained faithful and watched with their teacher through the wretched night which followed. When Mrs. Eddy left Lynn for Boston, Calvin returned to Lawrence, and immediately began to devote all his spare time to the work of healing.

So things went, until early one morning in August, 1882, he received a telegram. It was from Barton, Vermont, from Mrs. Eddy telling him that she was that morning setting out for Boston, and asking him to meet her at Plymouth. Calvin made his decision at once. He packed a few things in order to be ready for any contingency, and set out for Plymouth. It was a momentous move, for it changed the whole course of his life. From the time he joined her at Plymouth and travelled with her, as he did, to Boston, Calvin Frye never left Mrs. Eddy for a single day until she passed away twenty-eight years later. History records few such devotions.

The Mrs. Eddy that Calvin Frye met at Plymouth was a very different person from the forlorn almost defeated woman who had made her way from Boston to the little town of Barton a short two months before. The first few weeks had been for her a veritable Gethsemane. There was no clear light anywhere. The little circle at Lynn was broken up and the larger circle in Boston, which had promised so well, was shaken and dismayed, and in the death of her husband she had lost not only a companion and friend, but one of her chiefest supports in her work. She was sixty-two, at an age when most people have almost rounded out their life's task. She had only just begun, and now it must have seemed as if even that beginning was being swept away.

Nevertheless, although the sorrow must have been real enough and at times, poignant past belief, it never seems to have done more even from the first than "endure for the night".

In Arthur Buswell's old homestead at Barton she was surrounded with love and kindness which she most needed, and, gradually the light came again. "I have never found a kindlier people," she writes to her friend, Clara Choate. "I am situated as pleasantly as I can be in the absence of the one true heart that has been so much to me. O, darling, I never shall master this point of missing him all the time, but I can try, and am trying as I must—to sever all the cords that bind me to person or things material."

How well she succeeded as the weeks passed is seen in Arthur Buswell's account of those days. "However ill she might have been the night before, each day found her planning for the future of her church and college, arranging for lectures to be given by students, looking about for new practitioners, and tirelessly devising means to extend the movement." By the middle of July she had quite clearly won her way through and is found writing to Clara Choate: "Hold the fort for I am coming. Be wise as a serpent and harmless as the doves that are cooing at my window. I hope my forty days in the wilderness are about over."

That they were indeed over is quickly seen. Something had happened to Mary at Barton which was to change the whole tempo of her life if not its course. There is no record of the talk she had with Calvin Frye as the train took them from Plymouth to Boston or of the plans for the future they discussed, but that the period of tentative action and uncertainty was over is clear. From the moment she reached the Boston and Maine Station in Boston, on that August evening in 1882, she carried things forward and was herself carried, with an impulsion which within the space of a few short years was to make her teaching one of the most discussed subjects in the United States and far beyond its borders.

Within a few days of her reaching Boston she had reopened the Metaphysical College, and shortly afterwards moved its headquarters from Number 569 to Number 571 Columbus Avenue. The new house was slightly larger and more convenient. The lecture room was established on the first floor and another room on the same floor as a general office. The rest of the house was occupied by Mrs. Eddy and some of her students, who lived on a co-operative plan and used the office on the first floor in rotation to meet their patients. Among the students who lived there from the first were the faithful Julia Bartlett, Abbie Whiting, Hanover Smith, Arthur Buswell and Calvin Frye. It was Calvin Frye who at once and quite naturally "took charge", and he did it with that amazing adaptability which enabled him in after years to fill uncomplainingly and with great efficiency every conceivable position in Mrs. Eddy's household. Mrs. Eddy rightly described him once as her man of all work. He could serve equally well in the capacity of coachman, secretary, treasurer, real estate agent, major domo and general manager.

In the new headquarters in Boston it was Calvin Frye who supervised the household, did the marketing, engaged the servants, paid the bills, interviewed tradesmen, and, in his spare time, helped Mrs. Eddy with her letters, ran errands for her, and was ready to represent her on any and every occasion. A quiet, soft-spoken man, not specially small, but giving the impression of smallness. A man who moved about unobtrusively and always appeared to be on hand when he was wanted. In the 1880's his hair was dark, and a flowing moustache, after the fashion of the day, merged into a pair of full mutton chop whiskers. Twenty years later, the hair was white and the mutton chop whiskers had gone, but it is the same Calvin Frye. He changed very little, and, from the first, displayed those qualities of devotion and efficiency which always characterized his association with Mrs. Eddy.

He was just what Mrs. Eddy most needed. Years afterwards she was to tell him that he had done more for the cause of Christian Science than any other one of her followers. She needed, especially in these early years, someone who would be almost her second self, who, in the stress of work, would do what she wanted to have done as she would do it, carrying out her wishes exactly to the letter without the friction of questions or criticism. She found such a one in Calvin Frye.

CHAPTER 30

The Rising Tide

FROM THIS POINT onwards the tide of Mrs. Eddy's teaching rises steadily. There is to be much ebbing and flowing. There are to be times when the wash backwards is so extreme as to give the impression of almost complete reversal, but viewed over the months and years the move forward is steady and emphatic.

Something happened at Barton almost if not quite as important as that which had supervened upon the little disaster at Lynn sixteen years before. It may be venturing too far into the realm of inference to say that at Lynn Mrs. Eddy discovered to her satisfaction "the allness of God", and at Barton the "nothingness of evil", yet it is a fact that from the time she returned to Boston from Barton she moved forward with more certainty and incomparably less apprehension than she had ever done before. She does not lessen, indeed, she rather increases, her admonitions to her students to be on their guard. But she is more and more insistent on the position that evil is powerless in the presence of good, and that the only way to see evil, is to see it for what it is proclaimed to be in her teaching, nothingness—in other words, an illusion.

"The ship of Science is again mounting the waves, rising above the billows, bidding defiance to the floodgates of error, for God is at the helm." So she writes to one of her students after she had been back in Boston some few weeks, and her confident assurance was if anything an understatement. No one could study with any care the record of these months without being struck with the sudden burgeoning forth to be seen on all hands. It is like nothing so much as the coming of an eastern spring after a specially rigorous winter. Whereas before, students had come to Mrs. Eddy for teaching in ones and twos, now they came so many at a time that the little class room at the college was taxed to capacity. The elder students, moreover, were now better able to stand by themselves and even to take a hand in helping those less experienced.

The outstanding event of these days was the founding of the *Journal of Christian Science,* afterwards called *The Christian Science Journal.* The first issue appeared on April 14, 1883, with Arthur Buswell as associate editor. It was at first a little eight-page paper issued every other month, and in the opening editorial of the first issue Mrs. Eddy set forth her objective. "The purpose of our paper", she writes, "is the desire of our heart, namely, to bring to many a household hearth health, happiness and increased power to be good and to do good."

It was an unpretentious little paper and its difficulties, financial and otherwise, in its early stages were many, but it provided Mrs. Eddy with a much wider platform than had hitherto been available and one she was able to use to the uttermost, for, in spite of certain peculiarities of style and the influence of a laboured age in writing, from which she found it difficult to shake free, Mrs. Eddy was one of the most effective occasional writers of her day. She had a quite remarkable vocabulary. By actual count it was much larger than that of her most distinguished contemporaries, and all her life, with a freedom often irritating to the purist, she fitted language to her ideas rather than her ideas to language. Like Emily Dickinson or Walt Whitman, she coined words and misused grammar without compunction or apology. Most of her articles in these early issues of the Journals were afterwards reprinted in her book *Miscellaneous Writings,* and are among the most effective of her lesser writings.

295

A great difficulty about this time was the growing tendency to plagiarize her works, and early in 1883 she determined—possibly fulfilling Gilbert Eddy's wishes—to bring suit against Arens and stop the circulation of his pamphlet, most of which, as has already been noted, was simply a transcript from *Science and Health*. The case came up in the Circuit Court at Boston a few days after the publication of the first issue of the *Journal,* and in view of what was to follow in the same connection within a few years, Arens's defence was significant. Arens contended, through his counsel, that he could not have infringed Mrs. Eddy's copyright, because Mrs. Eddy's book *Science and Health* was not original with her but had been largely copied from the works of Phineas P. Quimby of Portland, Maine. When proof of this contention was in due course demanded, Arens could produce none. George Quimby of Belfast, Maine, who had his father's manuscripts in his possession, refused to submit them for inspection, and Arens had no proof to offer. The case was accordingly quashed, and the court issued a perpetual injunction against Arens restraining him from "printing, selling, giving away or distributing in any manner" his pamphlet, under pain of a fine of $10,000. It was further decreed by the court that the remaining copies of the pamphlet to the number of thirty-eight hundred should be "put under the knife and their unlawful existence destroyed". The costs of the suit, $113, were taxed against Arens. When the Quimby Manuscripts were finally published, as they were some forty years later, it was found that there was no ground for Arens's contention, but the subject was to come up again several times before it was finally laid to rest.

The immediate effect of the suit was to safeguard more certainly the contents of the *Journal.*

As will be clear enough later, these vigorous measures by Mrs. Eddy were not motivated entirely nor even principally by a desire to prevent her legal rights being infringed but to preserve the purity and integrity of her teaching as she understood it. As Christian Science gained in popularity and publicity, first one and then another student, dissatisfied with his position or prospects or the teaching he was given, would go off and found a sect of his own, teaching and preaching his own version of Mrs. Eddy's teaching, calling it Christian Science and contending for it that it represented an advance on what Mrs. Eddy taught or a correction of her errors. A succession of highly placed students did just this, and in less than two years from the Arens suit quite a number of "Christian Science Circles" had sprung up, the teachings of which had little or no relation with that set down in *Science and Health*.

But while the *Journal* to an increasing extent carried the word of Christian Science now here now there all over the world, the great forward movement, as far as Boston was concerned, was promoted by the Sunday services in Hawthorne Hall. These were becoming increasingly popular. The fact that the meetings were held on Sunday afternoon, instead of at the time of the regular church services on Sunday morning or evening, enabled many people to attend who would not have done so if it had involved being absent from their own church. The order of service was much the same as it had been in the Baptist Tabernacle on Shawmut Avenue; a hymn, silent prayer followed by the Lord's Prayer, then short readings from the Bible and *Science and Health*, another hymn and finally the sermon. But the character of a meeting was preserved by the fact that questions were allowed and even invited.

At first Mrs. Eddy spoke every Sunday, but later she sometimes delegated one of her students to take her place, and not infrequently invited a minister of one of the other denominations who had in any way shown himself sympathetic towards her teaching to occupy the pulpit. She generally let it be known when she was going to preach; but when she found, as she did, that when she was scheduled to speak, the hall was often crowded to overflowing and when she was not so scheduled the attendance was much less, she adopted the plan of purposely leaving it uncertain until the last moment who was going to occupy the pulpit. As a result, the attendance became more uniform, and meanwhile she had inaugurated a policy which she was to adhere to invariably in the future, that of discouraging dependence upon herself. She would often arrange with a student to give the address, and then change her mind at the last moment and speak after all.

Mrs. Eddy presented a striking figure on the platform. Always well-dressed, she carried herself well and had about her an air of distinction and command which seemed to compel attention even before she began to speak. She had, moreover—she had it all her life—a knack of wearing her clothes so as to make them appear much better and more costly than they were. Mary Harris Curtis, one of her students, in her recollections recalls an incident at one of the Hawthorne Hall meetings which illustrates the point. When it came to question time, a woman in the audience asked Mrs. Eddy if she thought it was Christian "to wear purple velvet and diamonds", alluding to her costume, to which Mrs. Eddy after a moment's hesitation replied:

"There are ladies here, I presume, with much more expensive dresses on, as this is velveteen, thirty-six inches wide, and one dollar a yard. The cross and ring were given me by those who have been healed in Christian Science with the request that I wear them." It would perhaps be hard to imagine a more effective reply.

But as the meetings in Hawthorne Hall grew in popularity and tales of healing began to be noised abroad with increasing frequency, the ministers of more orthodox faiths were roused to action, some of them to sympathetic investigation, but most of them to vigorous opposition and denunciation. Indeed, Boston in 1883 seems to have set the pace and quality for all future denunciations. There was about it all a venom and a "smouldering fury" which was at times reminiscent of nothing so much as the days of Salem witch-baiting. The two great protagonists of orthodoxy were the Reverend L. T. Townsend, D.D., member of the faculty of Boston University, and the Reverend Stacy Fowler, editor of the *Homiletic Review*.

Doctor Townsend came out straight from the shoulder on one occasion, the Boston Methodist Preachers' Meeting, when his topic was "Prayer and Healing". Alluding to Mrs. Eddy as "this woman", he denounced her in so many words as a fraud and a charlatan, declared that her teaching was "a crude attempt to resuscitate the defunct idealism of the nihilistic type which appeared in the Middle Ages", and that her views upon all metaphysical matters—"we speak very mildly"—are a "self-contradicting hotchpotch". When the meeting was over, some of the clergymen present urged Doctor Townsend to publish his address. This he subsequently did under the title of *The Boston Craze*.

With a rather engaging inconsistency, Doctor Townsend, at the close of his pamphlet, has this to say: "But notwithstanding these criticisms upon this misnamed Christian Science, fairness requires us to add that this woman, Mrs. Eddy, by her methods, is successful in healing disease. Our professional faith-workers are therefore in danger of losing their laurels at the hands of one whom they must regard as an infidel."

In other words, it is the old cry: "Give God the glory! As to this man we know he is a sinner."

The Reverend Stacy Fowler took another line. He is quite confident that the movement is already past the peak of its prosperity, and that nothing awaits Mrs. Eddy and her teaching in the future but steady decline and final extinction. Writing in the *Homiletic Review* for August, 1883, Fowler says confidently enough:

"While 'healers' are multiplying it is evident that the science is waning. Mrs. Eddy writes that her ability to teach the art of healing in her classes in twelve lessons is a greater wonder than her power of instantaneous healing. She may teach the principles of the science in twelve lessons, but she cannot impart her power, her personalism in twelve, nor in twelve hundred lessons. The real *ictus* is her personalism. Her pupils are but feeble imitators of their teacher. Hence the spell is losing its charm. The movement is losing its momentum. In its present form it is an epidemic and as an epidemic it will pass away, as did the Blue Glass mania. It is as transcendental as was Brook Farm, and like that experiment it may be useful in demonstrating that sentiment, fancy and fitful impulse are not the solid facts of science, nor the panacea for human ills."

Doctor Fowler can hardly have had more than a few weeks wherein he could have been accounted a true prophet, for it must quickly have become evident that the movement, far from losing momentum, as he confidently declared, was gaining momentum at a quite bewildering rate. Christian Science and the amazing way in which it was spreading became good copy for the newspapers. There is nothing that an editor likes better than a good controversy, provided that it can be kept within bounds and the newspaper itself not be involved, and Christian Science wherever it appeared in any community inevitably aroused controversy. Editors, it is true, often had a hard time, especially in small towns. A neutral attitude on their part was all too often construed by their orthodox readers as one of affording help and comfort to the enemy.

Later on, Mrs. Eddy herself entered the lists with vigour, and scarcely a Sunday passed at Hawthorne Hall without her replying to some newspaper or pulpit criticism, if not responding to disapproval voiced from the floor. Some of the issues raised were a little awkward, to say the least, but she parried them all successfully. More than once, for instance, someone would stand to ask, in accusing tones, why this exponent of Mind over matter occasionally wore spectacles during her platform appearances. She made short shrift of such inquirers, for in presenting her doctrine as a practical idealism she disclaimed any inconsistency in doing such things as seem needful until the student reaches the point in demonstrable understanding where such things no longer seem needful.[1]

In these early days of advance her energies were taxed to the uttermost to keep in touch with a movement which was rapidly outgrowing all

[1] Nevertheless, her use of glasses off and on throughout the years proved a stumbling block to many of her followers, who remained concerned, like the savants of old, with how many angels could dance on the head of a pin. And this same type of essentially superficial criticism was to plague her in other directions. As late as 1900, the Episcopal congress at Providence, in an effort to discredit the new movement, pointed to the fact that Mrs. Eddy had had teeth extracted under local anaesthesia by Dr. John M. Fletcher of Concord, and now wore artificial dentures, while claiming to restore carious bones. But far from evading the issue, Mrs. Eddy seized upon the challenge to write in the Boston Herald, December 2, 1900: "I have always instructed students of Christian Science to be wise and discreet, conforming, where conscience is not offended, to the usages of men." Asserting that there could be no logical objection to anaesthetics where pain was not otherwise dispensed with, she counseled full co-operation wherever the services of a dental surgeon were involved. As a matter of fact, she reminded her readers, this cardinal point was made on page 464 of *Science and Health,* in unambiguous words: "If from an injury or from any cause, a Christian Scientist were siezed with pain so violent that he could not treat himself mentally,—and the Scientists had failed to relieve him,—the sufferer could call a surgeon, who would give him a hypodermic injection, then, when the belief of pain was lulled, he could handle his own case mentally." After all, it was no more than a question of the individual doing what is practical to him until and unless something else becomes practical to him. This aspect of her teaching is clearly elucidated on pages 253 and 254 of her book, where she writes that "God requires perfection, but not until the battle between Spirit and flesh is fought and the victory won. . . . This task God demands us to accept lovingly to-day, and to abandon *so fast as practical,* the material. ."

bounds. By the spring of 1884, it was so well established in Chicago that urgent calls were coming to Mrs. Eddy to go out there and teach a class.

A journey from Boston to Chicago was much more of an undertaking then than it is today, and Mrs. Eddy was thronged with work. The *Journal,* the editing of which really devolved upon her, was gaining rapidly in circulation and brought inquiries from many quarters. Every day added to her mail. She was, moreover, teaching regularly in her college, lecturing every Thursday evening, as well as preaching most Sundays at Hawthorne.

In the circumstances, Mrs. Eddy felt she could not leave Boston for Chicago. It would mean a full month's absence, and it seemed as though there was no one quite fitted to be left in charge. They were all still pitifully dependent upon her for guidance. She finally decided to ask Clara Choate to go to Chicago in her stead. Mrs. Choate had held the fort faithfully and successfully during the difficult period when Mrs. Eddy was in Washington. She had not infrequently taken her place on the platform at Hawthorne Hall, and she was one of her oldest students.

But when Mrs. Eddy broached the question to Clara Choate, she found herself suddenly faced with a situation which, until she had finally ridden it down, was to face her frequently in the future. Mrs. Choate was doing very well in Boston. She had a large practice, and, moving as she did in a good social circle, she enjoyed a special distinction from her close association with a woman who was rapidly becoming one of the best discussed people in the country. Chicago was in those days to the average Bostonian very much "the West", and Mrs. Choate all too evidently feared that, if she went to Chicago, the more successful she was the greater likelihood would there be of her having to remain there. This did not appeal to her at all, and so she declined.

Mrs. Eddy seems to have realized that, with the movement growing as it was, many opportunities would be lost if her students were not ready to make sacrifices and go without question where opportunity offered. Years afterwards she was wont to maintain that Christian Scientists should be "minute men and women", and it would seem to have been the reluctance of Clara Choate to go to Chicago at her request that first aroused her to an exaction of instant willing service from her followers, such as was later to become characteristic of the movement as a whole.

The immediate step she took in the matter was one that afterwards occasioned her much trouble. Realizing the importance of the problem before her from the point of view of the movement as a whole, she gathered together all the students actually resident in her house and laid the issue before them, requesting them, as she did not wish any thought of dissension to get abroad, to regard the meeting as private. It was a mistake she never would have made in later years. The rock upon which the little church in Lynn had broken up—jealousy—was still a menace. Those who had been summoned to the meeting—some of them at any rate—could not resist the kudos such a summons would surely give them among their fellows. They took care to let the fact of the meeting be known and then surrounded its proceedings with the utmost secrecy. It was alluded to mysteriously as the P. M. Society, and quickly became a burning question of debate not only with the students in Boston but further afield.

It met only twice, but so widespread and lasting was the discussion it occasioned that four years later Mrs. Eddy, in reply to charges that the proceedings at these meetings were "terrible and too shocking to relate", felt obliged to explain their nature through the *Journal*. After declaring that the "Society" met only twice, she continues: "The first subject given out for consideration was this: 'There is no Animal Magnetism'. There was no advice given, no mental work, and there were no transactions at those meetings which I would hesitate to have known. . . . The second P.M. convened in about one week from the first. The subject given out at that meeting was in substance, 'God is All! there is none beside Him.' This proved to be our last meeting."

But the stir was sufficient to alienate Clara Choate. There was, as so often happens, no definite breach at first, but the two drifted further apart until some three years later her name was formally dropped from the roll of the Christian Scientist Association and Church.

Meanwhile, Mrs. Eddy determined to go to Chicago herself. She handed over the management of the *Journal* to one of the students, a Mrs. Emma Hopkins, suspended her classes at the college and her Thursday evening lectures and, accompanied by Calvin Frye as secretary and a Mrs. Sarah Crosse as companion, set out for Chicago, to teach a class of thirty-three—made up of eleven men and twenty-two women (according to the official history of First Church, Chicago). During her stay she gave a lecture to some four hundred people, "Whom do men say that I am?" at Hershey Hall. That was in April, 1884. She spent a month there, and could have spent much longer if she had taken everyone who wanted to enroll in her classes. Would-be students came not only from all over Chicago, but from much further afield, while shortly after her return to Boston applications began to be received from as far west as California. In the issue of the *Journal* for September, 1886, appears the name of one Ella Bradshaw, C.S.D., who, in accordance with the practice at that time, had opened the "California Metaphysical College" in San Jose, announcing that it afforded "an opportunity on the Pacific Coast for receiving a course of instruction in the rudiments of Christian Science".

The Quimby Manuscripts

FEW STRANGER OR more contradictory controversies have ever raged in
the realm of literature or philosophy than that which has surrounded the
manuscripts of Phineas P. Quimby and the allegation that the teaching
of Mary Baker Eddy is entirely derived from them. Commencing in 1883,
it still persists. The whole question, of course, depends on an understanding of what Mrs. Eddy actually taught. The protagonists of the claims of
Phineas Quimby maintain that she taught just what Quimby taught, while
at the same time insisting that if Quimby could have heard what she was
teaching he would have turned in his grave.

Thus George Quimby in a letter dated November 11th, 1901, quoted
by Horatio Dresser in his book *The Quimby Manuscripts*, is quite
emphatic on the point:

"The religion which she teaches certainly is hers, for which I cannot be
too thankful; for I should be loath to go down to my grave feeling that
my father was in any way connected with Christian Science."

As has been seen, Mrs. Eddy, for many years, certainly from 1862 to the time of her first class in Lynn in 1871, unhesitatingly attributed her teaching to Quimby. It is possible, however, from her first association with him that what she was attributing to Quimby was her own interpretation of what he was teaching, and not at all what he would have regarded as his teaching if he had understood the differences involved in her interpretation of it. In any case, she steadily, if quite unconsciously, grew further and further away from him, but it was not until she saw, as the result of her first class in Lynn, the incompatibility of her views with the Quimby system of manipulation that she realized, not only what she was teaching was not what Quimby had taught, but that her great task in the future was to be the freeing herself and her teaching from the essentials of Quimby's doctrine.

What it took Mrs. Eddy nine years to discover, the protagonists of Quimby never discovered, and Julius Dresser, who first publicly raised the issue in 1883, had no doubts at all on the subject.

Julius Dresser, it will be remembered, was the man who first brought Mrs. Eddy and Quimby together. It was he who came back to Doctor Vail's Water Cure establishment at Hill with a wonderful story of his own cure by the new doctor in Portland and about many other cures. Mary, of course, knew all about it. Indeed, as has been noted, it was with the express determination that Hill should only be a stopping place on the way to Portland and Quimby that she consented to Abigail's earnest solicitations that she go to Doctor Vail's establishment.

That was back in 1862, and during the four years of her association with Quimby which followed she had been in constant touch with Julius Dresser, and it was, of course, to Dresser that she sent her appeal for help after Quimby had died and she was struggling at Lynn to complete her recovery from a well-nigh fatal accident.

Shortly after Quimby's death, Dresser, who had married, went west, and for some years he and his wife practised a form of mental healing out there. By 1881-1882, word of the new system being taught in Boston reached him, and when he found that the Mrs. Eddy who was identified with the movement was the Mary Patterson he had known in Portland, he determined to make his way east again and see what was going forward.

His first impression, before he set out, was possibly that Mrs. Eddy was making a success of "Quimbyism", and, remembering her regard for himself and the appeal she had made to him for help, he may have thought that he might as well have his share in any success that was being achieved.

He did not approach Mrs. Eddy directly after his arrival in Boston. He decided to have all the facts before he made any move, and these facts when he discovered them were not at all to his liking. As the result of judicious enquiry and sundry visits to Hawthorne Hall, all he could see in Mrs. Eddy's teaching was something very like an "apostasy" from Quimby. As George Quimby was to write several years later, "the teaching was all too evidently her own," but it ought to be the teaching of Quimby.

The possibility that what Mrs. Eddy was teaching was something she herself had evolved never occurred to him apparently. Mrs. Eddy, the Mary Patterson who for four years had been associated with Quimby and himself, ought to be teaching Quimbyism and that was all there was about it as far as Julius Dresser was concerned. If she was not teaching Quimbyism, then she must be teaching something fraudulent and in any event was clearly guilty, in some inexplicable way, of plagiarism.

Julius Dresser opened his campaign in a roundabout fashion. He did not enter the field in person, but actually or fictionally in the guise of one "A.O." who, under date of February 8, 1883, wrote a long letter to the Boston *Post*.

After declaring that "many would remember with interest, the late Dr. P. P. Quimby of Portland, Me., who so successfully practised for about 20 years the mental method of treating disease, which is now claiming so much attention from all classes and is so widely accepted as the surest and best method of eradicating disease," "A.O." goes on to mention that at the time Doctor Quimby was practising his method was "new to the world", and that "although he did a vast amount of good, he had, like all minds that take the lead, to bow to the judgement of smaller minds and meekly accept the title of humbug, which ignorance always bestows on wisdom that it cannot understand".

"In speaking with a gentleman on this subject a short time since," he continues, "I was surprised and pleased to learn that he owed his life to the wisdom of that good man, that he had been a member of the same household for a length of time; and also a student of Dr. Quimby. . . . This gentleman informs me that Dr. Quimby did a great amount of writing on the subject of mental healing, or his theory which he termed 'Science of Health'."

Having thus made it perfectly clear who was meant—to Mrs. Eddy at any rate—"A.O." advances to a direct attack: "Some parties," he says, "healing through a mental method which they claim to have discovered, did, in reality, obtain their first thoughts of this truth from Dr. Quimby, and have added their own opinions to the grain of wisdom thus obtained, presenting to the people a small amount of wheat mixed with a great quantity of chaff. . . Dr. Quimby was, in many respects, a wonderful man; he feared nothing, and he dared to do anything that his wisdom taught him was right. He was no respecter of persons, and upheld only truth, without regard to whence it came. The opinions of the people, with regard to himself and his ideas, were of no importance in his eyes. When we see a few like him in the same field of action, who, while they are in the world are yet not of it, we shall see sin and sickness decreasing, instead of increasing."

Some ten days later, namely, on February 19, 1883, there appeared in the Boston *Post* an answer to this letter. It was signed "E.G." Whether these initials concealed the identity of Mrs. Eddy herself, as internal evidence would seem to indicate, or the letter was the work of one of her students, as is not impossible, certain it is that the letter itself lays the foundation for all further repudiation of similar charges.

If "E.G." at times seems ungenerous to Quimby, it must be remembered that, after all Mrs. Eddy had gone through in her own mental struggles and through the many misdemeanings in her students attributed

307

to Quimby's doctrine, her general estimate of his teaching must have undergone a great change. She still regards and speaks of him, as she always does even under the most trying provocation, with kindness and gratitude, but she no longer regards him as the inspired prophet such as he had appeared to her in the Portland days twenty years before, when surrounded by the aura of her own thought. And so "E.G." writes. Using the laboured editorial "we" of that day, she begins mildly, professing interest in "A.O.'s" letter because it had also been her privilege to know "the late Dr. Phineas P. Quimby, who died many years ago, and whom we regarded very highly". "He was", she continued, "a contemporary of the noted mesmerist Dr. Newton, and often amused us with his unique descriptions of their mesmeric performances. He, Dr. Quimby, told us, one evening on our way to a lecture at the city hall in Portland, that he would exhibit some of his powers to us in the hall. Accordingly, after we were seated, he said to us, 'I shall set them to coughing', and immediately one after another commenced coughing until the assembly in general joined in chorus, longer or shorter, according to directions. Then all of a sudden the coughing stopped, but our laughing was not over, for immediately the people commenced sneezing as if a sudden coryza had seized them, and pocket handkerchiefs were in quick requisition."

Having thus created the atmosphere evidently desired, that in which the subject should not be taken too seriously, "E.G." gets down to the real issue:

"Dr. Quimby's method of treating the sick was manipulation; after immersing his hands in water he rubbed the head, etc. He never called his practice a mental method of treating diseases to our knowledge, and we knew him and his history. He was very successful in many cases of lameness. We asked him several times if he had any system, aside from manipulation and mesmerism of treating disease, and he always evaded the subject. We were his patient, but he never gave us any further information relating to his practice, but always said it is a secret of my own, and I have thought best not to divulge it. After treating the sick he would retire to a side room and note with pen the especial case with such other paraphrase as he thought best. This copy he gave to certain individuals to bring out, or, as he said, 'put into shape'. His scribblings were fragmentary, but sometimes very interesting. He requested us to transform them frequently and to give them different meanings, which we did. He never took a student, to our knowledge, or gave information that was practical, of his healing. He called his scribblings, essays, but never the 'Science of Health'. *Science and Health* is a work of Mrs. Mary B. G. Eddy, issued in 1875. She discovered the science of healing embodied in that work, after years of practical proof through homeopathy, that mind instead of matter is the principle of pathology, and finally sealed her proof by a severe casualty, from which she recovered through her exercise of mental power over the body, after the regular physicians had pronounced her case incurable. . . . A grateful multitude acknowledge the blessings of her mental system of treating disease. Perhaps the following, in the words of her husband, the late Dr. Asa G. Eddy, best express it: 'Mrs. Eddy's works are the outgrowths of her life. I never knew so unselfish an individual.' . . .

E.G."

Five days later, Julius Dresser replies and this time comes at last right out into the open. On February 24th he writes once again to the Boston *Post,* characterizing "E.G.'s" letter as a tissue of falsehoods, accusing Mrs. Eddy of plagiarism and ingratitude, and winding up with what he evidently regards as a knockout blow, a republishing of Mrs. Eddy's pitiful plea to him for help in 1866.

"If 'E.G.' was ever a patient of Dr. Quimby's, as she claims," he says, "and 'knew the history', she knows that her article above referred to is false from beginning to end. The undersigned is a quiet, humble citizen of Boston, who seeks no controversy with anybody. But when he knows positively that truth is being outraged and dragged in the dirt, he will step forward and uphold the truth and let error become, as it always does, its own destroyer. As 'E.G.' has maligned and belittled a good man, who gave up his life for the cause of truth, and actually died for sick people,

I will call as a witness the same Mrs. Eddy whom 'E.G.' speaks of. This lady was a patient and a student of the late Dr. P. P. Quimby of Portland, Me., in the winter of 1862 and '63. She was then known as Mrs. Patterson, wife of Dr. Patterson, dentist. The writer of the communication was a patient and student of Dr. Quimby's at different times, from the year 1860 to 1865, including the period when Mrs. Patterson-Eddy was acting in the same capacity. There are other persons now in Boston who were likewise patients of Dr. Quimby at the same time, and who understand all the facts herein related.

"Now Mrs. Patterson-Eddy knows positively that the assertions of 'E.G.' in last Monday's *Post* are a tissue of falsehoods. There are only some shades of truth on mere minor points contained in 'E.G.'s' article. Mrs. Patterson-Eddy knows that the late Dr. P. P. Quimby of Portland, Me., was actually and solely originator and founder of a mental method of treating diseases. . . .

"She knows also that he called his peculiar theory the science of health, and that from him she got this name for the doctrine incorporated in her books. Dr. Quimby never had regular students, but to such of his patients as could understand him he freely explained his life-giving doctrine, for it was no secret, and such ones had access also to a portion of his writings, and copied them, as did Mrs. Patterson-Eddy. Such persons as herself and others of an inquiring mind were therefore in a sense students of the doctor, and they made the most of their opportunities.

"At the time of the 'severe casualty' stated by 'E.G.' as having happened to Mrs. Patterson-Eddy, the latter wrote to the undersigned a letter in part as follows:

" 'Two weeks ago I fell on the sidewalk, and struck my back on the ice, and was taken up for dead, came to consciousness amid a storm of vapours from cologne, chloroform, ether, camphor, etc., but to find myself the helpless cripple I was before I saw Dr. Quimby.

" 'The physician attending said I had taken the last step I ever should, but in two days I got out of bed *alone* and *will* walk; but yet I confess I am frightened, and out of the nervous heat my friends are forming, spite of me, the terrible spinal affection from which I have suffered so long and hopelessly. . . . Now *can't you* help me? I believe you can. I write this with this feeling; I think that I could help another in my condition if they had not placed their intelligence in matter. This I have not done, and yet I am slowly failing. Won't you write me if you will undertake for me if I can get to you? . . .

" 'Respectfully,

MARY M. PATTERSON'

"This letter is in the handwriting of Mrs. Patterson-Eddy, and can be seen by the truth-loving readers of the *Post* by calling at my office at No. 14 Chester Square, Boston. At the same place other papers and persons can be consulted to prove the statements above made. Do not take my word as evidence, reader, nor that of anybody else. Talk is too cheap. Call and get the facts. When Dr. Quimby's writings shall be given to the world in print, it will then be seen whether 'E.G.' has correctly called them 'mere scribblings', or whether truly they are the master delineations of a science of truth and health that shall become the healing of the nations.

J. A. DRESSER"

To this letter, on February 23rd, 1883, Mrs. Eddy replied over her own name. She is quite clearly not at all disconcerted. She re-asserts "E.G.'s" original statement and declares emphatically that far from being a tissue of falsehoods they are "strictly true", "for all time". She states:

"We had laid the foundation for mental healing before we ever saw Dr. Quimby; were an homeopathist without a diploma, owing to our aversion to the dissecting room. We made our first experiments in mental healing about 1853, when we were convinced that mind had a science which, if understood, would heal all diseases; we were then investigating that science, but never saw Dr. Q. until 1862. Mr. Dresser's statement that 'Mrs. Eddy knows positively that the assertions of "E.G." in last Monday's *Post* are a tissue of falsehoods', is untrue; we answer for all time that those assertions were strictly true. We never were a student of

Dr. Quimby's, and Mr. Dresser knows that. Dr. Q. never had students to our knowledge. He was a humanitarian, but a very unlearned man; he never published a work in his life; was not a lecturer or teacher. He was somewhat of a remarkable healer, and at the time we knew him he was unknown as a mesmerist. We were one of his patients. He manipulated his patients, but possibly back of his practice he had a theory in advance of his method, and, as we now understand it, and have since discovered, he mingled that theory with mesmerism. We knew him about twenty years ago, and aimed to help him. We saw he was looking in our direction and asked him to write his thoughts out. He did so, and then we would take that copy to correct, and, sometimes, so transform it that he would say it was our composition, which it virtually was, but we always gave him back the copy and, sometimes, wrote his name on the back of it. . . .

"At Swampscott, Mass., in 1866, we recovered in a moment of time from a severe accident, considered fatal by the regular physician, and regained the internal action that had stopped, and the use of our limbs that were palsied. . . . But the minds around us at that time were unacquainted with our mental theory. One individual of strong intellectual power, and little spirituality even occasioned us some momentary fears of our ability to hold on to this wonderful discovery. In one of these moments of fear we wrote to Mr. Dresser. . . . We sought for once the encouragement of one we believed friendly, also with whom we had conversed on Dr. Q.'s method of healing, and when we said to him, 'it is a mystery,' he replied to the effect that he believed no one but the Doctor himself knew how he healed. But lo! after we had found mental healing and nearly twenty years have elapsed during which we have taught some 600 students and published five or six thousand volumes on this subject, already circulated in the United States and Europe, the aforesaid gentleman announces to the public, Dr. Quimby, the founder of mental healing."

Shortly after the appearance of these letters, the Arens's Plagiarism Case, as already described, came up before the courts. Mrs. Eddy won her case on all counts, and her claims to copyright in *Science and Health* were finally established, but the great Quimby controversy continued almost unabated for many years. It may be disposed of shortly here. In 1885, Mrs. Eddy published a pamphlet entitled *Historical Sketch of Metaphysical Healing*. In this she once again covered the ground and re-affirmed her position. Then, in 1887, learning that an attempt was being made to secure the "Quimby Manuscripts" for publication, she boldly carried the war into the enemies' camp by offering to publish the manuscripts herself, at her own expense, and to hand over the proceeds to the owner of the copyright, on certain conditions. In due course there appeared in the Portland papers the following notice:

"Important Offer

"Mr. George A. Quimby, son of the late Phineas P. Quimby,—over his own signature, and before a witness—stated, in 1883, that he had in his possession at that time *all* the manuscripts written by his father. I hereby declare to expose the falsehoods of parties publicly intimating that I have appropriated matter belonging to the aforesaid Quimby, that I will pay the cost of printing and publishing the first edition of these manuscripts, with the author's name attached:

"*Provided*,—That I am allowed first to examine said Manuscripts, and that I find they were Mr. P. P. Quimby's own compositions, and not mine, that were left with him many years ago—or that they have not since his death, in 1865, been stolen from my published works; and also, that I am given the right to bring out this one edition under copyright of the owner of said Manuscripts, and that all the money accruing from the sale of book shall be paid to said owner. Some of Mr. Quimby's purported writings, quoted by J. A. Dresser, were my own words, as nearly as I can recollect them.

"There is a great demand for my book *Science and Health*. Hence Mr. Dresser's excuse for the delay in publishing Quimby's Manuscripts, namely, that this age is not sufficiently enlightened to be benefited by them (?) is lost; for if I have copied from Quimby, and my book is accepted, this acceptance creates a demand for his writings.

"MARY BAKER G. EDDY"

313

But George Quimby, who had the manuscripts in his possession, stead-fastly refused to allow them to be published. He rather unconvincingly claimed that Mrs. Eddy's offer was only a device to get the manuscripts into her own hands, where they could easily be "altered or destroyed". It could, of course, have been arranged for Mrs. Eddy to examine the manuscripts in the presence of a third party and make her decision there and then. However, they were not published and were not to be for many years more. Julius Dresser had to content himself with writing and publishing *The True History of Mental Science,* which he did in the spring of 1887. Mrs. Eddy replied in the *Journal,* and the following year George Quimby published an article on his father in the *New England Magazine.* In 1895 Julius Dresser and his wife, Annette Dresser, brought out a book, *The Philosophy of P. P. Quimby,* and since then the contro-versy has continued down to the present day. After the publication of the famous manuscripts in 1921, however, it has lost much of the mystery which up to that time had constituted its chief attraction.

George Quimby's statement to the effect that Mrs. Eddy's teaching "certainly is hers", and that he would be loath to think that his father was "in any way connected with Christian Science", would seem to be final.

Tremont Temple

BUT WHETHER IT was an attack on her doctrine by ministers of religion and others who differed from her, or an attack on her claim to be the true discoverer of that doctrine, as seen in the onslaughts of Julius Dresser and others, the only effect upon Mrs. Eddy and the progress of the movement she was fostering was to aid them. The effect of the Julius Dresser controversy was to stimulate public interest.

Mrs. Eddy and her teaching were rapidly becoming the most talked of subjects in Boston, and a situation arose which required all the woman's determination to offset. It became fashionable to know her, and still more fashionable to invite her to be present at various social gatherings. Whenever there was a prospect that by so doing she could promulgate her teaching, Mrs. Eddy was glad and even eager to accept, but when there was no such prospect and the motive for the invitation was curiosity or social prestige, she was vigorous and often curt in her refusals. It was, however, at just such gatherings that she found many of those destined later to become prominent in the movement.

The years 1883 to 1885 were particularly notable in this respect. Julia

Bartlett has already been mentioned. Another important figure was that of Ira O. Knapp, who later took a prominent part in the founding of The Mother Church and was one of its Directors. His long white patriarchal beard and kindly ways made him for years one of the most picturesque figures in the movement. Like many others, he was definitely attached to Christian Science through a remarkable healing, that of his wife, who, after years of helpless invalidism as a result of which she had lost the use of her limbs, was restored suddenly and completely to health.

Ira O. Knapp came of sturdy New England stock. Like Mrs. Eddy, he was born in the hills of New Hampshire—on June 7, 1839—having first seen the light in the little town of Lyman, not far from the great bend of the Connecticut River at Fifteen Miles Falls. He could trace his ancestry through his father's line to one Aaron Knapp, who settled at Taunton, Massachusetts, in 1639, about the time when "the son of Thunder", Thomas Hooker, and his followers were "planting" the three towns of Hartford, Windsor and Wethersfield, in the land which was afterwards to be called Connecticut. A later ancestor, Abeal Knapp, was a soldier in the Revolutionary War and was the first of his family to live in New Hampshire. Ira attended the district school of his town and the academies at Newbury and Peacham, Vermont. Afterwards, he farmed and taught school. He also, as time went on, held such local offices as school superintendent and selectman of his town and justice of the peace of his county. He took a wife, Miss Flavia S. Stickney, from among his own people in Lyman. That was in 1866, and some eighteen years later, this same Flavia, through her infirmities, brought Ira and herself into Christian Science and so changed the course of their lives.

Another figure was Joseph S. Eastaman, a retired sea captain of the old school, later, one of the Directors of The Mother Church. Replete with high adventure, shipwrecks and strange wanderings in India, China, Peru, he, too, was brought to Christian Science through the healing of his wife. He had, it seems, been to Hawthorne Hall several times, and at last applied directly to Mrs. Eddy for help. Not a little to his amazement, Mrs. Eddy, instead of offering to help his wife, surprised him by asking why he did not heal his wife himself. She then appears to have explained to him that if he would enter one of her classes he could learn how this might be done. Not a little incredulous, he agreed, with the result that within a few days, with the assurance of a man who all his life had been used to doing things, he began using what little he knew in the direction indicated, apparently with excellent result. As he puts it in his own record of the matter, "As I understood the rudiments, I began to treat her; and, so quickly did she respond to the treatment, that she was able to avail herself of the kindly invitation of the teacher to accompany me to the final session."

But perhaps the most notable adherents to the cause about this time, notable because of the strange part they were later destined to play in the history of the movement, were Josephine Woodbury and Augusta Stetson. Of these, Josephine Woodbury had known and admired Mrs. Eddy since 1879 when she and her husband, Edgar Frank Woodbury, had become interested through reading *Science and Health*. They were socially prominent people, with a town house in Boston and a summer place in Maine. Mr. Woodbury had helped Mrs. Eddy in the formation of the Metaphysical College and had been one of its Directors. In 1884, after several years of hesitancy, Josephine Woodbury decided definitely to cast in her lot with the new movement. She was an eloquent speaker, with a good voice and an unusually attractive presence. She was also something of a poet and a writer, and she had all the defects of her virtues. In these early days she carried all before her.

Then there was Augusta Stetson. When she first met Mrs. Eddy in 1884 she was a woman a little over forty who, after a period of study at the Boston School of Oratory, was just setting out on a career as an elocutionist. She was a striking woman, tall and generous in build, with a singularly compelling presence. She was not beautiful like Josephine Woodbury, but she had a way of commanding attention which was the subject of comment all her life. As a little girl in Damariscotta, Maine, where her father, Peabody Simmons, was engaged as an architect, she was devoted to music and when she was only fourteen played the organ in church. She married at twenty-two Captain Frederick Stetson, a veteran of the Civil War, who was associated with his father in the work of shipbuilding, and shortly afterward the two went out to India in connection with the shipbuilding business, living for several years in Bombay and then later on in Akyab, British Burma. In the early eighties, Captain Stetson's health—he had never recovered from privations suffered in the notorious Libby Prison during the Civil War—broke down completely, and the two returned to America where Augusta determined to make a living for them both. So it was, when Mrs. Eddy met her in the spring of 1884.

She had been invited to attend a lecture given by Mrs. Eddy in a private house in Charlestown. When the lecture was over, the two met and Mrs. Eddy seems to have recognized at once some exceptional ability in Augusta Stetson. She asked her to come and see her, assuring her, as she often did to a promising newcomer, that if she would study Christian Science she could do a great work in it. Mrs. Stetson did not respond at once, but she evidently maintained her interest in Christian Science, for in the fall of 1884 she invited Mrs. Eddy to give a lecture in her house, as the result of which she decided to join the next class which at that time was enrolling.

Augusta Stetson appears to have made the decision after much hesitation, even wondering whether she could spare the time from her work as an elocutionist, which just then was becoming more or less established. However, she decided to join, and within three weeks all else was forgotten. She came out of the class with only one thought, to devote herself completely to the practice of Christian Science. All thoughts of any other work were entirely put aside, and it was not long before her remarkable success as a healer began to be widely known.

But Augusta Stetson was not the only one who had amazing success about this time. Indeed, it would be impossible to explain the remarkable progress of the new teaching in any other way save on the basis of the spectacular exhibition of healing which seems to have been in evidence in many quarters. It is possible that a great deal of it was simply faith healing, intensified enormously, as in every case of religious revival, by the cumulative enthusiasm of increasing numbers. Many years later, Edward Kimball, one of the ablest exponents of Christian Science, was to admit frankly that a great deal of the healing in Christian Science, especially in these early days, was faith healing. But whether through faith or through understanding, there can be no doubt cast on the cures which from now on are to be recorded in increasing numbers.

From its first issue, cases of healing were given periodically in the *Christian Science Journal*, but it was not until about 1884 or 1885 that the records of cures became a regular feature. Up to then, practitioners in various parts of the country had sent in accounts of the cases they had handled, and some of these had been published. Later on it became the practice to have the original testimonials from the people themselves who had actually been healed.

One of Augusta Stetson's records, as found in Volume Three of the *Christian Science Journal*, is certainly a remarkable statement. Writing from Somerville, Massachusetts, she enumerates nine or ten cases of healing, among them a hopeless case of cancer, a case of diphtheria, chronic heart disease, and a badly sprained ankle which had failed to yield to medical treatment for some weeks. She gives her address, and states simply that she will be glad to give full details of these cases to anyone who is interested.

The record of Julia Bartlett is no less remarkable. Early in 1884, a young girl from Sugar Hill, New Hampshire, whose case had been pronounced hopeless by her local doctor, applied to Miss Bartlett for help. She was healed in nine days, and on returning to Sugar Hill her remarkable recovery attracted so much attention that Miss Bartlett received an earnest appeal to visit the little mountain town. She decided to go, and during the eleven days she spent there she is credited with having at many as seventy patients a day, many of whom were cured instantaneously.

When the widest margin is left for possible if unintentional exaggeration, the fact still remains that only by some extraordinary phenomena

319

as are here indicated can the tremendous impulse given to the movement about this time be explained. Especially in the early days, it was the healing work almost alone that attracted public attention and, as has been seen, attracted it to a remarkable extent.

Mrs. Eddy herself had a considerable reputation for healing work, but from the first she seems to have felt that her great mission was as a teacher and that, through her teaching, the demonstration of her Science could be made more universal by the ever widening practice of her students.

As a teacher she had in a marked degree an ability—shared in a measure by all great teachers—of arresting attention even before she began to speak. The first session of a class was in the nature of a revelation to those attending it.

Thus a Miss Lulu Blackman, who travelled about this time (1885) from Lincoln, Nebraska, to go through one of Mrs. Eddy's classes, remarks in her account of the matter upon this fact:

"When she entered the Class-room, I saw her for the first time. Intuitively, the members of the class rose at her entrance, and remained standing until she was seated. She made her way to a slightly raised platform, turned and faced us. . . . She stood before us seemingly slight, graceful of carriage and exquisitely beautiful even to critical eyes. . . . She was every inch the Teacher."

On the larger platform of the lecture hall, she seems to have been even more arresting. She had a remarkable poise and lack of all self-consciousness, and had at times a happy and quiet humour which tended to modify if not silence dissent. Word of her preaching had by this time travelled far. Hawthorne Hall had been outgrown, and the church now held its services in the much larger Chickering Hall; and then one day Mrs. Eddy appeared on the platform of Tremont Temple.

Tremont Temple was in those days, as indeed it still is, the scene of many notable gatherings and a platform for many notable people. In 1885, it was occupied every Monday by the Reverend Joseph Cook, a popular lecturer of his day, and the "Monday Lecture in Tremont

Temple" was one of Boston's favourite and fashionable occasions. It happened at a lecture of his early in March, 1885, that Mr. Cook read a letter from one of Mrs. Eddy's most bitter opponents, the Reverend A. J. Gordon, denouncing Christian Science and all its works with a thoroughness which was characteristic of those early days. Mrs. Eddy immediately demanded the right to reply to these denunciations and charges from the same platform. Mr. Cook agreed that she should have ten minutes on the following Monday, March 16.

And so at the time appointed, Mrs. Eddy appeared on the platform and, in exactly ten minutes, gave an exposition of her teaching which created much stir at the time and has since become historic. Recognizing, with what must be regarded as rare skill, that it would be impossible to present even the most general synopsis of her doctrine in a time so short, she confined herself to questions and answers, asking the questions she knew her audience was eager to ask, and answering them clearly and crisply and without evasion.[1]

The one evidently most asked she put first: "Am I a spiritualist?" Her answer was direct and emphatic enough: "I am not, and never was." And then she went on to explain how she understood the impossibility of intercommunion betwen the "so-called dead and living"; how her life had always been attended by phenomena of an uncommon order which spiritualists mis-called mediumship, but how she clearly understood that no human agencies were employed, but that "the divine Mind reveals itself to humanity through spiritual law". And then she continued: "To such as are 'waiting for the adoption, to wit, the redemption of our body', Christian Science reveals the infinitude of divinity and the way of man's salvation from sickness and death."

Her next question brought another vital issue into the open. Christian Science had been described by more than one minister in Boston as a Godless faith in which a kind of esoteric transcendentalism was substituted for true Christian doctrine, and so she asked the question: "Do I

[1] For text of her statement cf. *Miscellaneous Writings*, pp. 95-98.

believe in a personal God?" Her answer seems to have stood out as one of the great confessions of faith.

"I believe in God", she said, "as the Supreme Being. I know not what the person of omnipotence and omnipresence is, or what the infinite includes; therefore I worship that of which I can conceive, first, as a loving Father and Mother; then, as thought ascends the scale of being to diviner consciousness, God becomes to me, as to the apostle who declared it, 'God is Love'—divine Principle—which I worship; and 'after the manner of my fathers, so worship I God'."

She took each question slowly and deliberately, and it quickly became apparent, as question and answer followed each other, that she was working on a well-conceived plan. For having dismissed Spiritualism, and affirmed her faith in the fatherhood and motherhood of God, her next point was clearly the relationship of God to man, and so she asked, "Do I believe in the atonement of Christ?"

She paused a moment and then said simply, "I do; and this atonement", she continued, "becomes more to me since it includes man's redemption from sickness as well as from sin. I reverence and adore Christ as never before."

Another pause and then this question, "How is the healing done in Christian Science?" Here was the crux of the whole matter. The Tremont Temple was filled to overflowing. Many were standing at the back of the great gallery which circles the hall, and it is not difficult to imagine the wave of expectancy which swept over the audience. It was a question everyone was asking. How was the healing done?

Her answer was certainly remarkable for its succinctness. "This answer", she said, "includes too much to give you any conclusive idea in a brief explanation. I can name some means by which it is not done. It is not one mind acting upon another mind; it is not the transference of human images of thought to other minds; it is not supported by the evidence before the personal senses,—Science contradicts this evidence; it is not of the flesh, but of the Spirit. It is Christ come to destroy the power of the flesh; it is Truth over error; that understood, gives man ability to rise above the evidence of the senses, take hold of the eternal energies of Truth, and destroy mortal discord with immortal harmony,— the grand verities of being. . . . Christian Science is not a remedy of faith alone, but combines faith with understanding, through which we may touch the hem of His garment; and know that omnipotence has all power. 'I am the Lord, and there is none else, there is no God beside me.' "

Time was running short now, but she had measured it well. There was one more question, "Is there a personal man?" the Scriptures were clear enough, she said; man was made in the image and likeness of God. She commended the Icelandic translation of the passage in Genesis, "He created man in the image and likeness of Mind, in the image and likeness of Mind created He him." This image and likeness of Mind did not yet "appear", but it would appear more and more as the "perfect model" was "held in mind" and man's contemplation regarding himself turned resolutely "away from inharmony, sickness, and sin, to that which is the image of his Maker".

The Journal

IN MANY RESPECTS the founding of the *Christian Science Journal* in 1883 was a masterstroke of policy. The tendency of the movement, especially at first, was to spread sporadically. Word of a case of sickness healed in Salem, Massachusetts, would be sent by letter or carried by a friend to a sick person in Salem, Oregon, perhaps accompanied by a copy of *Science and Health*, and the sick person in Salem, Oregon, being restored to health, as many were while reading the book, would pass on the good news to others, and, very soon, a little group, intensely eager to learn more of the new teaching, would be formed. Members of this group would gather in each others' houses for discussion and the exchange of views and experiences, and letters any one of them might receive from Boston from those who were devoting themselves to the study and practice of Christian Science were read and re-read and then sent on further afield.

The one thing needed above all others was a connecting link, however slight, to bring these widely scattered groups together in some bond of fellowship. In those early days there were few—as there were always to be few—who could have understood Mrs. Eddy's steadfastly maintained counsel of perfection that the one true bond of perfectness was devotion to Principle. They felt deeply the need of personal guidance. The path they had set out to traverse was unaccustomed, and any assurance that they were not travelling alone would be gladly welcomed. Such assurance was supplied by the *Journal*. Even when it was only a little eight-page paper, published every two months, it was infinitely better than nothing. But by 1885 it had come to be quite a sizable magazine.

How clearly Mrs. Eddy realized the need is seen in her statement in the first issue.

"At this date, 1883," she writes, "a newspaper edited and published by the Christian Scientists has become a necessity. Many questions important to be disposed of come to the College and to the practising students, yet but little time has been devoted to their answer. Further enlightenment is necessary for the age, and a periodical devoted to this work seems alone adequate to meet the requirement."

The history of the little magazine was chequered from the first, as it was to be for many years. One after another, its editors or associates would enter upon their work full of enthusiasm and devotion, only to drift away after a year or two and embark on some course of their own. Arthur True Buswell, its first business manager, whose aid to Mrs. Eddy and his care for her after the death of Gilbert Eddy had been so faithful and unselfish, found the going too rough and was soon counted among the opposition, for Richard Kennedy, Daniel Spofford, Edward Arens, and others who had become alienated from Mrs. Eddy, were still active. Indeed, it quickly became clear that the more rapid the advance of the original movement, the more attractive to public interest would be any version of "mental healing." This presented a constant invitation to those who were discontented. In some cases, of course, the age-old human failing embodied in the conviction that it is better to be first man in a village than second man at Rome was particularly in evidence, and, in the early days of Christian Science, when the outside world had no sure way of distinguishing the original from the take-off, it was easy for the dissident to go out and build a village, secure a following, and persuade many into the new fold.

Arthur Buswell went out in January of 1884, and his place was taken by a Mrs. Emma Hopkins, wife of a professor of Andover. She was an able, well-educated woman, had been healed by Mrs. Eddy of a serious illness, had gone through one of her classes and now embarked on her new work as associate editor of the *Journal* with enthusiasm. Her position, bringing her, as it did, in constant association with Mrs. Eddy, gave her an outstanding place among her fellows, thus making her the target for both attack and temptation. The usual difficulties were not long in developing. In the summer of 1884, there came to the Metaphysical College to study, a woman from Detroit named Mary H. Plunkett, who was so impressed with Mrs. Hopkins' possibilities that the *Journal* editorship seemed to her of too limited a scope for such genius. Why not withdraw to freer expression and wider fields? Emma was not only a genius, so Mrs. Plunkett assured her, but a woman with a destiny. With her learning and her familiarity with the "mysteries of mind", she might well be a nineteenth-century Hypatia, and Mrs. Plunkett asked nothing better than to sit at her feet and forward her goings. She felt, too, that a way should be found to further her view that all marriages should be the result of selection "by soul affinity". She does not seem to have featured this theory until later but, however this may be, she had, within a few months, completely won over Emma Hopkins to the view that her abilities were being wasted in her subordination to Mrs. Eddy, and that she had better join with her in founding a new school of metaphysics.

And so they left Boston together, taught their own system for some time in Detroit and Chicago and other mid-western cities, published a magazine entitled *The International Magazine of Christian Science*, but before long faded out as a serious threat to Mrs. Eddy's leadership.

Mrs. Hopkins' history, as associate editor of the *Journal*, was the history of no fewer than three of her immediate successors. It was not until 1890 that the *Journal* was able to shake itself free, as far as Mrs. Eddy's partisans were concerned, from the taint of apostasy.

All through this long period, however, Mrs. Eddy remained firmly at the helm, directed the policy of the magazine, and wrote much of its contents. A copy of the *Journal* in the summer of 1885, shortly after Mrs. Eddy made her appearance at Tremont Temple, affords an interesting cross-sectional view of the movement as a whole about this time and of Mrs. Eddy's connection with it.

Thus the *Journal* for August, 1885, which is designated No. 5, Vol. III, is a magazine of some fifteen pages. It is well printed on good paper and is varied in its content. Opening with an article by Mrs. Eddy which was later used in part as a preface to her book *Miscellaneous Writings*, this is followed by an interview with her by Lillian Whiting, reprinted from the Ohio *Leader*. Thereafter come several articles signed variously, "Student", "Christian Scientist", or only with initials. They deal with various aspects of Christian Science, and one of them, entitled "Faith Works, Christian Science and other Cures", is a vigorous defence of Christian Science against the attacks of the Reverend L. T. Townsend already referred to.

Then there is poetry, quite a lot of it, some original and not so good, some quoted from famous poets and excellent not only in form but in appositeness. There are extracts from *Science and Health*, some well-written book reviews and three columns of testimonies from those healed. These testimonies are headed by a note to the effect that full particulars will be supplied on application to the editor of the *Journal*. They include among other things testimonies as to the healing of dyspepsia, kidney trouble, typhoid pneumonia, chronic dysentery, insanity, cholera, neuralgia and blindness.

But probably the most looked for features were those written by Mrs. Eddy herself entitled "Bible Lessons" and "Questions and Answers". There is a department bearing the heading "Humorous". It is not very successful, but then it lays no claim to originality save in the matter of selection. "You can easily tell a dogwood tree by its bark", from the Chicago *Sun*, has no special claim to distinction. Many of the jokes were on clergymen and doctors! Finally, there are several columns devoted to the names, addresses and office hours of practitioners, mostly in or around Boston, but some from New York and one at least from as far west as Omaha, Nebraska. A few pages of simple advertising round off the issue : garden swings, pianos, stationery, periodicals, and so forth. There are also notices from the "Massachusetts Metaphysical College" and two pages of advertising for *Science and Health*.

From the biographical point of view the most interesting feature in this issue is the interview with Mrs. Eddy by Lillian Whiting. Lillian Whiting of the Ohio *Leader* was a newspaper woman of the transitional school; that is to say, she was sufficiently near to the sentimentality and "highfalutin" of the Civil War period to be still touched by it and sufficiently near to the irrepressible story-getting afflatus of today to present some of its features. The fact that she was clearly "out for a story", while it would make one discount the value of the highlights, would intensify the importance of those more prosaic elements to which curiously enough she gives great prominence.

Whether she had been sent by her paper to Boston for the express purpose of interviewing Mrs. Eddy is not at all certain. As she tells the story, the idea came to her quite suddenly and without any preparation. She claims to have been so little interested in the subject that she had made no effort to hear Mrs. Eddy either at Hawthorne Hall or elsewhere, but acting on a sudden impulse wrote to her and asked for an interview. "My note of inquiry", she says, "was met by a very courteous invitation to come to her at an hour named, and accordingly at eight o'clock that evening I rang the bell of a large and handsome residence on Columbus Avenue near West Chester Park known as the Metaphysical College. A maid ushered me into a daintily furnished reception room where pictures and bric-a-brac indicated refinement and taste."

She then goes on to relate how that after she had waited for a few moments, appraising her surroundings, Mrs. Eddy came in and greeted her cordially and gracefully. She was, from what she had heard, prepared for this friendly greeting, but she was not prepared for something more, "an indefinable element of harmony and a peace that was not mere repose but more like exaltation".

She seems to have been a good interviewer, for, after some friendly talk back and forth on topics of the day, she got Mrs. Eddy down to telling the story of her early life and of how she arrived at Christian Science. The picture is complete. The sturdy New England ancestry, the devoted Abigail, the little girl sorely tried with sickness, but going on her way. Just a word or two about all the trials and troubles that intervened, and then a very vivid picture of the Sunday morning in Lynn when this little girl, grown to be a very tired, worn-out woman, saw something that enabled her literally to arise from a bed of sickness and walk.

One detail is added, not before recorded—how that after Mrs. Eddy had read the passage from Matthew recounting the healing of the man sick of the palsy, she lay for some time thinking over it, and how that with increasing persistency there came to her thought the words, "I am the Way and the Truth and the Life; no man cometh unto the Father but by me."

"And then", Lillian Whiting continues, telling the story, "she began to grow strong. She arose from her bed and walked into the adjoining room. . . . From that hour the power was revealed to her."

Lillian Whiting says that Mrs. Eddy impressed her "as a woman who is—in the language of our Methodist friends—'filled with the spirit'." And she relates her own personal experience as the result of the interview. It is interesting because similar accounts of similar experiences later come to be quite common.

"My own personal experience in the call was so singular that I will venture to relate it. I went as I have said in a journalistic spirit. I had no belief or disbelief, and the idea of getting any personal benefit from the call save matter for press use never occurred to me. But I remembered afterward how extremely tired I was as I walked rather wearily and languidly up the steps to Mrs. Eddy's door. I came away as a little child friend of mine expressively says, 'skipping'. I was at least a mile from the Vendome, and I walked home feeling as if I were treading on air. My sleep that night was the rest of Elysium. If I had been caught up into paradise it could hardly have been a more wonderful renewal. All the next day this exalted state continued. I can hardly describe it: it was simply the most marvellous elasticity of mind and body."

Many years before, Bancroft had noticed the same stimulation, not only on himself but on others who met her privately or heard her speak in public, and as years went by this stimulus seemed to increase rather than diminish. It attached also in a large measure to her writings, and even when every allowance is made for the influence of pure imagination, the effect often produced by the public reading of her letters must be accounted extraordinary.

In these early days of the *Journal*, this was specially noteworthy. A direct word from Mrs. Eddy was the thing most sought after, and through the *Journal* this word was going out everywhere. As Georgine Milmine, far from friendly, writing much nearer those days has left record: "Although her subscription-list was small, Mrs. Eddy knew what to do with her *Journal*. Copies found their way to remote villages in Missouri and Arkansas, to lonely places in Nebraska and Colorado, where people had much time for reflection, little excitement, and great need to believe in miracles. The metaphor of the bread cast upon the waters is no adequate suggestion of the result. Mrs. Eddy and Christian Science began to be talked of far away in the mountains and in the prairie villages. Lonely and discouraged people brooded over these editorials which promised happiness to sorrow and success to failure. The desperately ill had no quarrel with testimonials in which people declared that they had been snatched from the brink of the grave."

The *Journal* had taken as its motto Paul's statement, "For the weapons of our warfare are not carnal, but mighty through God, to the pulling down of strong holds." Any study of its history, especially in these early days, must compel the admission that it made good use of its weapons.

Chicago

VIEWED IN THE perspective of more than half a century, the outstanding characteristic of the Christian Science movement during the next three years, from 1885 to 1888, is expansion. This phase of it completely overshadows all others. It entered the period as a Boston Craze. It emerged from it as a national and even international religious movement. Comments and criticism, attack and defence, are no longer confined to local newspapers and periodicals. They appear with increasing frequency in national magazines and are often placed in the forefront of debate.

Mrs. Eddy made the utmost use of it all. No attack of importance was allowed to go unanswered, and so great was the interest in the subject that the circulation of the *Journal* increased rapidly not only among professed Christian Scientists, but much further afield. An attack in the *Century Magazine* one month—like that, for instance, of the Reverend Dr. J. M. Buckley, entitled "Christian Science and Mind Cure", which appeared in the issue for July, 1887—would be followed by a reply in the *Journal* in the next, and many *Century* readers would buy the *Journal* containing the reply in order to see how Mrs. Eddy or some one or other of her supporters handled the matter. Mrs. Eddy, it would seem, seldom replied to these attacks over her own name, but often the unsigned reply occupying a first place in the *Journal* would leave little doubt as to who was its author. How rapid was the expansion of the movement is well illustrated by the closing words in the reply to Doctor Buckley, in which the writer comments upon the change which has come over the face of things in one short year:

"It is a most gratifying sign that *The Century* devotes so much space to Christian Science. A year ago the editor 'returned with thanks' an article on this subject, giving as a reason for his refusal, that there was no such theme as Christian Science. Now this title heads the *Century* article. When the Metaphysical College was established in 1881, the President reluctantly accepted the title, because Christian Science was a thing unknown to legislators and this was the only fit name by which she could secure incorporation. Now the Massachusetts Legislature incorporates academies and societies under the caption, and without a murmur. The world moves spiritward."

But if it so moved it was largely because Mrs. Eddy determined that it should, or, rather, that nothing that could be done to make it so move should remain undone, as far as she was concerned. Her energy and resource were alike inexhaustible. In these three years she taught no fewer than twenty regular classes besides undertaking innumerable cases of special instruction. She wrote regularly and copiously for the *Journal*, and attended with her own hand to a correspondence which increased steadily week by week and month by month. In addition to all this, she had the personal direction of a movement which, having spanned the continent, stood in sore need of consolidation.

Her great aim about this time seems to have been the training of apostles in the simple sense of the word. She must have students who could undertake for her, who could be trusted to go into a new field and speak with authority and act with wisdom and teach and preach with understanding. And so in the *Journal* for February, 1886, she calls vigorous attention to the need for teachers and for teaching. In a circular letter which she sent out to students in different places throughout the country, she emphasizes the advisability of those prepared to teach to form classes as soon as possible and to carry on their work through some centre which might be known variously as "Christian Science Institute" or "Christian Science Academy".

Meanwhile, new churches were springing up everywhere. It was in the fall of this year, 1886, that she took the step—later to be fraught with so much import—of sending Augusta Stetson to New York to establish a church there. Mrs. Stetson was not specially eager to go. She had a large following in and around Boston, preached quite frequently at Hawthorne and Chickering Halls, and altogether occupied a position of no little prominence. She, however, decided to go, and although the work in New York was slow, so slow at first that she twice returned to Boston seeking release from her office, before two years were passed she was preaching to large congregations at Crescent Hall, Number 138 Fifth Avenue, and Christian Science was spreading rapidly throughout the state.

It was, however, towards the west that Mrs. Eddy, with a sure instinct, persistently turned her attention. In 1887, she sent Josephine Woodbury on a special mission to Denver, Colorado. A minister by the name of Reverend W. D. Westervelt had been conducting a vigorous campaign in Denver against the new teaching, and the leading article in the September *Journal* was devoted to an examination of one of his essays. Josephine Woodbury was an able speaker with, as has been seen, an attractive personality, and her mission was a complete success. She returned to Boston with word of the growth of the cause in all directions.

But while Mrs. Eddy was thus sending envoys further and further west—an academy was established in San Francisco early in 1887—her highest hopes were centred in Chicago. Ever since her visit in 1884 she had seen the movement grow there in a way that was not being equalled anywhere else. From the first it seems to have attracted people of influence and wealth, who in the freer atmosphere of the Middle West were less hide-bound than the settled Easterners, and so more contagiously demonstrative. It is true that in Chicago as elsewhere, of those called and chosen, many in time fell away, but great and increasing numbers remained faithful, and within a few years Chicago had gained a reputation in the movement for soundness which it never lost.

In the early weeks of 1888, Mrs. Eddy began to receive urgent calls to revisit Chicago. A way had opened out for her to do so with excellent effect. Some two years previously she had advocated through the *Journal* the formation of a National Christian Scientist Association. A Christian Scientist Association had existed, of course, for many years, ever since the earliest Lynn days, but, as Mrs. Eddy points out in her notice in the *Journal* for January, 1886, this Association was exclusively a society connected with the Massachusetts Metaphysical College and thus necessarily limited in its scope.

"I deem it advisable", she says, "that an organization be formed on a broader basis, by which all Christian Scientists and their students may come together; and I would recommend that steps be taken by my students throughout the United States to organize a National Christian Scientist Association."

This was promptly done, and within a few weeks, namely, on February 11, 1886, the first meeting of the new Association was held in New York City. At that meeting, which was necessarily small owing to the shortness of the notice, plans were laid for the development of the larger organization, and in the following year the first annual meeting of the Association was held in Boston at Tremont Temple on Wednesday afternoon, April 13, 1887.

The list of delegates to this first annual meeting shows the extent to which the new teaching had spread throughout the country. No fewer than fourteen states were represented: Maine, New Hampshire, Rhode Island, New York, District of Columbia, Kentucky, Michigan, Ohio, Illinois, Wisconsin, Missouri, Nebraska, Iowa and Colorado.

The report of the meeting, which later appeared in the *Journal*, dwells upon the evidence afforded of the rapid growth of the movement.

"This Association", the report said, "only a year old shows by the interest manifested in all parts of the country the deep root it has taken in the minds of the people, and the attendance shows how many were anxious to see and hear the leader of this great movement."

The meeting lasted two days, and at the end of the second day adjourned "to meet a year hence". This next meeting was held in Chicago.

The choice of Chicago was another excellent stroke of policy. As the far west developed, Chicago was rapidly becoming the favourite city for conventions of all kinds. Then as now, perhaps the greatest railway centre in the country, it offered facilities for the gathering of people from a much wider area than the old convention towns on the Atlantic coast.

Mrs. Eddy decided to attend the convention in person, and in order to ensure that it would be a gathering fully representative of the movement, she issued a special plea to Christian Scientists everywhere to attend.

"Let no consideration", she wrote in the *Journal,* "bend or outweigh your purpose to be in Chicago on June 13."

She herself left it in doubt until almost the last moment that she would be present. Indeed, it was formally announced in the May issue of the *Journal* that she would not be. She was insisting more and more on the need to divert attention from herself and concentrate it on her teaching. If sometimes the methods she adopted seem unnecessarily severe, there can be no question as to the excellence of her objective. She finally decided to go, and a few days before the convention was scheduled to open she left Boston accompanied by Captain and Mrs. Eastaman, Calvin Frye, and a young physician named E. J. Foster, who was later to figure prominently in the movement.

What Mrs. Eddy and those around her actually expected to find in Chicago it is not easy to say, but there can be no doubt that it exceeded all their expectations. Nothing that had happened up to that time could have afforded more dramatic evidence of the extraordinary growth of the movement. Even before the meeting opened, it was apparent that interest throughout the country in the gathering was sufficient to give it all the advertising and publicity it needed, and as the Christian Scientists

335

from all quarters began to come into Chicago, the newspapers, with a sure instinct of what would be news, published long preliminary descriptions and issued periodical bulletins, most of them familiarly inaccurate, on such vital questions as to whether Mrs. Eddy herself really would or would not be present. The actual number of delegates belonging to the National Association which assembled was about eight hundred, but within a very short time after the doors of the Central Music Hall, where the public meeting was scheduled to be held, were opened, the hall was filled to overflowing with an audience considerably in excess of four thousand people.

Mrs. Eddy, apparently, was unprepared for anything of the kind. She had come to the meeting without any intention of making a formal address, and when told on their way to the platform by the Reverend George B. Day, who was then pastor of the First Church in Chicago, that he had already announced her as the speaker of the day, she was at first quite vigorous in her dissent but next moment, as she reached the platform, evidently realizing her opportunity, she went to the front and faced the audience.

According to the Boston *Traveller's* report, as soon as she appeared, the audience rose to their feet as one man and remained standing until she motioned them to be seated. Then, "without notes of any kind and evidently depending entirely on the inspiration of the moment," she delivered an address which, in spite of the inadequacy of its recorded form, has come to be regarded as one of her most effective public utterances.[1] The report, preserved in her book *Miscellaneous Writings*, although excellent in substance and affording occasional views of the strangely compelling quality which must have been in the original, only illustrates anew how much at all times the power of Mrs. Eddy's utterances were deepened when they were delivered in person.

"Science is absolute and final. It is revolutionary in its very nature; for it upsets all that is not upright. It annuls false evidence, and saith to the

---

[1] An accurate transcription of the original address appears in full on pages 288-294 of the book *Christian Science Class Instruction*, by Arthur Corey.

five material senses, 'Having eyes ye see not, and ears ye hear not; neither can you understand'."

So, after a few words of quiet greeting, outlining the purpose of the gathering and pleading for individual consecration, did she move into her subject and set the pace for what was to follow.

The speech comprised in all some three thousand words. There is no attempt at an outline, as was the case with the address in Tremont Temple, but there is a quite remarkable wealth of eloquent reasoning, culminating in telling phrases and unexpected legends of rhetoric such as may well have roused the audience to eager attention even when their full import was not gathered.

"Past, present, future, will show the word and might of Truth—healing the sick and reclaiming the sinner—so long as there remains a claim of error for Truth to deny or to destroy."

So it went, culminating in this final statement: "Because God is Mind, and this Mind is good, all is good and all is Mind. God is the sum total of the universe. Then what and where are sin, sickness, and death?"

There was a moment's silence when she had finished, followed by a scene which, judging from the various reports, must have been indescribable. According to one account a few days later in the Boston *Traveller*, the whole audience seemed to rise and move forward towards the platform where Mrs. Eddy was standing. Men and women climbed up, dozens at a time, eager to shake her hand. "Those whom she had never seen before—invalids raised up by her book *Science and Health*—attempted hurriedly to tell their story." Women lifted up their children so that they might see her, and when she finally released herself it was only with great difficulty that she made her way through the throng blocking her passage from the door to her carriage.

That evening a reception was given for her in the Palmer House where she was staying. Again it was all unexpected, and although she went down from her suite and stayed for a few minutes, seeking not to appear ungracious, it was evident to those who were with her that this aspect of her visit filled her with doubt. Once again, people thronged her,

337

and she had to appeal to Calvin Frye, who stood near, for help. It was only with great difficulty they were able to withdraw.

Publicly, she never said anything about it. In her message to Chicago, published later in the *Journal*, she has no words but thanks. Privately, however, she implied, as she had done on several previous occasions, that she did not think the cause of Christian Science was advanced by such methods. Only once afterwards did she have a similar experience. That was in New York, about a year later, when she addressed a large audience in the Steinway Hall. After that, she never appeared at any public gathering of a similar kind.

But whatever else Chicago did for Christian Science, it gave to the movement an unquestioned national character. From now on it moves forward in this way.

Science and Health Again

AMONG THE MANY activities crowded into the three years covered in the previous chapter, not the least, as far as Mrs. Eddy was concerned, was the revision of *Science and Health*. For more than thirty years this was for her a constant devoted labour. Her main purpose in these revisions was, of course, to elucidate her meaning. True, in the earlier editions she used the book as a platform to deal with special developments and to right wrongs as she believed, adding chapters or inserting paragraphs which were afterwards deleted or modified as the occasion for them passed, but in the main her one thought was to make more readily apprehensible the principle set forth in the first edition.

As already stated, the book is unique. The fact that its author never read it through consecutively in the thirty or more years that elapsed between the first edition and the last is proof sufficient that she had no thought of fashioning it after any accepted model. Like Emily Dickinson, Walt Whitman, Carlyle, Saint John and not a few others, this woman had very little respect for convention either in her grammar, her style, or her use of words. She bent and even twisted all three to her service in any way she wished if by so doing she could bring out her point more clearly or more strikingly. In the fashion of some advertising she would, it may be ventured, have gladly turned a word upside down or spelled it backwards, if by so doing she could have compelled for it the attention she desired.

As has been seen also, she formed her style in a tortuous age of English literature. The florid grandiosity of the forties and fifties of last century was a handicapping period in which to serve an apprenticeship for one whose objective was not literature in the ordinary meaning of the word, but merely the use of language for the promulgation of a revolutionary idea. The more clearly did she see this idea, the more easily did she divest herself of the "ornamentation" of her earlier style, until in her later years she had a terseness of presentation and a cogency of content which place her in a class by herself. In her earlier writings, she "labours with the rest".

As the demand for her book increased and as a consequence was subject to more widespread criticism from a literary point of view, Mrs. Eddy seems to have realized that however little she might care for literary convention, the fact remained that breaches of it tended to divert attention from the main purpose of her writing and concentrate it on a very minor essential. Early in 1885, therefore, she determined that the next edition of *Science and Health*, as far as literary form was concerned, should be more in line with accepted usage. To this end she adopted a wise course. She enlisted the services of one of the editors of the University Press, a retired Unitarian minister named James Henry Wiggin, to act as proof reader for the fifteenth edition of her book which she was then preparing. She was quite explicit with Mr. Wiggin as to what she wanted done. In a statement made to the New York *American* some twenty years later, she declares that because some critic had insisted that her book was "as ungrammatical as it was misleading", she employed Mr. Wiggin, a man whose authority was generally recognized, to "defend my grammatical construction", and also "to avail myself of his criticisms of my statement of Christian Science, which criticisms would enable me

340

to explain more clearly the points that might seem ambiguous to the reader".

Any comparison of the first edition of *Science and Health* with the fifteenth or sixteenth or any later edition shows clearly that this is exactly what Mr. Wiggin did. The actual diction in all editions is as unquestionably from the same hand as are different varieties of an individual signature. Often it is possible to trace the hand of Mr. Wiggin all too clearly, as when one of the author's refreshing departures from literary convention is rather pedantically sacrificed to the demand of the purist, but, for the most part, his work seems to have been confined to the very valuable and necessary task of bringing the style into line with accepted standards.

James Henry Wiggin was an interesting character. If fate had decided that he should have flourished in London in the closing years of the eighteenth century instead of in Boston in the closing years of the nineteenth, he might have found a place along with Paley and Butler and a host of lesser lights among the immortals. He revelled in dialectics. Like Sheridan, he had no sooner won his case than, if nothing better offered, he would gladly turn around and argue with eager conviction for the other side. For several years he wrote for the *Christian Science Journal* over the *nom de plume* "Phare-Pleigh", defending Mrs. Eddy's teaching against all comers, but, as his private correspondence sufficiently shows, he did so only because he saw the weak places in the attackers' armour and the cut and thrust of the *melée* gave him much joy.

He did a good work on *Science and Health*, and the sixteenth edition is rightly regarded as one of the landmarks in the history of the book. A formal announcement of the appearance of this edition in the *Journal* for January, 1886, says: "Attention is called to this volume. It is worth the notice, not only of Christian Scientists, but of all who are interested in the progress of truth. It is from the University Press, Cambridge, and this is a guaranty for its typographical appearance. All the material of other editions is herein retained, but all of it has been carefully revised and rewritten by Mrs. Eddy, and greatly improved. The arrangement of the chapters has been changed. One new chapter has been added, on the Apocalypse, giving an exposition of the bearings on Christian Science of the twelfth chapter of Revelation, to which it is believed by Mrs. Eddy to particularly relate. A special feature is a full index, prepared especially for this edition, by a competent gentleman. In these days no important book has a right to come before the public without a proper index."

The "competent gentleman" did a good job. His index proved to be an excellent one and served the readers of *Science and Health* well for many years.

All the time that this work was going forward, the Quimby controversy already alluded to was moving unremittingly from point to point. In fact, controversy over Mrs. Eddy or some form of her teaching was the order of almost every day. Wherever the movement planted itself in however small a way, right there within a very short time a flame of debate would spring up like that caused by a wind-blown spark in a grass fire. But throughout, in spite of, or rather it would seem because of it all, the movement prospered prodigiously.

For Mrs. Eddy, the days of poverty were left a long way behind. In the winter of 1887 she purchased as a residence the large house, 385 Commonwealth Avenue, in Boston, which is still used as a residence for the First Reader of The Mother Church. She retained the house on Columbus Avenue as the headquarters of the Metaphysical College and thus secured for herself greater privacy, which she sorely needed. The move also served to lessen, for a time at least, the growing tide of sycophancy and adulation which more and more at this period seems to have filled her with anxiety.

One last thread to be gathered up in these years, before going on to consider the amazing aftermath of the Chicago triumph, is another visit which George Glover paid to his mother in the summer of this year. George Glover is now a man of forty-five. He has a wife and several children, and they live in Lead City, South Dakota, and he is still interested in mining. When Gilbert Eddy died in 1882, Mrs. Eddy had written to her son begging him to come to her, but George Glover did not even answer this letter. All his life, as far as his mother was concerned, it was the same.

Almost from birth, his feet were planted in a road which led him away from his mother, and just so long as they both were alive, their intercourse, if so it may be called, was characterized by the same trend. Long efforts to secure reunion, at any rate on the mother's part, were marked when achieved by an outward semblance of happiness all too surely doomed to disappointment and failure; then long periods of silence or intermittent communication; then another effort at reunion, with the same results. This had been the way of it in Boston in 1877, at the time of George's strange encounter with Richard Kennedy, and it is not surprising that when in the summer of 1887 Mrs. Eddy received a letter from her son announcing his intention of coming to Boston with his family to pay her a visit, she should have regarded the matter with no little uneasiness.

Their lives had grown utterly apart. If they had little in common in 1877, they had practically nothing in 1887. Mrs. Eddy wrote to him frankly, telling him how she must have quiet in her home and opportunity to do her work without distraction; how that she still looked forward to a day when they could be reunited if he would only reform his ways, but that now she had a duty to others to perform, and it was a duty that must be performed.

George Glover was, it appears, the kind of man who simply could not realize the importance of such niceties, as he would have called them. A prospector's life could be interrupted at any moment, and he evidently felt very much in the mood for a trip east with his wife and children. He wrote to Mrs. Eddy notifying her that he was on his way. Mrs. Eddy, on receipt of his letter, determined to make the best of it. She received him gladly when he arrived, introduced him and his wife to her students, took a house for them in Chelsea and appeared with the children on one or two occasions on the platform at the Sunday afternoon meetings.

But George Glover was still very much the square peg in the round hole, and his wife, likely much more at home in a mining camp than in

343

Boston, fitted no better than her husband into the very special *menage* which Mrs. Eddy at this time was obliged to maintain. Slowly but steadily as the weeks passed, the futility of the effort became more and more apparent, and at last George Glover and his family went out west once more, not to reappear on the scene for another decade.

Meanwhile, Mrs. Eddy was feeling more and more the need for someone who would stand to her in the same relation as her son might have stood if things had been different. Calvin Frye was faithful and efficient, but he was a man singularly lacking in any imagination. To him, routine was one of the great joys of life and one of its outstanding satisfactions. He was devoted to Mrs. Eddy, and whatever happened to be her vision of the moment was the limit of his desire. Mrs. Eddy, in whom the maternal instinct in spite of its many frustrations, was very strong, felt always the need for warm affection in those with whom she lived and worked, as there is abundant evidence to prove.

True, she had already written in her book *Science and Health* that if existence without personal friends would be to anyone a blank, then the time would surely come when he would be "solitary, left without sympathy. . . . Friends will betray and enemies will slander, until the lesson is sufficient to exalt you; for 'man's extremity is God's opportunity'." But, whatever her meaning and purpose in writing these words, she herself always sought the love that is expressed in personal friendships and hesitated not at all to say so. The memoirs of her household associates show this time after time. Caroline Foss Gyger speaks of her fond kisses, and Martha Wilcox tells how Mrs. Eddy, with tears streaming down her face, begged her never to leave her side. The laborious efforts of the traditionalists to paint a pale and unearthly Leader, forever platitudinizing on love instead of practising it, are effectively discredited by any one of a thousand episodes such as that in which she drew Mrs. Wilcox to her, patted her affectionately and said, "How nice and fat you are!"

And so, in the first moments of her final rather bitter conclusion that she had nothing to hope from her son in the way of aid for her work or comfort for her daily living, she cast around to see if there was not

344

someone who would take the place of what he might have been. As she did so, she seems to have thought more and more about the young physician, Ebenezer Foster, who had accompanied her party when they went to Chicago.

Ebenezer J. Foster was a graduate of Hahnemann Medical College in Philadelphia. About forty years of age, he had until 1887 been practising homeopathy in Waterbury, a little mountain town in Vermont, and the whole course of his life seemed to set towards his establishment there as a country and small town doctor. Then one day an old friend, who had long been sick, came to him and told him how he had been healed completely through reading a book called *Science and Health*, by a woman named Mary Baker Eddy. Doctor Foster was very deeply impressed, and shortly afterwards, being in Boston on a visit to an aunt, he went to call on Mrs. Eddy, with the result that next day he had joined one of her classes which was just then forming.

He was completely won over, returned to Waterbury for a time, but later gave up his practice there and came to live in Boston, opening an office and devoting himself with enthusiasm to the practice of the new teaching.

From the first, Mrs. Eddy seems to have seen in Ebenezer Foster someone who might afford her the help she so sorely needed. She invited him to accompany her to Chicago, and shortly after her return to Boston, grateful for all the help he had been to her and faced with another bitter crisis in her movement, she offered to adopt him as her son. He gladly assented, and so it was arranged. In her petition to the Court, Mrs. Eddy stated that "said Foster is now associated with your petitioner in business, home life and life work, and she needs such interested care and relationship." And so, on the 5th of November, 1888, the legal arrangements being complete, Ebenezer Foster assumed the name of Foster-Eddy, and entered Mrs. Eddy's household as her son.

But before this had been accomplished, the whole face of things in Boston had been changed. Through all the years of her progress, Mrs. Eddy had been slowly learning to distrust—as she expressed it—"both tear and triumph". It was not without reason that she had viewed the outbursts of enthusiasm in Chicago with a heavy heart. The train carrying her back to Boston had scarcely reached the South Station before she was faced with a crisis which threatened to disrupt the whole movement and caused her to make a decision which for audacity and courage has scarcely been equalled in the history of any great movement.

College Closed and
Church Dissolved

FOR SOME TIME before Mrs. Eddy left for Chicago, serious trouble had been developing among her followers in Boston. This trouble had its origin in two main tendencies, both present from the first, which were to maintain themselves in various forms as thorns in the flesh of the movement right up to the time of Mrs. Eddy's passing and beyond. The first of these was the tendency of certain of her students and followers to adulterate her teaching by the introduction of all manner of strange doctrine, and the second was sycophancy and its inevitable repercussion in its most rabid form. Richard Kennedy going out frankly as a dissident in 1872, and George Barry, after years of abject devotion, bringing suit against his patron and teacher to recover compensation for his every act of service, are typical instances of both tendencies, and they were to be duplicated again and again.

In the early days of 1888, the great problem confronting Mrs. Eddy was the protection of her teaching against adulteration by her students, and misrepresentation by her enemies. Of these, the former was by far the most dangerous, and she rightly so regarded it. For several years, as has been seen, Julius Dresser had been urging the claims of Quimby to be the real discoverer of Mrs. Eddy's teaching or rather of what he conceived Mrs. Eddy's teaching ought to be. There was, of course, a curious inconsistency in his position. On the one hand, the more fully he developed his concept of what Quimby actually taught, the more indignant he became over Mrs. Eddy's glaring departure from that teaching, and, at the same time, the more insistent was he that she was a plagiarist of the worst type. In 1887 Julius Dresser had published his book *The True History of Mental Science*, and the foundations for what came to be called the "New Thought" movement, as it exists today, were being laid.

Not a few of Mrs. Eddy's students were attracted by restatements and variations of Quimby's teaching. The appeal to manipulation, mental and physical, which underlay it, was much more readily comprehended by some mentalities than the appeal to spiritual law which was the basis of Mrs. Eddy's doctrine. Quimbyism would inevitably appear to them much more rational and simple. It put forward no such revolutionary ideas as that involved in denying the "sure-enough-isness", as one critic put it, of matter and the material creation, while it preserved, at all times, intact, the nexus with matter. In other words, it was easy to believe that mind could influence the body so long as there was some outward means provided by which the contact could be effected, even if it were only the making of passes with the hands or the manipulation of the head with wet fingers.

Even more misleading, because much more subtle, than the teaching of Quimby, as adapted by Dresser, was the adaptation of Christian Science to the Quimby doctrine. Quimbyism was always much more of a philosophy or a method of medicine than a religion, and as a consequence fell short in its appeal to many people. This shortcoming it was the objective of the ever recurring "new and improved system of mental healing" to make good.

One of the main attractions of all such teaching, to the less fervid among Mrs. Eddy's followers, was the "freedom" it seemed to offer the individual student. The suggestion that there was more than one way, that Christian Science was all right, but something else might be discovered that was just as good, if not better, had a tremendous appeal, especially to those who resented the stern discipline meted out by Mrs. Eddy in her insistence that it was no more possible to deviate by a hair's breadth from the principle of Christian Science and succeed in its demonstration than it was to deviate from the principle of mathematics and expect to solve its problems.

Mrs. Eddy was uncompromising in the matter. "Having seen so much suffering from quackery," she wrote in her book *Science and Health*, "the author desires to keep it out of Christian Science. The two-edged sword of Truth must turn in every direction to guard 'the tree of life'."[1] And so, as the danger increased, the Christian Scientist Association, under her direction, passed a series of resolutions, each one more drastic than the last, calculated to curb this tendency to go after other gods. Members of the Association were forbidden to use any other books as textbooks than *Science and Health* and the Bible. Later on, they were forbidden to meet in small groups to discuss Christian Science unless all members of the Association were invited to attend.

In spite of everything, however, the unrest and fermentation continued, and Mrs. Eddy knew when she set out for Chicago that she was leaving behind her in Boston a situation very much like that which had confronted her in Lynn, seven years before.

A typical instance of such "deviating doctrine" may be seen in the teaching of the Reverend Warren F. Evans which about that time was attracting much attention. Doctor Evans never was a student of Mrs. Eddy. Neither did he, as far as can be gathered, ever claim that he had evolved a rival system. Indeed, he seems to have been one of the earliest exponents of pure Quimbyism, having been treated by Quimby in 1863, and, as early as 1869, writing a book on the subject. His history was an interesting and significant one. Born in Rockingham, Vermont, in 1817,

[1] *Science and Health*, p. 458.

349

he was educated at Chester Academy, Middlebury College and Dartmouth. Later, he received a diploma which entitled him to the degree of M.D. from a chartered board of physicians of the Eclectic School. He left Dartmouth before he had finished his course there, and entered the ministry of the Methodist Episcopal Church, and, for some twenty years, held charges in various towns in New Hampshire and Massachusetts. Always somewhat frail, in the latter years of his ministry he suffered from persistent ill-health. This was in the early sixties of last century, when, as has been seen, all manner of excursions were being made into the occult and the mystic in the simplest meanings of those words, spiritualism, mesmerism, electromagnetism and so forth, while great impetus was given to the more spiritual and mystic teaching of Emanuel Swedenborg. And so, in these years of broken health, Evans began the study of the works of Swedenborg, and came to believe strongly in the possibility of curing physical disease through "the power of living faith".

About the year 1863, Evans went to Quimby for treatment. It was just a year after Mrs. Eddy's first meeting with him and, like her, Evans seems to have been convinced that he had found the truth for which he had long been seeking. The difference between the reaction of the two was, however, fundamental, for whereas Mary Patterson manifestly read into the Quimby doctrine views of a radically different kind, later to appear in Christian Science, Evans seems to have grasped Quimbyism more nearly as Quimby taught it than Dresser or anyone else. After a second visit to Portland, he told Quimby that he felt sure he could practise his teaching, and, on receiving cordial encouragement from the always generous little doctor, he returned to his home at Claremont, New Hampshire, and at once began to practise. He later set up a kind of mind cure sanatorium known as the "Evans Home" at Salisbury, Massachusetts, and in the latter years of his life devoted himself to writing books on the subject of mental healing. It is true, he surrounds it all with an atmosphere of religion and faith.

To Dresser and Evans were added several other minor "schools". Indeed, one of the causes of unrest among Mrs. Eddy's students was the temptation the situation presented to many of them to go out and found a school of their own, it would appear.

This was not the only reason for unrest, in this medley of personalities which constituted her following. About this time dissension from another direction was to shake the young movement to its very foundations. It happened that in the spring of 1888, Mrs. Abby H. Corner, one of Mrs. Eddy's students in West Medford, Massachusetts, attended her own daughter in childbirth, and that both the mother and the child died. An outraged community saw to it that Mrs. Corner was indicted for murder, seeing that she did not have medical attention for her daughter, and the case was given enormous publicity in the papers.

It was by no means unheard of for Christian Scientists to be dragged before the courts in those days charged by their religious and medical opponents with everything from practising medicine without a license to manslaughter. In the majority of such instances the Scientists won out, establishing their constitutional right to freedom of religious practice and free choice in the method of treatment to be followed. But this case was to have greater repercussions than any of the others.

Not a few in the Christian Scientist Association looked upon the situation as a test of their religion and called for a rallying to the support of their persecuted colleague at a special meeting. Although invited, Mrs. Eddy did not attend and, more disquieting still, the following letter appeared in the Boston *Herald* under date of April 29, over the signature of the "Committee on Publication, Christian Scientist Association":

"The lamentable case reported from West Medford of the death of a mother and her infant at childbirth should forever put a stop to quackery. There has been but one side of this case presented by the newspapers. We wait to hear from the other side, trusting that attenuating circumstances will be brought to light. Mrs. Abby H. Corner never entered the obstetrics class at the Massachusetts Metaphysical College. She was not fitted at this institute for an accoucheur, had attended but one term, and four terms, including three years of successful practice by the student, are required to complete the college course."

Not only had the Committee no knowledge of this letter before it was published, but the College had no more than three—not four—terms, practitioners did not "specialize" in their treatment of diseases and disorders, and all had been handling cases of every type without a three-years' apprenticeship.

Such was the position of affairs when thirty-six members decided to withdraw. But a formidable obstacle stood in their way. There was, it will be remembered, the stipulation in the organization by-laws that anyone who wished to resign his membership was guilty of immorality and should be publicly so branded. They were well aware of the fact that Spofford had suffered this fate.

So, when Mrs. Eddy was away on her memorable trip to Chicago, the dissident thirty-six, taking advantage of her absence, secured the Association books from the Secretary's wife, Mrs. William B. Johnson, and turned them over to a lawyer to be held until such time as they should receive letters of honourable discharge. Mrs. Eddy urged them to remain within the fold, writing in a circular letter to them: "At the first special meeting called in behalf of Mrs. Corner, I was absent not because unready or unwilling to help her, but that she needed no help and I knew it." Unmoved by this plea, the secessionists clung to the books, justifiably or otherwise, for nearly a year, at which point Mrs. Eddy yielded, granting each a letter of release, no strings attached.

Meanwhile, Mrs. Corner was tried in due course and acquitted, expert medical testimony being adduced that the cause of death was such as could not have been averted had a physician been in attendance.

But things could not be allowed to slip back into the old rut, where the danger of rebellion stood as a constant threat. The triumph in Chicago, followed within a few short weeks by apparent defeat in Boston; the bewildering contrast presented almost continuously among her followers of utter devotion or bitter rebellion; the silent, ill-concealed struggle everywhere apparent along the age-old lines of which should be greatest; her own seeming helplessness, in the presence of open rebellion, to settle the issue in any other way but by drastic material action; all these questions evidently began to culminate in a realization that the organization which she had so eagerly and gratefully built up might somehow be at fault, her college, her church, her association, with all the vision she had had for all three.

She did not act hastily, but she determined to get away from Boston, from the struggle and strife which seemed to be everywhere, and give herself time and opportunity to think it all out, and see if possible what was meant for her to do. Early in 1889 she sent her adopted son, Foster-Eddy—Bennie, as she called him—up into Vermont to look for a place for them to live. A few months previously she had written to a friend in the country, "Oh how I want, need, the sweet peace you are enjoying. But when I fall it must be with my armour on. He girdeth me. He is my shield and buckler. He alone can discharge me from this battle." Now apparently it came to her that the kind of stand she was being called upon to make was a much more difficult one than any she had contemplated.

On February 15, 1889, she addressed the huge audience at Steinway Hall in New York—already referred to—and had been almost mobbed by over-zealous followers and students; yet here in Boston the fight still smouldered. She was clearly being required to do something different. And so, on her return from New York, when she got word from Bennie that he had found a house for her in the little town of Barre in Vermont, she decided to leave Boston and try to solve her problem in the solitude of the snowbound countryside.

It was a slow and all too bitter process. In spite of all the difficulties with which she had to contend, the year 1888 had been for her one of tremendous activity. Applications for admission to her classes were coming in from all over the country. Between March, 1888, and February, 1889, she taught nearly two hundred students. Among those who went through her classes in this year were many who were later to become well known in the movement, such as General Erastus Bates, Edward A. Kimball, Julia Field-King, Lanson P. Norcross, Clara Shannon, Edward P. Bates, James A. Neal, Alfred Farlow and others. There could be no doubt in her mind but that the movement was going forward and at a rate she could hardly have thought possible. Evidently it was just this that was troubling her. Between her disturbing experience in New York on February 15, and her departure for Barre at the end of the month, she taught a class in Boston of over sixty students, and she had before her many applications for admission to future classes. Money was no longer a question. Men and women with wealth and substance were willing and eager to pay anything for her teaching, and although she never deviated from the fee of $300 established years before—save to reduce it or forego it altogether—money seemed now to come to her without effort on her part. This then was the picture as she took the train for Barre from the North Station in Boston the day following the last session of her class—it was to be her last for many years. It was a picture bewildering enough, presenting such glaring contrasts as unity and disaffection, devotion and treachery, outward and visible prosperity past belief, shot through in the most unexpected quarters with conspiracy and unseemly scramble for power, while in and out and over and above it all was an attachment to her own person, whether in love or hate, which evidently cast her into the depths.

She found no rest at Barre, and as the long winter gave way to spring she moved to Concord, New Hampshire, the scene of so much in her early life. It must have been a strange homecoming. Abigail, away over at Sanbornton Bridge, now Tilton, had been dead these many years, her last written words to her sister, words of bitter reproach. The family was scattered, and most of those who had known her were dead or had moved away. She took a house at 62 State Street, and it was here that she reached the strange decision which appeared to her as the solution of her problem. She would scrap everything and build again from the ground up, and in this new building she would eliminate the opportunities for personal conflicts as far as possible and cause the new structure to be founded on principles instead of persons.

She does not seem to have seen it all clearly at first. She made one last effort to withdraw herself and yet save her college by appointing Foster-

Eddy to teach her next class, and when that only gave rise to bitter dissatisfaction, she appointed General Erastus Bates to teach the next one. General Bates was more successful, but the clamour for Mrs. Eddy's own personal instruction continued unabated. And so some time in these days she evidently reached the final decision that the college should be closed and the church dissolved and the future progress of the movement left to unorganized voluntary effort and "the providence of God".

Her first step was with the *Journal*. She turned it over completely to the National Christian Scientist Association, and in her "seven fixed rules", which were published in the May issue, she declared emphatically that in the matter of leadership she desired to turn her followers away from her own personality to the principle of her doctrine. She laid it down, therefore, that she should not in future be consulted "verbally or through letters" on any questions such as the following:

"As to whose advertisement shall or shall not appear in the *Christian Science Journal.* . . .

"As to the matter that should be published in the *Journal* and *Christian Science Series.* . . .

"On marriage, divorce, or family affairs of any kind. . . .

"On the choice of pastors for churches. . . .

"On disaffections, if there should be any between students of Christian Scientists. . . .

"On who shall be admitted as members, or dropped from the membership of the *Christian Science Churches* or *Associations.* . . .

"On disease and the treatment of the sick; but I shall love all mankind and work for their welfare."

In June, when the National Christian Scientist Association held its annual meeting in Cleveland, the *Journal* was formally handed over to it, and the control vested in the "Publication Committee", which then consisted of Edward P. Bates of Syracuse, New York; Joseph Armstrong of Nebraska; William G. Nixon of Boston; and Augusta Stetson and Caroline D. Noyes of New York.

Having thus disposed of the *Journal*, Mrs. Eddy next turned her attention to her college. She hesitated here. When the rumour got abroad, as it did early in the year 1889, after her large class in February, that she really contemplated closing the college, protests from all quarters were so vigorous that, as has been seen, she hesitated and strove to compromise the situation by appointing others to teach in her place. When, in the late summer, it became apparent that this was no solution, she decided to take the drastic step of closing the institution entirely.

In a letter of explanation of her action, published in the Boston *Traveler*, she put the matter simply yet forcibly:

"There are", she wrote, "one hundred and sixty applications lying on the desk before me, for the Primary class in the Massachusetts Metaphysical College, and I cannot do my best work for a class which contains that number. When these were taught, another and a larger number would be in waiting for the same class instruction; and if I should teach that Primary class, the other three classes—one Primary and two Normal—would be delayed. The work is more than one person can well accomplish, and the imperative call is for my exclusive teaching.

"From the scant history of Jesus and of his disciples, we have no Biblical authority for a public institution. This point, however, had not impressed me when I opened my College. I desire to revise my book 'Science and Health with Key to the Scriptures,' and in order to do this I must stop teaching at present. The work that needs to be done, and which God calls me to outside of College work, if left undone might hinder the progress of our Cause more than my teaching would advance it: therefore I leave all for Christ."

Later on, in her book *Retrospection and Introspection*, she suggests how deeply she pondered the question at this time, when she writes: "The apprehension of what has been, and must be, the final outcome of material organization, which wars with Love's spiritual compact, caused me to dread the unprecedented popularity of my College."

Her followers, although stunned and not a little dismayed at her action, seemed to have apprehended with surprising rapidity, if only dimly at first, what she was seeking to do. When a meeting of the Metaphysical College called for the purpose assembled on October 29, 1889, the dissolution was effected in a series of resolutions, which later became historic.

After reciting the purpose and history of the College, its admittedly temporary nature, and the fact that its president at the height of the institution's prosperity was willing to sacrifice it all, if thereby greater spirituality might be gained, the statement continued:

"RESOLVED, That an Institution for instruction in Christian Science, which is the highest, purest and noblest of all teaching, should be of a spiritual formation wholly outside of material regulations, forms or customs," for which, with other reasons listed, the unanimous vote is, "That as all debts of the Corporation have been paid, it is deemed best to dissolve this Corporation, and the same is hereby dissolved."

So the College was closed and the right by charter to confer degrees permanently surrendered.

After the College came the Church. Here, in a way, the situation was simple. The dissolution of the material organization did not debar, and was evidently not intended to debar, any voluntary meeting. But in her letter urging dissolution, written from Concord under date November 28, 1889, Mrs. Eddy makes it perfectly clear that if any material organization was to be maintained, it would have to be along far different lines from the one that was being dissolved. And so she wrote:

"The Church of Christ (Scientist) in Boston was my patient seven years. When I would think she was well nigh healed a relapse came and a large portion of her flock would forsake the better portion, and betake themselves to the world's various hospitals for the cure of mortal maladies." She was referring, she explained, to those straying sheep who either claimed improvements on her doctrine or disappeared in ignominy. She had put up with this condition of her Church for a decade, but must now say, as to a patient who is relapsing because of dependence upon physical hygiene, "quit your material props and leave all for Christ, spiritual power, and you will recover." If they would agree "to drop all material rules whereby to regulate Christ, Christianity, and adopt alone the golden rule for unification, progress, and a better example," by the simple procedure of disorganizing, she promised to provide them with a plot of ground suitable for the erection of a shining edifice all their own. The deadline was set for their annual meeting to be held December 2, 1889, at which time their decision must be embodied in official action.

When the members met at this meeting, they voted to disorganize, and in the next issue of the *Journal* the whole strange series of incidents was brought to a close in a simple statement by Mrs. Eddy which sought to emphasize once again the purpose of it all.

"The dissolution of the visible organization of the church", she wrote, "is the sequence and complement of that of the College Corporation and Association. The College disappeared that the spirit of Christ might have freer course among its students and all who come into the understanding of Divine Science, the bonds of the Church were thrown away so that its members might assemble themselves together to 'provoke one another to good works' in the bond only of love."

A Troubled Scene

OF THE OLD organization there now remained only the National Christian Scientist Association. It had been loosely formed and was loosely held together, and it is possible that, after she had closed her College and dissolved the organization of her Church, Mrs. Eddy had hoped that the National Christian Scientist Association might survive. It was not long, however, before she became convinced that in the future it would have to be one safeguarded as never before by mutual agreement against attack from without or disintegration from within. Surrounded on all sides, as her movement was, by those who sought to pull it down and out of the wreckage to fashion something more after their own liking, she held that an obligation was owed to the public that, if they sought what she taught, they should be sure of getting what they wanted, and not run the risk of unwilling entanglement in all manner of strange doctrine.

When she closed her College and dissolved her Church, she was clearly passing through a stage when she thought and hoped that the way out was a complete abandonment of all organization. "From the scant history of Jesus and of his disciples, we have no Biblical authority for a public institution," she declared in her notice closing the College, adding that that point had not impressed her when she opened it. The directors of the College in their closing resolutions had echoed the same thought, declaring that they found "no platform in Christ's teachings for such material methods of instruction". It was the same when she disbanded her Church and urged its members to "drop all material rules whereby to regulate Christ, Christianity".

It is hard to be sure what she really had in mind about this time, probably because her own thought was in a state of flux, torn between the counsel of perfection as seen in the "Christly method" and the insistent demand of human nature for the outward and visible sign of united action involved in an organized church.

But whatever she was thinking, she pursued undeviatingly her course towards the dissolution of old bonds. When the National Christian Scientist Association met in New York in the year following the dissolution of the Church, it received a letter from its President couched in much the same terms as the notices regarding her College and Church and urging the body to disband.

This letter, dated from Concord, throws much light on her state of mind. The hope that the way out was to be an abandonment of all organization is still very much in the ascendant, for she clearly views with distrust the elaborate preparation that had gone to the gathering of the convention. There is more than a shade of impatience in her opening sentence, "Accept my thanks for your card of invitation, your badge, and order of exercises, all of which are complete," and more than a little reflection on the value of such meetings in her recalling of the fact that at a previous meeting at which she was present the atmosphere had been such that no thoughtful conference had been possible. "I remember my regret, when, having asked in general assembly if you had any questions to propose, I received no reply."

After thus preparing the ground, she moves forward at once to the purpose of her letter. She is gently persuasive, but the immense strength of her conviction is clear enough.

"Now, dear ones, if you take my advice again, you will do—what? Even this: Disorganize the National Christian Scientist Association! and each one return to his place of labour, to work out individually and alone, for himself and for others, the sublime ends of human life."

In thus recommending the dissolution of the National Association, Mrs. Eddy makes it clear that individual groups of Christian Scientists are to be left free to do as they think best in the matter of organizing among themselves. "My students can *now* organize their students into associations, form churches, and hold these organizations of their own,—until, in turn, their students will sustain themselves, and work for others." But she goes on to show that she has no illusions as to the final value of the time-honoured system of "getting together".

"For students to work together is not always to co-operate, but sometimes to co-elbow! . . . I once thought that in unity was human strength; but have grown to know that human strength is weakness,—that unity is divine might, giving to human power, peace."

And so the National Christian Scientist Association was disbanded, and the abandonment of organized effort was complete.

It was only just in time. Nothing, it is to be imagined, is more dangerous to the integrity of any cause than an organization so loose that its members cannot be held to a common objective. A movement that can depend solely upon the demonstration of a principle is always safe. The proof of works is final and incontrovertible, and it was clearly towards this final satisfaction that Mrs. Eddy was looking as she left Boston for Barre in the spring of 1889, and for several years thereafter. As long as the only passport to fellowship was an ability to heal the sick in the fullest meaning of that term, spurious doctrine should eliminate itself through its inability to meet the demand.

Be that as it may, unorthodox—if not spurious—doctrines continued to grow apace. Of such bids for attention perhaps the most extraordinary was that put forward by Josephine Woodbury. Josephine Woodbury with her husband, Edgar F. Woodbury, were, it will be remembered, among Mrs. Eddy's earliest students, and their social position in Boston gave them from the first a prominence not enjoyed at that time by other followers of the new teaching. Mr. and Mrs. Woodbury entertained considerably, both at their town house in Boston and at their summer place at Ocean Point, Maine, and as the years passed, Mrs. Woodbury attracted a large coterie, mostly of young people, who under her leadership, developed a romantic and emotionalized version of Christian Science —if we are to judge from both the words of her critics and the dramatic events which were to follow in time.

Josephine Woodbury was an able woman, and in her association with Mrs. Eddy seems to have done some devoted work. She made lecture tours as far west as Denver, wrote frequently for the *Journal* and later became a qualified teacher. She was, however, of an eager, romantic disposition, the type of woman upon whom it was not easy to impose restraints. Almost from the first, Mrs. Eddy seems to have had difficulty with her, and the outstanding characteristic of Mrs. Eddy's letters to her over a period of some ten or fifteen years—many of them have been preserved—is her constant efforts to keep Mrs. Woodbury in line. In 1888-89, the years when so much else that was ominous and troubled was rising up, Josephine Woodbury increasingly indulged the unconventional until finally, in the summer of 1890, she announced to her friends and students that she was about to give birth to a child which had been immaculately conceived. The announcement immediately became a front page story, and Mrs. Eddy, struggling with a thousand other problems as to the future of the movement, found this burden of ridicule added to all the others.

Very wisely she took no public action in the matter, but her letters show that she begged Mrs. Woodbury to retreat from the position she had taken up, insisting that such claims were utterly inconsistent with her understanding of Christian Science. Mrs. Woodbury, however, not only refused to change her stand, but when the child—a boy—was born, as he was early in June, she named him "The Prince of Peace".

362

Doubts may have assailed some of Mrs. Woodbury's followers, but quite a number rose enthusiastically to the occasion and accepted her statements at their face value. Mrs. Woodbury, meanwhile, far from modifying her claims, even increased them, going so far as to declare that Mrs. Eddy herself foretold the event, and a few weeks after the child was born she had it publicly baptized in a pool on her Ocean Point estate, which she had for the purpose named Bethesda. In a strange book written some years later, entitled *War in Heaven* Mrs. Woodbury gives a vivid description of the scene.

"There occurred the thought of baptizing little Prince in a singularly beautiful salt pool, whose rocky bottom was dry at low tide and over-flowing at high tide, but especially attractive at mid-tide, with its two feet of crystal water. A crowd of people had assembled on the neighbour-ing bluffs, when I brought him from our cottage not far away, and laid him three times prayerfully in the pool and when he was lifted therefrom, they joined in a spontaneously appropriate hymn."

Such an incident, to which the newspapers did not fail to do full justice, created a difficult situation. Ridicule had been heaped upon Mrs. Eddy's teaching from the first and was to be heaped upon it repeatedly in the future, but, in all previous and all subsequent cases, ridicule had no fundamental justification and so fell ultimately by its own weight. Here, on the contrary, was something that invited ridicule; while any serious protest could but add to the flames.

Did not Mrs. Eddy say that if spiritual healing was possible in the day of Jesus it must be possible in our own age and clime? By the same token, demanded Mrs. Woodbury, would it not follow that, if the immaculate conception actually took place at Bethlehem, virgin-birth must be fully as possible today? Very wisely, Mrs. Eddy did not pick up the gauntlet. After the tumult had died down, she re-affirmed her faith in "the Scriptural narrative of the Virgin-mother and Bethlehem babe," but cautioned against "speculative theories as to the recurrence of such events." Would anyone presume to take the place of the Virgin Mary? was the burden of her argument. Then, in *Science and Health* she forestalled all future claimants among her followers with this sentence: "The perpetuation of the floral species by bud or cell-division is evident, but I discredit the belief that agamogenesis applies to the human species."

So the incident passed. Josephine Woodbury was to enter the story of the movement once again, even more vividly, within a few years, but now, so far as the outside world was concerned, she was quite forgotten. Within the ranks of Mrs. Eddy's followers attention was now more and more preoccupied with speculation and surmise as to the future which their leader was planning for her church and the cause as a whole.

It is not possible to say when, in the course of these nearly two years of retirement, Mrs. Eddy reached the conclusion that the human mind was not yet ready for the "Christly method", as she described the completely unorganized plan. Almost from the first, through the *Journal,* she was urging upon her students in various quarters to form churches of their own. She evidently regarded these churches just as loose gatherings together of her followers in almost apostolic simplicity, and it is possible she thought that ultimately the Church in Boston might be re-established and go forward in the same way. But that she had no idea of the Church in Boston being abandoned is evidenced by her letter of November 28, 1889, urging its dissolution.

In that letter she announced that she had "deeded to those who shall build a church edifice the plot of land designed for the site of such an edifice and which is now valued at $15,000."

The idea that such a church would one day be builded had been in her mind for years. As far back as 1886, her followers had begun to collect money for such a building, and the plot of land upon which The Mother Church now stands in Falmouth Street had actually been secured. The contributions had paid off a substantial portion of its cost. Now, however, the mortgage was falling due and this situation presented a clear opportunity to at last establish her church on a rebellion-proof foundation. Acquiring title to the property personally at a fraction of its value, she proved her altruism in the affair by immediately handing over the land in trust to one of her students, Ira O. Knapp, for reconveyance to three trustees, namely, Alfred Lang, Marcellus Monroe and William G. Nixon. While the church was thus the beneficiary, her control thereafter was to be assured through her own by-laws governing the trustees, the exercise of such by-laws in key instances to be contingent always upon her written signature of approval. This unchallengeable control, which she deemed vital to the welfare of the movement, was the whole purpose of the elaborate transaction which she describes in *Miscellanous Writings* as "circuitous," "morally and spiritually inalienable but materially questionable." Her maneuver was astute and successful, and perhaps the only way in which the movement could be stabilized at that time.

At first all went well, until William Nixon, who was then Mrs. Eddy's publisher, raised the question as to the legality of the Trustees' receiving contributions for the building of a church which was without charter or organization or legal standing of any kind. Perhaps it was then that Mrs. Eddy decided that in a social order built up and held together by rules, conventions and regulations of all kinds, it would be impossible to develop a church which should exist "alone", as she was to put it later on a memorable occasion,"in the affections, and need no organization to express it."

The three trustees were so convinced that their position was questionable at law—as indeed it was—as the law was then understood, that they all three resigned, after making their position secure by returning all the subscriptions received for the building fund to the amount of about $23,000 to the donors. Mrs. Eddy tried in vain to prevent this being done, insisting that "the title was from God, and no material title could affect God's temple." The trustees were thoroughly scared. The Massachusetts Insurance Title Company had refused to insure the title and advised that the position was entirely illegal, and so when the money had been returned, Ira O. Knapp conveyed the property once again to Mrs. Eddy for a consideration of one dollar, and the work was begun all over again.

Mrs. Eddy was insistent that subscriptions to the building fund should be received and the church built in the way she had planned, and that if research were carried far enough it would be found that the method she proposed was perfectly legal. "Unity prevailed," she wrote in the *Journal*, "till mortal man sought to know who owned God's temple, and adopted and urged only the material side of this question. . . . I believe—yea, I understand—that with the spirit of Christ actuating all parties concerned about this legal quibble, it can easily be corrected to the satisfaction of all."

And so in the end it proved. A long disused statute, originally passed in behalf of the Methodist Church, was discovered which provided that "the deacons, church wardens or other similar officers of church or religious societies" could be "deemed bodies corporate for the purpose of taking and holding in succession all grants and donations, whether of real or personal estate, made either to them or their successors, or to their respective churches, or to the poor of their churches."

It was then further discovered that, although the church had been dissolved, its charter had never been surrendered. Mrs. Eddy set to work at once. On September 2, 1892, she deeded the Falmouth Street property to four trustees, Ira O. Knapp, William B. Johnson, Joseph S. Eastaman and Stephen A. Chase, who undertook to erect thereon within five years a church building to cost not less than $50,000.

This deed of conveyance has always and very justly been looked upon as one of the important landmarks in the history of the movement, for in it the plans for a "Mother Church", which Mrs. Eddy had evidently been formulating for some time, were first unfolded. Up to now the Boston Church had been like any other church, a local organization with a local membership. Henceforth, it was to draw its membership from all over the world. Members of local churches could be members of The Mother Church, whilst it also opened its doors to those who had no local affiliations but felt that they could subscribe to its tenets.

These tenets were at first of the simplest nature. They were only three in number and the whole confession of faith was comprised in about one hundred and fifty words. They were as follows:

"1. As adherents of Truth, we take the Scriptures for our guide to eternal Life.

"2. We acknowledge and adore one supreme God. We acknowledge His Son, the Holy Ghost, and man in His image and likeness. We acknowledge God's forgiveness of sin, in the destruction of sin, and His present and future punishment of 'Whatever worketh abomination or maketh a lie'. And the atonement of Christ, as the efficacy of Truth and Love. And the way of salvation as demonstrated by Jesus casting out evils, healing the sick, and raising the dead,—resurrecting a dead faith to seize the great possibilities and living energy of the Divine Life.

"3. We solemnly promise to strive, watch and pray for that Mind to be in us which was also in Christ Jesus. To love the brethren, and, up to our highest capacity, to be meek, merciful, and just, and live peaceably with all men."

Nothing could well be broader but Mrs. Eddy was determined that, as far as her new church could safeguard it, its membership should be limited to those who would strive to live up to the spirit as well as the letter of their undertaking.

First of all, the Trustees were constituted a "perpetual body" to be known as the "Christian Science Board of Directors". This board was empowered, as soon as the church was built, to elect the pastor, speaker or reader and to make all necessary rules for this purpose. It was required to maintain public worship, while the deed further provided that, "whenever said Directors shall determine that it is inexpedient to maintain preaching, reading or speaking in said church," the property must be reconveyed forthwith to Mrs. Eddy, her heirs or assigns.

The method of forming the church body was simple but effective. Twelve Charter Members were appointed by Mrs. Eddy. These Charter Members in turn elected First Members nominated by Mrs. Eddy, who, until their duties, always somewhat ill defined, were turned over to the Board of Directors, as they were in 1901, constituted a kind of seldom summoned "privy council" whose main duty was to get the church started.

The work once begun was pushed through with remarkable rapidity.

Mrs. Eddy knew exactly what she wanted, while her experience through the years, many of them bitter enough, had shown her clearly whom she could trust and whom she could not. The deed was signed on September 2, 1892. On September 21, with the Charter Members duly appointed, the election of First Members took place, and on October 5, at a general meeting called for the purpose, the enrolment of regular members began. On this occasion, fifty-nine persons were admitted to membership. Two years later, the membership had risen to nearly three thousand, ninety-five per cent of whom lived outside Boston. The Mother Church had become a national institution.

The Building of the Church

THE BUILDING OF the original Mother Church edifice, like so much else in the history of the Christian Science movement, presents on the surface a picture of conflict clearly demanding for its resolution the understanding of motives and purposes not apparent to the casual observer. No more satisfying objective could well be imagined—if traditional views are to be accepted—than the project advanced and expanded in successive issues of the *Christian Science Journal* by the Board of Directors for the building of a permanent home for the Church in Boston.

So it was accepted by Christian Scientists everywhere. Those who had had their original contributions returned to them, now sent them back again to Boston, often doubled and trebled. In order that the work might go forward more rapidly, some forty of Mrs. Eddy's students were asked to contribute one thousand dollars each immediately. Mrs. Eddy made the request—and yet it is clear from letters and statements about this time that her great concern was to turn the thoughts of her students and followers away from what they were doing in the matter of material achievement to its spiritual significance. The louder and more exultant grew the rejoicing, the more surely did Mrs. Eddy come out with some reminder that what they were doing amounted to very little if anything in comparison with what they were thinking.

Thus the issue of the *Journal* for March, 1892, might well have been regarded as a "Church Building Number". It contained the architect's plans for the proposed Mother Church Building and Publishing House, a full list to date of subscribers to the building fund, a poem by Adelaide Proctor on giving, and a vigorous editorial dealing with the whole question of church and church building. The issue is pervaded by enthusiasm and evidently designed to arouse Christian Scientists everywhere to renewed effort.

It might reasonably be expected that Mrs. Eddy would have placed herself unequivocally in the forefront of this appeal and used her immense influence to supplement the efforts of the Trustees. Instead, she uses this issue of the *Journal* to emphasize the fact that the whole enterprise has no other basis than that of "suffer it to be so now".

"It is not indispensable", she wrote, "to organize materially Christ's Church. It is not absolutely necessary to ordain pastors and to dedicate churches; but if this be done, let it be in concession to the period, and not as a perpetual or indispensable ceremonial of the Church. If our Church is organized, it is to meet the demand, 'Suffer it to be so now'. The real Christian compact is love for one another. This bond is wholly spiritual and inviolate."

Nothing, however, could lessen the enthusiasm of Christian Scientists everywhere. Neither did Mrs. Eddy seek in any way to lessen it. That was quite clearly not at all her purpose. She never failed to express her appreciation of what was being done, and when a fund was started by the children to furnish and decorate the suite of rooms which were being planned for her in the tower of the church, it seems to have touched her deeply. She was, however, firmly determined that the substance should not be lost in the shadow.

The corner stone of the new building was laid on May 21, 1894, and in the course of her address Mrs. Eddy once again emphasized the same point. Nevertheless, it is possible to read into what she said on this occasion a more satisfied sense that what they were doing had to be done and should be done at that particular time. "The Church," she said, "more than any other institution, at present is the cement of society, and it should be the bulwark of civil and religious liberty. But the time cometh when the religious element, or Church of Christ, shall exist alone in the affections, and need no organization to express it. Till then, this form of godliness seems as requisite to manifest its spirit, as individuality to express Soul and substance."

There was much else, of course, in the address. It was a joyful happy gathering and Mrs. Eddy made it clear that she thought it was so. She briefly went over the story of the building as it had progressed and was to progress, spoke of the donations that had come in from all over the world so promptly and gratefully, of the children's fund and of the many letters she had received. She then went on to tell of how the stone—granite—for the building was coming from her native New Hampshire, and of how that day they were laying away under the foundation stone the names of all those who had subscribed to the building fund, "in your own handwriting", together with a copy of the Bible and *Science and Health*.

The ceremony, as described later in the June issue of the *Journal*, was of the simplest character:

"It consisted of silent prayer, and the audible repetition in unison of the Lord's Prayer by the Christian Science Board of Directors, thus quietly fulfilling the Scripture, 'His voice was not heard in the street'. And thus unostentatiously was consummated the laying of our corner stone,—the type of that stone which of old the builders rejected, but which 'is become the head of the corner; this is the Lord's doing and it is marvellous in our eyes'.

"As evidence of the watchfulness and faithfulness of those having immediate charge of the matter," the account went on to say, "we deem it but just to state, that through three successive stormy nights, two trusted students—James A. Neal and Thomas W. Hatten—watched the stone with its precious contents. This was made necessary by certain delays, which prevented for the time being, the final completion of a part of the mechanical work."

Referring in conclusion to the ease and rapidity with which the necessary funds had been raised, the account says: "With an analogy almost approaching the miracle of the Master in bringing out of the mouth of a fish the money with which to pay tribute, the large sum of money referred to in the Address, rolled into the treasurer's hands in prompt response to the Leader's simple call. No doubt, if the history associated with the 'demonstration' of these respective sums were known, it would make a chapter which would amaze even the most credulous."

Some six months later, namely, on January 6, 1895, the new Church was dedicated. The final cost of the building was something over $250,000.

The dedication of the original Mother Church in Boston served, as nothing else could have done, to focus public attention on a movement vaguely realized for many years but now suddenly taking shape as a national institution. Practically every newspaper in the United States of any importance and many abroad carried long descriptions of the new Church and the dedication ceremonies, while the story of Mrs. Eddy's life and the movement of which she was the recognized leader was given prominent place both in the newspapers and magazines.

What seemed to impress the general thought most was that, in spite of the fact that the dedication ceremonies were held in the depth of winter when Boston is almost surely frost-bound and snow-bound, thousands of Christian Scientists travelled from all over the country and often from beyond its borders to attend the opening ceremonies. The Boston newspapers especially, all too familiar with their own climate at that time of the year, found it hard to understand such enthusiasm.

"Surging crowds of Christian Scientists", said the Boston *Globe,* "from all parts of the United States poured in and out of the new edifice. . . . More than 6,000 of the faithful worshipped in the beautiful temple and participated in the dedicatory exercises. . . . The cars were loaded all day, and the church was the centre of attraction to the travel. It was interesting to watch the people stand in the cold, with the snow beating down upon them, gazing with loving eyes at their beautiful temple."

The New York *Sun,* after referring to the fact that it was necessary to hold five services in order to accommodate all those who wanted to attend, went on to relate how Mrs. Eddy had "announced her intention of being absent on the occasion, and sent a communication ordaining the Bible and *Science and Health* as the rightful pastor of the Church."

The first service, as described in the *Journal's* account of the matter, began promptly at nine o'clock a.m., and was attended largely by the local congregation for whose accommodation it was specially given. Another was held at ten-thirty a.m.; another at twelve mid-day; another at one-thirty p.m.; and the last at three o'clock p.m. The same order was repeated at each service except the second, at which the children, who had contributed the funds for the building and furnishing of the Mother's Room, were present in a body.

Mrs. Eddy, as has been noted, was not there, but she sent a dedicatory address which was read at all the services. It is in many ways a remarkable document, chiefly because of its restraint. There is, it is true, running through it a quiet note of triumph. "No longer are we of the church militant, but of the church triumphant; and with Job of old we exclaim, 'Yet in my flesh shall I see God'." But, for the most part, she is as usual concerned with turning the thoughts of her auditors away from the outward and visible to the inward and spiritual. "There is a thought higher and deeper than the edifice. Material light and shade are temporal, not eternal." Nevertheless, she allows herself to look backwards and re-traverse some of the path, often stony enough, by which she had reached that day and occasion, the persecution and derision of the early days, the encouragement of such men as Bronson Alcott, who had been her friend, and Wendell Phillips, who had said, "Had I young blood in my veins, I would help that woman"; and the steady winning of the way by her book *Science and Health*. And so she came to a concluding prayer or invocation, the effect of which in the circumstances may well have been remarkable:

373

"Divine presence, breathe Thou Thy blessing on every heart in this house. Speak out, O Soul! This is the newborn of Spirit, this is His redeemed; this, His beloved. May the kingdom of God within you,—with you alway,—reascending, bear you outward, upward, heavenward. May the sweet song of silver-throated singers, making melody more real, and the organ's voice, as the sound of many waters, and the Word spoken in this sacred temple dedicated to the ever-present God—mingle with the joy of angels and rehearse your hearts' holy intents. May all whose means, energies, and prayers helped erect The Mother Church, find within it home, and *heaven*."

So, as the world would view it, was a great work completed. But Mary Baker Eddy was far from sharing the world's view. For her the work had only just begun. She accorded what had been done no more than a passing glance. It was fully three months after the dedication of her Church before she took time to make the journey to Boston in order to see it. Apparently, she viewed with misgiving the flood of personal adulation and publicity the whole episode had evoked, and it is evident from her letters, about this time, that she was casting around in ever-increasing doubt for some means of saving for herself some small measure of that peace and quiet for which she greatly longed and which she greatly needed.

It is quite evident that the woman, about this time, was literally thronged. The more earnestly she strove to safeguard her movement from alien teaching, the more inevitably was she called upon to settle questions of doctine and give her endorsement to what conformed. She was nothing if not plain-spoken on the matter. Some of her public statements are veritable whips of thongs which she laid about her, quite regardless apparently of consequences. Thus, in the very issue of the *Journal* describing the laying of the corner stone, in fact on the very next page to the rather fulsome account of the matter, she has a statement under the title "Take Notice" which leaves no doubt as to her meaning:

"I hereby state publicly and *positively*, that until I advertise through these pages, or send special requests to individuals to the contrary of this statement, I shall not receive a call from anyone, nor read letters,

374

MSS., etc., which I have not myself first solicited. I advertise this, after waiting over two years for sufficient time of my own to arrange my writing desk, and while having on hand packages of sermons, with request that I examine them, other people's correspondence to read, heaps of MSS. sent for approval, pyramids of letters requiring immediate answers, tiered columns of applicants to call on me, business letters innumerable, etc.

"My work for The Mother Church *is done*; and be it remembered that five years ago I came to Concord, N.H., for the purpose of *retirement.*

"If I know myself this is my sole desire—that all whom I have taught Christian Science, and all its teachers and its students by whomsoever taught, yes, that all mankind, shall have one Shepherd, and He shall gather them into His fold (unto Himself) Divine Love.

MARY BAKER EDDY"

With individuals seeking an interview whom maybe she would have been glad to see but simply could not from lack of time, Mrs. Eddy was less emphatic, but there was always, as in the notice above, attached to her most vitriolic utterances a revealing note of kindness which softened the blow and, as many later testified, served to open their eyes to their own lack of consideration and failure to "do their own work". Thus, in one of her letters evidently dealing with some such situation, Mrs. Eddy says: "I cannot and do not receive visits any more from anyone but from those who come at my request to help me or who are my students. This, dear one, is the reason, viz. I have so much writing and care as a leader in a cause to which I devote my entire life that I have not time to visit or to be visited. Now this is not because I would not enjoy seeing you, but because I *cannot* give more than one hour to anyone unless it is to work with me in my field of labour."

To a friend who had apparently written to her regretting how seldom she was seen in Boston, Mrs. Eddy replies wearily. "The fact is I am allowed no earthly peace and it is this that keeps me from visiting my church oftener."

However, the day came when she determined to make the journey and see for herself that about which she had heard and read so much. In her

375

dedication message she had spoken happily of how sure she was that if she had been there in person she would have felt like the Queen of Sheba before the treasures of Solomon and would have to say like her that the half had not been told her. But when she did go she went alone and unannounced.

It was on April 1, 1895. Winter was just giving way to spring and it was the week before Easter. She had heard that her followers when she came were eager to have the chimes rung in the tower and to greet her with flowers, and so she told no one of her plans until the last minute and then, attended only by one or two of her household, left Concord for Boston. When she arrived, she drove at once to the Church, prepared to spend the night in the Mother's Room in the tower. Her first view of the auditorium was from the door at the end of the centre aisle. It was late afternoon and the light was failing, so she asked that the lights in the auditorum might be turned on. When this was done, she walked up the aisle until she came under the dome. There she stood for a moment and then, advancing towards the platform, knelt down on the first step. She was seventy-four now, and her hair, always one of her beauties, was snow white. Clara Shannon, who describes the scene in her recollections, goes on to tell how that, after a little while, she rose slowly and mounted the platform, going to the desk on the right. There she waited a moment and then very softly but quite audibly repeated the Ninety-first Psalm through to the end. "With long life will I satisfy Him; and show Him my salvation." She waited again a little while and then, going over to the other desk, repeated one of her favourite hymns, "Guide me, O Thou great Jehovah", through the prayer of the first verse to the quiet affirmation of the second:

> Open is the crystal fountain,
> Whence the healing waters flow;
> And the fiery, cloudy pillar
> Leads me all my journeys through.
> Strong Deliv'rer. Still Thou art my strength and shield.

Next day—it was Sunday morning—she left the Church quite early and returned to Concord.

Pleasant View

WHEN MRS. EDDY left Boston, in the summer of 1889, and went to Concord, seeking the refuge of her native hills in which to work out the strangely mixed problems that confronted her, Concord took little note of her coming. As has been seen, most of those who had known her in the days of her youth or young womanhood had passed away or had joined in the great national movement westward and found new homes in new states. The old familiar landmarks were still there: the old elm on North State Street under which as a child she used to play on Sundays, "between the morning and afternoon services," when her father drove in with the family from Bow; the building in which Franklin Pierce had his office; the winding road to Sanbornton Bridge, the straight stretches and great bends of the Merrimac; and the hills and brooks of Bow, amid which she and Andrew Gault had taken things so seriously when she was all of fifteen and Andrew not quite twenty.

A new Concord was to open for her in the near future, a Concord wherein she was to be reckoned a leading citizen; but when she rented a house there in the summer of 1889 at 62 State Street, the townsfolk took little notice of it. She was already a well-known and greatly loved or greatly opposed woman to thousands of people throughout the country and beyond its borders, but Concord through many years had been used to hearing strange stories out of Boston and gave little heed to them. This was exactly what this tired, much enduring woman needed. With the faithful Calvin Frye and Foster-Eddy to help her, she could carry on her work vigorously and yet be free in a measure from the thousand and one intrusions which threatened at times to overwhelm her in Boston. It was in Concord that she worked out her plan to pull down her organization, and it was here in Concord that she laid the foundation for its rebuilding.

Through the first two years of her retirement she lived in the house on State Street, and then one day in the spring of 1892, in the course of one of the daily drives she allowed herself, she found at a point about a mile and a half west of the city on Pleasant Street—at that distance a country road again—an old farmhouse for sale. It stood not far from the road on a little knoll whence the view southward was along a narrow valley, at the end of which rose the gentle green hills of Bow, one above the other, their sides covered as she always remembered them with fields and woodlands. She seems to have decided there and then that that was where she wanted to live, and within a short time she had bought the house and the land that went with it.

It was a more important move than appeared on the surface. In the troubled times that followed and thereafter for many years—seventeen in all—Pleasant View, as Mrs. Eddy called her new possession, was for her a haven of refuge without which it might have been impossible for her to do what she did do. Concord was just far enough from Boston so that anyone would think twice, especially in those days, about making the journey, and yet near enough to be accessible within a few hours. Moreover, Pleasant View afforded her, particularly at first when she was rebuilding the house and planning the garden, a relaxation and diversion she greatly needed. And she certainly went to it with a will. The original house was quite small and commonplace, but Mrs. Eddy added bow windows and wide verandas, built a *porte-cochère* at the front of the house and a tower room with a balcony at the south-east corner, whence the best view of the hills and valleys was to be had. Later on she bought more land, built a gardener's cottage, stables and out-buildings. She sought privacy, but always seems to have had a strong objection to anything that looked like seclusion. There were no high fences around Pleasant View, the hedges were kept low and neatly trimmed, while the lawns and gaily stocked flower beds were always plainly visible from the road.

The project occasioned tremendous interest among her students and followers everywhere. In that mysterious way common in such cases whereby information is spread abroad, word of what Mrs. Eddy was doing reached the most distant parts of the Field—as the wide spread of the movement was coming to be called—and Mrs. Eddy began to receive gifts large and small for her new home. Among these, perhaps the most interesting, because it gave rise to one of her most important shorter writings, was the gift by a group of students of a little pond for her garden. It is still there, fed as always by two or three small springs and such surface waters as seep in from the hillside. Not to be outdone, another group, this time in Toronto, Canada, sent her a boat for the pond, and the little boat house that was built for it was long one of the features in the grounds of Pleasant View. To the donors, she wrote: "Across lakes into a kingdom, I reach out my hand to clasp yours."

But if Pleasant View tended to become more and more of an establishment, Mrs. Eddy continued to maintain the simplicity which had always characterized her life. She rose at six in summer and seven in winter, and after breakfast usually walked for a while, either pacing up and down the veranda at the back of the house, or, if the day was fair, strolling with some of her household round the little pond or along the paths through the trees beyond it. She loved her garden and delighted in doing things that others thought impossible, like moving trees in summer or having things planted too late or too early, and seeing them come to perfection just the same. There was something at times almost pathetic in her love for flowers and natural beauty. It had been one of the great passions of her childhood, and one of her sternest condemnations was directed against a misinterpretation of her teaching which sought to make little of physical beauty. "To take all earth's beauty into one gulp of vacuity and label beauty nothing, is ignorantly to caricature God's creation, which is unjust to human sense and to the divine realism. . . . Earth is more spiritually beautiful to my gaze now than when it was more earthly to the eyes of Eve."[1]

There was always something behind her indulgence. She might sit for an hour or more at a time in the dusk of summer evening doing nothing apparently but watch the light fade from the hills, but it would be found next day by her household that she had not spent her time in "dreamy absentness", as she would express it, but had something very concrete to show for her apparent idleness. "Improving moments before they pass into hours"[2] was a practice she only urged upon others after she had applied it rigorously to herself.

And so, at the time of the dedication of the Church and her brief visit to Boston, as described in the preceding chapter, the daily round at Pleasant View had settled into definite ways. All her life Mrs. Eddy had been punctual in the true meaning of that word. She accounted it just as much unpunctual to be too early as too late. She always had a clock where she could see it, and, especially in later life, she insisted that there should be a time for everything and everything should have its time. She seems to have felt very keenly that the more the essentials of the day's work could be reduced to a routine, the freer were she and those around her to do what she regarded as their real work, to "pray without ceasing" in the widest meaning of that injunction.

At Pleasant View, as afterwards at Chestnut Hill, meals were always served to the minute and every member of the household was expected to be on time. Dinner was in the middle of the day, and after dinner punctually every day at two o'clock Mrs. Eddy went for a drive. Year by year, as she became more and more of a public figure, Concord people

[1] *Miscellaneous Writings*, p. 86-87.
[2] Ibid., p. 230.

looked forward to seeing her, and one of the regular daily incidents in the city's daily life was the appearance of Mrs. Eddy's carriage on State Street with its pair of well-groomed horses and Calvin Frye in livery on the box seat.

Mrs. Eddy was now becoming a wealthy woman. She had ceased to teach, but the circulation of her book *Science and Health* was rapidly increasing. With the closing out of the 1891 edition, over one hundred and fifty thousand copies had been sold, while later royalties paid to her amounted to approximately $12,000 in 1893; $15,000 in 1894; and $18,000 in 1895. But no matter how much riches increased, Mrs. Eddy never relaxed anything of her almost rugged simplicity. She was the recipient of many gifts, but she spent little on herself, and the furnishings of Pleasant View although comfortable were far from luxurious.

Her writing was still her chief work; besides her articles for the *Journal,* her constant literary labour was the revision of *Science and Health.* There had been a new edition in 1891 and another in 1894, and at the time the Church was dedicated she was hard at work on yet another edition which was brought out in 1896. Generally speaking, the trend of each succeeding edition is towards simplicity. Apt quotations from other writers, whether in prose or verse, which, in the earlier editions, were used so freely as chapter headings or embodied in the text, are curtailed or eliminated, while now a sentence or now a paragraph is rewritten in order to elucidate her meaning.

The great work in 1895, and the first of the many far-reaching developments to come out of Pleasant View, was the compiling of the *Church Manual.* Rules and regulations governing The Mother Church had been promulgated and adopted from time to time as occasion demanded, but by 1895 they had become so numerous that some form of codification was clearly demanded. It had always been Mrs. Eddy's custom to originate these rules and then send them to the Board of Directors with orders that they be officially adopted. Now the need was for a systematic marshalling of the various controls in a convenient and comprehensive booklet.

And so, early in the summer of that year, the First Members at Mrs. Eddy's direction appointed a committee of four to go into the matter and "prepare the *Church Manual*". The committee appointed consisted of four well-tried members, namely, Edward P. Bates, Julia Bartlett, Judge Hanna and William B. Johnson. They got to work at once, and within a few months the first edition of the *Church Manual* made its appearance. Mrs. Eddy changed it, adding or deleting up to the year of her death, but its broad provisions remained the same. It set forth the scope within which the Directors should act, the provisions governing the constituent departments and agencies of The Mother Church and the terms under which branch churches might be formed. It provided for discipline, how and in what circumstances it should be applied, promulgated the terms of membership, and published in full the deeds and other documents relating to the founding of the Church. Strictly speaking, the *Manual* was binding only on actual members of The Mother Church, but as it became the almost universal practice for branch churches to adopt by-laws embodying the essential features of the *Manual*, the *Manual* quickly became a code of conduct for church members everywhere.

How Mrs. Eddy viewed the matter is not easy to say. It is quite clear that from the moment she concluded the age was not ready to do without a visible church and decided that her own church should be reorganized, she determined that she was going to safeguard it in every way possible, not only from false doctrine, but from the dissensions which had characterized so disastrously the early days of its history. Nevertheless, it is again clear from her statements in regard to the *Manual* at the time of its first publication, and also later, that she viewed it, as she did her Church, as a "concession to the period".

In replying to the acclaim which some years later greeted the appearance of a new edition, Mrs. Eddy left no doubt as to her position:

"Will those beloved students," she wrote in the *Journal,* "whose growth is taking in the Ten Commandments and scaling the steep ascent of Christ's Sermon on the Mount, accept profound thanks for their swift messages of rejoicing over the twentieth century Church *Manual*? Heaps upon heaps of praise confront me, and for what? That which I said in my heart would never be needed,—namely, laws of limitation for a Christian Scientist."[1]

At another time, as though defending herself and her actions against any possible charge of autocracy, she insisted that the rules and by-laws of The Mother Church "were written at different dates, and as the occasion required. They sprang from necessity, the logic of events,—from the immediate demand for them as a help that must be supplied to maintain the dignity and defense of our Cause."[2]

And so she went forward, her patience often tried by the fact that she was compelled to take half measures where the full measure alone would have fulfilled her hope, and to take the course nearest right when she herself knew that in the long run it would have to be abandoned. More and more was she led to make "Suffer it to be so now" her daily prayer.

But Pleasant View was a great comfort to her. Although beset on all hands, as has been seen, by those who sought her aid and counsel or made claims upon her time for less worthy reasons, Mrs. Eddy nevertheless as time went on, succeeded in securing for herself some measure of the quiet she so earnestly desired. Three periods every day she devoted to prayer and meditation, and at these times she was never disturbed. It was all much simpler at Pleasant View than it had been anywhere else. Calvin Frye, always faithful, stood guard. He sometimes made mistakes, denying people who ought not to have been denied and admitting people who ought not to have been admitted, but, on the whole, he did a work that perhaps nobody else could have done. The faults of his virtues must often have tried Mrs. Eddy to the uttermost, as they did without doubt many of her household, but Mrs. Eddy, in appraising him, would come back again and again with a sense of gratitude and returning peace to his one outstanding virtue that seemed to have no fault—his faithfulness. Whoever else fell away, Calvin Frye always remained. Pleasant View without Calvin would not have been Pleasant View.

[1] *Miscellany*, p. 229.
[2] *Miscellaneous Writings*, p. 148.

383

Defections and Loyalties

SHE NEEDED ALL Calvin's faithfulness. Although the number of those attaching themselves to her company and remaining faithful increased year by year, those who fell away were still very many and were often from among those who had been nearest to her. Mrs. Eddy seems to have recognized, almost from the first, that in the end her work would have to be done alone, but she parted reluctantly from the "sense of personal joys",[1] as she sternly characterized the small bonds of human affection with which she sought to fill a void in her life. In the end, she realized and with tremendous abundance that the "seeming vacuum is already filled with divine Love",[2] but when she lavished her affection on Richard Kennedy or Daniel Spofford or Miranda Rice or begged her son George to come to her when she was widowed and homeless, or adopted as a son one whom she thought would be a strong arm in her support and in support of the Cause she had made her own, she was casting round for human help and encouragement.

For a short time, in the summer of 1892, just after she moved into

[1] *Science and Health*, p. 266.
[2] *Ibid*, p. 266.

Pleasant View, her son George had come east to visit her. He left his wife behind but brought with him his little son, George III. Mrs. Eddy was delighted. She took a great fancy to the little boy, but George came and went as he had done in the past, and, when he had gone, it seemed to her a greater comfort than ever before that she had by her one like her adopted son, Bennie, who seemed to understand so well what she wanted to do and was so ready to help her. Foster-Eddy was now President of The Mother Church and Manager of the Publishing House. He spent most of his time in Boston, but came out to Concord frequently, and "Bennie's room" at Pleasant View was always kept ready for his reception.

But Ebenezer J. Foster-Eddy was to prove a sore disappointment. Disturbing stories began to reach Pleasant View about his personal conduct, not the least of which was the rumour that he was guilty of improprieties with a married woman in his office. *Journal* subscriptions were lagging, even if book royalties were increasing. Suspicion and dissension grew, until an open break could not well be averted. It did not take long for Mrs. Eddy to make up her mind that her protege was being victimized by animal magnetism and that she, as the leader of the movement, was the ultimate object of evil's onslaught. No sooner had this become her clear conviction than she took action—action at once bold, stern and final. The fate of the cause, her very life's blood, seemed again in jeopardy, and one cannot recount what followed without painting the vivid picture of a seasoned general at war—the quiet reconnoitering, the mobilizing of forces, the ebb and flow of morale, the excitement of open conflict, the flicker of mutiny, the call to allegiance, rallying to the standard.

It may be supposed that Mrs. Eddy endeavoured earnestly to bring her adopted son around to her way of thinking. It is certain that recrimination fell with increasing frequency until at last there was left nothing but drastic measures to be taken. Already his mentor had written him, under date of March 17, 1897, that his work was unsatisfactory, his attitude and conduct reprehensible, his protests and reassurances valueless. "I was not 'falsely' referring to your mind on me. I am not and cannot be mistaken now in whose mind is on me," she wrote. "But you were governed by hypnotism to work against me and yourself . . ."

This fruitless controversy, which boded so much evil to the great Cause, as its leader saw the matter, could be, must be terminated. Seizing upon the occasion of the First Members' meeting currently in session, she dispatched a special letter directing the adoption of this startling by-law:

"A member of this church who is a student of Rev. Mary Baker Eddy and refuses to leave a place in the field that she knows it is for his or her interest to leave and so advise him or her yet they do not comply with my request, this member shall be dropped from the roll of membership and he or she treated by this church as a disloyal student. This by-law can only be amended or annulled by the unanimous vote of every member of this Church."

The immediate enactment of this statute was imperative if the movement was to survive, the accompanying letter explained, for "I cannot be your leader unless I have the power to guide you when you need this guidance."

Foster-Eddy, who was uncomfortably enough in the chair, must have put up a convincing defense, for the members wavered. In fact, they found it necessary to repair to Concord and confer with Mrs. Eddy herself before taking a vote.

Needless to say, the tide had turned, for to be in disfavour with Mrs. Eddy was to be in disrepute with the membership. Dr. Ebenezer J. Foster-Eddy was unceremoniously stripped of his offices and his titles and swiftly relegated to the ranks. The remaining story is a long and involved one, but it may be briefly summarized in the observation that he drifted into obscurity, not to be heard of again until his reappearance ten years later in the "Next Friends" suit, to be described in due order.

The whole proceeding may not be above criticism, but it needs to be remembered that the movement was "in a state of war", and that Mrs. Eddy had no alternative but to deal ruthlessly with what she saw as treachery. As to the justice of her appraisals and verdicts, of those who insist upon interpreting the record, opinion must be divided. Not a few believe that Mrs. Eddy's judgement was infallible because of her ordination from above to lead humanity out of the wilderness. Others feel that many who fell before her onward march were the victims of "court intrigue." Certain it is that few survived, whatever their faults or virtues, and that all had to defend themselves against household gossip as the sainted Leader grew steadily more secluded with her work and her immediate associates. Available correspondence with the abjectly devoted Dr. Julia Field-King and a wealth of other documentary evidence show this over and over again. Even the impeccable Edward Kimball, writing to Judge Septimus Hanna as late as November 29, 1907, lamented that there were those prominent enough to command the Leader's ear who were beating a constant pathway to her door to carry the evil insinuation that his teaching was wrong in order to discredit him in her eyes and thus dispose of an interloper. How could anyone, however great, be wholly unmoved by the constant stream of provocative reports, unrelieved by any counteracting statements? That Mrs. Eddy did as well as she did is surely to her everlasting credit.

As has been before noted, it was from the first characteristic of the movement that for every one who dropped out there was always one and sometimes many to take his place. In 1895 and the years which followed, this was increasingly true. When the church was dedicated, Mrs. Eddy already had around her or within immediate call a group of people whose names were later to become well known in the movement, and the great majority of them were to remain faithful right through to the end. Of these, among the most notable were Judge Septimus J. Hanna, William B. Johnson, Edward A. Kimball, James A. Neal and William P. McKenzie. Judge Septimus Hanna was perhaps the most prominent in the period under consideration. He had become interested in Christian Science in 1886 while practising as a lawyer in Leadville, Colorado, famous for its altitude above sea level—10,200 feet—and for its mines of gold and silver. His wife, Camilla, had been healed of a serious physical trouble and they both took up the study of Christian Science with much earnestness, corresponding with Mrs. Eddy in regard to receiving instructions from her and making plans for devoting themselves exclusively to the work. In 1890 they moved to Scranton, Pennsylvania, where Judge Hanna—he had served for a time as County Judge in Council Bluffs, Iowa, hence the title—was elected "Speaker" of the church there. About this time he began to contribute articles to the *Journal* which attracted much attention, and in the summer of 1891 he was invited to deliver the sermon for the original Church of Christ, Scientist, in Boston. Next year he was appointed editor of the *Journal* and his wife assistant editor, positions they continued to occupy for more than ten years.

Of the others, William B. Johnson, already mentioned as accompanying Mrs. Eddy on her memorable journey to Chicago in 1888, had become interested in 1882 through a healing of rupture and chronic ill-health, the result of hardships suffered during three years' service in the Civil War. He later became a director of The Mother Church, and appears and reappears in the story. Edward A. Kimball, destined afterwards to become the first great apostle of the movement, was from Chicago; James A. Neal, later a director, was from Boston; and William P. McKenzie, also a director, was from Almonte, Canada. These three, however, do not appear very prominently on the scene until several years later. They are mentioned here because they are among the most notable of those who, amidst much defection, maintained their loyalty to the end.

It was about this time, too, when the wonder aroused over the spread and scope of the movement as revealed in the dedication of the Church in Boston had somewhat subsided, that Christian Science began to be accepted as an important new theology, and to be considered as something that would have to be reckoned with in any future record of religious history. The voice of ridicule was by no means silenced—Mark Twain's onslaught was still ten years away—but now, wherever the movement established itself, although it made enemies aplenty, it also made friends among those who were far from subscribing to the demands of its teaching. With the press, the activities of the movement, especially when they related to Mrs. Eddy, became "news" to an increasing extent, not from the point of view of ridicule, as had so often been the case in the past, but for fundamental reasons.

In Boston, from now on, Christian Science, with its Church and Publishing House and all their activities, is taken for granted, while it is possible to detect in the tone of the press a certain civic pride in the fact that the city was the headquarters of a world-wide movement, for so it was now rapidly becoming. But the larger it grew and the more eager its adherents, the more surely did Mrs. Eddy withdraw from any public contact with it. It was, as has been noted, fully three months after the completion of the Church that she first saw it, and another two months were to pass by before she occupied its pulpit for the first time. When she did—it was Sunday, May 26, 1895—the fact that she was to be present at the morning service was known only to very few; the fact that she was to speak, only to herself.

"Her presence was unknown", says the *Journal's* account of the matter, "until her appearance in the aisle of the auditorium on her way to the pulpit. The services had proceeded as usual until they were more than half concluded when she stepped upon the platform. After listening to the organ and a solo . . . she stepped to the desk and without text or note addressed the congregation for upwards of twenty minutes. Her glowing words of kindly greeting, love, admonition and warning, were intently and eagerly listened to by all. At the close of the benediction the audience were requested to remain seated until Mrs. Eddy passed out, as it would have been impracticable to have personally met all the large audience."

The *Journal* adds that the event was "a memorable one", and expressed the hope that there would be "many repetitions of it".

But there was to be only one more such appearance. One Sunday in the following February, Mrs. Eddy preached again in The Mother Church, coming unexpectedly, as she had done the first time, and returning immediately afterwards to Concord. After that, although in the remaining fifteen years of her life she made several public appearances of a similar nature, she never preached again in The Mother Church.

Immediately following the account of the first sermon, the *Journal* prints a letter written by a boy to his mother after he had attended the service and heard Mrs. Eddy speak. It is an interesting letter as affording a glimpse of Mrs. Eddy at this time and of the impression she made on those who saw and heard her. The letter runs:

"DEAR MOTHER:

"I have just returned from church, where I had the pleasure of seeing and hearing Mrs. Eddy. I think only a few of the congregation knew any more than I did that she was going to be there; I do not know now why she came this particular day. Anyway when the lesson was half through to verse 27, the reader stopped, and she came into the auditorium and passed up on to the platform. The audience rose to their feet when they saw her coming in. She did not stop in the centre or step to the most prominent point behind the desk, but simply to one side, and after bowing a welcome to the audience, she sat down and rested her head in silent prayer. Then a lady in the choir sang a beautiful solo, after which Mrs. Eddy arose and stepping to the desk, spoke in a quiet pleasant voice, very distinct—for you could easily hear every word—and yet she seemed to be talking as if she were in a small room sitting only a few feet from you instead of in that large church.

"Mrs. Eddy did not preach; she took no text, but I wish I could write you all she said. She must have spoken for twenty minutes. . . . She said it all in such a simple, loving way. . . . I don't wonder that she is loved,— she is all love. You simply feel as if she was your best friend."

For several Sundays after this, the church was thronged in the hope that Mrs. Eddy would speak again, so much so that in the *Journal* for August she published a statement to the effect that, in the future, she would notify the Church Directors when she would be present, emphasizing once again that the only pastor of the church was the Bible and *Science and Health*. "Therefore, beloved," she added, "my often coming is unnecessary; for though I be present or absent, it is God that feedeth the hungry heart, that giveth grace for grace, that healeth the sick and cleanseth the sinner."

The *Journal* carried her message, if not round the world, certainly all over the United States and Canada, for the movement was growing now prodigiously. An examination of an issue of the *Journal* about this time shows that it was devoting no less than forty-three pages to announcements of church services and practitioners in the United States and Canada, while, as its records show, the new teaching had already gained a foothold at the other side of the Atlantic.

London

ON THE MORNING of May 26, 1885, many people in London heard of Christian Science for the first time. *The Times* published a two-column article from a correspondent in Boston describing some of the phases of mental healing that had sprung up in the United States, but giving foremost place to Mrs. Eddy and the teachings of Christian Science. *The Times* in that year was moving forward under a new editor. Thomas Chenery, who had followed the great Delane, had died in 1884, and George Earl Buckle had succeeded to his chair in Printing House Square. Delane had, as used to be said of him, "turned the favourite broadsheet of the English public into the leading journal of the world," and Buckle was eager to maintain the standard. Politics and war were Delane's great activities. Buckle, while maintaining the standard of his paper in these directions, sought also news of the more fundamental development in the realms of science and literature.

The article published in the issue of May 26 was in every way a fair article. It recognized the fact that Christian Science differed from all other methods in that it had a definite theology and claimed to work on lines that could be understood and demonstrated, while it adduced several instances of healing and other positive testimony from people whose honesty and reliability, the correspondent declared, could not be gainsaid.

The correspondent himself was, it is true, inclined to find his own explanations for the healings, but was quite clearly determined to be unbiased, and present the situation as it was, as nearly as he could. He was, moreover, far from underrating the stir the new teaching was creating, and his description of a service he attended at Hawthorne Hall depicts a scene in interesting consonance with those described in earlier chapters of this record.

"Hawthorne Hall, where the Christian Scientists worship, is thronged for an hour before the time for service each Sunday. So eager are people to hear that after the standing room is all taken people crowd around outside the doors, where they can catch only an occasional word or two. The service consists of ordinary devotional exercises preceding a sermon by Mrs. Eddy."

The Times also had a leader or editorial on the subject, running to a full column in length. On the whole, like the original article, it is fair in its comments, but, in the light of all that has happened since, it cannot be said to have caught a prophetic glimpse of the future. It regarded the letter from Boston as "entertaining", and attributed the success of mental healing in general and Christian Science in particular to the "credulity of the Boston people", maintaining firmly that such things were to be expected from people who still retain "a large share of fresh receptiveness of an earlier age".

The Times' article and leader aroused little interest. The flame flickered upwards for a moment and then went out again. It was two years before there was any further sign. Then one day a Mr. and Mrs. Graves Colles, who lived in the little village of Killiney overlooking Dublin Bay, received a letter from a friend in the United States telling them about Christian Science, what it was, and what it claimed to do. It must have been a persuasive letter, for Mr. and Mrs. Colles acted promptly. They sent at once to Boston for a copy of *Science and Health*, and, when it arrived, read it through with an increasing conviction that they had found something of which they had long been in search. So impressed, indeed, were they that nothing would do but that they must cross the Atlantic to learn more about Christian Science from Mrs. Eddy herself.

That was in the fall of 1887. A few months later they were in Boston, and after several interviews with Mrs. Eddy they arranged to enter the class she taught in the March of 1888—shortly before her journey to Chicago. It was, as may be remembered, a notable class for the reason that so many of those enrolled in it afterwards became well known in the movement, among them General Erastus Bates, Edward A. Kimball, Hannah A. Larminie, Anna Dodge and several others. The Colleses seem to have developed a special regard for Hannah Larminie. Mrs. Larminie had studied with Mrs. Eddy three years previously, and when the March class was over, the Colleses begged her to return with them to Ireland and commence the work in earnest in Dublin. Mrs. Eddy was consulted and with her approval the three set out on what was the first missionary journey of Christian Science beyond the shores of America.

Reaching Dublin late in June, it was not long before Mrs. Larminie had established herself in offices at 40 Mountpleasant Square. She seems, almost at once, to have secured a following, did considerable healing work and taught at least one class. Mrs. Eddy, however, was eager that Christian Science should gain a foothold in London. In a letter to a friend several years later she recalled that in the very earliest days of her work, as far back at 1868, she had remarked to a student that she felt sure she could "introduce Christian Science in England more readily than in America".

Indeed, a study of her letters shows that her thoughts turned constantly to England as a more than favourable field. At the time that Mr. and Mrs. Colles conferred with her as to the advisability of Mrs. Larminie's joining with them to make a start in Dublin, Mrs. Eddy seriously considered going to London herself in order to teach one or more classes. The turmoil which followed her return from Chicago and the momentous developments in the years immediately afterwards prevented her from carrying out her project, but, as her correspondence with Mrs. Larminie clearly shows, she was in touch with the movement at the other side of the Atlantic all the time.

Thus, in November, 1888, she wrote Mrs. Larminie in Dublin, urging her to extend her mission to London. Perhaps the chief reason actuating Mrs. Eddy at this time was the fact that several dubious versions of her teaching were already establishing themselves in London. Mrs. Larminie complied at once, for in December, 1888, she writes to Mrs. Eddy from London that she is "putting the dividing line between the false and the true, that the people may not be deceived".

In the following year another member of the March, 1888, class, namely Miss Anna Dodge, at the instance of Mrs. Eddy, went over to London to help Mrs. Larminie and the Colleses, who had now left Dublin and lived in Monmouthshire, having a house also in London. All four seem to have been impressed with the extent to which false teaching had gained a foothold and, as shown by a letter from Miss Dodge to Mrs. Eddy, determined to take up the very wise position of carrying conviction to the outside world by their works rather than by any enunciation of their faith. In other words, they set to work to heal the sick, thus beginning, as Mrs. Eddy had begun and as all the most successful extensions of Christian Science had begun.

Writing to Mrs. Eddy under date of September, 1890, in a letter published in the October *Journal*, Miss Dodge said: "Let Christian Science do healing work here, seen and acknowledged, and it is established for all time; consequently I shall devote myself to healing, and do no teaching at all for the present—further than to recommend the textbook to all."

Miss Dodge later leased a house at 48 Stanhope Gardens, and it was in this house that the first public Christian Science services were held in England. They continued, however, only for a couple of months, and then the little group apparently decided once again that they should devote themselves simply to healing. As a consequence, three years passed before public services were held again. Then, finally, in the summer of 1896, the First Church of Christ, Scientist, of London was definitely established at 57 Bryanston Street and advertised its regular services in the *Journal*.

Shortly before this was done, Mrs. Colles and other members of the group had written to Mrs. Eddy asking her to send to them a teacher of recognized standing who could help them for a time in the work of establishing and expanding the Church and teaching. In response to this request, Mrs. Eddy arranged with one of her students, Mrs. Julia Field-King, to undertake the work, and so early in the summer of 1896 Mrs. Field-King sailed for England.

She was in many ways a remarkable woman. Born on an Iowa farm, she early displayed a more than usual aptitude for study, and ultimately went to Oberlin College in Ohio. There, after taking her baccalaureate degree, she studied medicine, practised for eleven years and taught in Chicago Medical College. She married early and was widowed within a few years, and then, in the early eighties, became interested in Christian Science through a lecture delivered by Emma Hopkins, who, it will be remembered, was one of the first editors of the *Journal*. She went through a class with Mrs. Eddy in September, 1888, and later settled in Seattle, where she quickly developed a large practice.

From the first, she seems to have attracted the attention of Mrs Eddy, who, early in 1891, invited her to come to Boston and assume the editorship of the *Journal*. Mrs. Field-King did good work. Although in the end she suffered the fate common to the favourites, her star was for the moment in the ascendancy. She had been a successful practitioner in Seattle and also a successful teacher. She was, moreover, a cultured woman well versed in all social amenities, and so taking her all in all, Mrs. Eddy evidently thought she would be a suitable woman to send as special envoy to London. This judgement was well founded, for although at first disappointed with the situation—she wrote to Mrs. Eddy in the July of 1896 that the general thought in England was "as far back as it was in the United States fifteen or twenty years ago"—nevertheless, she seems to have achieved almost instant success as a teacher, and in unexpected quarters.

Christian Science in the United States had its beginnings among the humblest people; in England, it began rather among those at the other end of the social scale. The Earl and Countess of Dunmore, Sir Douglas Galton, Sir William Marriott, Colonel Hamilton and many other well-known people became interested.

All went well for a time, and then in the winter of 1896 occurred one of those amazing onslaughts on the new teaching which were so characteristic of the early days of its history.

In November, Harold Frederic, the American novelist, died in London, and at the inquest it was shown that he had been attended by a Christian Science practitioner. In spite of the fact that Frederic had been treated by an orthodox physician before he appealed to Christian Science for help and was also under the care of a physician at the time of his death, the practitioner, a Mrs. Mills, was arrested and charged with murder. She was ultimately exonerated, but the case attracted a tremendous amount of attention. Such notoriety was bound to hamper in some degree the spread and prosperity of the movement abroad. Christian Science had not yet achieved a sustaining momentum in England and Mrs. Eddy quickly made it plain that she considered the Frederic affair a serious set-back. To Mrs. Field-King she wrote that students should "never take a case of so doubtful a kind." And, according to the report of Sue Harper Mims, the Atlanta teacher, she told her gift-minded students that she "would rather have had the demonstration made in that home in London where Harold Frederic was than to have all the gifts on earth." Nothing in twenty years had harmed the Cause so much, she insisted, since the survival of her doctrine depended wholly upon its healing works. "By their fruits ye shall know them."

In spite of these difficulties, the definite establishment of Christian Science in London and the extraordinary appeal it made to people of culture and influence placed the movement finally on a recognized international basis. Ten years before *The Times* had regarded it complacently as a "rather naive product of a rather naive people". But from now on, as far as the outside world was concerned, the movement was able to point to a large and increasing number of adherents drawn from all walks in life, from the highest to the most humble, on both sides of the Atlantic.

As far as the elderly woman in Concord was concerned, there were times when a very human sense of satisfaction would reign for a moment, as when she wrote to her son George that "Lords and ladies, earls and princes, marquises and marchionesses" came to see her or corresponded with her; that Hoke Smith declared she was the most illustrious woman on the continent; and that senators and congressmen sought her advice. But, next minute, she had deflated her own balloon with the cryptic remark that she was "not made the least proud by it or a particle happier."

She goes calmly forward. In her letters, as in a few isolated cases in her writings, may be seen arising again and again the old Adam of the Baker heritage: Mark's terrible sternness with backsliders and unbelievers; his masterfulness and intolerance; his pride of place and family. But the course of final victory was all on the Ambrose side. Just as Abigail always won in her struggle with Mark, so the Abigail in her daughter Mary rode more and more to victory, until it was, in the end, completely triumphant. Mark comes out at times and suns himself, as in her short autobiography *Retrospection and Introspection*, where she dwells for a page or two upon her family history and seeks to make the best and more than the best of her strangely failing son. She indulges it all for a moment, and then the Abigail and the Mary in her are found writing that it all amounts to just nothing at all:

"It is well to know . . . that our material, mortal history is but the record of dreams, not of man's real existence, and the dream has no place in the Science of being. It is 'as a tale that is told', and 'as the shadow when it declineth'."[1]

And then she adds, almost impatiently: "Mere historic incidents and personal events are frivolous and of no moment, unless they illustrate the ethics of Truth."[2]

Her one thought, now, more than ever, was the extension of the Cause, and it may be ventured that the only abiding satisfaction she got

[1] *Retrospection and Introspection*, p. 21.
[2] *Ibid.*, p. 21.

out of the lords and the ladies, the senators and congressmen, was the evidence it all afforded of the progress of that Cause. And so she writes:

"I learned long ago that the world could neither deprive me of something nor give me anything, and I have now one ambition and one joy." And then, as if reflecting on even this, she adds: "But if one cherishes ambition unwisely, one will be chastened for it."[1]

[1] *Miscellaneous Writings,* p. 281.

Two Years

THE TWO YEARS, 1897 and 1898, were for Mrs. Eddy, very notably, years of attainment. Out of the turmoil with which she was constantly beset, she brought to fruition two plans which she had long been maturing, the establishment of the Christian Science Publishing Society on a sure basis as an irrevocable Trust, and the founding of a weekly magazine in the form of the *Christian Science Sentinel*. They were years, too, of many other outward and visible signs of expansion. In the summer of 1897 she received a great assembly of Christian Scientists to the number of some three thousand at Pleasant View, while towards the close of 1898 she gathered around her in Concord, on two bleak November days, a group of chosen men and women students, summoned for what she evidently designed as a new missionary effort, to whom she delivered what was to prove her valedictory in the matter of class teaching.

The gathering at Pleasant View—on the afternoon of Monday, 5th July, 1897—must have had about it an inescapable air of triumph, of joy at last in the morning after a very long night of struggle and no little sorrow. It was Independence Day, for the Fourth, falling on a

Sunday that year, the national holiday was kept on the following day. In order to avoid anything in the nature of a pilgrimage to Concord from distant parts of the country, Mrs. Eddy had not issued her invitation until the Sunday morning service the day before. Addressing her letter to "My Beloved Church", she wrote:

"I invite you, one and all, to Pleasant View, Concord, New Hampshire, on July 5th, at 12:30 p.m., if you would enjoy so long a trip for so small a purpose as simply seeing Mother."

The letter, however, was dispatched from Concord on June 30, and somehow or other news of its contents got abroad almost immediately and word was telegraphed to newspapers all over the country, with the result that hundreds of Christian Scientists from as far west as Kansas City set out at once for Boston.

On Sunday morning The Mother Church was thronged. The First Reader, after reading the letter already quoted, gave notice as to the arrangements that had been made for the journey to Concord, the time and place of departure of the trains, the cost of tickets, and so forth. Trains were to leave Boston at half-past nine in the morning. Ushers were appointed to show the way to the cars. The sale of tickets was provided in such a way that all could be accommodated.

July is one of the hottest months of the year in Boston, and the heat almost proverbially reaches its peak on Independence Day. This year was no exception. As the heavily laden special trains pulled out of the North Station, there was every indication of "the wrath to come", and it was amply fulfilled later on. All of the newspaper accounts of the matter dwell on the heat, but also on the fact that nobody seemed to care what the weather was like.

When the trains arrived at Concord, the travellers numbering well over two thousand, found every available vehicle that could be requisitioned in and around Concord waiting to carry them to Pleasant View, and by 12:30 the entire party had reached its destination and the visitors spread themselves over the lawn beneath the tower window.

All Concord joined in the celebration. The Honourable A. B. Woodworth, mayor of the city, was present in the chair, and about one o'clock Mrs. Eddy came out of the house, accompanied by the Chairman of the Board of Directors of The Mother Church, Edward P. Bates. Very many of those present had never seen her before and pressed eagerly forward to get a glimpse of her, as cheers of greeting went up from all sections of the crowd.

The Mayor was the first to speak, and his commendably short address served to indicate not only the standing which Mrs. Eddy had by this time attained in her own community, but also the personal regard in which she was held by those who did not share her faith.

"Ladies and gentlemen: It gives me great pleasure", said the Mayor, "to comply with the request of Mrs. Eddy, that, as Mayor of Concord, I should welcome you to our city. This I do with the most cordial feeling possible, for I recognize the fact that I see before me a great company of men and women who have come from all parts of the country to express their devotion to the religion of God and of Christ, the great Healer, as it has been the more clearly revealed through the insight and the power of her who has bidden you here. May this day be one long to be remembered as the occasion when you saw her whom you most delight to honour, in her beautiful home and surrounded by the charming scenery she loves so well."

At the conclusion of the Mayor's address, Mr. Bates remarked that the audience needed no introduction to Mrs. Eddy nor she to it, as all knew her though some had never seen her before. And then Mrs. Eddy spoke in her usual calm, unhurried way and in a voice which carried to the limits of her audience. In the atmosphere of all that had grown up around her and her teaching, it must have been an impressive scene. The Boston *Herald* in a report of the matter presents a vivid picture, the view over the valley bathed in sunshine, the blue summits of the distant hills and the great throng in bright summer clothing, set off against a background of green. And then the tall, slim figure of Mrs. Eddy, clad in lavender and black lace, outlined clearly against the shadows of the veranda.

"The profile", said the Boston *Globe*, "is sharp and keen. the face in full view is extremely delicate and tender—motherly more nearly expresses it, and her hair is silver white. She wore her badge of ruby and diamonds as a Daughter of the American Revolution."

Mrs. Eddy's address on this occasion, afterwards republished in her book *Miscellaneous Writings,* is one of the most interesting of her public utterances. In many ways, as might be expected, it is a quiet paean of triumph.

"Today", she said, "we commemorate not only our nation's civil and religious freedom, but a greater even, the liberty of the sons of God, the inalienable rights and radiant reality of Christianity, whereof our Master said: 'The works that I do shall he do'; and, 'The kingdom of God cometh not with observation' (with knowledge obtained from the senses), but 'The kingdom of God is within you,'—within the present possibilities of mankind."

Then she went on with no little eloquence to tell how from the "falling leaves of old-time faiths" men might learn the parable of that hour, namely, that all error, physical, moral, or religious, would "fall before Truth demonstrated, even as dry leaves fall to enrich the soil for fruitage".

And so she spoke for some ten minutes or more, and then with that indescribable ease which was one of her great attractions she spread out her hands to the audience, and, having turned for a moment to those who were beside her on the veranda, she concluded:

"Friends, I am not enough the new woman of the period for outdoor speaking, and the incidental platform is not broad enough for me, but the speakers that will now address you—one a congressman—may improve our platforms; and make amends for the nothingness of matter with the allness of Mind."

There were more speeches and letters and telegrams. The last speech was that by General Erastus N. Bates. As will be remembered, he was a veteran of the Civil War and had been a man noted for his courage.

With all the simplicity of a soldier he told what he owed to Christian

Science, how at the close of the war he had returned to his home a physical wreck, his days numbered by his friends and physicians, his own expectation of life limited to a very short time; how Christian Science had brought him out of what was virtually his grave, and how, knowing this, his audience would not wonder that his heart should now overflow with love and gratitude toward her whom in an especial sense he owed the preservation of his earthly life so that he had now reached well nigh his, not three, but four score years and ten.

The meeting which assembled in Concord, some eighteen months later, was very different in character. The gathering at Pleasant View on Independence Day had been a veritable jubilee of achievement. The meeting in November of the following year was the inauguration of new labours. Mrs. Eddy, full of plans for the future, sought to determine the materials she had to work with; in other words, to review her resources and find out by personal test whom she might count upon to be faithful.

The problems to be met were many. She was confronted with a tremendously expanding movement, and experience in the past had shown her that nothing was more dangerous to orderly progress than zeal without knowledge. As far as her own personal contacts with the movement were concerned, she had been steadily withdrawing for over ten years, with mixed results. As far back as 1888, in a letter to the National Christian Scientist Association, she had said that for two years she had been gradually withdrawing from active membership and that this policy on her part had "developed higher energies on the part of true followers, and led to some startling departures on the other hand".

Similar registration of advantage and disadvantage was characteristic of all the years that intervened. Mrs. Eddy's great and increasing difficulty, as the movement developed, was to find men and women capable of faithful service and work, without entering into the age-old competition as to which should be the greatest.

Late in 1898, she determined upon an inventory. And so on Tuesday, November the 15th, she sent out an identical telegram to some sixty or seventy of her students scattered east of the Great Divide, telling them that if they would be in the Christian Science Hall in Concord at four o'clock on the following Sunday afternoon, November the 20th, she would have "a great blessing in store" for them.

If nothing else, it was a test of obedience and willingness to act without question, and it was successful, for everyone of those thus invited immediately set out for Boston and Concord. They came from as far west as Kansas City, from as far south as Memphis, and as far north as Toronto. Some of those invited reached Concord only just in time, but the great majority were present at the Sunday morning service in the Concord Church. No one knew it at the time, but, later, many of them looked back with interest on the fact that the reading from the Bible at that service was the Tenth Chapter of Luke relating the sending out of the seventy disciples.

By four o'clock in the afternoon, all those invited had assembled in the Christian Science Hall. Mrs. Eddy was not present but Edward A. Kimball from Chicago, who was rapidly coming into prominence in the movement, stepped up on the platform and read a letter from Mrs. Eddy, explaining that she had not in advance divulged the purpose of her summons as she did not wish to stir up those others who would "wish to share this opportunity." The purpose? This representative group was "to receive from me one or more lessons in Christian Science," the number to be determined by the results shown but, in any case, not to exceed three. The work, designed to impart a fresh impetus to the movement, would be without money and without price.

In the years to follow a cloak of mystery was to be drawn about this memorable event, but at the time it was regarded as anything but esoteric. Two newspaper reporters—one of whom, at least, was never a Christian Scientist—were among those invited and no one was pledged to secrecy. Many recorded the experience in considerable detail and, since there is virtually no disagreement as to the content of the material covered and on the general impression created, the reader of today is not without an accurate picture of an historic moment.

Mrs. Sue Harper Mims, the Atlanta teacher, describes the "class" as "principally an examination, with some teaching." Arriving promptly at four, Mrs. Eddy spryly and gracefully mounted the platform. Her snow-white hair, in loose waves or curls about her forehead, was uncovered. Handsomely attired in a skirt of black moire and a waist of white silk covered with net and heavily trimmed in jet, her cape was thrown back to reveal the large diamond Cross, given her by Mrs. Stetson, and the diamond and ruby badge of the D.A.R. Against the red-plush chair she was a striking figure. Her gestures, as always effective, were accentuated by white-kid gloves, which she did not remove.

In her greeting, she said she had been waiting fifteen years to meet such a band of faithful workers. Then, without more ado, she got down to the business on hand by asking each one in turn, "What is God to you?" The replies, largely in words borrowed from *Science and Health*, elicited little comment. But when one hapless youth defined God as Life, Truth, Love and also "destruction," he was gently but devastatingly asked, "Will you tell me how God is destruction? Is there anything but God? What is there to destroy?"

It took quite some time, naturally, to get around the large class, but this session was to last two hours and there was still some attention reserved for other matters. "You have told me wonderful things today," Mrs. Eddy said, "and now you must live up to them." If Science was to be practical, they must prove their precepts by works rather than words. For herself, she had three times raised the dead, she assured them, and cited one instance. She was sent for by a woman crying that her child was dead. Putting the mother out of the room, she took the child up into her arms and prayed. In an hour she called the mother back and the child ran to meet her, restored not only to life but to health. The very first revelation that ever came to her, she recalled, was that she could not die. "She saw life and that it was impossible for her to die."

She went on to relate how those who merely called for her were healed before she could get to them and then were loath to admit that God heals. So anxious was she to have them acknowledge the truth that she said to herself on one occasion, "He (the patient) must not get well until I get there!" This one did not get well even after she got there,

406

and it was a bitter lesson for her. "When I reached home, I threw myself on the floor, put my head in my hands and prayed that I might not be for a moment touched with the thought that I was anything or did anything, that this was God's work and I reflected Him."

There was a pause, and then the students one after another stood up to recite their experiences. Judge Hanna said that he, too, had raised the dead. Several spoke of revelation coming to them as a marvelous burst of light, some describing it as literally flooding *Science and Health* as they read. The scene in the little hall was so impressive that when a Dr. Stockman rose he was too overcome by emotion to speak.

Before closing, Mrs. Eddy had a few words to say on supply. Because God is All, man cannot lack. When one stands before a mirror, the reflection is the same as the original. "Now you are God's reflection. If His hands are full, your hands are full. If you image Him, you cannot lack."

The class had been so very satisfactory, their teacher observed as she left the platform, that there would be but one more session—this to be held next day at one o'clock.

The second and final session lasted about four hours and emphasized, according to George Wendell Adams, the basic and vital truth that one infinite Principle can only be manifested as one infinite idea, or reflection, "which, of course, was the compound idea, man."

How, though, to get down to cases, is instantaneous healing to be done? Many were the answers to this question, ranging all the way from "Realize the ever-presence of God" to "Deny the claims of evil." When all had been heard from, Mrs. Eddy smilingly said the answer was simple. "It is to love!" If one lives love and knows only love, nothing is impossible in the way of healing. "*Be* nothing but love!" But was not the practitioner required to discriminate between good and evil? Ah, yes. Not only must he, like Jesus, love righteousness but, by the same token, he must hate iniquity. Bearing out this theme, she was later to denounce to John Lathrop the Three Monkeys—"See no evil, hear no evil, speak no evil"—as a symbol of heathen philosophy, saying, "Christian Scientists do not close their eyes to evil but open them." Those who were un-
407

able or unwilling to recognize error as something to be corrected she found "unteachable." The general tendency, on the other hand, to become fascinated with error instead of going on through to the truth, she dismissed with the story of the man who killed a fox, stuck its tail out through a hole in the door and then laughed at the crowd which soon collected to discuss "how the fox got through that little hole." Human beings were "always trying to find the reason for something that never happened," she concluded.

At another point she said: "In the human, it is good to think of God as our Father and Mother, with us every moment, giving us everything good and beautiful, caring for our human bodies." Divine provision was like a scale, she explained, with infinite good on the side of Spirit. Everything put into the scale of Spirit would be on the side of infinity, while everything put into the scale of matter weighed on the side of limitation.

The Trinity of old was now to be understood as Life, Truth, Love, wherein man reflects all that God is. With God triune, man must be triune, the idea of Life, Truth, Love and "living in the thought of his ever-present, infinite Life, Truth, Love." (As an afterthought, she was to send each student a written statement on the Trinity, defining *Father* as man's divine Principle, *Son* as His spiritual idea or image, and *Holy Ghost* as divine Science, making "Jesus in the flesh" the wayshower to Life, Truth, Love, while "out of the flesh Jesus was the Christ.")

Dismissing as absurd the literal interpretation of the Bible, she said it reminded her of the farmer who claimed scriptural authority for refusing to let his hired hands go for water on a hot day. "Hoe, everyone that thirsteth!" was the Biblical injunction, he insisted.

Who among those present would like to translate for her into the "new tongue" some passage from the Bible? The youthful John Lathrop, asked about the women who brought sweet spices to the tomb of Jesus, said: "Well, Mother, you know they were women and women have the highest idea of God." But Mrs. Eddy was heard distinctly to murmur, "I don't know about that." She let him finish and then she asked Mrs. Mims to come up onto the platform with her. "I want them all to see you." The stone that was rolled away from the sepulchre, Mrs. Mims

408

volunteered, was the concentrated human belief that Life was limited, and removing this stone meant seeing immortality. But Mrs. Mims had something else in mind and here was the ideal opportunity for bringing it out. Those at the tomb, disciples of another day, "saw what our beloved Mother has, through *Science and Health,* enabled us to see. Through this book we have seen all that they saw and more, and we owe it all to her, this beloved one who is God's messenger today." Like an awaited signal, this brought a flood of tributes from the assembled students. "How could we forget you?" was heard on all sides. Judge Hanna came to his feet again, this time to say that in his position he was such a target for evil that blackness hid the horizon except when he turned to Mrs. Eddy as "the Revelator for this Age." Few if any present failed to voice the same thought. "My dear children," Mrs. Eddy said when they had all finished, "if you had not seen it, I should have had to teach you this. I could not have avoided telling you that when my students become blinded to me as the one through whom Truth has come to this age, they go straight down." Tears of joy were upon her cheeks, according to the written accounts, and she brought her class to a close with the joyous benediction of one who has drunk deeply of the Holy Grail that is a sacred goal attained.

These two meetings in Concord are perhaps specially important to the purpose of this record in that they afford an interesting glimpse of the inner life of the Christian Science movement about this time and of Mrs. Eddy's relation to it. The struggles and trials, defections and disloyalties, which seem to crowd themselves into every period of this woman's life were, it now becomes increasingly clear, very far from being the whole of the story. Back of them all and apparently quite unaffected by any of them was a tremendous development constantly reaching new expansions only to exhibit unmistakable signs of going on further still.

Some twenty years before, Mrs. Eddy had written in her book *Science and Health*: "Undisturbed amid the jarring testimony of the material senses, Science, still enthroned, is unfolding to mortals the immutable, harmonious, divine Principle,—is unfolding Life and the universe, ever present and eternal."

409

Josephine Woodbury Again

WHATEVER PEACE MRS. EDDY attained at almost any period of her life, but especially in her latter years, was attained in spite of, rather than because of, circumstances. It is true that she was now surrounded by faithful friends and helpers, and that she was daily the recipient of messages of gratitude and loyalty from all over the world, yet hardly a week passed but that some friend disappointed her, or some trusted lieutenant failed in a given task, or someone she had long striven to help finally fell away. Worse still, others proved to be sources of great embarrassment.

A notable instance of this last was Josephine Woodbury, who here once again makes a rather tragic entrance. Mrs. Eddy had no doubt gone far out of the way to keep this spectacularly unconventional student in the fold and out of the public limelight. Despite the notoriety occasioned by her housetop proclamation two years before that her child had been virginally conceived, when the Church was reorganized in 1892 her application for membership was accepted—albeit conditionally.

Incidently, this ingenious device of keeping a member in line by placing him on probation instead of excluding him, was to be employed there-after by the Church with astonishing success in case after case, although it must be admitted that it failed in this instance.

The irrepressible Josephine was not to be easily harnessed. Before very long she was found to be involved in two law suits, one with a certain Fred D. Chamberlain, who charged her with alienating his wife's affections, and the other a divorce action brought by a Mrs. Evelyn I. Rowe on the grounds that her husband had been devoting practically all his earnings to the support of Mrs. Woodbury's son, the little "Prince of Peace."

The Boston *Traveler* published a spicy and embroidered article on these affairs, but Mrs. Woodbury was not the type to submit to ridicule without a fight. Greatly daring, she brought action against the *Traveler* for libel. This, Mrs. Eddy indicated by one of those sternly inexorable letters which she knew so well how to write when faced with an impasse, was the last straw. "How dare you in the sight of God and with your character behind the curtain of your students ready to lift it on you pursue the path perilous?" she demanded. Swiftly, then, the Church acted and Mrs. Woodbury was "forever excommunicated," a notice to this effect being inserted in the *Journal* for June, 1896. Her libel suit against the newspaper collapsed and she found herself ostracized by the world she had built up for herself, adrift in what must have seemed a desolate and uncharted sea.

But Josephine Woodbury had been taught there was no living without religion and no religion without a church and so it was not long before she hired rooms in the Legion of Honour Hall in Boston, and there every Sunday afternoon she or her daughter, Gwendoline, preached to a group of her followers and others to the number of some one hundred and fifty.

The following year, namely, 1897, about the time of the gathering at Concord recorded in the last chapter, Mrs. Woodbury published a pamphlet entitled *War in Heaven*. In this she gave what purported to be an account of her experiences in Christian Science. Later on still, she published a series of articles in the *Arena*, in which she launched an attack on Mrs. Eddy which for simple violence had hardly been equalled up to that time. She ridiculed the English in *Science and Health*, accused Mrs. Eddy of "trafficking in the temple", and with fine indignation charged her with teaching the doctrine of spiritual conception. Mrs. Eddy's title, "Discoverer and Founder of Christian Science," she derided as paradoxical, saying: "Surely a 'Discoverer' cannot be the 'Founder' of that which she has been under the necessity of discovering; while a 'Founder' would have no need of discovering her own foundation."

She insisted that all she had "discovered" were "ways of perverting and prostituting the science of healing to her own ecclesiastical aggrandizement, and to the moral and physical depravity of her dupes. . . . What she has 'founded'," she added, "is a commercial system, monumental in its proportions, but already tottering to its fall." Another unfortunate excursion into prophecy!

Mrs. Eddy, in the course of her message to The Mother Church delivered on June 4, 1899, and later republished in her book *Miscellany*, made a statement which, although it did not mention Mrs. Woodbury by name, was construed by her and her followers into a direct attack.

"The doom of the Babylonish woman", Mrs. Eddy declared, "referred to in Revelation, is being fulfilled. This woman, 'drunken with the blood of the saints, and with the blood of the martyrs of Jesus', 'drunk with the wine of her fornication', would enter even the church,—the body of Christ, Truth; and, retaining the heart of the harlot and the purpose of the destroying angel, would pour wormwood into the waters—the disturbed human mind—to drown the strong swimmer struggling for the shore,—aiming for Truth,—and if possible, to poison such as drink of the living water."[1]

Josephine Woodbury was outraged. Within a few weeks she brought a suit for libel against Mrs. Eddy. Mrs. Eddy in her reply maintained that in speaking as she did she was dealing with a situation, not a person, and that in mentioning the "Babylonish woman" she had been speaking, "not of an individual, but of a type." Mrs. Eddy called to Boston her

[1] *Miscellany*, p. 125.

foremost disciples—including Mrs. Stetson and Mr. Kimball—to handle mentally this new crisis.

There were many delays, but when the action did come up, the court dismissed the case at the end of the plaintiff's evidence.

That, as far as Mrs. Woodbury was concerned, was the end. Insisting that she was being mentally hounded by Mrs. Eddy and her followers and in serious danger of her life, she declined to appeal, as some of her friends wished her to do, and shortly afterwards she withdrew definitely and finally from the scene, to live out her days in England.

Such an incident, dragging itself out anxiously over the weeks and months and even years, was only one of many with which Mrs. Eddy and her movement were beset in these years. Almost every issue of the *Journal* contains some reference to cases wherein Christian Science practitioners had been haled before the courts charged with the unlicensed practise of medicine, with manslaughter, and so forth. It is true that practically all such cases resulted in acquittal and that some of the decisions later became historic, establishing precedents for the future, but for the much-enduring woman at Concord they must have represented only trial added to trial of faith and patience, and she had had so many.

Nevertheless, looking back on it all in the perspective of the years, the outstanding feature of these times, as far as the Christian Science movement was concerned, was sustained and amazing growth, and if this record were a history of the movement rather than a biography of its founder, it would be necessary to travel far afield to get a true picture year by year of what was happening. For at the turn of the century Christian Science had literally spread all over the world. The *Journal* for March, 1900, shows Christian Science practitioners established in Sophia, Bulgaria; Peking, China; in Hawaii and the Philippines; in Australia, England, France and Germany. Within a few years Mark Twain, one of its most caustic critics, was to admit that it was spreading at the rate, as he put it, of a new church every four days. And Mrs. Eddy at Pleasant View never lost touch with any of it. More and more, did those around her seek to take over routine business and as much else as possible, but that Mrs. Eddy kept in touch with anything and everything that had any important bearing on the spiritual or physical growth of the movement is amply shown by her letters and messages. Always she had been a remarkable correspondent, and although now she dictated a good deal, yet, even at eighty and afterwards, she spent long hours each day at her desk writing letters, messages, articles for the *Journal* or *Sentinel*, or working at a task which was never done, revising *Science and Health*.

It had become a practice, when a new church was built and dedicated, to write to Mrs. Eddy, notifying her of the fact and inviting her, no matter what the distance, to be present. Mrs. Eddy always replied to the invitation, personally, either by letter or by telegram, and these letters to churches are today among the best-known of her shorter writings. They cover a wide field; from a nearby town, such as Lawrence, Massachusetts, to San Jose in California; Toronto, Canada; Sydney, Australia; or London or Edinburgh. Several of them were published in her book *Miscellaneous Writings*, which appeared in the spring of 1897, but most of them appear in her book *The First Church of Christ, Scientist and Miscellany*, published shortly after her death.

One of the most interesting of these letters is that written to the church in her own Concord on the occasion of its final organization, February, 1899. It was at a time, as has been seen, when newspaper attacks on Mrs. Eddy and her teaching were particularly virulent. Josephine Woodbury was preparing her broadsides in the *Arena* and, a few months previously, had published her *War in Heaven*. And so Mrs. Eddy's letter to the Concord Church is full of exhortation to patience and to a recognition of the fact that those who attacked them did so for the most part in ignorance and were deserving of compassion rather than resentment. She herself had patience, she said, with the attacks of the newspapers because she "sympathized with their ignorance of Christian Science", and because she knew that "no Christian can or does understand this Science and not love it".

"Rest assured", she added, "that the injustice done by press and pulpit to this denomination of Christians will cease, when it no longer blesses this denomination."

Yet in spite of the bitterness of the attacks upon her from without, Mrs. Eddy was even more beset by adulation from within. Her writings maintained that as far as her followers were concerned, while attacks would only serve to strengthen them, deification of herself was only a hindrance if not a fatal obstacle to progress.

Her letters and writings, about this time, are full of exhortations against personal attachment to herself. Her teaching could not be expected to survive if a person were to displace Principle for the student. "Those who look for me in person or elsewhere than in my writings, lose me instead of find me," she wrote to one correspondent, and in a vigorous article entitled "Personal Contagion", published in the *Journal*, she said: "There was never a religion or philosophy lost to the centuries except by sinking its divine Principle in personality."

And then she adds in a passage eloquent of patience sorely tried: "I left Boston in the height of prosperity to *retreat* from the *world*, and to seek the one divine *Person*, whereby and wherein to show others the footsteps from sense to Soul. To give me this opportunity is all that I ask of mankind."

But it was a problem to be taken up again and again. All her life she had been particularly sensitive to human affection, and, for years, in spite of repeated betrayals and pitiful failing, she had accepted it with new hope whenever it had been sincerely offered. And so in these times of adulation and hero worship she often found it hard to deprive others of what apparently meant so much to them.

An interesting instance is afforded in an article published in the *Journal* for June, 1899, by one Martha Sutton-Thompson, giving an account of a visit she paid to Boston and Concord. She had come to Boston for the purpose of attending a class in Christian Science and, after describing how much she kept hoping that before the class was over Mrs. Eddy herself might come to see them, she goes on to tell how when the class had come to an end without Mrs. Eddy's appearing, she and her friend determined to go to Concord in the hope of catching a glimpse of their leader. They were successful, for she writes:

"The following day five of us made the journey to Concord, drove out to Pleasant View and met her face to face on her daily drive. She seemed watching to greet us, for when she caught sight of our faces, as our carriage turned a little, she instantly half rose with expectant face, bowing, smiling, and waving her hand to each of us; then as she went out of sight, kissed her hand to all."

The writer then goes on to describe what it all meant to her, and when it is remembered that Mrs. Eddy was in daily receipt of letters from all quarters expressing similar sentiments, it is not difficult to understand how she might be torn between a desire to reciprocate it all unrestrainedly in kind, and a recognition of the fact that undue devotion to personality was one of the great foes to progress.

"I will not attempt to describe the Leader," Martha Sutton-Thompson wrote, "nor can I say what this brief glimpse was and is to me. I can only say I wept, and the tears start every time I think of it. Why do I weep? I think it is because I want to be like her, and they are tears of repentance. I realize now what it was that made Mary Magdalene weep when she came into the presence of the Nazarene; it was not his personality."

Towards affection such as this Mrs. Eddy was full of compassion—at any rate there was here some semblance of an attempt to look away from effect to Cause—but there was another kind of "gratitude" towards which Mrs. Eddy always showed herself stern and relentless.

"A person wrote to me," she writes in the *Journal*, "naming the time of the occurrence, 'I felt the influence of your thought on my mind, and it produced a wonderful illumination, peace, and understanding'; but, I had not thought of the writer at that time. . . . When will the world cease to judge of causes from a personal sense of things, conjectural and misapprehensive!"[1]

And so it went. The pathway of what the world would call success was no more easy for this woman than the long road of toil and struggle she had traversed in the earlier days of her pilgrimage.

[1] *Miscellaneous Writings*, p. 290.

Widening Recognition

WITH THE FADING out of the hue and cry which supervened on the Woodbury libel suits and the Woodbury articles in the *Arena*, there followed three or four undisturbed years. As far as the outside public was concerned, the articles in the *Arena* had overstepped the mark. Their malicious intent was apparent, and the rapid growth of Christian Science all over the world, but especially in the United States, and the respect which it was gaining resulted in the attacks upon it having, in many cases, the reverse effect of what was intended. On any issue which really attracts public interest, the demand for good sportsmanship on both sides becomes more insistent, and the attacks on Christian Science, especially on its founder, began to savour more and more of bad sportsmanship.

The general public, moreover, was as always interested in success, and every day that passed showed the Christian Science movement more successful. And so the years 1901 to 1906 were years of quiet, both as far as Mrs. Eddy personally was concerned and her teaching.

Christian Science lectures became periodic features of public life in most cities large and small, and some Christian Science lecturers, like

Edward A. Kimball, became famous for their eloquence and the convincing nature of their presentation. They attracted large audiences and could command almost unlimited space in the daily press.

Edward A. Kimball, who has already appeared several times in this record, was perhaps the most outstanding instance of really effective apostleship. Born in Buffalo, New York, on August 27, 1845, he was a lineal descendant of one Richard Kimball, an Englishman of gentle birth who landed in New England in 1684. Edward's father died when he was three years old, and the support and care of the children, two sons and two daughters, devolved upon the mother, Elvira St. John Kimball. She seems to have been a remarkable woman, one of those rare people who combined a cultured sensitive mind with a simple capacity for management such as enabled her to raise her family and afford them more than ordinary opportunities for advancement.

Edward got to work early. At the age of seventeen, after attending public schools in Buffalo, he moved to Saginaw, Michigan, and soon afterwards went on to Chicago. There he got a job as bookkeeper with a firm of manufacturers, and rose steadily in their employ until he became a partner in the firm.

In the early eighties both he and his wife—he had married in 1873—suffered from persistent ill-health, and they both seem to have heard of Christian Science about the same time, though through different channels. Mrs. Kimball was healed almost at once. Edward was not so fortunate. It was fully a year before he finally got relief. When he did, however, it was complete, and thereafter both he and his wife took up the study of the new teaching with devotion. As already recorded, they sought and obtained instruction from Mrs. Eddy in 1888, being members of the historic class which met in Boston after Mrs. Eddy's return from Chicago, and just before she took decision to dissolve her College and Church and seek retirement in Concord. Ten years later, they were members of Mrs. Eddy's last class, the one she taught in Concord in the November of 1898. Kimball was then a lecturer and a member of the Board of Education, and recognized as one of the ablest men in the movement. In the latter years of his life as a lecturer he could apparently fill any hall of any size in any part of the world.

In these years, Edward Kimball and his fellow-lecturers carried their message everywhere, and from time to time there would come out of Pleasant View a word of commendation, published in the *Journal* or *Sentinel* for this one or that one who had done well. And Mrs. Eddy's "well done" had come to mean much.

Another important move at this time was the resumption of the practice of certifying teachers. The Massachusetts Metaphysical College, it will be remembered, had been dissolved in 1889 and its charter surrendered. The state law under which the College was chartered originally had since been revoked and it became necessary to set up a different arrangement. Accordingly, Mrs. Eddy issued a new by-law in 1899 creating a "Board of Education," to be constituted of three of her appointees and authorized to send out twenty-one teachers annually. (Later the number was changed to thirty triennially.) Edward A. Kimball was designated to teach the first class under the new auspices. Indeed, he was to continue in this office for five years and Mrs. Eddy was to publicly declare, after his passing, that his "clear, correct teaching of Christian Science has been and is an inspiration to the whole field."

Still another step was the establishment on an orderly footing of what was later known as the Committee on Publication. Ever since its first appearing, as has been seen, Christian Science had been subject to attack in the public press. It had invariably found a great cloud of defenders, always earnest, but not always judicious, and in many cases it had much need of being delivered from its friends. As the teaching spread, it became clear that its defence was better left to those who really understood the subject and could deal with objections "after knowledge" rather than "after zeal".

And so it became the custom to appoint in different centres a committee to correct in every possible way, but especially by means of open letters to the press or private letters to editors, all utterances that were regarded as misstatements of Christian Science. It was also his duty to send reports to headquarters in Boston of any developments affecting the movement, and especially to aid practitioners who became involved in difficulties with medical doctors and others, as they often did in the early days. The office of "Committee" was to develop into a base for concerted action more and more as the years rolled on, for the Committee could instantly bring effective pressure to bear on editors and legislators through floods of officially inspired letters, and could well nigh swamp with protests any hapless bookseller who undertook to handle literature which the Church authorities deemed "objectionable."

Meanwhile, as the great organization—for so it was by this time—was perfecting itself, Mrs. Eddy in her retirement at Pleasant View was keeping track of it all and seeking at every turn to safeguard it against the obvious danger to all organizations, namely, materialization. When New York built and dedicated a magnificent church—at the time, it was one of the finest ecclesiastical structures in the country—Mrs. Eddy in her dedicatory message bade its members always to keep before them that the letter of their work must die, "as do all things material, but the spirit of it is immortal". "Remember", she added, "that a temple but foreshadows the idea of God, the 'house not made with hands, eternal in the heavens', while a silent, grand man or woman, healing sickness and destroying sin, builds that which reaches heaven."

It was in these years, too, that a pilgrimage to Concord, at the time of the annual meeting of The Mother Church, tended to become one of the most eagerly anticipated privileges of those journeying to Boston for the annual gatherings. Mrs. Eddy did not issue invitations every year, and ultimately ceased to issue them at all, seeking, as she did persistently at this time, to check the all too vigorous tendency to focus on her personality. She was, however, constantly torn between a sympathy with those who naturally desired to see her from motives of gratitude and genuine human affection, and disapproval of the unwholesome adulation with which she was continually burdened.

The great gathering of 1898, already described, was several times repeated. In June, 1903, no fewer than ten thousand people journeyed from

Boston to Concord and spread themselves over the lawns at Pleasant View and were addressed briefly by Mrs. Eddy from the balcony outside her tower window. In 1903, she was eighty-two years of age, as slim and erect as ever, with a voice to the strength and beauty of which Arthur Brisbane some five years later still was to testify. It carried her brief address to the utmost limits of the great crowd.

There are several records of the scene at the gathering. When Mrs. Eddy came out on to the balcony, she stood for a moment looking out over the throng, and then, stretching out her hands with a characteristic gesture, bade them welcome "to your home in my heart". "Welcome to Pleasant View," she continued, immediately adding quaintly, "but not to varying views." And then she went on:

"Beloved, some of you have come long distances to kneel with us in sacred silence in blest communion—unity of faith, understanding, prayer, and praise—and to return in joy, bearing your sheaves with you. In parting I repeat to these dear members of my church: *Trust in Truth, and have no other trusts.*"[1]

The following year, the Church at Concord was completed, and at the time of the annual meeting Mrs. Eddy addressed an invitation to the members attending to come out to Concord and see the new Church, "in the afternoon, Monday, June 13, 1904". There was no indication in the invitation that Mrs. Eddy expected to be present, but an interesting little ceremony had evidently been planned beforehand. Punctually at two o'clock in the afternoon, Mrs. Eddy started out from Pleasant View on her daily drive. She took her usual route towards the courthouse. The town was thronged with visitors and as she passed the lawn of the Unitarian Church and the high school and other vantage points, she was received with cheers and waving handkerchiefs. Her carriage came to a standstill on North State Street, and she was greeted on behalf of the church by the President, Mr. E. P. Bates, to whom she presented a little rosewood box containing a gavel which, as an enclosed note explained, had been made from a tree grown on her father's farm at Bow. It was

[1] *Miscellany*, p. 171.

a great day for Concord, and, as was the case with all these pilgrimages, it was made a civic occasion.

A few days afterwards, Mrs. Eddy wrote to the Concord newspapers expressing her gratitude to all concerned for the welcome which had been extended to the members of her Church. She spoke simply of the pleasure it had all given her. "It was a glad day for me—sweet to observe with what unanimity my fellow-citizens vied with each other to make the Christian Scientists' short stay so pleasant."

And so Mrs. Eddy at eighty-three could settle back with the thought that the earth was at least beginning to help the woman. There was much to be done. About this time it became evident that The Mother Church Building in Boston, less than ten years old, was quite inadequate to accommodate even its local congregation. It was necessary to hold additional services on Sundays, and at the time of the annual meeting one of the largest halls in the city had to be requisitioned to accommodate the visitors. Early in 1902, Mrs. Eddy sent a letter to the Board of Directors suggesting that they give the matter their careful consideration, and at the annual meeting in June a resolution was taken pledging any part of $2,000,000 for the purpose of acquiring additional land and enlarging The Mother Church so as to accommodate at least five thousand people. No sooner was the need made known generally through the *Sentinel* and the *Journal* than money began to flow in from all parts of the world.

In October of 1903, sufficient sums had been secured to acquire the necessary land and commence the work of clearing it. Early in 1904, the foundation stone was laid, and for the next two years the great structure was in building. Fashioned of Bedford stone and granite, its huge dome, which still dominates the sky, rose to a height of 224 feet, higher by one foot than the Bunker Hill Monument. In the late spring of 1906, the building was completed and the dedicatory ceremonies were set for Sunday, June 10.

Nothing in the history of the Christian Science movement, it may be ventured, served to awaken public attention all over the world to the fact and the growth of Christian Science more than the building of The

Mother Church extension or annex, as it has come to be called. Nothing quite like it had ever been seen before. There were no appeals for money in the ordinary sense of the word; no suggestion of a bonded indebtedness; and long before the Church was completed notices to the effect that no more subscriptions were desired were inserted in both the *Journal* and the *Sentinel*. Newspaper men especially were impressed by this fact more than any other. The spontaneity of the whole thing made it clear to these men, accustomed as they were to witnessing the struggles of other denominations to raise sufficient funds for anything connected with their work, that Christian Science evidently contained some incentive to action not shared by all religious bodies. When the day for the dedication of the great structure came, the acclaim from the press was complete and almost unanimous.

Long before the dedication date, railway companies throughout the country had announced special excursion rates to Boston and most of them ran special trains. So great, indeed, was the influx that between 30,000 and 40,000 Christian Scientists were in Boston ready to attend the ceremonies. It is, of course, difficult to be sure of such figures, but the fact that the new building held between five and six thousand people, that the dedication ceremonies were repeated six times in the course of the day and that the building was filled to overflowing at each service seems to argue that the estimate of 40,000 was not far from the truth.

Each of the six services was the same and of the simplest character, the main feature being the reading of a dedicatory message from Mrs. Eddy. This message was dated from Pleasant View the day before, June 9, and in many ways, while characterized by a quite remarkable restraint, was an appeal of conciliation to all those who had so vigorously opposed her in the past. "A genuine Christian Scientist", she said, "loves Protestant and Catholic, D.D. and M.D.,—loves all who love God, good; and he loves his enemies."

It was also a message of thanks to each and everyone who had helped to bring their hopes to fruition.

"Beloved," she said, "I am not with you *in propria persona* at this memorial dedication and communion season, but I am with you 'in spirit and in truth', lovingly thanking your generosity and fidelity, and saying virtually what the prophet said: Continue to choose whom ye will serve!"

And then, looking backwards upon herself and upon the little Church which had been the original building, she added: "The modest edifice of The Mother Church of Christ, Scientist, began with the cross; its excelsior extension is the crown. The room of your Leader remains in the beginning of this edifice, evidencing the praise of babes and the word which proceedeth out of the mouth of God. Its crowning ultimate rises to a mental monument, a superstructure high above the work of men's hands, even the outcome of their hearts, giving to the material a spiritual significance—the speed, beauty, and achievements of goodness."[1]

At each service was sung one of her hymns, the same one: "Shepherd, Show Me How To Go". It had been played on the bells before the first service in the early morning and before each of the five thereafter, and in the course of the day it was sung by thirty thousand people or more. Mary Baker Eddy was not a great poet or even a poet at all in the strict sense of the word, but she was a genuine hymn-writer. Her harshest critics have been compelled to silence before "O'er Waiting Harpstrings of the Mind", or "Saw Ye My Saviour", "O Gentle Presence" or "Shepherd, Show Me How To Go".

> So, when day grows dark and cold,
>   Tear or triumph harms,
> Lead Thy lambkins to the fold,
>   Take them in Thine arms;
> Feed the hungry, heal the heart,
>   Till the morning's beam;
> White as wool, ere they depart,
>   Shepherd, wash them clean.

If the dedication of the new church roused the press to special interest

[1] *Miscellany*, p. 6.

and all manner of articles and editorial comment, this was nothing to the discussion evoked by the series of testimony meetings which were held throughout Boston on the following Wednesday evening. There was no attempt on this occasion to accommodate everyone desiring to attend in the new church by having a series of meetings throughout the day. The meeting was held in The Mother Church edifice at eight o'clock in the evening, but it had overflow meetings in practically every hall of any size throughout the city. At each of these meetings, those desiring to testify were asked to introduce themselves simply by announcing the city from which they came. It must have been a memorable scene, for in good, bad, indifferent and broken English came out the cities of the world from Moscow to Los Angeles and so on west to Moscow again, with voices welling up from "down under" all the way. And they bore testimony to the healing of all manner of disease. *Zion's Herald* perhaps most nearly summed up the effect of it all on a large cross-section of public thought when it described the whole development as "audacious, stupendous and inexplicable".

In these weeks of June, 1906, Mrs. Eddy was doubtless the most discussed woman in the world. She must have distrusted "tear or triumph" but triumph more than tears. She had grown accustomed to storm, and to her there was perhaps something even ominous in this loud acclaim.

Mark Twain

AS FAR BACK as 1899, Mark Twain had fired his first gun at Christian Science and its founder in two articles which appeared in the *Cosmopolitan Magazine*. The first, in the August issue, was entitled, "At the Appetite Cure", and the second, which appeared in October, "Christian Science and the Book of Mrs. Eddy". There was nothing malicious in the articles and, as Mark Twain's biographer, Bigelow Paine, justly remarks, "Their delightful humour awoke a general laugh, in which even devout Christian Scientists were inclined to join." Mark Twain was willing to admit that Mrs. Eddy and her book had benefited humanity, but he could not resist the fun-making which to his mind her doctrine invited. Today, although worn rather thin in the light of subsequent history, the articles are still delightful clowning. No one knew better than Mark Twain how to build up an inference of his own into a solemn announcement by his opponent and then use it to excellent purpose as a foil for some quite hilarious comment. His insistence that *Science and Health* could not, as he averred Mrs. Eddy claimed, have been written by the Almighty because no foreigner could secure copyright in the United States, is a case in point.

Nothing, however, roused Mark Twain to more violent explosion than an issue quite impervious to his attacks, and there was something about Christian Science, especially about Mrs. Eddy, which he evidently found little short of exasperating. To him, one minute, Mrs. Eddy was "easily the most interesting person on the planet, and in several ways as easily the most extraordinary woman that was ever born upon it"; the next, she was a liar and a fraud, a crook and a charlatan.

Only once did Mrs. Eddy reply to him—in a letter to the New York *Herald*. One of the most difficult things to answer successfully is a clever satire. Humanly speaking, any engagement in kind must meet satire with more pungent satire, must at every point out-Herod Herod. Mrs. Eddy made no attempt to do anything of the kind. To Mark Twain's direct charges, she makes direct answers without heat or irritation. Mark Twain had lampooned her for being styled "Mother" by her followers. She says simply that she had begged them not to do so, but that "the word spread like wild fire", and then she continues:

"I still must think the name is not applicable to me. I stand in relation to this century as a Christian Discoverer, Founder, and Leader. . . . I may be more loved, but I am less lauded, pampered, provided for, and cheered, than others before me."[1]

To Mark Twain's implied charge that she regarded herself as a "second Christ", she says that she considers "self-deification as blasphemous", and his further charge that if she does not regard herself as a second Christ she certainly regards herself as a second Virgin Mary, she dismisses in few words:

"I have not the inspiration nor the aspiration to be a first or second Virgin-mother—her duplicate, antecedent, or subsequent. What I am remains to be proved by the good I do. We need much humility, wisdom, and love to perform the functions of foreshadowing and forecasting heaven within us. This glory is molten in the furnace of affliction."[2]

But if Mrs. Eddy dismissed Mark Twain's attack thus briefly, there was among her followers one at least who thought it might be done

[1] *Miscellany*, p. 302.
[2] Ibid., p. 303.

more thoroughly; and when Mark Twain in the early days of 1906 collected his articles together, added to them others not previously published and issued the whole in book form under the title of *Christian Science*, Edward Kimball undertook to make reply in the *Cosmopolitan Magazine*. His article appeared in the May issue and immediately attracted widespread attention, not only for the skill with which it dealt with Mark Twain and his book, but because of its simple yet masterly exposition of his concept of Mrs. Eddy's teaching.

The problem before Mr. Kimball was a difficult one. Mark Twain was at the height of his popularity and he was armed with the deadly weapon of satire which no one in his generation knew better how to handle. Kimball himself admired Mark Twain immensely, and he made no effort to conceal his admiration. His line of attack, if so it should be called, is that of Mark Antony. "Brutus is an honourable man; they are all honourable men", is its underlying theme, and the effect in the case of Mrs. Eddy runs true enough to form. By the time he is finished with the "honourable man" and his friends they seem somehow to have lost no little caste and importance.

Mark Twain's objections were in many respects very human objections. When the pure fun-making in them had been eliminated, they were the objections of the man in the street. Edward Kimball's replies are very human replies. His opening sentence is certainly calculated to arrest attention.

"By way of justification, in part, of the Christian Science propaganda," he writes, "the reader of this article is asked to consider for a moment the startling statement of fact, afforded us by medical authority, to the effect that of the fifty million people who die every year, one-half die prematurely. . . . It may be presumed that before dying nearly all of these people tried to get well, and that in this effort they had recourse to some form of material means. . . . Finally, it may be concluded that at least twenty-five million people die annually because of the insufficiency of material means to cope with disease."

Having thus laid before the readers an incontrovertible statement,

Kimball goes on to pay warm tribute to the "grand men and women, who, as medical practitioners, have struggled on through the fluctuations of success and failure, ever deploring the instability of medical theories and the inadequacy of material remedies."

Thus, in two brief paragraphs, he laid before his readers what most people would be compelled to admit was a tragic need and the tragic inadequacy of the means so far devised to meet it. Christian Science, he insisted, had no quarrel with any man who sought by any means to meet so urgent a need, but it did "lift its voice inquiringly to those who are dying" and asks if "they are doing the best that can be done to live in peace".

There was, therefore, he went on, quite clearly room for another healing method. Indeed, there was an urgent call for one, and where the need was so great and the provision for help so utterly inadequate, it surely ill became anyone to heap contumely on a woman who had it in her heart to render what aid she could.

"Nearly forty years ago," he writes, "Mrs. Eddy proclaimed to the world certain postulates of a religio-scientific nature and declared that the verity thereof can be demonstrated with scientific accuracy. . . . She insisted that God, the sole creator of all that has actual, legitimate existence, has not created or procured disease and does not make use of it or co-operate with it for any purpose. She declared that sickness is an abnormality, wholly illegitimate, unlawful, and unnecessary; that it is not a natural, indispensable, or irresistible incident of man's normal experience; and, finally, that sickness, being at most but a disorder of human procurement, can be and will be exterminated."

And then, warming to his subject, he continues: "She declared that the demonstrations of Jesus, instead of being works of mystery, were in attestation of the divinely scientific verity that the nature, power, and law of God are adequately available to a sick man and are spontaneously responsive to his need.

"To scientists, philosophers, and metaphysicians she declared that, the chief mischief-maker of the world and the primary cause or essence of disease is what Paul designated the carnal mind, represented by the sum of an aggregation of human fear, ignorance, superstition, sin, and erroneous and perverted beliefs and illusions.

"She declared that the one supreme potentiality of the universe is the divine Mind or Spirit, which correctly has been termed omniscience, and furthermore that this mind which was also in Christ, is equal to, and is all that will ever effect, the redemption of mortals from sin and sickness. . . .

"If these things be true, then it follows that the verity thereof sanctions the unlimited hope and favourable expectations of everyone whose earthly sojourn is beset by disaster. A million people who have tested the truth of this Science insistently bear witness that by its means they have been delivered from every form of disease, sin, vice, fear, and misery."

Having thus presented his case and established in some degree an appreciation of the almost pathetic urgency of the situation—how in the presence of so great a need, such bitter hopes deferred and despair, any honest effort to bring help and comfort should not be met with derision and contumely—Kimball, evidently feeling that his readers were now with him, turns suddenly on Mark Twain:

"A man whose wit has been the object of a nation's admiration; a man who actually won his way to the generous affection of his countrymen by reason of his genial and unmalicious humour and good cheer—this man, whose mission in life was to tinge with gentle glow the rugged peaks of human existence and, perchance, even to dry the tears of some who were being stung by the bitterness of 'man's inhumanity to man', comes with deliberate offensiveness to denominate Mrs. Eddy a liar and a fraud."

Thence onwards, Kimball has an easy time of it. The reader is inclined to agree with him when he declares that there is a certain "venerable staleness" about Mark Twain's statement that Christian Scientists do not think; that they have no discriminating faculty; that they are the dupes of folly and duplicity; that they have no mental integrity; and that most of them are engaged in "an unholy pursuit of money". He does not attempt to answer these charges, but comes quickly to Mark Twain's main theme, namely, that Mrs. Eddy did not and could not have written *Science and Health*. Here Kimball is certainly at his best.

"Mr. Clemens has written a book", he says in conclusion, "through which runs an unbroken thread of purpose to procure the discomfiture of Mrs. Eddy. In this behalf, he presents a riot of inconsistency which we may with propriety consider. In order to gain his point he is obliged to present *Science and Health* as possessing some merit. Then he insists that Mrs. Eddy never rose to an intellectual altitude that was on a plane of excellence with the book. Then follows the deduction that she did not write it and that her pretence is fraudulent. He thus used the book for the obliteration of Mrs. Eddy, in apparent disregard of the fact that in another place he has written 'of all the strange and frantic, and incomprehensible books which the imagination of man has created, surely this one is the prize sample'. He declares that in several ways Mrs. Eddy is the most interesting woman that ever lived and the most extraordinary—that 'she launched a world-religion which is increasing at the rate of a new church every four days'; that 'it is quite within the probabilities that she will be the most imposing figure that has cast its shadow across the globe since the inauguration of our era'; that 'she is profoundly wise in some respects'; 'she is competent', and so forth; and then he declares his conviction that she could not have written 'the most frantic and incomprehensible book which man has ever created'. And this is the testimony of an expert!"

And so he rides to this finish: "After concluding that the founder and leader of this religious movement is a fraud and a cheat, and a tyrant, and that the textbook of this church is an unconscionable lie; that the church organization is venal, its laws outrageous, and its aims degrading, he declares, 'I believe that the new religion will conquer half of Christendom in a hundred years,' and adds concerning this statement, 'I think perhaps it is a compliment to the human race.'"

It was not long before Mark Twain regretted it all very deeply. The man who suffered all his life and especially in his later years when he thought of the unkindness and cruelty inflicted by man upon his fellow-man, came to see that what he had done in his articles and in his book was something he would have condemned roundly in another. His biographer, Albert Bigelow Paine, records how one day in conversation with Mark Twain he referred to the matter and elicited a very unexpected comment.

"I was at this period", Paine writes, "interested a good deal in mental healing, and had been treated for neurasthenia with gratifying results. Like most of the world, I had assumed from his published articles that he condemned Christian Science and its related practices out of hand. When I confessed rather reluctantly one day the benefit I had received, he surprised me by answering: 'Of course, you have been benefited. Christian Science is humanity's boon. Mother Eddy deserves a place in the Trinity as much as any member of it. She has organized and made available a healing principle that for two thousand years has never been employed, except as the merest guesswork. She is the benefactor of the age.'"

Mark Twain's fun-making, as far as Christian Science was concerned, remained for many years and still remains, but the sting has long since gone from it.

There was, however, already developing, even before Mark Twain launched his satires, a far more deadly attack and by a man of very different character. For several years Joseph Pulitzer, the strange dynamic genius who had raised the New York *World* from a "bankrupt sheet" in 1883 to one of the most widely circulated newspapers in the United States by 1906, had been watching Christian Science and its founder. With that sure instinct for news which helped to make him one of the outstanding figures in modern journalism, he saw from the first the news possibilities of Christian Science in general and Mrs. Eddy in particular.

A man of strong intellect, amazing ability and insatiable ambition, he had in his latter years, when stricken with blindness, withdrawn from the world of men and women as far as his own personal appearance was concerned, but from the cabin of his yacht or from some place of seclusion in the south of France or the coast of Maine he kept control of every detail of his great paper, and every day and many times each day some one of the small army of secretaries, always at his command, would cable instructions to New York as to what was to be dealt with prominently and how it was to be dealt with.

He seems to have worked up to the conclusion that the Christian Science movement was a gigantic fraud and that Mrs. Eddy, although in her day the high priestess of this fraud, had, in her later years, simply become the tool of designing people.

The tremendous stir created throughout the country by the dedication of The Mother Church evidently decided Pulitzer that he was right. Mrs. Eddy's absence from the scene of her triumph was something he found it difficult to understand save on the assumption that she was incapable of being present. Her message, so he thought, anyone could have written. It was quite possible that she was sick and incapable, even mentally deficient, and that those around her in Concord, in collusion with the church authorities, were keeping up the pretence of her leadership to further their own ends. She might even be dead. To be sure, report had it that she went out for a drive daily, but the carriage was a closed one, and it would be the simplest thing in the world for someone moderately resembling Mrs. Eddy to impersonate her.

For Joseph Pulitzer it was sufficient, it would seem, to conceive such a picture to believe that it represented the true condition of affairs. Always he had had what he would have called a passion for truth, and so it might justly be described, but the truth was the truth of Pulitzer's own determining. He was often right, far more often than not, and this perhaps makes no little excuse for him; but the fact remains that, once he had made up his mind as to what should be regarded as the verities of a situation, nothing could change him. Facts might prove to be against him, but, if so, then so much the worse for the facts. No one knew better than did Joseph Pulitzer how to get facts to prove his case.

And so in the summer of 1906, when everyone was talking of Mark Twain's book, as his yacht was cruising off the coast of Maine, Pulitzer seems to have formulated a plan for an attack on Mrs. Eddy and the Christian Science hierarchy—for so he would have called it—the like of which had never been attempted before. The *World* never did anything in a small way, and the *World* would show the world how exposures should be made and misdemeanants brought to justice.

Joseph Pulitzer

"Concord, New Hampshire.

"Mr. Joseph Pulitzer, Bar Harbour, Maine.

"MY DEAR MR. PULITZER:—You are a comparatively old man, and your years, your character, and your accomplishments entitle you to the respect and kindly regard of your fellows. That which is due you, and which you have a right to expect at the hands of men, is due from you and yours to others under like or similar conditions.

"Few, if any, women, living, have done so much to pass their names to posterity as has Rev. Mary Baker G. Eddy of this city and state, and we of Concord, regardless of religious beliefs, have great respect for this woman, and we resent any indignity aimed at her or passed upon her, and every decent man and woman in Concord experiences a sense of disappointment and shame on realizing that a great newspaper like *The World*, through the overzeal of its representatives, would annoy her or cause her discomfort by appealing to low natures or those given to gossip or envy, to secure guesses or opinions about her, unworthy of *The World*, unworthy of Mrs. Eddy, and unworthy of the intelligence, integrity, and manhood and womanhood of New Hampshire's capital city.

"My dear Mr. Pulitzer, I have met and talked with you once. I have met and talked with Mrs. Eddy more than once. I know her; she knows me. I have been in her home, in her study with her within a few months, and discussed with her many things; I have bowed to her in her carriage within forty-eight hours, and my salutation has been returned by her.

"If the intent of *The World's* representatives to Concord be carried out in its columns, *The World* will say in substance that Mrs. Eddy is dead, and that a mummy or substitute, and not she, is in the carriage each day when it passes through the main streets of our city, and its occupant is greeted by our people; or it will say Mrs. Eddy is enfeebled and decrepit, and that those brilliant faculties which in the past made her wonderful accomplishment possible have departed.

"To every statement, or even insinuation, of this kind, I, as one who knows, say it is not true, in whole or in part, but on the contrary is unqualifiedly false.

"This letter to you is not occasioned by any special zeal on my part in the cause of Christian Science, nor is it occasioned by any blind adherence to or worship of persons or advocacies, but solely in a spirit of justice, truth, square dealing—a becoming regard for brains and respectability as well as reverence for age and motherhood. I am,

"Very truly yours,

"October 26, 1906."   (Signed) MICHAEL MEEHAN".

So did Michael Meehan, Editor of Concord's daily paper *The Patriot*, seek, at the eleventh hour, to stave off the blow. As a newspaper man, he, in common with many others in Concord, knew what was coming.

About the middle of September, two reporters from the New York *World* had made their appearance in Concord, evidently with instructions to allow nothing to stand in the way of a ruthless investigation of Mrs. Eddy and all that concerned her such as none knew better than Pulitzer how to set in motion. They came armed with all manner of "evidence". A few months previously, Georgine Milmine had undertaken

436

to write a life of Mrs. Eddy for *McClure's Magazine*. She set about the task with a will, and, after interviewing Frederick Peabody, who had acted as attorney for Mrs. Woodbury in her abortive suit against Mrs. Eddy some years previously, returned to New York with such amazing "revelations" that McClure's felt sure they had the story of the century, and at once detailed other members of the staff, namely Will Irwin, Burton Hendrick and Willa Cather, to collaborate with Miss Milmine in its production.

As rumours of the coming story spread throughout the journalistic world of New York, they lost nothing in the telling, and it was not long before *The World*, at Pulitzer's insistent demand, was hard at work seeking to anticipate the McClure "revelations" and render them even more sensational. Two reporters were sent to Concord to commence the work there. They delved into Mrs. Eddy's past with earnest enthusiasm. They traced carefully her every transaction in real estate away back to her first purchase of the little house on Broad Street in Lynn. They investigated her copyrights, and, in both connections, viewed with rising suspicion Mrs. Eddy's practice, specially noticeable in her later years, of apparently turning over her equities to others. Thus, in 1899, they found that she had transferred the copyrights of her books to Edward Kimball, and that he, for no good reason that they could see, had in 1906 turned them over to Calvin Frye. Surely this was just what the Chief had insisted: that Mrs. Eddy, mentally incapacitated, was in the hands of designing persons who were taking it turn about to share her substance between them.

So sure, indeed, were *The World* men that they had discovered something momentous such as could not be gainsaid, that they determined to confront some well-known Concord business men with the facts they had unearthed and secure the support of their admissions as to their correctness. The two chosen were Frederick N. Ladd, Mrs. Eddy's cousin, who was secretary of the Loan and Trust Savings Bank of Concord, and J. Wesley Plummer, treasurer of the Concord Church. Both men seem to have received the suggestion of the reporters that Mrs. Eddy was mentally incompetent, with a quite disconcerting amusement; were entirely unimpressed by the evidence they had accumulated, and possibly advised them to go to Pleasant View and find out for themselves whether Mrs. Eddy was mentally competent or not.

Anyway, within a few days, the two men did actually present themselves at Pleasant View and demanded to see Mrs. Eddy. No previous announcement had been made of their intentions, and, at first, Calvin Frye and other members of the little household were quite at a loss to know what to do. They had heard of the rumours that were going around, and it seemed a simple matter to settle the question of Mrs. Eddy's existence and mental capacity once and for all by acquiescing in the demand in spite of the evident truculence with which it was made. But Mrs. Eddy was in her eighty-sixth year. Save in her daily drives, she had little contact with the world, and what little she had, never exposed her to anything but gentleness and consideration. These two New York newspaper men had evidently little of either quality about them. They did not ask to see Mrs. Eddy, they demanded the right to see her, and virtually made it clear that they did not propose to leave the house till they had seen her. Frye finally compromised the situation by asking them to come back at three o'clock in the afternoon, when he would see what could be done. Mrs. Eddy would be back from her drive by that time, and it might be possible for them to see her.

As far as Calvin Frye and Laura Sargent and the other members of the household were concerned, this action represented no more than an effort to gain time. They shrank from the prospect of exposing Mrs. Eddy to such a contact, but there seemed no other way out of it, and at last reluctantly they took their problem, as they always did in the end, to Mrs. Eddy herself, and Mrs. Eddy solved it promptly by saying that she would see the two men. When three o'clock came round and the reporters returned, they were shown into her study.

As they stood in the doorway, Mrs. Eddy rose from her desk to greet them. Next moment, the two men were overwhelming her with questions. They had done what no other reporters had done, and they were determined to make the most of it. Mrs. Eddy answered calmly at first, but it was not long before Frye and Lewis Strang, another member of her household, intervened, and the interview was brought to a close. The two reporters, realizing no doubt that, interpreted as they intended to interpret it, they already had more than enough material to make the story Pulitzer wanted, left the house without further protest.

One thing, however, remained to be done. Pulitzer was insistent that Mrs. Eddy, if not actually dead, was at any rate so incapacitated that she could not leave the house, and that the woman who took a daily drive in her carriage through Concord was not Mrs. Eddy, but some other woman made up to impersonate her. If they could establish this as a fact, their work would be complete and their commendation sure. They laid their plans carefully. Every day, punctually at two o'clock, Mrs. Eddy's carriage swung through the gates of Pleasant View on its way to Concord. The carriage, however, was a closed one, and, in the bright afternoon sunlight, its interior was very much in shadow; and so, after haunting the entrance to the drive for several days without being able to make quite sure, they determined to make their evidence such as could not be controverted. A day or two later, as the carriage slowed down near the entrance, they jumped on the running board, one on each side, calculating that if Mrs. Eddy turned her head away from one, the other would only get the better view.

It all happened in a moment, and was all over before Mrs. Eddy had recovered from her surprise or Calvin Frye, who was on the box as usual, from his indignation, but the two *World* men had got what they wanted. As was subsequently shown beyond doubt, the occupant of the carriage was Mrs. Eddy, as it always was, but, in the account of the matter these men were writing for *The World*, Mrs. Eddy had already been portrayed as in the last stages of senile decay. It would, therefore, be a simple matter for them to find that the Chief was right and that the occupant of the carriage was not Mrs. Eddy.

It was a lurid story, and Michael Meehan, with the sixth sense of a good journalist, knowing what was contemplated, had determined to

439

make an eleventh hour attempt to prevent the appearance of anything so scandalous. Hence his letter to Pulitzer. The hope was a forlorn one and he must have known it. Joseph Pulitzer did not even answer Meehan's letter, and in the columns of *The World* on the following Sunday morning, October 28, appeared an article on Mrs. Eddy and her household at Pleasant View, which, by reason of its quite shameless malice and misstatement, was within a few days to arouse a large section of the American Press to vigorous protest.

In a series of scare headlines which spread themselves over the front page of one of *The World's* many sections it was announced that Mrs. Eddy was dying, that she was controlled by a footman and impersonated by a dummy, that she was hopelessly affected with cancer and "immured at Pleasant View, while another woman impersonates her on the streets of Concord". "Calvin A. Frye, Secretary-Footman, Supreme Power at the Eddy Home," the headlines went on; "Mrs. Eddy's Fortune Estimated at $15,000,000, Her Income at $1,000,000 a Year. Members of her Coterie Say She Spent it all in Charity, though No Records of Large Gifts Can be Found."

And then came the story of the interview; surely, in the light of what subsequently transpired, one of the most amazing travesties that ever was published. Distasteful as is the task, the historian is compelled to quote, at least in part, the *World's* article, for in no other way could the incredible malignancy of the attack be shown and the forces behind a vastly more ambitious attack to follow understood. Here are typical passages:

"Mrs. Eddy looked more dead than alive. She was a skeleton, her hollow cheeks thick with red paint, and the fleshless, hairless bone above the sunken eyes pencilled a jet black. The features were thick with powder. Above them was a big white wig.

"Her body was pitifully emaciated, and her throat, on which sparkled a horseshoe of brilliants, was shrivelled.

"Her weakness was pathetic. She reeled as she stood clinging to the table. Her sunken faded eyes gazed helplessly, almost pleadingly, at her visitors. The air of the room reeked with the odours of powerful stimulants. In a corner, as though hastily pushed aside, stood a galvanic battery with its surgical basin half full of water and a sponge wet from use.

"To every eye it was clear that the unfortunate old woman had been doped and galvanized for the ordeal of identification. But it was equally clear that the utmost stimulation could not keep the tortured woman upon her feet much longer.

"Strang glided to her side and held an outstretched arm behind her in readiness for the threatened collapse. But old Mrs. Eddy was nerved to supreme effort.

"Her listless eyes were fastened upon Professor Kent[1] as he stepped towards her. As he bowed formally she released her hold upon the table, swayed toward him, clutched him with her shrivelled fingers and held on with desperate strength. Had Professor Kent withdrawn his support she must have fallen.

" 'My-dear-dear-pro—fessor,' she cried in the high cackling voice of extreme age. 'H-h-how glad I am to see you. Let me co-congratulate you on getting back your position. I-I am so glad that you are at the head of your school again.' It was the senseless chatter of senility. Professor Kent years ago severed all connections with the Concord School.

"As he stammered out a reply and gently freed himself from the quivering fingers, Mrs. Eddy turned reeling again to the table and clung to it for support. Her fictitious strength was almost gone.

"Turning to the others for the first time, she gasped, 'I-I-I ca-cannot understand your in-terest in poor me. B-but I ca-nnot be interviewed.'

"She had just strength enough left to extend a palsied hand to each visitor and motion appealingly to Strang. The interview was at an end. It had lasted only three minutes."

No so-called "scoop" in the history of modern journalism has received more emphatic or more general condemnation than did this *tour de force* of the New York *World*. Concord, on that Sunday morning was literally out in the streets about it before the sun was well up. As soon as possible,

---

[1] Professor Kent, a neighbour of Mrs. Eddy and at one time Principal of Concord High School, had been persuaded by the reporters to accompany them for the purposes of identification.

the mayor, the Hon. Charles R. Corning, accompanied by General Streeter, a member of the National Republican Committee and one of the foremost lawyers in New England, drove out to Pleasant View to place their services at Mrs. Eddy's disposal, and on their return to Concord gave to a representative of the Associated Press, who had come hot afoot to Concord, statements combating in detail the absurdities and misstatements of the *World's* article. Mayor Corning declared indignantly that he had known Mrs. Eddy for years, that he saw her driving past his office almost every day, that he had just seen her, talked with her for half an hour, that he had found her as usual, "keen of intellect and strong in memory . . . a surprising illustration of longevity, with bright eyes, emphatic expression, and alertness rarely encountered in a person so venerable."

General Streeter testified to much the same purpose. Mrs. Frank Leonard from New York, who had been accused by *The World* of impersonating Mrs. Eddy, wired that she had never in her life stepped inside Mrs. Eddy's carriage. Michael Meehan, editor of *The Patriot*, Josiah E. Fernald, president of the National State Capital Bank, J. Wesley Plummer, deputy state treasurer, and George H. Moses, then editor of the Concord *Evening Monitor*, and later United States Senator from New Hampshire, all denied emphatically that there was a word of truth in *The World's* story.

Next day, the press of the country left no doubt as to its reaction. Led by the New York *Journal, The World's* great rival, condemnation of the most emphatic kind was almost universal.

"The New York *World*", said the *Journal*, "continues its personal and vicious hounding of Mrs. Eddy, leader of the Christian Science religion. The account which it publishes of recent events in Mrs. Eddy's home could reflect credit upon no newspaper and upon no man."

The effect of it all upon Joseph Pulitzer can only be surmised. He was used to storms and had weathered many, but in each and all of them he had always managed to preserve some claim to be heard, justification for his action, which enabled him to out-ride even the most violent storms

442

of protest. But here *The World* stood before the country, not only as the perpetrator of a deliberate slander, but as doing it with a naïvete and clumsiness past belief.

Pulitzer said nothing at the time. He made no attempt to justify his action, but during the next few weeks, in the cabin of his yacht at Bar Harbour, he laid plans for a revenge which, less than a year later, stood revealed in the form of a lawsuit which must rank as one of the most remarkable in the history of American courts.

The "Next Friends" Suit

THE NEW YORK *World* in the first decade of the century was a great institution. It dominated the field of journalism in the United States, and Joseph Pulitzer completely dominated *The World*. His word was law, and he exacted and received willingly from *The World* men a loyalty and devotion seldom if ever equalled in similar circumstances. He could not afford to lie under the stigma of having allowed his paper to trump up a case reflecting on a woman and upon the religion of a large body of people and based on nothing more substantial than, as his critics insisted, a desire for sensationalism. It was a new thing to Joseph Pulitzer to be thus called to account and to find himself with nothing to say in his defence. He must confound his enemies somehow, and it seems to have been clear to him from the first that whatever action he took would have to be such as to compel circumstances rather than any open and direct action on his part to produce his vindication.

Joseph Pulitzer's immense driving force had got him much that he wanted in his early days. This same force, plus almost unlimited resources, seemed, in his later years, capable of getting him literally anything he wanted and enabled him to make or unmake anyone he pleased. He still firmly believed that most of the charges he had brought against Mrs. Eddy and her household were true, and he was determined that they should, somehow or other, be "substantiated".

And so he set about it. There was nothing to show for some time, and then in its issue for March 2, 1907, *The World* announced that a petition had been made to the Courts of New Hampshire by Mary Baker Eddy, "who sues by her next friends, George W. Glover and George W. Baker, *against* Calvin A. Frye, Alfred Farlow, Irving C. Tomlinson, Ira O. Knapp, William B. Johnson, Stephen A. Chase, Joseph Armstrong, Edward A. Kimball, Hermann S. Hering and Louis C. Strang," to compel them to give an accounting of her property to make restitution if it should be proved that they were in any way in default and to enjoin them while the suit was pending from receiving or disposing of any funds. They further prayed the court to appoint a receiver to take possession of Mrs. Eddy's estate.

As far as the outside world was concerned, neither Joseph Pulitzer nor his paper had anything to do with the move. That *The World* should give prominence to it, to news which seemed to indicate a development tending towards the justification of its contentions in regard to Mrs. Eddy and the Christian Science movement, was only natural. Hence when it devoted several columns in its issue of March 2 to the story of the case, no one was surprised and no other newspaper had the temerity to suggest that such full reporting had anything to do with a connection of *The World* with the case. Indeed, so complete was Pulitzer's hold on the press at that time, that never once during the long drawn-out legal proceedings which followed was such connection openly averred. It was hinted at often enough, but that was as far as it ever got.

Pulitzer had laid his plans carefully, and the story is an interesting one. On a cold winter day in the latter part of 1906, a traveller of unmistakable New York cut alighted from the train at Lead City, South Dakota. There was nothing unusual in that. Lead City in 1906 was enjoying the great mining boom in its history. Gold was being brought into the town from the snow-clad Black Hills at the rate of $5,000,000 a year, and the huge mining plant of the Homestake mine was rapidly becoming one of the largest in the world. New York was much interested, and there was much traffic back and forth between the two cities.

This particular traveller, however, had no interest in mining, although the driver of the hackney which he hired at the station might have so assumed, for he asked to be driven to the house of a well-known mining prospector in the city, one George Glover.

George Glover, at that time, was well settled in a comfortable home which his mother, Mrs. Eddy, had built for him some years previously, and was energetically seeking to secure that share in the boom which always somehow evaded his grasp. Mrs. Eddy had from time to time given him money for his mining ventures, but he was in chronic need of "capital". Five thousand dollars to secure a share in something that was "absolutely beyond question". Thirty thousand dollars to erect a new quartz mill which for many years to come "would secure unlimited business". These are some of the things mentioned in his letters to his mother about this time. And so, when a traveller from New York was landed at his door and announced his desire to discuss a very private and confidential matter, he was no doubt filled with pleasurable expectancy.

The traveller introduced himself as Mr. James Slaght of New York, and after warning George Glover that his mission was highly confidential and being assured by the latter that his confidence would be respected and that he might speak with the utmost frankness, Mr. Slaght at once went on to explain that he came from the New York *World,* that *The World,* in spite of all the statements to the contrary which had appeared broadcast in the press, was convinced that its charges in regard to the condition and treatment of Mrs. Eddy were true. Mr. Slaght insisted to George that it had no quarrel whatever with Mrs. Eddy, that the whole purpose of its disclosures was to save a woman, who in her day had deserved well of her fellows, from falling in her old age into the hands of designing people, who sought to seize and dissipate a fortune which rightly belonged, in large part at any rate, to George Glover himself.

George was impressed. He evidently, as subsequent correspondence disclosed, found it difficult at first to believe that his mother was dominated mentally by anyone, but when Mr. Slaght went on to dilate upon the enormous proportions of his mother's estate; how that *The World* had reckoned its net value at no less than $15,000,000 and that the income approximated $1,000,000 a year, George, no doubt asking himself what he could not do with a twentieth of such a sum, began to have his doubts.

At the right moment, Mr. Slaght produced a letter from Senator Chandler of New Hampshire. George knew him, of course, by reputation, and as he commenced to read the letter he could see that it was most friendly in tone. Dated, "Washington, D.C., November 22, 1906," it ran:

"MY DEAR MR. GLOVER,—I have consented to act as legal counsel concerning certain questions which arise in connection with Mrs. Mary Baker G. Eddy. They are stated in a letter from me to Mr. Slaght, who will call upon you and show you my letter to him.

"It is important for public and private interests that these questions should be investigated and met and fairly and justly disposed of as questions involving doubts which from large and commendable motives, all good citizens, and especially all relatives of Mrs. Eddy, should help to solve and settle. Therefore, please be sure and give Mr. Slaght a full hearing and possess yourself fully of all the facts which he will be able to give you.

"Very respectfully,

(Signed) WILLIAM E. CHANDLER"

As soon as George had finished reading, the adroit Mr. Slaght had the letter referred to ready and handed it over. The senator came at once to the point. Writing to Slaght from Washington, under date November 22, 1906, he said:

447

"My dear Mr. Slaght: I consent to act as counsel concerning certain questions which arise in connection with Mrs. Mary Baker G. Eddy. It seems that there are several doubts about several points.

"1. Mrs. Eddy may be detained in the custody of strangers against her will.

"2. She may be so nearly worn out in body and mind as a confirmed invalid that she is incapable of deciding any questions whatever, according to any will or pleasure of her own, and necessarily, therefore, incapable of managing her business and property affairs.

"3. Being thus restrained or incapable, or without relatives near her, she may be surrounded by designing men who either have already sought or may hereafter seek to wrongfully possess themselves of her large property, or induce her to make a disposition of it contrary to what would be her sane and deliberate intentions if she were in perfect possession of her liberty and mental faculties.

"These doubts have arisen in connection with investigations recently made. Beyond all question, steps should be taken to solve the doubts, to correct the wrong, if it exists, and to establish the right in every respect.

"This new work should be done, if possible, in co-operation with Mrs. Eddy's son, or any other relative who may be impressed with his duties in this regard; and if the relatives do not move, it should be done by such right-minded citizens as are in sympathy with the commendable movement.

"Yours truly,
William E. Chandler"

It is not surprising that, in the circumstances, George Glover was easily won over, and, when told that his cousin, George W. Baker, only son of George Sullivan Baker—of the far-off days in Sanbornton Bridge —had decided to join in the petition, he consented to take the lead, and, shortly afterwards, on the advice of Senator Chandler, he set out with his daughter Mary for Washington.

Meanwhile, in Concord, there was no thought of what was coming.

The popular condemnation of *The World's* attack in October had been so emphatic and complete that it looked as if Mrs. Eddy and her household might reasonably look forward to some measure of peace, in the immediate future. And then one day, just before Christmas, Mrs. Eddy to her surprise received a letter from George from Lead City telling her he was just setting out for Washington with his daughter Mary and that they looked forward to seeing her in Concord before they returned home. He said nothing as to the purpose of his visit in Washington, and immediately on receipt of his letter Mrs. Eddy sent word for him to come to Concord as soon as he could, and telling him that although they had not room for him and Mary at Pleasant View, she had arranged for them to be guests in the home of one of her friends in Concord.

On the advice of Senator Chandler, George, in his reply, did not set any date for his visit, but on January 2 he and Mary went up to Concord unannounced. Mrs. Eddy received them at once, and although, as written up in *The World* three months later, she was again pictured as in the depths of senile decay, subsequent testimony was abundant to show that such allegations were untrue to the point of absurdity.

There was as yet, however, no word of the contemplated suit, and the announcement in *The World*, as already quoted, broke on the little household in Concord quite unexpectedly.

The petition of the "Next Friends", as published practically verbatim in *The World*, was a formidable document, and indicated an investigation as to the property and position of Mrs. Eddy such as could only have been achieved as the result of the expenditure of much time and resources. The charges amounted to the same as those advanced in the notorious articles in *The World* some six months previously, namely, that Mrs. Eddy was mentally incapable; was kept a virtual prisoner in Pleasant View, and that there was reason to suppose that those who had her in custody were dissipating or misappropriating her property. The petition then went on to set forth the alleged character and worth of this property in detail, going back over the years to Mrs. Eddy's first classes, and setting forth exactly how much she received from each. The income from her books and the computed value of the *Journal* and the *Sentinel* and The Mother Church "as a going concern" were all set down, and the whole concluded with the usual prayer that the defendants be required "to disclose and give an account"; "be restrained from further action"; and that "a receiver or receivers be appointed".

Mrs. Eddy felt it all keenly, especially the fact that the leader in the attack should be her own son. But, in moments of crisis, she had found that she had to take the lead. Those around her might strive valiantly to solve this problem and that, but, if they could not do it, the burden, in the end, devolved upon her. It had been the case when she first embarked on her self-appointed task in middle life; it was the same when she was eighty-six.

From a legal point of view, she had always been singularly well-advised, and this was certainly the case in regard to the "Next Friends Suit". General Frank Streeter, who immediately took charge of matters, was a distinguished and resourceful lawyer, and his first act was little short of an inspiration. He advised Mrs. Eddy to turn over her entire estate to three trustees of her own choosing, and give them paramount power to manage her affairs. In this way, the sole question which would be before the court when the case came up for trial would be whether or not Mrs. Eddy, at the time of granting the trusteeship, was mentally capable.

Accordingly, on March 6, 1907, Mrs. Eddy signed a deed of trust which gave ownership of property in trust to three individuals: Archibald McLellan, editor-in-chief of her publications and periodicals; Josiah E. Fernald, president of one of the Concord banks; and Henry M. Baker, a cousin and a lawyer.

From the moment that the petition was formally filed and the inevitable trial of the case in the newspapers had begun, it became clear that time was going to be on the side of the aged woman at Pleasant View. The press in the country was thoroughly roused. Newspapers everywhere that had told *The World* just what they thought of its policies and methods, some six months previously, had no intention of allowing *The World* to prove itself right and themselves wrong without a struggle. Newspaper correspondents flocked to Concord with urgent petitions that they might be allowed to interview Mrs. Eddy, and, in several notable instances, the request was granted. William E. Curtis of the Chicago *Record Herald*, Edwin J. Park of the Boston *Globe*, Arthur Brisbane of the New York *Evening Journal*, all went to Pleasant View and came away with the same story: that instead of the mental and physical derelict they had been assured was held in durance vile, they had found a woman "physically and mentally phenomenal", whose people were "absolutely devoted to her", who "selected the food for her table", "supervised the work of her retainers", and took "the keenest interest in the disposition of all her affairs and belongings". "The idea that this strong-minded woman", declared impatiently yet another interviewer, Dr. Allan McLane Hamilton, "is ever a victim of coercion, is manifestly absurd."

Of these journalists and others who interviewed Mrs. Eddy at Pleasant View in the early summer of 1907, while the "Next Friends Suit" was awaiting the convenience of the courts, the record of Arthur Brisbane is perhaps the most remarkable. Arthur Brisbane, at this time, was in his early forties. He was editor of the New York *Evening Journal*, and was rapidly coming to the front as an able if somewhat ruthless journalist. He was the last man in the world to commit himself to statements which he knew might well be disproved within a few weeks. He went to Pleasant View, as he admits himself, full of prejudice, but, from the first, he seems to have been captivated by what he found there; his first glimpse of the house, "a very pleasant quiet abode . . . on the side of a most beautiful New Hampshire valley"; the "brightness and light" to be found everywhere; the "Christian Science ladies" with "peaceful happy expressions", who greeted him so kindly.[1]

"One of them came forward to say: 'Mrs. Eddy is very glad that you have come, and will see you. Please come into her sitting-room.'

"She led the way upstairs into a corner room at the rear of the house, with wide windows overlooking the valley and the distant hills.

---

[1] The interview was published in due course in the New York *Evening Journal* and republished in book form in 1930 by M. E. Paige, publisher, New York, under the title *What Mrs. Eddy said to Arthur Brisbane*.

"Beside a writing desk, in an armchair, sat a white-haired woman, who rose and walked forward, extending her hand in friendly greeting to a stranger. That was Mrs. Eddy, for whom many human beings in this world feel deepest reverence and affection, and concerning whom others have thought it necessary or excusable to write and say unkind and untruthful things.

"It is quite certain that nobody could see this beautiful and venerable woman and ever again speak of her except in terms of affectionate reverence and sympathy. There are hundreds and thousands of Christian Scientists who would make almost any sacrifice for the privilege of looking on Mrs. Eddy's face. It is impossible now for her to see many, and it is therefore a duty to make at least an attempt to convey an idea of the impression created by her personality."

And then Arthur Brisbane goes on to paint his picture. It is easy to see that his heart is in his task:

"Mrs. Eddy is eighty-six years old. Her thick hair, snow white, curls about her forehead and temples. She is of medium height and very slender. But her figure is straight as she rises and walks forward. The grasp of her thin hand is firm; the hand does not tremble.

"It is hopeless to describe a face made beautiful by age, deep thought, and many years exercise of power. The light blue eyes are strong and concentrated in expression. And the sight, as was soon proved, is that of a woman half Mrs. Eddy's age.

"Mrs. Eddy's face is almost entirely free from wrinkles; the skin is very clear; many a young woman would be proud to have it. The forehead is high and full, and the whole expression of the face combines benevolence with great strength of will. Mrs. Eddy has accumulated power in this world. She possesses it; she exercises it; and she knows it. But it is a gentle power, and it is possessed by a gentle, diffident, and modest woman.

"Women will want to know what Mrs. Eddy wore. The writer regrets he cannot tell. With some women you see the dress; with Mrs. Eddy you see only the face. She wore a lace collar, no jewellery of any kind, and a simple dress. That much is remembered."

452

With that good journalistic sense which, in later years, enabled him to scale dizzy and uncertain peaks in his profession, Arthur Brisbane then goes on faithfully to cover the whole ground. He fills in his picture, which he evidently designs to be a full-length portrait not only of the woman, but of her surroundings also. He records how she pointed out the beautiful view to him from her study window; how she spoke simply "of her own life and work and of her absolute happiness in her peaceful surroundings"; how she discussed business matters with him "for ovei half an hour with equal interest and without any sign of flagging", and in the turn of his sentences he manages to convey quite accurately that sweeping away of prejudice which seems to have been a characteristic effect on many people who visited Mrs. Eddy.

He asked her to read aloud to him a passage of his own selection, and later declares that "among young public speakers there are few with voices stronger, deeper, than the voice of Mrs. Eddy at eighty-six. She read the ordinary magazine type without glasses, as readily as any woman of twenty-five could do, and with great power of expression and under-standing."

Finally, in describing their leave-taking, he writes: "Her face, so remarkably young, framed in beautiful snow-white hair and supported by the delicate, frail, erect body, seemed really the personification of that victory over matter to which her religion aspires."

C H A P T E R   4 8

The Case in Court and
Its Outcome

"Pleasant View, Concord, May 16, 1907

"Hon. Judge Chamberlin, Concord, N.H. RESPECTED SIR:.

"It is over forty years that I have attended personally to my secular affairs, to my income, investments, deposits, expenditures and to my employees. I have personally selected all my investments except in one or two instances and have paid for the same.

"The increasing demands upon my time, labours and thought, and yearning for more peace and to have my property and affairs carefully taken care of for the persons and purposes designated by my last will influenced me to select a board of trustees to take charge of my property, namely, Hon. Henry M. Baker, Mr. Archibald McLellan, Mr. Josiah E. Fernald.

"I had contemplated doing this before the present proceedings were brought or I knew aught about them and I consulted Lawyer Streeter about the method. I selected said trustees because I had implicit confidence in each one of them as to honesty and business capacity.

"No person influenced me to make this selection. I find myself able to select the trustees I need without the help of others.

"I gave them my property to take care of because I wanted it protected and myself relieved of the burden of doing this.

"They have agreed with me to take care of my property, and I consider this agreement a great benefit to me already.

"This suit was brought without my knowledge and is being carried on contrary to my wishes. I feel that it is not for my benefit in any way but for my injury, and I know it is not needed to protect my person or property.

"The present proceedings test my trust in divine Love.

"My personal reputation is assailed and some of my students and trusted friends are cruelly and unjustly and wrongly accused.

"Mr. Calvin Frye and other students often ask me to receive persons whom I desire to see but decline to receive solely because I find that I cannot 'serve two masters'—I cannot be a Christian Scientist except I leave all for Christ.

"Trusting I have not exceeded the bounds of propriety in the statements herein made by me, I remain,

"Most respectfully yours,

MARY BAKER EDDY"

This letter, written in her own unmistakable hand, although not made public until later, marked an important point in Mrs. Eddy's defence. The case, as has been seen, had been narrowed down to the single question of Mrs. Eddy's competence at the time she executed her trust deed, and her letter to Judge Chamberlin, to which both sides would have had access, must have filled Senator Chandler and his colleagues with misgiving. The defence, in fact, as far as the press was concerned, was having it all its own way. The letter to Judge Chamberlin was clearly not that of a woman either physically or mentally incapacitated, and the testimony of Curtis, Park or Brisbane and several others all went to show that the very reverse was the case. The petitioners, moreover, had been

naturally inspired; (3) that she could heal miraculously; (4) that her philosophy was destined to supplant others; (5) that there is such a thing as malicious animal magnetism; (6) that malicious animal magnetism is the cause of terrible evils. The Court, however, emphatically upheld General Streeter's contention that however interesting such matters might be in themselves, they clearly had nothing to do with the case.

"As a matter of law", General Streeter declared, "these suggestions of delusions,—which simply mean that Mrs. Eddy believes in some things that Mr. Chandler and others don't believe,—unless they are in some way connected with the transactions of her business affairs, are absolutely incompetent."

The discussion was continued back and forth for some time, but in the end the Court decided that the only way to reach an answer to the issue and the readiest way was for the Court itself to examine Mrs. Eddy, and to this end Judge Aldrich proposed that the Court adjourn to Pleasant View rather than require Mrs. Eddy to undertake a personal appearance in Concord. In deciding to journey to Pleasant View rather than require Mrs. Eddy to appear in court, the Masters concurred in pointing out that such action on their part should not be construed into an assumption that Mrs. Eddy was not able to come to Concord.

"It is no disrespect", Judge Aldrich declared, "to say of any woman of Mrs. Eddy's years that she is entitled to every court clemency . . . we think it entirely reasonable, out of deference to her, to go there if desired."

And so on the afternoon of August 14, 1907, the Court, accompanied by leading counsel on both sides, adjourned to Pleasant View.

The coming of the Court seems to have made no unusual stir there. It was a lovely summer day with just that wisp of haze and that breath of sweet odour which tell of approaching fall. All the windows at Pleasant View were wide open, and Mrs. Eddy, as she entered her study on her return from her customary drive, remarked with quiet humour as she looked out on it all from her tower window, "Well, the Nexters have a fine day for their visit."

Some weeks previously, Edwin J. Park, news editor of the Boston *Globe*, had interviewed Mrs. Eddy at Pleasant View and had given an intimate picture in his paper of Mrs. Eddy at home. Like Brisbane, he seems during the interview to have been kept in a constant state of astonishment at her memory for dates, names and circumstances which appeared to him "marvellous", at the ease with which she moved from one subject to another, and at her vivid interest in the world around her. He seems, however, to have been specially impressed with the fact that Mrs. Eddy still ran her house and household in the full tradition of a New England housewife. Several times he reverts to the subject and tells how in the end, Mrs. Eddy, seeking to convince him, rang for her housekeeper, who appeared shortly afterwards, "a neat wholesome looking young woman, in the attire which she had worn in her duties about the house". And then he continues:

"She started in to apologize for her appearance, although there was nothing about it that required apology. Mrs. Eddy quieted her with the remark, 'Never mind, dear, you are all right,' and then continued—smiling:

" 'Are you my housekeeper?'

" 'Yes, Ma'am,' affirmed the pleased and radiant girl, bowing and smiling.

" 'Do I go downstairs and look around every day and see that everything is running smoothly?' asked Mrs. Eddy.

" 'Yes, Ma'am, you surely do,' answered the housekeeper.

" 'Am I careful and observant?' asked Mrs. Eddy.

" 'You surely are, Ma'am.'

" 'Have I arranged the furniture and shown just how I wanted it?'

" 'Yes, Ma'am, you told me just how everything should be.'

" 'That will be all, dear,' concluded Mrs. Eddy, and the housekeeper bowed herself out."

And then Edwin Park goes on to tell how Mrs. Eddy dwelt happily on the harmony of her household and the devotion of its members; how Mr. Frye had been with her for twenty-five years, Mrs. Sargent for eighteen, her cook for fifteen, and how all were most faithful.

Promptly at two o'clock the carriages from Concord drove up to the front door, and a few minutes later Mrs. Eddy was receiving the Court and attending counsel in her study. It must have been a curious scene of quickly changing emotions. The Justices, having regard for Mrs. Eddy's years, had evidently prepared themselves to act with the utmost gentleness and consideration, and when the first greetings were over, Judge Aldrich at once set out to reassure her.

"Mrs. Eddy," he said, "the gentlemen here wish to have an interview with you, and we desire to make this call as comfortable as possible for you, and we want you to let us know if we weary you."

Even as he spoke he must have felt that circumstances, as they were, were not at all as he had fancied them. There was nothing of *The World's* lurid picturing in this quiet, composed, venerable woman, who sat at her desk by the big open window and surveyed them all so calmly and kindly.

"I am very glad to see you," she said, "and I thank you."

For a time the Court endeavoured to maintain its formality. The first questions were depressingly routine. What was her native town? How long had she lived in Concord? And then Judge Aldrich made another brave show of kindness and consideration.

"Well, the gentlemen present want to ask you some questions, and we all want to make this interview as pleasant as possible for you."

"Thank you very much," Mrs. Eddy interjected, and the judge continued: "We want to have regard all the time to your comfort and convenience, and if you feel at all fatigued, we want to have you say so at any time."

Mrs. Eddy again thanked him, assured him that, save for a slight deafness, she was perfectly well, and could work many hours day or night without any fatigue when it was "in the line of spiritual labour".

And so Judge Aldrich went on for a time with his formal questions, but it was not long before a change came over the scene. The Judge had asked Mrs. Eddy about Pleasant View and how she acquired it. Doctor Jelly had supplemented Judge Aldrich's questions by asking if the place had been laid out under Mrs. Eddy's directions, and Justice Parker had asked about the fruit trees, and it was not long before they were all discussing the questions raised with keen interest, with Mrs. Eddy in the lead, telling how she cut down scrub pine and planted fruit trees; how people had laughed at her, but how she had said, "You will see, it will be pretty, pretty soon." And now instead of the decrepit old woman to whom they had come prepared to help along to her answers with tender encouragement, they found themselves enjoying a summer afternoon visit with a delightful hostess, who kept them all at ease and immensely interested. They asked her about Concord, about the gifts she had made from time to time to the city, about the church she had built there, and about her friendly connections in the countryside.

Then Judge Aldrich turned to the question of finance. He had, he said, some insurance maturing in the near future; what would Mrs. Eddy consider a good investment for it? If she had $100,000 to invest, what kind of investment would she consider sound? And Mrs. Eddy on the whole preferred municipal bonds. Stocks might be all right for anyone who could look after them, but she preferred not to have the trouble of it, and the only time she had gone contrary to her judgement in this respect, she had lost by it. How did she judge as to the value of municipal bonds? Well, she had a little book which gave definitely the population of the cities and their money value, and when she saw that they were large enough in population and valuation to warrant an investment, she made it. And Judge Aldrich remarked that he thought such judgement pretty sound.

Next they took an excursion into Christian Science, became tremendously interested and then had misgivings, misgivings as to whether they were justified in bringing the religious question into it, and so, after a brief private consultation, abandoned the subject and went on to discuss such questions as books, letter-writing and accounts. From these they passed to music. Doctor Jelly wanted to know if she was fond of music, if she was musical in her younger days, and Mrs. Eddy replied that she used to be very fond of music, and, although as a child had never been taught, she used to be fond of composing music. And then, as though suddenly remembering something, she told them that she had "an artificial singer" in her home and she would be glad for them to hear it before they left. As they got ready to leave, she rang for Calvin Frye and asked him to let her visitors hear the "artificial singer" on their way out. Mr. Frye assented gladly. "Yes," he said, "it is a gramophone, gentlemen."

But the Court was in no hurry to leave. Judge Aldrich wanted to tell Mrs. Eddy about his mother, who was eighty-seven and still quite happy, and Mrs. Eddy was full of interest. "Give her my love," she said, "God bless her; she is not a day older for her eighty-seven years if she is, as I am sure she is, growing in grace." And then as she took his hand in hers, she said simply: "If we keep our mind fixed on Truth, God, Life and Love, He will advance us in our years to a higher understanding. He will change our hope into faith, our faith into spiritual understanding, our words into works and our ultimate into the fruition of entering into the Kingdom."

And so there were leave-takings all round, and she remembered everyone, even the stenographer. "We have kept you very busy," she said. "Thank you for your services."

In the hall below, the Court and the rest of the company stopped to listen to the gramophone, greatly interested in Mr. Frye's explanation and no doubt marvelling at the dizzy heights modern invention was achieving.

Then, as the last record was being played, a message came from Mrs. Eddy. As she had sat at her desk when the door had closed behind the last of her visitors, she had evidently come to the conclusion that although the Court had done with her she ought not to have done with the Court. She owed it something yet. They had all learned from what they had seen and heard that none of the things that were being said of her was true, but all that was nothing compared with her message, and her message had been misrepresented and misinterpreted even more than her life and person. She must bear testimony to her message, and the Court, she was sure of it, would listen.

461

And so she sent down word, and asked them all to come up to her room again as she had forgotten something of importance. When they were assembled once more, she stood by her desk, her back to the great window which gave a view across the valley to where Mount Monadnock rose up above the skyline, and said how she had a great desire to tell them something, quite briefly, of "the footsteps of Christian Science."

And so, as they stood around her, she told them very simply how she had gone in search of healing from orthodox medical practice to homeopathy, from that to a realization that it was not the drug but the human mind that was the healer; how she had laboured with this human mind through spiritualism, mesmerism and hypnotism, only to find that God was not in any of it, until at last she came to see that the human mind was but a counterfeit of the real Mind, the mind that is God, the mind that was in Christ Jesus.

When she finished, everyone was silent for a moment, but if there was any sense of strain it was immediately broken by Mrs. Eddy. She shook hands around once more. "I thank you", she said, "for your kindness and attention—very much."

The interview of the Masters with Mrs. Eddy at Pleasant View really involved the collapse of the "Next Friends" case. As the Court and the rest of the company made their way down the stairway leading from Mrs. Eddy's study to the hall below, Senator Chandler was heard to remark in a tone of no little bafflement, "She is sharper than a steel trap."

Nevertheless, the hearing was resumed immediately on their return to Concord. Judge Aldrich had been careful before dismissing court—as they were about to leave for Pleasant View—to impress upon the counsel that the hearing was not adjourned, that no recess had been taken. "We do not take a recess really," he said. "The hearing is going on, but going on at another place."

And so, at the close of the interview, the Masters and those with them returned at once to the court room, where the hearing was continued. Senator Chandler and his colleagues made a brave show for three days of carrying on, but it must have been clear to them from the first that the Masters would inevitably interpret their evidence and argument in the light of what they had seen and heard for themselves. In addition to this, the reports of the various alienists appointed to examine Mrs. Eddy in regard to her physical and mental condition were coming in and, although they were not made public until later, they were known by the plaintiffs' counsel to be very unfavourable to their case. This was particularly true in regard to the report of Doctor Allan McLane Hamilton, who declared quite unequivocally that far from displaying any sign of mental incapacity, he did not hesitate to say that Mrs. Eddy was "both physically and mentally phenomenal".

When the Court convened on the sixth day of the trial, namely, August 21, 1907, Senator Chandler, as senior counsel for the plaintiffs, arose and announced the withdrawal of the suit. Rumours of what was about to happen had spread rapidly, and the little court room was crowded as soon as the doors were opened.

"May it please the Court," Senator Chandler said, "it will doubtless be a relief to the Masters to be informed that the counsel for the 'next friends' have this day filed with the Court a motion for the dismissal of the pending suit, and that they hereby withdraw their appearance before the Masters without asking from them any finding upon the questions submitted."

It was an astute move, for, in the matter of law, it not only saved the "next friends" from riding on to what was inevitable defeat, but effectually barred defendants' counsel from bringing into court, and so making public, the great mass of evidence that had been accumulated to prove Mrs. Eddy's complete physical and mental competence.

General Streeter pleaded with the Court to refuse the motion, urging that his clients were entitled to every opportunity to clear themselves of the charges so recklessly made against them and to establish beyond all peradventure the complete competence of the venerable lady who had been rendered the involuntary petitioner in the case. Judge Aldrich, however, ruled that the Masters had no choice in the matter, and that in view of the withdrawal of the plaintiffs there was "nothing left to be answered by Mrs. Eddy or decided by us". The case, therefore, stood dismissed, without any ruling on the part of the Court.

The result was, however, accepted everywhere as a signal triumph for Mrs. Eddy and a complete proof of her capacity. As far as Joseph Pulitzer and the New York *World* were concerned, the outcome of the proceedings was the reverse of all they had hoped. If the press, after the attack on Mrs. Eddy in the previous October, had scourged *The World* with whips, it now proceeded to scourge it with scorpions. Even the newspapers most notoriously antagonistic to Mrs. Eddy and her movement registered a changed attitude almost overnight. The press throughout the country seemed suddenly to develop a pride, not only in the vigour displayed by this woman so long past the age of active service, but in the work she had done and was doing. Everywhere Mrs. Eddy became "good copy"; stories about her were eagerly read. The accounts given of her quiet good humour, her, at times, quite disconcerting wit; her freedom from all bitterness; her kindness; her charity; her infectious sense of fun; her refusal to ask for help or cry quarter, seemed to appeal specially to the sporting instinct of press and people.

"The dismissal of the suit brought by 'next friends' against Mrs. Mary Baker G. Eddy", declared the New York *American*, "will be gratifying to all fair-minded people without regard to religious belief . . . it is now to be hoped that Mrs. Eddy, like all other persons who are acting within their rights, will be left in peace and security."

The *Free Press* of Detroit declared that it had been proved to the satisfaction of the reading public that the "venerable woman was in full possession of her mental faculties" and that any reports to the contrary were "destitute of foundation". The *Daily Herald* of Omaha declared editorially: "The entire proceeding was disgusting. It was redeemed only by the impressive scene that resulted when Mrs. Eddy was 'examined' at her home, where her courtesy and unfailing good nature, no less than the clarity of her thought and the force and vigour of her expressions, put her persecutors to shame. The effect on the enlightened sentiment of the country was such that the dismissal in short order was an inevitable consequence."

Mrs. Eddy's comment on it all was her accustomed one, "When these things cease to bless, they will cease to occur."

And so within a week or less, its customary calm had descended once again upon Pleasant View, and Concord had returned to its familiar ways. The many reporters who had hovered around the Court House at all hours or gathered in knots at the street corners had gone home, and the lobby of the Eagle Hotel was no longer the scene of momentous off-record discussions.

The Return to Boston

BUT FOR MRS. EDDY, her victory was only a breathing spell, if that. As always, apparent defeat or actual victory merely served as incentives to renewed effort and on a larger scale. She had claimed the right to live her life in Concord secluded from the world, if she so desired, without having her motives or capacity questioned and she had won her case. She now claimed the right to reverse her policy, if she had a need to. She would leave Concord and make her home in Boston.

It was no hasty or whimsical decision. The movement was growing rapidly, and although Mrs. Eddy—as successive notices in the *Sentinel* and *Journal* about this time sufficiently show—was withdrawing more and more from active participation in the work, nevertheless, the new fields of activity constantly presenting themselves tended to increase rather than diminish the amount of actual labour that devolved upon her. Concord was too far away. When anything of importance was to be done, she always dealt directly with those responsible, and a trip to Concord requisitioned a whole day for something which, if she were nearer, could be despatched in a few hours. And so, soon after the conclusion of the "Next Friends Suit", Mrs. Eddy decided to return to Boston.

As soon as the decision was taken, the project moved forward rapidly, and it was not long before negotiations were in progress for the purchase of a small estate in Chestnut Hill in the suburbs of Boston. Formerly known as the Lawrence estate, it comprised a large house of twenty-five rooms situated in some twelve acres of well-wooded ground, and commanding a wide view across the valley to the Blue Hills. The purchase was completed late in the year, and on Sunday, January 26, 1908, this strangely venturing woman, at the age of eighty-seven said goodbye to Pleasant View. She looked out of her study-window for the last time over the river towards Bow, up the valley toward Mount Monadnock, and then set out for her new home.

It was a beautiful day as she drove through Concord for the last time, snow everywhere, but the air was mild and the sun shone brightly. She walked across the station platform unaided and, as the newspapers put it, "with the ease and grace of a much younger woman," to the special train waiting to take her and her household on the first stage of their journey. Three hours later, in the red half-light of a winter evening, she drove through the gates of Chestnut Hill, which was to be her home until she died some three years later.

Concord was sorry to see her go. The old town had known her all her life, and its people, especially in these latter years, had come to look upon her as one of their particular possessions. The appearance of her carriage on State Street of an afternoon, summer or winter, was something that Concord, now these many years, had taken for granted. And so, a few days after she and her household had departed for Boston, the mayor and the city council met together in special session and passed resolutions of regret, causing them to be spread on the records of the city and forwarded to Mrs. Eddy at Chestnut Hill.

And Mrs. Eddy promptly replied, thanking them "deeply" for the "kindly resolutions passed by your honourable body"; telling them how rich were the recollections of her associations with Concord and its "good folk", and praying that she might deserve the friendship and esteem "of people of my native state".

But if Concord was sorry to see her go, Mrs. Eddy was sorry to leave, and many times, especially during the immediately ensuing months, must her thoughts have returned regretfully to the compact old-fashioned house on the side of the hill which she had called her home for so long.

Chestnut Hill was beautiful and convenient and supplied with the last word in everything, but it was so vast. When anyone had entered the door of her study at Pleasant View, by the time she had looked up from her desk to see who it was, he was almost beside her, but at Chestnut Hill there seemed to be so much walking to do before anyone could come within hail of anyone else. She endured it all for a time, and then, in one of those sudden decisions she had a way of making the moment she became convinced that something was wrong that could and should be righted, she took counsel with Calvin Frye and other members of her household.

Adam Dickey in his memoirs describes how she clinched the matter by remarking humorously: "When I call a student to come to me I cannot wait until he walks across such a great expanse of carpet from the door to my desk. Something must be done to conserve my time."

In the end, a plan was worked out with the aid of the architect whereby her bedroom and study were reduced to the same size as the bedroom and study in Pleasant View and the two rooms arranged in as nearly as possible the same way. The change, moreover, it was found, added greatly to the comfort of the house. It allowed Calvin Frye to have a sitting room as well as a bedroom, afforded space for an elevator, and widened the landing outside of Mrs. Eddy's study. She could almost imagine herself back again in her old home.

She must have been glad of it, glad when she could think of Concord without regret and Chestnut Hill without misgiving, for, as subsequent events showed, she had great things yet to do. Of these, first place must be given to the launching of a great daily newspaper, which she was to name *The Christian Science Monitor*. Perhaps she had envisioned something of the sort twenty-five years earlier when she said, with the first issue of the *Journal*, that there was an urgent need for a publication devoted to counteracting the unwholesome influence of the newspapers of the world. Much water had gone under the bridge since then, but the colour of the stream had not changed much. All through the history of her movement, Mrs. Eddy had suffered many things from the press generally, and while she recognized that much of the misrepresentation and sensationalism which characterized the newspaper approach to her teaching was inevitable, she must frequently have longed for some medium through which she could make known the facts as she saw them. It was plain by now that little could be done through a monthly periodical, such as the *Journal*, in this direction, in so far as reaching the general public was concerned, and practically nothing in presenting the news of the day in the way she felt it ought to be presented.

And so, with the merciless notoriety attendant upon the "Next Friends Suit" so fresh at hand, she was prepared to regard warmly the suggestion from one John L. Wright that "a general newspaper owned by Christian Scientists and conducted by experienced newspaper men who are Christian Scientists" be started. Mr. Wright was First Reader of the Church at Chelsea, had been for three years substitute night city editor of the Boston *Globe* and for fifteen years a reporter on that paper. From this impressive background of experience, he wrote Mrs. Eddy in March of 1908 that he was convinced a large public would be ready to support a wholesome paper "that takes less notice of crime, etc., and gives attention especially to the positive side of life, to the activities that work for the good of man and to the things really worth knowing." A few months later, in August of that year to be exact, the Trustees of the Christian Science Publishing Society received a laconic note from Chestnut Hill signed by Mrs. Eddy requesting that a daily newspaper be started at once, the same to be called *The Christian Science Monitor*.

Whether the Trustees knew what was involved in starting a metropolitan daily newspaper, not only in the matter of capital but in a thousand details of management and promotion, it is impossible to say. Even

469

if they did there were by this time few, if any, connected with the work who would question any request from Mrs. Eddy.

Experience had taught them that she never asked them to do anything until she was satisfied that it was feasible, while the rapid, orderly fulfilment of her plans had become almost a commonplace in the records of the Cause.

The Trustees replied at once, expressing their joy at the "good news", their confidence that the "move is timely", and that the new paper would be "a mighty instrument for the promotion of Christian Science", that it would be "a success from a business standpoint", and that they rejoiced "to have this additional opportunity of assisting in your plans for the welfare of humanity".

The exact nature of the new project was not announced immediately, but within a week or so a notice appeared in the *Sentinel* to the effect that a large addition was necessary to the Publishing Society's building in Boston, and that all who desired to subscribe to this object could send their contributions to the Church Treasury in Boston. Without any further effort, the sum of $400,000 was subscribed within a few weeks, additional land was purchased, and the work of constructing what was required in the way of new buildings, and of strengthening existing buildings to the extent that they could carry the weight of the printing presses was commenced. Then in October appeared the formal announcement of the forthcoming appearance of the new daily, in which the Trustees said:

"It is their intention to publish a strictly up-to-date newspaper, in which all the news of the day that should be printed will find a place, and whose service will not be restricted to any one locality, or section, but will cover the daily activities of the entire world.

"It will be the mission of the *Monitor* to publish the real news of the world in a clean, wholesome manner, devoid of the sensational methods employed by so many newspapers. . . . "

Meanwhile, throughout the country letters had gone out in all directions to newspaper men and women who were known to be interested in Christian Science, inviting them to send in their names to the Publishing

Society to the end that a suitable staff might be selected to serve on the new paper. The response was immediate and emphatic. Many hundreds of men and women in all parts of the country wrote in expressing their willingness to serve the new daily in any capacity. The work of selection must have been difficult; nevertheless, it was carried through rapidly, and, early in November, some three months after the Trustees had received the first request from Mrs. Eddy, the new building was completed, the machinery installed and the staff ready to commence work. Then on November 25, 1908, the day before Thanksgiving, the first issue of *The Christian Science Monitor* appeared.

Mrs. Eddy attached great importance to the name and especially to the point that the definite article should be an integral part of the title. Then she seems to have had quite a struggle to retain the words "Christian Science" in the title. Some members of the Board of Directors and many others were of opinion that the title should be simply *The Monitor*, without any indication as to the religious body that was sponsoring it, but Mrs. Eddy, while rigidly limiting the actual presentation of Christian Science teaching to one short article each day, was determined that the new daily should carry the name of Christian Science wherever it went. She spoke of it and wrote of it as the *Monitor*, but in any official reference she insisted on the full title.

In all this Mrs. Eddy was consistent. Nothing seems to have aroused her more sternly to protest at any time than an appearance of sailing under false colours. In the far-off days in Lynn she had boldly put up the blue and gold notice, "Christian Scientists' Home", over the door, and she had been insistent to keep the words "Christian Science" in the forefront of her work ever since. Even up to the time that Archibald McLellan carried the proof of the first issue of the *Monitor* out to Chestnut Hill, he seems to have still had some hope that Mrs. Eddy would accept the point in regard to the name of the new periodical he and others were trying to make, but Mrs. Eddy, once again, left no doubt as to her wishes. On his return to Boston, McLellan made it clear to his colleagues that the matter was most certainly settled. "The name of the paper", he said, expressively, "is *The Christian Science Monitor*."

To her followers as a whole Mrs. Eddy contented herself with a short notice which appeared in the first issue of the new paper in which she related how she had given the name to all the Christian Science periodicals, *The Journal, The Sentinel, Der Herald der Christian Science,* and now *The Monitor*. "The object of *The Monitor*", she added simply, "is to injure no man, but to bless all mankind."

CHAPTER 50

Keeping the Faith

FROM THE DAYS of her first struggle with Richard Kennedy to maintain the integrity of her teaching, Mrs. Eddy had always regarded this as the great field of her warfare. Attacks upon herself and upon her doctrine from the point of view of the orthodox religionist might seem to occupy a larger and more frequent place in the limelight of her life, but, in her own mind, she never seems to have had the least doubt but that the real enemy of the Cause at all times was the false prophet. Richard Kennedy, Edward Arens, Josephine Woodbury, to mention a few of the most outstanding, constituted the only serious menace she seemed to feel, not as individuals but as the lo here! and lo there! of mortal mind, as she would have put it, which could and would, if not resisted, deceive even the elect.

In the "Next Friends Suit" she had won a final victory over the enemies of her person, over those who sought to restrict her liberty and abridge the rights and privileges of her movement. She had still to measure swords in an equally momentous struggle with the "false Christ", in the—for her—broadest possible meaning of the term.

473

The scene of it all was New York and the central figure one of Mrs. Eddy's oldest and most devoted students, Augusta Stetson.

Augusta Stetson, it will be remembered, had gone to New York at Mrs. Eddy's request, as far back as 1886, in order to start the Christian Science movement there. From the first she had been successful and more than successful. A woman of striking personality and tremendous force of character, she had literally carried all before her and gone from strength to strength. From a room over a drug store at the corner of Fifth Avenue and Forty-seventh Street, she had moved her church steadily at intervals to more commodious quarters. From the room over the drug store to Crescent Hall at 138 Fifth Avenue, in 1890; to Hardman Hall on the corner of Fifteenth Street two years later; and from Hardman Hall, in 1894, to the Scottish Rites Hall in Madison Avenue and Twenty-ninth Street; thence in 1896, to still more commodious quarters at 145 West Forty-eighth Street. Finally, in 1899, unable to obtain sufficient accommodations in any other way, it was decided to build a church of such a size as to meet all reasonable needs of the near future, and to this end a lot was purchased at the corner of Central Park West and Ninety-sixth Street.

There was nothing in all this to occasion any misgivings at first. Between Mrs. Eddy and Augusta Stetson there seems to have existed for years a very real affection and mutual admiration. There was, however, between the two this fundamental difference that, whereas Mrs. Eddy was ever attaining to clearer views of the ultimate of her teaching and was always ready to abandon a practice the moment she saw that it tended to impede progress towards this ultimate, Augusta Stetson, like many others, remained through the years exactly at the point of her entrance. With the more obscure of Mrs. Eddy's followers, this tendency to stulti- fication might pass unnoticed, but Mrs. Stetson's outstanding achieve- ments made her the centre of the movement's scrutiny so that her perpetu- ation of the outgrown concepts of a by-gone period—namely, that day in the eighties when marriage was looked upon as something to be risen above and one's woes were so easily attributable to telepathic bombardment by others—brought her into irreconcilable conflict with the newer generation and its less personalized doctrine. But after the die was once cast against her, the criticisms were by no means confined to these issues. Her undeniable eloquence was regarded by her detractors, who were perhaps not so articulate, as symptomatic of arrogant vainglory, and every questionable pronouncement she made was transmitted promptly to Boston and to Chestnut Hill. She was quoted as telling her students:

"We need health and strength and peace, and for these we look to God. But let us not forget that we also need *things,* things which are but the type and shadow of the real objects of God's creating, but which we can use and enjoy until we wake to see the real. We surely need clothes. Then why not manifest a beautiful concept? Clothes should, indeed, be as nearly perfect as possible, in texture, line and colour. . . . It is certain, too, that we need homes. Then why not have beautiful homes? Our homes should express the highest sense of harmony and happiness. If we have a carpet, why not a beautiful, perfect one, intead of a dingy half-worn one? . . . We have a right to everything that is convenient, most comfortable, most harmonious. God made all things, though we only see their shadows, and all things are for His Children. Everything is *ours.* It does not belong to mortal mind."

This, said her critics, elevated money-making and the ability to make money to the point where it was regarded as the supreme test of understanding. A case was in the building. Her individualistic speech and manner were cited as departures from what were becoming the canonical writings of the Church, and the initiative with which she built her New York church became a sign of inordinate ambition. All this led readily into the ancient charge of aspiring to displace the God-ordained Leader of the movement. Worse still, she was accused—and she never denied the accusation—of "taking up" her enemies by name and "working" mentally to destroy these "incarnate evils" which she declared inimical to the cause.

There can be no question that Augusta Stetson knew all about the downfall of so many of her distinguished predecessors through such backstairs gossip—the Julia Field-Kings, the Arthur True Buswells, the Clara Choates—but with her superior intelligence, indomitable will and closer friendship with Mrs. Eddy she should be able to weather the storm. Anyway, far and above all these considerations, she had unquestioning faith in the absolute infallibility of her divinely inspired Leader and, as her correspondence and subsequent events prove, she felt that in any final test Mrs. Eddy would come to her rescue.

But as "Gussie's church," as Mrs. Eddy called it in her letters, flourished ever more spectacularly, so did the disquieting stories flourish. The anti-Stetsonites saw a threat to the supremacy of The Mother Church, to the purity of the doctrine upon which the whole movement was based and to the leadership of Mary Baker Eddy. When the great edifice at Ninety-sixth Street was completed in 1903, they pointed to its unorthodox design and appointments and to its unorthodox activities within. All around the building had been fitted out with luxurious practitioners' rooms where clients were received, advised and treated, while every day at noon Mrs. Stetson was wont to have practitioners' meetings in which she gave advice, not only as to how certain problems should be met, but as to how certain people whose attitude was not regarded as satisfactory should be treated and dealt with.

It all seemed innocent enough, and could be explained by skillful casuistry as being absolutely in line with the teachings of Mrs. Eddy, but from the first it seems to have filled Mrs. Eddy herself with great misgiving. So it was not long before she formulated a by-law which forbade practitioners' rooms being in the same building with churches. Mrs. Stetson, who always made a great point of complete obedience to her Leader, immediately complied, and the practitioners' rooms at First Church, New York, were vacated overnight and remained permanently closed. The practitioners carried on their work and in the same spirit in other quarters, of course.

And so things went on until the summer of 1908, when rumours began to be heard in Boston that Mrs. Stetson was seeking to elevate her church in New York to a position similar to The Mother Church in Boston, and to establish branches throughout the city. A few months later, such a scheme was discussed in the New York *American,* and it was said that subscriptions were already coming in to carry through the project.

The announcement appeared in the New York *American* on November 30, and in the issue of the *Sentinel* five days later, instead of a simple statement as to the falsity of the report, appeared a vigorous editorial setting forth the unsound nature of the whole proceeding and restating the fundamental organization of the movement wherein there was one Mother Church and its branches. Mrs. Stetson met the situation by a statement through the New York *Times* in its issue of December 7, in which she declared that there had never been any thought in her mind of establishing a branch church of the First Church of New York, but that, on the contrary, the new church would be styled Seventh Church, and its only connection with First Church was that the funds for the new building would be supplied by First Church.

The situation was continuing to get more and more out of hand. With the principal actors coming out from behind the scenes to take up their battle positions on the open stage, what appeared to be a grave schism was developing within the Church. To a public conditioned to think of the Christian Science movement as an organization, Mrs. Stetson's blatant independence was a challenge to the constituted authority that was Boston and, indeed, a threat to the very integrity of the cause itself. Whatever the merits of Mrs. Stetson's stand and whatever her personal deserts, Mrs. Eddy could not deny that she was a dangerously disturbing element and she must have recognized that she was the only one at this time with great enough influence to cope with such a contingency. But to the venerated warrior at Chestnut Hill, any direct action must have promised a veritable Armageddon. Perhaps some sort of strategy could forestall a ruinous battle.

And so on the day Mrs. Stetson's repudiation appeared in the New York *Times,* Mrs. Eddy dispatched a letter to her in New York proposing a visit together.

Mrs. Stetson lost no time in accepting the invitation. She received the letter on the morning of the 8th and the same evening took the midnight train for Boston. Early next morning she notified Calvin Frye of her arrival, and Mrs. Eddy promptly invited her to come out to Chestnut Hill at one o'clock and go for a drive with her.

According to Mrs. Stetson's account of the matter, and there is no reason to doubt its accuracy, Mrs. Eddy showed herself tender and understanding. When Mrs. Stetson arrived, Mrs. Eddy was already in her carriage waiting at the door, and, after greeting her kindly, insisted on sharing her robe with her. Then the two set off together. From notes found among Mrs. Stetson's papers after her death, Mrs. Eddy seems to have concentrated all her attention on dissuading Mrs. Stetson from anything savouring of inordinate or unseemly initiative. She deprecated strongly the idea of one branch church founding another branch church, and warned her to take a lesson from her, Mrs. Eddy's, own experience and the difficulties she had when she sought to relieve her students of labours rightly devolving upon them by giving them land and money to build a church when they ought to have provided both themselves.

Mrs. Eddy's efforts were apparently rewarded, for within a few days after their drive together she received a letter from Mrs. Stetson announcing that the whole project of the new church had been abandoned. So far, Mrs. Eddy evidently might feel satisfied that she had won her battle, but this would prove a forlorn hope.

In the summer of the following year Mrs. Stetson's students presented her with a gift of gold, accompanied by a "composite letter", which ran in part as follows:

"Our hearts are filled with gratitude and awe as we see, in you, Christianity demonstrated . . . May a purified life attest the endless gratitude I feel for the manifestation of the Christ you have given us, while, with Mary of old, I cry, Rabboni—Teacher . . . Your unselfish life, fast approaching the perfect idea of Love, is to my hungry sense for Truth 'the bread of heaven and the water of Life'. Eating this bread and drinking this water is to me eating the body of Christ, and drinking his blood . . . The voice of the Father-Mother God is ever speaking through you. . . . our blessed teacher, as the manifestation of Truth."

Mrs. Stetson, in a covering letter to Mrs. Eddy said she counted herself far from worthy of such adulation, and so sent it on to her, with the assurance that she did so because she felt that all the devotion it contained really belonged to her "forever Leader."

Mrs. Eddy was thoroughly roused. She sent the letter on to the Board of Directors and urged them to act upon it in accordance with *Science and Health* and the *Mother Church Manual;* while to Mrs. Stetson herself she wrote:

"Awake and arise from this temptation produced by animal magnetism upon yourself, allowing your students to deify you and me."

Mrs. Stetson replied immediately, and in that vein of complete submission with which, however, Mrs. Eddy could no longer be swayed. The Board of Directors had already summoned her to appear before them and Mrs. Eddy determined to let the summons stand. About the middle of July, Mrs. Stetson appeared before the Board in Boston, and a preliminary examination of the whole situation at First Church, New York, was commenced.

The proceedings, however, had not gone far before Mrs. Eddy advised that the examination be suspended and the whole matter referred back to First Church, New York, for action.

At this point, the first reader of the church, one Virgil O. Strickler, called upon the Board in Boston and laid before them some startling claims in the form of a diary which he had kept of some of Mrs. Stetson's private meetings that he had attended. Virgil Strickler was a lawyer from Omaha. He had been healed, he said, through Christian Science, had gone through Mrs. Stetson's class and had joined First Church, New York. As first reader, he had the privilege of attending Mrs. Stetson's "practitioners' meetings", and being greatly troubled at some of the proceedings at these meetings, he had kept a diary which he now laid before the Board. So serious were the claims set forth that the Board continued its investigations, and during September various practitioners, students of Mrs. Stetson, were summoned to Boston to answer inquiries. Before long the Board, satisfied that drastic action was necessary and, acting under a special provision of the *Manual*, removed Mrs. Stetson's card and those of her practitioners from the *Journal*, withdrew her licence as a teacher and served upon her informal notice of their "findings and orders".

Among these findings were that Mrs. Stetson attempted "to control and to injure persons by mental means; this being utterly contrary to the teaching of Christian Science"; that she was responsible for "perverted sex teaching", for "encouraging self-deification", and for "seeking despotic control over her students".

Mrs. Stetson, on receipt of this indictment, immediately turned it over to the Trustees of her Church for examination, and it quickly became apparent that, although the revolt against her was gaining ground rapidly, she was still sufficiently strong to secure from her Trustees some formal exoneration. When this became apparent, Mrs. Eddy wrote to the Chairman of her Board of Directors, Archibald McLellan, under the date of October 12, 1909, this directive:

"Beloved Student: Learn at once if The Mother Church can be prosecuted for suspending a student or even expelling them, who is giving us so much trouble as Mrs. Stetson does, and if it can be done safely drop Mrs. Stetson's connection with The Mother Church. Let no one know that I have written you on this subject. Lovingly yours." No dimming of that astuteness that had founded an empire and perfected the greatest crusade is here apparent.

The regal Augusta was again summoned to Boston where she was to be questioned by the Board for three days—ten hours the first day, ten the second and six the last. During the second session, the harried Mrs. Stetson sent word to her church in New York that Mrs. Eddy had "requested us all to unite with those in our church who are supporting the Mother Church directors" on the pending issue, and that she herself was now induced "to believe that I may have been wrong where I felt that I was absolutely right."

The day before this, December 15 namely, at a meeting of First Church, New York, a letter was read from Mrs. Eddy pleading for loyalty to the Board in this "momentous question." Naturally, this was oil upon the waters, for to Mrs. Stetson's opponents such a letter could portend nothing less than her defeat, while the Stetson students had been taught to expect divinely infallible judgement from their Leader and this meant to them that their teacher must be gloriously vindicated.

The reign of Augusta Stetson was over. She returned to face a hostile majority in the temple she had builded with her own hands. Her resignation from the branch church came on November 22, 1909, following close upon her public excommunication from The Mother Church, November 18.

Defeat in Christian Science? Never. Well had Augusta Stetson learned at least this lesson from her adored teacher and forever Leader. She could now write with poignant sincerity:

"I learned during this severe trial that the hour had come when I must see that this experience was to exalt me by severing me from material organization. . . . I am confident that I burst the bonds which held me to a *material* organization when I finished my church edifice and taught Truth to those who were ready to assimilate it and rise higher and 'build on a wholly spiritual foundation' . . . Watching over Israel, our beloved Leader, Mrs. Eddy, foresaw from the summit of her spiritual vision the answer to her prayer, namely, that her child, a loyal branch of the Vine, First Church of Christ, Scientist, New York City, should bear fruit for Immortality, lay the foundation for the Church Triumphant and Universal, in which Christ, in His second appearing, must tabernacle in visible and tangible presence to reign on earth forever and forever." Mrs. Eddy remained her saviour.

Armageddon's receding thunderings were no longer audible at far-off Chestnut Hill. Here, too, the same serene satisfaction of Victory prevailed—and Mrs. Eddy must have enjoyed the more tangible evidence she held that "what blesses one blesses all." Surely, as she settled back into the sweet calm of that westering light of her long crusade, she might have heard these longed-for words, "Well done, thou good and faithful servant."

The End and the Beginning

MRS. EDDY WAS now eighty-eight years old, and, as the days passed, it must often have seemed to those around her that she was living almost in a world apart, while the world of everyday—as she once put it—"flutters in my thought as an unreal shadow."[1]

She was setting her house in order, doing the things she felt ought to be done, providing for everyone she felt ought to be provided for—for George and his family, for Calvin Frye and many others, even for Ebenezer Foster-Eddy, the Benny of happier days. She was making her will with its many carefully thought out provisions, which were to mean so much in the future of the Cause she had founded.

Troubles came and went, but above and beyond them all, and through them all, was ever, now, more and more, "the eternal sunshine and joy unspeakable," of which she was wont at times to talk. And so she moved quietly, faithfully on into the closing years and the last phase.

She was still above all the teacher. Indeed much of her time seems to have been taken up with just this. Every morning she would summon her household around her to instruct them on some question, either one raised

[1] *Miscellany*, p. 268.

by a simple Bible reading or prompted by some happening of the day before. She was often hard to the point of sternness with them. Calvin Frye's diary, which he kept in a kind of shorthand of his own on the scratch pad on his desk, reveals at times a grief almost childlike over Mrs. Eddy's rebukes and shows a littleness of outlook, which, however natural from a human standpoint, must have been a sore tax on the patience of a woman of Mrs. Eddy's temperament. She met it all with a sweetness and light which ever prompted her household to renewed devotion.

The steadfastness of her faith was often tried in other ways. Her teaching allowed no place for death any more than it did for sickness. She made no claim for herself. "I cannot speak of myself as 'sufficient for these things'," she had written years before in her book *Unity of Good*. "I insist only upon the fact, as it exists in Science, that man dies not." But she met every onslaught of death upon herself or her friends with unshaken confidence that even if the victory was not yet, yet surely it would be.

In the August of 1907, just after the close of the "Next Friends Suit", one of her most devoted adherents in England, the Earl of Dunmore, died suddenly in London, and, a few months later, big, burly Joseph Armstrong, who had served her faithfully as the publisher of her books, passed away. Later still, Edward Kimball, who had on so many occasions come to her defence and the defence of her teaching, followed Joseph Armstrong. She was nothing daunted. Each passing only served to call forth a new message of confidence to all her world. "Our brothers are not dead, neither do they sleep nor rest from their labours and their works do follow them," was the tenor of her word. And so her peace returned to her.

But if the way was not easy for anyone, on the other hand, there seem to have been times, many of them, when the whole household would be caught up into a kind of seventh heaven, and an atmosphere of indescribable joy was everywhere. It was no sudden flash in the pan that made her write a few months before the end:

"The Christian Scientists at Mrs. Eddy's home are the happiest group on earth. Their faces shine with the reflection of light and love; their footsteps are not weary; their thoughts are upward; their way is onward, and their light shines."

She was still hard at work, almost as hard at work as ever. Visitors came and went at Chestnut Hill as they had done at Pleasant View. A study of the department in the *Sentinel* entitled "Letters to Our Leader" shows how many and varied were her interests in these years. Her own letters grew shorter. There is no sign in them of waning power, but they are brief and to the point, constantly having recourse simply to fundamental fact as she saw it. There is only one enemy now—a belief in a power apart from God. Every phase of wrong thinking could be reduced to that, just as every phase of right thinking could be reduced to love. If love is all there is to life, is the fulfilling of the law, then the belief in the opposite of love is all there is to death and all that leads up to it. Just as John in his extreme old age is traditionally supposed to have said to his disciples whenever they appealed to him for help, "Little children, love one another," so this latter day Michael of a new-old faith, as she reached the limits of her earthly course, could see only one enemy, in whatever guise he appeared, a belief in a power apart from God, wrong thinking, wrong practice in a realm of thought, of mind; in a word, mental malpractice.

Again and again, they failed her, as had Richard Kennedy, Arens, Josephine Woodbury, and now, only the other day, Augusta Stetson, drifting into witchcraft and necromancy, or if not wandering so far afield, going about under a cloud of fear over the presence of something that "is not but seemeth to be".

The way at times must have seemed very hard for her. Calvin Frye, in his diary, tells of how, on one occasion, after she had struggled valiantly with weakness for several days, she called some of her students to her and with something of her old fire bade them get about it and heal her. And then suddenly realizing by their answers that she had nothing to hope from them, in this direction, she bade them take their thought away from her and know that she was well.

484

After this she goes on alone—she is in her ninetieth year now—through periods of struggle into periods of great calm and no little glory, and so, at last, as summer gives place to autumn and autumn to the first touch of winter, full circle is made.

It was the 1st of December, 1910, "a pleasant day", as one record has it, "with all the bright frosty beauty of early winter lying on the wooded country". In the afternoon Mrs. Eddy went out for her usual drive, seeming to her household much as she always was. On her return, she rested for a while in her study, and then asked for her writing tablet. When it had been brought to her she wrote, in a firm hand, "God is my Life". They were the last words she ever wrote.

The next day, although she rose at her accustomed time and went to her desk, she did no writing or reading. Every now and again someone would come into the room to see if she needed anything, or to lay some paper on her desk. They found her always the same, calm and motionless, quite clearly wrapped in thought.

Her study at Chestnut Hill, as has been seen, looked out over the valley towards the Blue Hills. And her desk was close to the bay window whence the best views might be had. Members of her household have told how much she loved this view, especially in the evening light, and how she would sit for an hour or more at a time quietly contemplating it. She had a copy of the Bible and her book *Science and Health* on a reading stand near by, and every now and again she would turn on the little light, read awhile and then resume her thinking.

So it was all day on this Friday in December and, as hour followed hour, it began to be clear to those accustomed to her ways that a change was taking place. Outwardly she was the same. She talked to those about her with her usual serenity and she retired at her usual time.

But she did not get up on the next morning. In the evening she passed quietly away.

On the following day—Sunday—the congregation in The Mother Church building in Boston heard the news. Just before the benediction at the accustomed morning service, the first reader, Judge Clifford P.

Smith, read from the desk part of a letter written by Mrs. Eddy some twenty years before. "You may be looking to see me in my accustomed place with you," he read, "but this you must no longer expect. . . . I am still with you on the field of battle, taking forward marches, broader and higher views, and with the hope that you will follow." [1] The reader then added: "Although these lines were written years ago, they are true today, and will continue to be true. But it has now become my duty to announce that Mrs. Eddy passed from our sight last night at 10:45 o'clock, at her home in Chestnut Hill."

By the next day it was known, throughout the world, that *finis* had been written to an earthly record that is one of the most remarkable in human history.

[1] *Miscellaneous Writings*, pp. 135-136.

Index

Baker, Abigail (Ambrose), mother of Mrs. Eddy, 12-15; her premonitions before Mary's birth, 13, 18; character of and attitude toward Mary, 18, 19, 20, 21, 22, 398; advice to Mary, 24; letters and book sent to Mary after marriage to Glover, 57-58, 59, 68; after Mary's widowhood, 72, 73; last days and death of, 78-79.

Baker, Abigail, sister of Mrs. Eddy — See Tilton, Abigail (Baker).

Baker, Albert, brother of Mrs. Eddy, 15; childhood and early companionship with Mary, 20-21, 28, 31; education of, 20, 28, 29, 32, 34, 45; association with Franklin Pierce, 27, 28, 32, 33; correspondence with Mary, 44-45, 50, 51; letters to brother George Sullivan, 49, 50; legal and political career of, 46, 49-50, 51; attitude toward religion, 44-46, 50-51; ill health and death of, 49, 50, 51, 55, 57.

Baker, George Sullivan, brother of Mrs. Eddy, 15; letters of Mary to, 33-34, 36-38, 43, 44, 46, 69, 76, 78-79; letters from Albert to, 49, 50; trip with Mary to White Mountains, 56; letter concerning George Glover's death, 71-72; marriage of, 76, 78; ill health, refuses Mary's help, 144, 145; death of, 144.

Baker, George W., nephew of Mrs. Eddy, joins in petition in "Next Friends" Suit, 445, 448.

Baker, Henry M., cousin of Mrs. Eddy, one of Trustees during "Next Friends" Suit, 450, 454.

Baker, John, son of Robert Baker, ancestor of Mrs. Eddy, of Lyminge, England, refuses to pay church tax, 5, 6.

Baker, John, immigrant ancestor of Mrs. Eddy, 4, 6; joins Massachusetts Bay Company, 7; prospers in new land, 7-8, 214.

Baker, Joseph (1st), great-grandfather of Mrs. Eddy, early history of, 10-11; marriage of, 10.

Baker, Joseph (2nd), grandfather of Mrs. Eddy, early history and marriage of, 11.

Baker, Marion (or Ann) Moor McNeil, grandmother of Mrs. Eddy, 11, 12, 79; marries Joseph Baker, 11, 16; background and ancestry of, 11, 12, 137; Mary's devotion to, 15-16; relates stories to Mary as child, 16, 18; Mrs. Eddy's recollections of, 16, 19; death of, 57.

Baker, Mark, father of Mrs. Eddy, birth of, 11; heritage of, 4, 5-8, 9-11; marriage, birth of daughter Mary, 12; character of, 14-15, 17-19, 21, 22, 23, 79, 398; distress over Mary's views, 18-19, 20, 21, 22, 23, 24; friendship with General Pierce, 28; at Mary's marriage to Glover, 57; writes to Mary, 68; death of wife, 78-79; Mary keeps house for, 79; remarriage of, 79-80; disapproval of Daniel Patterson, 85-86; final approval of Mary's marriage to Patterson, 87; estrangement from Mary, 125; death of, 144.

Baker, Martha (Rand), sister-in-law of Mrs. Eddy, Mary's letter to, 76-77; marries Mary's brother, George Sullivan Baker, 76, 78.

Baker, Martha, sister of Mrs. Eddy—See Pillsbury, Martha (Baker).

Baker, Robert, earliest known Baker ancestor of Mrs. Eddy, 5, 6.

Baker, Samuel, brother of Mrs. Eddy, 15; goes to Boston, 34; marriage of, 35, 52; letter from George Glover to, 53, 54.

Bakers, immigrant ancestors of Mrs. Eddy, 4-6, 7-8, 10-11.

Bancroft and Purington, shoe factory in Lynn, 168; Samuel Putnam Bancroft as foreman with, 168; dissolution of, 191.

Bancroft, Samuel Putnam, member of Mrs. Patterson's first class, 168, 169, 170, 171, 196; foreman in shoe factory, 168; writes his recollections, 168, 171, 175, 184, 185, 223; describes first class, 168-171; records her happiness in work, 184, 200, 210; character of, 188; marriage of, 188; Mrs. Patterson makes home with, 188, 189; she leaves Bancrofts, 189; correspondence of Mrs. Patterson and, 189, 190, 191, 192; opens office in Cambridge, 191, 192; signs resolution to help Mrs. Patterson's work, 199; mentions favorable notices of Science and Health, 210; describes Mrs. Patterson's appearance, 211; Mrs. Patterson advises concerning his lack of patients, 212; her complaint about students to, 213; unable to aid Mrs. Eddy in "Conspiracy to Murder Case," 245; helps found Massachusetts Metaphysical College, 274; notes beneficial effect of Mrs. Eddy's presence, 330.

Barnard, Lydia, mother of Calvin Frye, 289; marriage of, 289; illness and healing by Clara Choate, 289, 290.

Barre, Vermont, Mrs. Eddy and Dr. Foster-Eddy make short stay in, 353, 354.

Barry, George W., member of Mrs. Patterson's first class, 169, 184, 195; association with Mrs. Patterson at Lynn, 195-196; character of, 196; signs resolution to help Mrs. Patterson's work, 199; helps form The Christian Science Publishing Company to publish and sell *Science and Health*, 200, 202, 207, 209, 229; breaks with Mrs. Patterson over Gilbert Eddy, 218, 219, 222; received by Alcott, 224; sues Mrs. Eddy for payment for services, 225, 232, 347; writes poem to Mrs. Patterson, 232; Mrs. Eddy's testimony in case of, 232-233; compromise verdict in legal suit of, 233; in controversy regarding Spofford, 233, 234; fails to involve Mrs. Eddy in plot against Kennedy, 242-243.

Bartlett, John M., suitor of Mary Glover, 77-78; engagement to Mary, 78; death of, 79.

Bartlett, Julia, student of Mrs. Eddy, 272; story of life, 272; opens office in Boston, 272; Mrs. Eddy's reliance on, 272, 277, 280, 287, 315, 316; at Metaphysical College, 283; with Gilbert Eddy day before his death, 285; lives with Mrs. Eddy, 292; records of her healings, 319; works on *Church Manual*, 382.

Bartlett, Mrs. Mary Ellis, granddaughter of Mrs. Nathaniel Webster, 150; writes of Mrs. Patterson's residence in Webster home, 150-154.

Barton, Vermont, Mrs. Eddy's stay in Arthur Buswell's home in, after Gilbert Eddy's death, 287; she leaves for Boston, 290; receives kindly care in, 291; her important metaphysical discovery made in, 291, 294.

Bates, Edward P., student of Mrs. Eddy, attends class of 1888, 353; member of Publication Committee, 355; works on *Church Manual*, 382; Chairman, Board of Directors of Mother Church, at celebration at Pleasant View, 402; as President of Concord church, receives gavel from Mrs. Eddy, 421.

Bates, General Erastus, student of Mrs. Eddy, attends class of 1888, 353, 394;

teaches classes, 355; at Pleasant View celebration, 403-404.

Bean, Luther, early suitor of Mary Glover, 76.

Belfast, Maine, early home of Quimby, 107; life in 1830's, 108; Poyen's lectures in, 108-109; Quimby's exhibition of Mesmerism in, 109; Quimby's retirement and death in, 128.

Besse, Frances E., deeded Lynn property to Mrs Patterson in 1875, 193.

Bible and its Spiritual Meaning, The, by Mary Baker Eddy, manuscript of, 160.

Blackman, Lulu, student of Mrs. Eddy, describes her as teacher, 320.

Board of Education, creation of, 419.

Boston, Massachusetts, heading Chapter 27, 269-278; heading Chapter 49, "The Return to Boston," 466-472.

Bow, New Hampshire, Mrs. Eddy's birthplace, 4; her grandfather settles in, 11; General Pierce visits Mark Baker's at, 28, 32-33; Mary Baker's first letters written from, 33-34, 36; heading Chapter 4, "The Last Year at Bow," 35-40; comparison with Sanbornton, 38, 39, 42, 43.

Bradshaw, Ella, opens "California Metaphysical College" in San Jose, 303.

Braid, James, his research on hypnotism and surgery, 99.

Brisbane, Arthur, editor of *New York Evening Journal,* pays tribute to Mrs. Eddy in interview, 211, 451-453, 455, 458; interview published by M. E. Paige in book, *What Mrs. Eddy Said to Arthur Brisbane,* 451.

Brown, Lucretia L. S., patient of Mrs. Eddy, her healing and relapse, 237-239; sues Spofford in "Ipswich Witchcraft Case," 237, 239-241; complete recovery of, 241.

Brush, Ada E., marries Calvin Frye, 289; death of, 298.

Bubier, S. M., Mrs. Patterson carried to home of, after ice accident, 130.

Buckley, Dr. J. M., attacks Christian Science in *Century,* 331, 332; *Journal* publishes reply to attack of, 332.

Burkmar, Lucius, youthful mesmeric subject of Quimby, 109, 110; diagnoses cases for John Bovee Dods, 110; Quimby's experiments with, 110, 215.

Burnham, "Priest," friend of Mark Baker, 17, 28.

Burt, John M., early suitor of Mary Glover, 76.

Buswell, Arthur True, student of Mrs. Eddy, 262, 272, 287; director of first Church organization, 262; takes charge after Gilbert Eddy's death, 287, 291; lives at headquarters, 292; associate editor of first *Christian Science Journal*, 295; joins opposition, 325, 326, 476.

Carr, Oren, student of Mrs. Eddy, director of first Church organization, 262.

Carter, Mary Esther, directs Mrs. Patterson to Webster home, 148, 149.

Case, Reverend Albert, writes of George Glover's death, 69-70.

Cather, Willa, on staff of *McClure's Magazine* re Mrs. Eddy's life, 37.

Century, The, publishes Dr. Buckley's attack on Christian Science, 331, 332.

Chamberlain, Fred D., involved in lawsuit with Josephine Woodbury, 411.

Chamberlin, Judge, Mrs. Eddy's letter to, in "Next Friends" Suit, 454-455.

Chandler, William, immigrant ancestor of Mrs. Eddy, joins Massachusetts Bay Company, 7; religious character of, 11-12.

Chandler, Senator William E., legal counsel in "Next Friends" Suit, urges George Glover to join in petition, 447-448, 449; charges against Mrs. Eddy, 455, 456, 457, 462, 463; withdraws suit, 463, 464.

Chandlers, ancestors of Mrs. Eddy, of Hertfordshire, England, 7; seek freedom, 7, 11; reputation for godliness, 11.

Chaplin, H. W., attorney for prosecution in "Conspiracy to Murder Case," 247-248.

Charleston, North Carolina, George Glover moves to, 52; recounts life in, 53-54; conveyance of land to Glover in, 54; Glover's return to, 54, 55; Glover and bride Mary arrive in, 56, 58, 59, 63; early days of, 60-63; the Glover's life in, 63, 64; social and political life in, 64-69; Mary Glover's attitude toward slavery in, 66, 67; heading Chapter 7, 60-70; the Glover's leave, 69.

Charlestown, Massachusetts, John Baker, ancestor of Mrs. Eddy, registered as freeman in, 7-8.

Chase, Stephen A., trustee for establishment

of Mother Church, 366; defendant in "Next Friends" Suit, 445.

Cheney, Mahala (Sanborn), wife of Russell Cheney—See Sanborn, Mahala.

Cheney, Russell, marries Mahala Sanborn who took charge of young George Glover, 80.

Chestnut Hill, home of Mrs. Eddy, arrangement of furniture at, 164; she moves to, 467, 468; remodeling of, 468; Mrs. Eddy's final days at, 380, 484, 485, 486.

Chicago, heading Chapter 34, 331-338.

Choate, Clara Elizabeth, early student of Mrs. Eddy, 267; her healing and moving of family to Lynn, 267-268; describes Mrs. Eddy's life in Lynn, 268; Dr. and Mrs. Eddy share home with, 271; tells of withdrawal of members from Christian Scientist Association, 277; her work in Boston, 280; Mrs. Eddy's letters from Washington, D. C. to, 280, 281, 282; gives reception to Eddys, 283; Mrs. Eddy's letter to, after Dr. Eddy's death, 286, 290; heals Calvin Frye's mother, 290; withdrawal from Mrs. Eddy, 301, 302, 476.

Choate, George D., husband of Clara Choate, 267-268.

Choate, Warren, son of Mr. and Mrs. George D. Choate, 268; Mrs. Eddy's interest in, 281.

Christian Advocate, Buffalo, New York, gives favorable review of *Science and Health*, 210.

Christian Science, by Mark Twain, 428.

Christian Science Board of Directors, duties of, 367, 381.

Christian Science Journal, The, founding of, 295, 324, 472; Arthur Buswell, associate editor of, 295; purpose, and difficulties in early stage, 295, 296, 469; Arens' plagiarism suit safeguards, 296; publishes history of Augusta Stetson's and other healings, 319; heading Chapter 33, "The Journal," 324-330; unifies movement, 324, 325; Buswell joins opposition, 325, 326; Emma Hopkins and other editors abandon position, 326, 396; Mrs. Eddy directs policy and writes for, 327, 328; article forms preface to *Miscellaneous Writings*, 327; publishes reply to Reverend Townsend, 327; reprints Lillian Whiting's interview with Mrs. Eddy, 327, 328-330; Georgine Milmine records influence of, 330; publishes reply to Dr. Buckley, 331-332; Mrs. Eddy urges need for teachers, 332-333; examines essay of Reverend Westervelt, 333; publishes report of first annual meeting of National Christian Scientist Association, 334-335; announces second annual meeting, 335; announces 16th edition of *Science and Health*, 341-342; Mrs. Eddy turns it over to Christian Scientist Association, 355; publishes Mrs. Eddy's statement re dissolution of College and Church, 358; Mrs. Eddy urges to form own churches, 364; plans for building Church, 369; describes cornerstone laying and dedication of Mother Church, 370, 371, 372; publishes Mrs. Eddy's notice of retirement, 374-375; gives her statement on *Church Manual*, 382-383; Judge Hanna as editor, 388; describes Mrs. Eddy's first sermon in Mother Church, 389; publishes boy's letter describing occasion, 390; publishes Mrs. Eddy's statement concerning her appearance at Church, 390; carries message to U. S. and Canada, 391; publishes Anna Dodge's letter on work in London, 395; announces first services of London church, 395-396; Mrs. Field-King as editor of, 396; notice of Josephine Woodbury's excommunication, 411; reports cases of legal difficulties, 413; indicates world-wide movement, 413; publishes Mrs. Eddy's article on "Personal Contagion," 415; contains Martha Sutton-Thompson's description of Mrs. Eddy, 415-416; Mrs. Eddy writes against thought influence in, 416; publishes notices of new Church Annex, 422.

Christian Science Monitor, The, Hugh A. Studdert Kennedy, Foreign Editor of, XII; founding of, 468-472; naming of, 471-472.

Christian Science Publishing Society, The, foundation of, 200, 233; publishes *Science and Health*, 200; Foster-Eddy, manager, final demotion from, 385, 386; establishment by Mrs. Eddy on Trust basis, 400; expands and issues *Monitor*, 469, 470, 471.

Christian Science Sentinel, The, founding of, 400; notice re founding of *Monitor*, 470; editorial on Stetson case, 477; reveals Mrs. Eddy's activities, 484.

Christian Scientist Association, The, organization of, 233, 260; action against Spofford, 233-234; certain members withdraw from, 276-277; resolutions concerning seceding members, 281-282; formation of National Association and early meetings, 334, 335; annual meeting in Chicago, 335, 336; Mrs. Eddy's Chicago address to, 336, 337; resolutions to curb "strange doctrine," 349; dissenting members' attitude in "Corner Case," 351; dissenting members demand honorable discharge from, 352; Mrs. Eddy grants demand, 352; *Journal* handed over to, 355; dissolution of, 359, 360, 361; Mrs. Eddy's letter regarding withdrawal from activities of, 404.

Chronicle, Wilmington, publishes George Baker's letter on George Glover's death, 71-72.

Church Manual, Mother, compilation and provisions of, 381-382; Mrs. Eddy's statement on, 382-383; in Stetson case, 479-480.

Church of Christ, Scientist, early establishment of meetings, 198-200, 260; resolutions to provide for expenses of, 198-199; early meetings and discontinuance, 198-200; heading Chapter 26, "The Church," 259-268; Mrs. Eddy's attitude toward organization, 260-261; formation of chartered organization and naming of, 261-262; first officers and directors, 262; Mrs. Eddy ordained as pastor, 278; moves to Boston, 278; Augusta Stetson establishes church in New York, 333, 474, 476; heading Chapter 36, "College Closed and Church Dissolved," 347-358; Mrs. Eddy's dissolution of, 357-358, 364; Mrs. Eddy's reestablishment of, through trusteeship, 364, 365, 366, 367, 368; contributions and cornerstone ceremonies, 364, 365, 369, 370, 371, 372; Board of Directors, 367; heading Chapter 38, "The Building of the Church," 369-376; dedication and Mrs. Eddy's address, 372, 373, 374, 376; Mrs. Eddy's first visit to Mother Church, 374, 376; Foster-Eddy, president of, 385; first public services in England, 395; first church in London, 395-396; gatherings and annual meetings at Concord, 400-403, 420, 421; Josephine Woodbury's difficulties and dismissal from, 410, 411; Mrs. Eddy's letters to new churches, 414; Mrs. Eddy presents church to Concord, 421, 422; enlargement of Mother Church and dedication of Annex, 422-425; Augusta Stetson's difficulties and dismissal from church, 474-481; Judge Smith announces, in Mother Church, death of Mrs. Eddy, 485-486.

Clapp, Catherine, cousin of Lucy Wentworth, comments on Mrs. Patterson, 159, 160.

Clark, Ellen J., student of Mrs. Eddy, 272.

Clark, George D., Jr., son of Mr. and Mrs. George D. Clark, his recollections of Mrs. Patterson, 136, 187; literary efforts of, and trip to publisher with Mrs. Patterson, 187, 188.

Clark, Mr. and Mrs. George D., Mrs. Patterson's stay with, 136, 137, 139; she leaves their home for Stoughton, 140; her return to, 187, 188.

Clay, Henry, Mrs. Glover's attitude toward, 65-66.

Clement, Sarah, pupil in Mrs. Glover's infant school—See Kimball, Sarah Clement.

Clement, Zenas, father of Sarah, friend of Mark Baker, 81.

Colles, Mr. and Mrs. Graves, students of Mrs. Eddy, 393-394; return to Dublin, Ireland, to teach, 394; teach in London, 395, 396.

Collier, George, witness in "Conspiracy to Murder Case," 247, 248, 250; confession of, 251, 252, 253.

Committee on Publication, in "Corner Case," 351, 352; control of *Journal* in, 355; members in 1889, 355; establishment of, 419; activities of, 420.

Cook, Reverend Joseph, permits Mrs. Eddy's lectures at Tremont Temple, 320, 321-323.

Concord, New Hampshire, state capital, 4, 38; General Pierce's duties in, 28; legal case, with Franklin Pierce and Mark Baker, decided at, 32, 33; Samuel Baker marries Eliza Glover in, 35, 36; George Glover meets youthful Mary Baker in, 35, 36; Glover leaves, 36, 52, 53; Albert Baker handles Franklin Pierce's law practice in, 50; Glover writes to Samuel Baker from, 53, 54; Franklin Pierce opens office in, 57, 377; Mrs. Eddy moves to, 354, 375, 377, 378; Mrs. Eddy's letter from, re dissolution of Church, 357-358; Mrs. Eddy's letter from, re dissolution of National Christian Scientist Association, 360, 361;

Pleasant View at, 378-381, 383, 384-385; assemblage of Christian Scientists at, 400-404; Mrs. Eddy's final class in, 404-409; Mrs. Eddy's letters from, 413, 414, 415, 420; Martha Sutton-Thompson visits Mrs. Eddy in, 415-416; annual church meetings at, 420-421; Mrs. Eddy presents church to, 421-422; *World* investigates Mrs. Eddy's life at, 435-441; citizens uphold Mrs. Eddy, 441, 442; trial of "Next Friends" Suit in, 445, 448-465; Mrs. Eddy moves from, 466-468.

"Conspiracy to Murder Case," heading Chapter 24, "Conspiracy to Murder," 244-253; Mrs. Eddy claims case supports thesis of mental influence, 256; included in various attacks, in *Science and Health*, under "Demonology," 257; helped drain Mrs. Eddy's finances, 262; causes fear in movement, 263, 267; public opinion re case, 273; Arens' activities at conclusion of, 275.

Conwell, Russell H., attorney for Dr. Eddy and Arens in "Conspiracy to Murder Case," 247.

Corey, Arthur, edits manuscript of *Mrs. Eddy*, XIV, XV; states views on Plagiarism, XV, XVI; author of *Christian Science Class Instruction*, records Mrs. Eddy's Chicago address therein, 336.

"Corner Case," legal case involving Christian Scientists and Mrs. Abby H. Corner, 351-352.

Corning, Charles R., mayor of Concord, New Hampshire, defends Mrs. Eddy, 442.

Corser, Reverend Enoch, Mrs. Eddy's early pastor, receives her into church, 48; marries George Glover and Mary Baker, 58.

Corser, Bartlett, son of Reverend Enoch Corser, relates father's early admiration of Mary Baker, 48.

Cosmopolitan Magazine, publishes Mark Twain's articles against Christian Science, 426, 427; Kimball's reply in, 428-431.

Courier, Portland, Maine, contains Mrs. Patterson's letter on her healing by Quimby, 112.

Covenant, The, fraternal magazine, edited by Reverend Richard S. Rust, Mrs. Glover's early contribution to, 75, 76.

Crafts, Hiram S., student of Mrs. Patterson, 139; she makes home with Crafts, 140, 143, 165; he opens office, 140-141; Mrs.

Eddy, Dr. Ebenezer J. Foster-, adopted son of Mrs. Eddy, accompanies Mrs. Eddy to Chicago, 335; Mrs. Eddy's interest in, 345; early history of, 345; joins Mrs. Eddy's class, later is legally adopted as her son, 345, 384; they make short stay in Barre, Vermont, 353, 354; he assists Mrs. Eddy in her work, 354-355, 378, 385; is President of Metaphysical College and Manager of Publishing House, 385; proves to be disappointment and subject of scandal, 385; Mrs. Eddy writes him regarding conduct, 385-386; she directs adoption of by-law causing him to lose status, 386; drifts into obscurity, 386; Mrs. Eddy makes final provision for him, 482.

Eddy, Mary Baker, birth and childhood of, 4, 12-25, 28, 29; beauty of, 16-17, 41, 42, 57, 136, 158, 211, 320; early religious convictions, 21-25, 45; early schooling, 29, 30, 31, 32; correspondence with brother Sullivan, 33, 34, 36, 37, 38, 43, 44, 46, 69, 76, 78-79; meets George Washington Glover, 35, 36; correspondence of brother Albert, 44-45, 46, 49, 50, 51; joins church, 46, early poetry, 56; marries Glover, 57, 58; letters from mother to, 57, 58, 68, 73; life in Charleston, attitude toward slavery, 63-67; illness and death of husband George Glover, 69, 70; journey home, 71, 72, 73; birth of son, illness of, 72, 73; early separation from son, 73, 80; poem in Glover's memory, 74; letter to Martha Rand, 76, 77; engagement to Bartlett, his death, 77, 78, 79; death of mother, 78, 79; keeps house for father, 79; remarriage of father, 79, 80; enters sister Abigail's home, 80; opens infant school, 81; letter to Daniel Patterson, 83; marries Patterson, 83, 85, 86, 87; unsettled married life, separation from son, illness of, 87, 91, 92, 95, 96, 97, 98; interest in homeopathy, 92, 93, 94; her faith healing, 94-95; Abigail provides home for, 96; Patterson enters war work, 98, 99, 103, 104; investigates Mesmerism and Spiritualism, 99, 100; desires Quimby's treatment, 102, 105, 110, 111; son enters war, 103; Patterson in Libby Prison, 104, 105; enters Vail's Sanitorium, 106; correspondence with Quimby, 102, 103, 105, 106, 110, 111, 115, 116, 117, 118, 120, 122, 123, 132, 137; healing by Quimby and relapse, 112, 115, 117, 118; studies with Quimby, 112, 113, 119-120, 123; Patterson joins wife, his unreliability, 113, 114, 115, 117, 118, 123, 124, 127; begins healing work, 119, 120, 121, 122; lecture at Warren, 121-122; spiritualistic experiments with Mrs. Crosby, 125, 126, 127; Quimby's death, 127, 128; her poem on him, 128; injury from ice accident and healing, 130, 131, 132; correspondence with Julius Dresser, 132, 133, 134; desertion by Patterson and divorce, 135, 136; healings at Lynn, 136, 137, 138; estrangement from Abigail, 138, 142-145, 146, 221; association with Crafts, 139, 140, 141, 143, 146, 157; absorption in writing, 141, 152, 157, 160, 163; death of brother Sullivan, 144; situation regarding niece Ellen, 145, 146; at Webster home, 148-155, 156; Richard Kennedy studies teachings of, 152, 155, 156, 161, 164; at Sarah Bagley's, 155, 156, 157; experiences at Wentworths and "Wentworth Manuscripts," 157-160, 162, 163; returns to Bagley's, 161, 163, 164; meets Whittier, 165; partnership with Kennedy, 165, 166, 167; first class, 167-171, 173, 175; Wallace Wright controversy, 170, 176, 177, 178, 181; disapproves Kennedy's methods, 174, 175; dissolution of Kennedy partnership, 175, 178, 179, 180, 181; works on Science and Health, 183, 184, 187, 189; association with Bancroft, 184, 185, 188-192; purchases Lynn property, 193, 194; completes Science and Health, 195, 200; Barry's devotion to, 195, 196, 209, 218; relations with Spofford, 196-198, 202, 203, 209, 212-213, 218-234, 236; holds public meetings, 198, 199, 200; forms Christian Science Publishing Company, 200; publication of Science and Health and sale of, 202, 203, 207, 209, 212, 213, 218; meets Alcott, 208, 209, 224; association with Asa Gilbert Eddy, 217, 218; marries Gilbert Eddy, 221, 222, 223; Barry's suit against, 225, 232, 233; controversy with Spofford, 225-230, 232, 233, 234; Arens enters class, urges litigation, 236; meets difficulties of "Ipswich Witchcraft" and "Conspiracy to Murder" Cases, 237-253; attitude toward organization, 260, 261;

organizes church, 261-262; moves to Boston, 263; visit of son, 264-267; secures charter for Massachusetts Metaphysical College, 273-274; problem of Arens and plagiarism, 275, 276, 279, 296, 297; students' defection, 276, 277, 278; ordained as pastor, 278; moves church to Boston, 278; visit to Washington, D.C., 279-282; Gilbert Eddy's illness and cause of death, 283-287, 342; association with Calvin Frye, 290-293, 344, 383, 458, 468, 482, 483; founds *The Christian Science Journal*, 295, 296; preaches in Hawthorne Hall, 297, 298, 300; difficulties with Clara Choate, 301, 302; establishes work in Chicago, 301, 303; Dresser controversy regarding Quimby and, 304-314, 342, 348; wins Arens plagiarism case, establishes copyright claims to *Science and Health*, 312, 313; difficulties regarding Quimby manuscripts, 313, 314; prominent followers of, 316-319; lectures in Tremont Temple, 320-323; directs policy of *Journal*, 324, 325, 327, 331, 332; Lillian Whiting interviews, 328-330; sends Mrs. Stetson to establish church in New York, 333; sends Mrs. Woodbury to Denver, 333; organizes National Christian Scientist Association, 334; receives ovation in Chicago, 335-338; revises *Science and Health* with James H. Wiggin, 340-342; purchases home in Boston, 342; George Glover's visit, 342-344; adopts Foster-Eddy, 345; attitude toward dissenting students, 347-349, 352, 386, 387; action in "Corner Case," 351, 352; moves to Concord, 354; disbands Christian Science organizations, 354-361; urges students to form churches, 361, 364; difficulties with Mrs. Woodbury, 361-364, 410-414, 417; establishes Mother Church by Trusteeship, 364-368; visits Mother Church, 374, 375, 376; moves to Pleasant View, 378-381; compiles *Church Manual*, 381-383; visit of Glover, 385; defection of Foster-Eddy, 385, 386; loyal adherents of, 387, 388; preaches in Mother Church, 389, 390; introduces Christian Science to Great Britain through Mr. and Mrs. Colles, Mrs. Larminie, Mrs. Dodge, 392-397; sends Mrs. Field-King to London, 396; attitude in case of Harold Frederic, 397; guests' assemblage at Pleasant View,

400-404, 420, 421, 422; final class, 404-409; life at Concord, 413, 420-422; presents church to Concord, 421, 422; message to Mother Church Annex, 423, 424; Mark Twain's attack on, 426-433; Pulitzer's attack on, 432-441; citizens uphold, 441, 442; Pulitzer counterattacks through "Next Friends" Suit, 443-449; Glover in suit against, 445-450; charges in suit against, 448-450; assigns trusteeship, 450; Brisbane's interview with, 451-453, 455; Park's interview with, 451, 455, 458; writes letter regarding trusteeship, 454-455; hearing of "Next Friends" Suit, 456, 457, 459-463; plaintiffs withdraw suit against, 463; case dismissed, 464; vindicated by press, 464; moves to Chestnut Hill, 466, 467, 468; founds *The Christian Science Monitor*, 468-472; efforts to maintain integrity of teaching, 473-476, 479; difficulties regarding Mrs. Stetson, 474-481, 484; urges Church to act in Stetson case, 479, 480, 481; makes will and provision for family and friends, 482; final activities, 482, 483, 484; last days of, 485; death of, 485, 486.

Eddye, John, immigrant ancestor of Asa Gilbert Eddy, leaves England, 214.

Eddye, Reverend William, Vicar of Cranbrook, England, ancestor of Asa Gilbert Eddy, 214.

Eddye, Samuel, brother of John Eddye, 214.

Eddyes, ancestors of Asa Gilbert Eddy in England, 214.

Edwards, T. M., Congressman, worked to release Patterson from Libby Prison, 105.

Eliot, John, pastor of William Chandler, Mrs. Eddy's ancestor, 12.

Ellis, Fred, schoolmaster, describes Mrs. Patterson's life at Swampscott, 147.

Ellis, William, son-in-law of Mrs. Webster, causes Mrs. Patterson's ejection from Webster home, 153, 154.

Emerson, Ralph Waldo, exponent of new freedom, 99, 288; Alcott and, 207, 208, 209; interest in Mrs. Eddy, 209, 210; death of, 270.

English Reader, by Lindley Murray, used by Mrs. Eddy as child, XV, 30, 31, 36.

Evans, Reverend Warren F., follower of Quimby, 349; practices and writes books on Quimbyism, 350.

Evening Journal, New York, publishes Brisbane's interview with Mrs. Eddy, 451-453.

Glover, George Washington (III), grandson of Mrs. Eddy, visits her, 385.

Glover, Mary, granddaughter of Mrs. Eddy, her trip to Washington, D. C., and Concord, 448, 449.

Godfrey, Mr. and Mrs., friends of Gilbert Eddy, 216, 217; Mrs. Patterson heals Mrs. Godfrey, 217.

Goodhue, Nicholas, immigrant ancestor of Mrs. Eddy, leaves England, 7.

Goodhues, ancestors of Mrs. Eddy, of Kent, England, 7; join Massachusetts Bay Company, 7; arrival in new world, 11.

Gordon, Reverend, A. J., opponent of Mrs. Eddy, she answers his denunciation, 321-323.

Gray, Judge Horace, in "Ipswich Witchcraft Case," 240.

Gyger, Caroline Foss, records Mrs. Eddy's kindly disposition, 344.

Hahnemann, Friedrich, his system of Homeopathy, translation into English, 92; its introduction into United States, 92, 93; his statement regarding nature of healing agent, 93.

Haiti, Glover's project to build cathedral in, 54, 67, 69, 70.

Hamilton, Dr. Allan McLane, alienist in "Next Friends" Suit, testifies to Mrs. Eddy's mental powers, 451, 463.

Hanna, Camilla, wife of Judge Hanna, her healing by Christian Science, 387; assistant editor of Journal, 388.

Hanna, Judge Septimus J., follower of Mrs. Eddy, helps prepare Church Manual, 382; devoted work in Church and as editor of Journal, 387, 388; in class of November 1898, 407.

Hatten, Thomas W., follower of Mrs. Eddy, guards cornerstone of Mother Church, 371-372.

Hendrick, Burton, on staff of McClure's Magazine re Mrs. Eddy's life, 437.

Herald, Boston, Mrs. Eddy tells of Dr. Eddy's death, 285; on "Corner Case," 351; reports celebration at Pleasant View, 402.

Herald der Christian Science, Der, Mrs. Eddy gives name to, 472.

Herald, Newburyport, articles on Spofford case, 234; reports "Ipswich Witchcraft case," 237; Mrs. Eddy writes on Malpractice in, 239.

Herald, New York, publishes Mrs. Eddy's reply to Mark Twain, 427.

Herbert, Mr. and Mrs. John, Mrs. Patterson makes home with, 96.

Hering, Hermann S., defendant in "Next Friends" Suit, 445.

Hill, New Hampshire, location of Dr. Vail's Water Cure Sanatorium, Mrs. Patterson's stay there, 106, 110, 111, 305.

Hillsborough, New Hampshire, General Pierce settles in, 26-27, 28; birthplace of Franklin Pierce, 27.

Historical File of the Mother Church, contains letter to Mrs. Eddy from her stepmother, 190.

Historical Sketch of Metaphysical Healing, by Mary Baker Eddy, 313.

"Holbrook, Old Asa," spiritualist healer with Mrs. Wentworth, 157-158.

Holmes Academy, school attended by Mrs. Eddy as girl, 47.

Holmes, Augusta, schoolgirl friend of Mrs. Eddy, Mary's correspondence with, 47, 55-56, 116; marriage of, 55.

Holmes, Nathaniel, father of Augusta Holmes, 47.

Homeopathy, Patterson's study of, 82, 83, 92; Patterson's belief he can cure his wife by, 85; Hahnemann and, 92-93; in the United States, 92-93; Mrs. Patterson's interest in, 92, 93, 94, 311; healing agent in, 93; Mrs. Patterson cures case by, 93, 94; her conclusion that faith is healing power in, 94; Dr. Foster-Eddy practices, later gives it up, 345.

Homiletic Review, Reverend Stacy Fowler, editor of, 298.

Hopkins, Emma, student of Mrs. Eddy, associate editor of Journal, 303, 326; leaves Mrs. Eddy to found new system, 326.

Howard, James C., treasurer and one of founders of Massachusetts Metaphysical College, 274; withdraws from Christian Scientist Association, 276, 277, 282.

Huntington, Constant, President, Putnam & Company, publishers, London, states favorable views on Mrs. Eddy, XIV.

Huntoon, Mehitable, youthful cousin of Mrs. Eddy, hears Mary's childhood "voices," 19.

from, XII, 20, 145, 186, 281, 383, 412, 414, 421, 424, 427.

Monroe, Marcellus, follower of Mrs. Eddy, Trustee to establish Mother Church, resigns as, 365.

Moors, ancestors of Mrs. Eddy, of Northern Ireland, character of, 11, 16.

More, Hannah, tradition as to relationship to Mary Baker, 16.

Morrison, Mrs. Amos, first nurse of Mrs. Eddy's son, George Glover, 72-73.

Moses, Senator, George H., upholds Mrs. Eddy against *World* attack, 442.

Mrs. Eddy As I Knew Her in 1870, by Samuel Putnam Bancroft, publication of, 168; quotations from, 169-171, 184, 185, 189-192, 200, 210, 211.

Murray, Lindley, *English Reader* and *Grammar* of, Mrs. Eddy's study as child, XV, 30, 31, 36.

McClure's Magazine, Georgine Milmine's articles on Mrs. Eddy in, 41, 132, 156; describes Webster household, 150-154; publishes Milmine's life of Mrs. Eddy, 436-437; staff conducts investigations of Mrs. Eddy, 437.

McKenzie, William P., follower of Mrs. Eddy, Chairman, Board of Directors of Mother Church, correspondence between author of *Mrs. Eddy* and, regarding publication of book, XII, XIII, XIV; devotion to Mrs. Eddy, 387, 388.

McLellan, Archibald, editor in chief of publications for Mrs. Eddy, 450; Trustee in "Next Friends" Suit, 450, 454; regarding name for *The Christian Science Monitor*, 471-472; Mrs. Eddy's letter to concerning Augusta Stetson, 480.

McNeil, Fanny, niece of Franklin Pierce, sees Mrs. Eddy in Washington, D. C., 281.

McNeil, General John, cousin of Mrs. Eddy's grandmother, 2; in War of 1812, 2; father of Fanny McNeil, 281; Mrs. Eddy visits grave of, 281.

McNeil, Marion (or Ann) Moor, grandmother of Mrs. Eddy—See Baker, Marion (or Ann) Moor McNeil.

McNeils, ancestors of Mrs. Eddy, in Northern Ireland, emigrate, 11.

Neal, James A., follower of Mrs. Eddy, 353;

guards cornerstone of Mother Church, 371-372; Director of Church, 387, 388.

New England Magazine, publishes Quimby article by his son, 314.

Newhall, A. C., the Pattersons' home with, 131; Mrs. Patterson carried there after ice accident, 131; she tries to help sell house of, 135.

Newhall, Elizabeth M., student of Mrs. Patterson, helps finance publication work, 199, 229; helps form Christian Science Publishing Company, 200; regarding Spofford case, 234.

New Hampshire, early days of, 1-4.

Newman, Anna B., student of Mrs. Eddy, withdraws from Christian Scientist Association, 277.

New Thought, foundation of, 348.

"Next Friends" Suit, The, heading Chapter 47, 444-453; *World* announces suit, 445, 449; Glover leads in petition, 448, 450; Mrs. Eddy's legal actions in, 454-456; heading Chapter 48, "The Case in Court and its Outcome," 454-465; Mrs. Eddy's letter re trusteeship, 454-455; hearing on Mrs. Eddy's competence, 456-457; adjournment to Pleasant View, 457, 459; Court's interview of Mrs. Eddy, 459-462; plaintiffs' withdrawal, case dismissed, 463-464; vindication of Mrs. Eddy, 464-465, 473.

Nixon, William G., follower of Mrs. Eddy, member of Publication Committee, 355; Trustee to establish Mother Church, 365; resigns as Trustee, 365.

Norcross, Lamson P., follower of Mrs. Eddy, attends class, 353.

North Groton, New Hampshire, residence of Cheneys and George Glover in, 89; the Patterson's life in, 89, 90, 91, 92, 93, 94, 95, 100, 131, 285; Mrs. Patterson leaves, 95, 96.

Noyes, Caroline D., follower of Mrs. Eddy, member of Publication Committee, 355.

Noyes, Dr. Rufus K., diagnoses case of Gilbert Eddy, 284, 285-286.

Oliver, Mrs. Clarkson, Mrs. Patterson and Kennedy reside with, 166.

Oliver, Mr. and Mrs. George, friends of Mrs. Patterson, 137, 143, 191; Mrs. Patterson heals Dorr Phillips, brother of Mrs.

Oliver, 137, 138; withdraw from Mrs. Patterson, later Mrs. Oliver becomes Christian Scientist, 138, 139.

Orne, Edward A., Director in first Church organization, 262.

Paige, M. E., publishes book, *What Mrs. Eddy Said to Arthur Brisbane*, 451.

Paine, Albert Bigelow, biographer of Mark Twain, 426; his interest in mental healing, tells of Mark Twain's change of heart, 432.

Park, Edwin J., of Boston *Globe*, interviews Mrs. Eddy, 451, 455, 458.

Parker, Hosea W., Co-master in "Next Friends" Suit, 456, 459-460.

Patriot and State Gazette, New Hampshire, Mrs. Eddy's early reading of, 32; recounts Patterson's prison escape, 114-115; publishes editor Meehan's letter to Pulitzer supporting Mrs. Eddy, 435-436.

Patterson, Daniel, second husband of Mrs. Eddy, heading Chapter 9, 82-95; early life and character of, 82, 83, 88, 89, 96-99, 113-115, 117, 123, 124, 135; correspondence with Mary Glover, 83, 85, 86, 87, 88; as Mary's suitor, 83, 84, 85; Mark Baker's opposition to and final approval of, 85, 86, 87; marriage of, 87; forbids George Glover's return, 88; life in Franklin, 87, 88, 89; life in North Groton, 89-95; at Rumney Station, 95, 96, 97; war work, capture, prison experience, 98, 99, 103-105, 113-115; correspondence with Quimby, 102-103; trip to Saco, 117-118; unfaithfulness to and desertion of wife, 118, 124, 135, 136; return to Lynn, 123-124, 135; Mary obtains divorce from, 135-136; return to birthplace, 135; aided by Mrs. Eddy in last years, 135; death of, 135.

Patterson, Lieutenant-Governor George W., brother of Mrs. Elizabeth Patterson Duncan, second wife of Mark Baker, 80.

Peabody, Frederick, attorney for Josephine Woodbury, interviewed by Georgine Milmine, 437.

Pembroke, New Hampshire, Joseph Baker settles in, 10; Nathaniel Ambrose, Mrs. Eddy's grandfather, builds meeting-house in, 11.

"Phare-Pleigh," non de plume of James Henry Wiggin, in *Journal*, 341.

Philbrick, Chase, detective in "Conspiracy to Murder Case," 250.

Philbrick, Martha, pupil of Mary Baker, describes Mary's appearance, 56-57.

Phillips, Dorr, Mrs. Patterson's healing of, 137, 138.

Phillips, Mr. and Mrs. Thomas, friends of Mrs. Patterson, parents of Dorr Phillips, 137, 138, 139, 143.

Philosophy of Electrical Psychology, The, by John Bovee Dods, 110.

Pierce, Franklin, birth of, 27; friendship and association with Albert Baker, 27, 28, 29, 32, 33, 50, 57, 377; as Senator and political views of, 50; Mrs. Patterson regarding his election to Presidency, 84; Mrs. Patterson asks his aid for Patterson, 105.

Pierce, General Benjamin, father of Franklin Pierce, life of, 26-28; friend of Bakers, 28, 32, 33; death of, 57.

Pillsbury, Ellen, niece of Mrs. Eddy, 144; healing by aunt and association with her, 145-146; estrangement from aunt, 146.

Pillsbury, Martha (Baker), sister of Mrs. Eddy, 15, 17, 20, 29, 36, 38, 46; marriage of, 57, 144; Mrs. Patterson's association with and estrangement from, 95, 144, 146.

Pinkham, Hollis C., detective in "Conspiracy to Murder Case," 246, 247, 250.

Pinney, Frances, member of Mrs. Patterson's first class, 169.

Pleasant View, home of Mrs. Eddy, 37; heading Chapter 39, 377-383; purchase and remodeling of, 378-379; Mrs. Eddy's life at, 379-381, 383; assemblages of Christian Scientists at, 400-409, 415-416, 420-422; *World* interviews Mrs. Eddy at, 438-439, 440-441; Glover visits Mrs. Eddy at, 449; interviews of Mrs. Eddy by Brisbane and Park at, 451-453, 455, 458; "Next Friends" Suit held at, 457-462; Mrs. Eddy moves from, 467-468.

Plummer, J. Wesley, treasurer of Concord Church, denies *World's* accusations, upholds Mrs. Eddy, 437, 442.

Plunkett, Mary H., student of Mrs. Eddy, secedes with Emma Hopkins, 326.

Portland, Maine, home of Quimby, 101, 102, 103, 106, 110, 306, 308; Dresser visits Quimby in, 110-111; Mrs. Patterson visits Quimby in, 111-113, 119-120.

son's first class, 169, 184, 191; Mrs. Patterson stays with, 186-187; Mrs. Patterson leaves, 187; connection with purchase of Mrs. Patterson's Lynn home, 195; signs resolution to help finance Mrs. Patterson's work, 199; joins George Barry in selling *Science and Health*, 207; fails in Lucretia Brown's relapse, 238; makes charges and withdraws from Christian Scientist Association, 276-277, 282.

Record Herald, Chicago, William E. Curtis interviews Mrs. Eddy regarding *World's* charges against her, 451, 455.

Reporter, Lynn, relates account of Mrs. Patterson's fall on ice, 130-131; records post-wedding celebration of Dr. and Mrs. Eddy, 222-223.

Republican, Springfield, gives *Science and Health* favorable notice, 203.

Retrospection and Introspection, by Mary Baker Eddy, citations from, 14, 15, 16, 19, 24, 25, 29, 30, 37. 78, 80, 88, 91, 92, 94, 128, 129, 168, 202, 356, 398.

Rice, Miranda R., member of Mrs. Patterson's first class, 169, 184, 191, 384; signs resolution to help finance Mrs. Patterson's work, 199; rejoinder re Spofford's expulsion from Christian Scientist Association, 234; aids Mrs. Eddy in "Conspiracy to Murder Case," 245; makes charges and withdraws from Christian Scientist Association, 276-277, 282.

Rounsevel, R. D., attests to Patterson's failure as a husband, 124.

Rowe, Mrs. Evelyn, I., involved in lawsuit with Josephine Woodbury, 411.

Roxbury Lane and Church Records, refer to John Baker, 8; contain Reverend John Eliot's tribute to William Chandler, 11-12.

Ruddock, Mrs. Mary, director in first Church organization, 262.

Rumney Station, New Hampshire, Patterson's move to, 96, 97.

Rumney Village, New Hampshire, Patterson's move to, 97, 132; Patterson writes to Quimby from, 102; Mrs. Patterson begs Quimby to come to, 105, 106, 110; she leaves, 106, 143.

Russell, Mr. and Mrs., the Pattersons take rooms with, 135; opposing views cause Mrs. Patterson's departure from, 136.

Rust, Reverend Richard S., Principal of Methodist Seminary and Editor of *Covenant*, offers teaching position to Mrs. Glover and publishes her writings, 74-76; visitor at Baker home, 76.

Saco, Maine, visit of Pattersons to, 117-118; Patterson returns to birthplace, 135; Patterson's death in, 135.

Sanborn, Mahala, servant in Baker household, 68-69; writes letter to Mary Glover in Charleston, 68-69; nurses Mary and cares for her son George, 73, 89; George Glover sent to live with, 80, 89, 90; marriage to Russell Cheney, 80, 264; relationship of George Glover to, 91, 264; takes George Glover west, 92, 264.

Sanbornton Bridge, New Hampshire, Baker family moves to, 37; Mary Baker writes to brother of farm at, 37, 38; Baker family life in, 39, 42, 43, 44, 46, 47; heading Chapter 5, 41-51; early history of, 42, 43; marriage of Mary's sister Abigail in, 42, 43, 52; Mary received into church at, 46; wedding of Mary Baker to Glover at, 56, 57, 58; departure of couple from, 58-59; heading Chapter 8, "The Return to Sanbornton," 71-81; return of Mary Glover as widow to, 72; birth of Mary Glover's son and her illness in, 72, 73; Mary's life and literary work in, 74-81; death of Mary's mother in, 78, 79; Mary opens infant school in, 81; Mary Glover's marriage to Patterson in, and departure from, 87; Mrs. Patterson's illness and short stay in, 106; heading Chapter 14, "Sanbornton Revisited — and Afterwards," 142-149; Mrs. Patterson's visit to, 143-146; her final departure from, 146.

Sargent, James L., Boston saloonkeeper, involved in "Conspiracy to Murder Case," 246-253.

Sargent, Laura, follower of Mrs. Eddy, at Pleasant View, 438, 458.

Science and Health with Key to the Scriptures, by Mary Baker Eddy, citations from, 93, 134, 135, 139, 140, 162, 171, 174, 185, 202, 204-213, 218, 219, 220, 224-234, 236, 239, 241, 242, 255, 256-257, 258, 260, 261, 267, 271, 274, 275, 279, 281, 282, 296, 297, 300, 309, 313, 317, 324, 327, 328, 337, 339-346, 349, 363-364, 371, 373, 381, 384, 393, 406, 407, 409, 412, 414, 426, 431, 479, 485; heading

Chapter 19, "Completing the Book," 193-203; heading Chapter 20, "Science and Health," 204-213; heading Chapter 22, "The Second Edition," 224-234; heading Chapter 35, "Science and Health Again," 339-346.

Science of Man, The, by Mary Baker Eddy, given in manuscript to Mrs. Wentworth, 162, 163; comparison with Quimby manuscripts, 162-163; published by Bancroft in his book, 171.

Shannon, Clara, student of Mrs. Eddy, 353; describes Mrs. Eddy's first visit to Mother Church, 376.

Shaw, Jane L., student of Mrs. Eddy, signs notice of withdrawal from The Christian Scientist Association, 277.

Sibley, Alice, companion to Mrs. Eddy on Vermont trip, after Dr. Eddy's death, 287.

Sigourney, Lydia, Abigail Baker gives her poems to George Glover after his marriage to Mary Baker, 59.

Slaght, James, of New York *World*, persuades George Glover into legal action against Mrs. Eddy, 446-448.

"Sleeper," early admirer of Mrs. Glover, 76.

"Sleeping Lucy," Lucy Cook, mesmeric healer, consulted by Dr. Eddy's mother, 215.

Smith, Hanover, student of Mrs. Eddy, makes home with, 292.

Smith, James, early admirer of Mrs. Glover, 76.

Smith, Judge Clifford P., Editor, Bureau of History and Records of The Mother Church, in letter to author of *Mrs. Eddy* declares source material authentic, XIII; as First Reader of The Mother Church, announces death of Mrs. Eddy, 485-486.

Smith, Myra, blind servant of Mrs. Patterson, 90-91; recollections of her in Groton, 91; association with Mrs. Patterson, 94, 95.

Soul's Inquiry of Man, The, written by Mrs. Eddy for her first class, published in Bancroft's book, 171.

Spiritualism, Mrs. Patterson's repudiation of, 125-126; her experiences with Mrs. Crosby, 126-127; her discussion with Hiram Crafts concerning, 139; interest in, 142; Mrs. Webster and, 150-152; after Civil War, 179; disturbances caused by Mrs. Patterson's condemnation of, 200.

Spiritualism and Individuality, written by Mrs. Eddy for her first class, published in Bancroft's book, 171.

Spofford, Daniel H., his interest in Mrs. Patterson's teachings, 168-169, 196, 384; practices healing in west, 196; returns for further study with Mrs. Patterson, 196; practices in Lynn, 196-197; character of, 197-198; signs resolution to help finance Mrs. Patterson's work, 199; in charge of sales of *Science and Health,* 202-203, 209, 212-213; his relationship with Dr. Eddy, 217, 218, 219, 222; Mrs. Eddy's correspondence with, 220-221, 225, 226-230; meets Alcott, 224; breaks with Mrs. Eddy, 229-230, 232; expulsion from Christian Scientist Association, 233-234; Mrs. Eddy explains expulsion of, 234; involvement in Ipswich case, 237-241; in "Conspiracy to Murder Case," 244-253; in opposition to Mrs. Eddy, 384.

Spofford, Mrs. Daniel H., wife of Daniel Spofford, member of Mrs. Patterson's first class, urges Bancroft to join, 168-169, 196; healed by Kennedy, 168-169, 196.

Stanley, Charles, member of Mrs. Patterson's first class, 169; requested to leave class, 170; Arens' suit against, 237.

Stetson, Augusta, student of Mrs. Eddy, early history and marriage of, 317-318; joins Mrs. Eddy's class, 318; as successful healer, 318, 474: records of healings published in *Journal,* 319; establishes church in New York, 333, 474; member of Publication Committee, 355; her gift to Mrs. Eddy, 406; treats in Woodbury case, 413; her interpretation of Christian Science doctrine, 474-476; controversy over New York branch of church, 476-477; visits Mrs. Eddy at Chestnut Hill, 477-478; Mrs. Eddy's attitude towards, 478, 479, 480, 481, 484; Mrs. Eddy's letter to, 479; Virgil Strickler's findings against, 479; excommunication and resignation from Church, 481.

Stevens, Oliver, district attorney in "Conspiracy to Murder Case," 251.

Stickney, Flavia S., married Ira O. Knapp, 316; her healing through Christian Science, 316.

St. John's Lodge, Wilmington, North Carolina, Masonic Lodge, sends invitation to funeral of George Glover, 70.

Strang, Louis C., follower of Mrs. Eddy,

intervenes in *World* interview with Mrs. Eddy, 439, 441; defendant in "Next Friends" Suit, 445.

Streeter, General Frank, attorney for Mrs. Eddy in "Next Friends" Suit, 450, 456, 457, 463; protests dismissal of case, 463.

Strickler, Virgil O., First Reader in First Church, New York, makes charges against Augusta Stetson, 479.

Stuart, Elizabeth G., student of Mrs. Eddy, signs notice of withdrawal from Christian Scientist Association, 277.

Sun, New York, describes dedication of Mother Church, 373.

Suncook, New Hampshire, Joseph Baker settles in, 10.

Sutton-Thompson, Martha, describes Mrs. Eddy at Concord, 415-416.

Swampscott, Massachusetts, Mrs. Patterson's fall on ice at, 130-131; her life there, 131, 135; her account of accident and healing, 131, 312; Mrs. Patterson stays at Bancroft's home at, 188.

Swasey, Samuel, marries Augusta Holmes, friend of Mary Baker, 55.

Swedenborg, Emanuel, Mrs. Eddy and, XV; mystic teaching of, 350; Reverend Warren F. Evans' study of, 350.

Taunton, Massachusetts, the Crafts and Mrs. Patterson share home in, 140, 141, 143, 158, 165; Hiram Crafts opens office in, 140-141; Mrs. Patterson returns to, 146; she leaves Crafts at, 146, 147.

Theology, or the Understanding of God as Applied to Healing the Sick, by Edward J. Arens, 275.

Tilton, Abigail (Baker), sister of Mrs. Eddy, 15, 17, 20, 29, 44; marriage of, 42, 52; increasing prosperity of, 57, 79, 84, 144; takes Mary into home, 80, 81, 82, 83, 84, 85; provides for Pattersons, 89, 90, 95, 96, 104, 105, 114; sends Mary to Vail's Sanitorium, 106, 143; takes son Albert to Quimby, 115-116; Quimby's failure with Albert causes estrangement from Mary, 116, 125, 138; character of, 125, 142, 144; makes offer if Mary abandon theories, 142, 143, 154-155; death of husband and care of estate, 144; breaks relationship with Mary, 144, 145, 146, 190, 354.

Tilton, Albert, nephew of Mrs. Eddy, son of

sister Abigail, 80; receives no benefit from Quimby, 115, 116, 117, 125.

Tilton, Alexander Hamilton, brother-in-law of Mrs. Eddy, mill-owner, marries Abigail Baker, becomes wealthy, 42, 52, 57, 144; death of, 144.

Tilton, Nathaniel, ancestor of Alexander Hamilton Tilton, 42.

"Tilton Tweed," invented by Alexander Hamilton Tilton, increases revenue, 42.

Times, The, London, policy of editors of, 392; publishes article on Christian Science, 392-393, 397.

Tomlinson, Irving C., defendant in "Next Friends" Suit, 445.

Townsend, Reverend L. T., Boston clergyman, denounces Mrs. Eddy, 298-299; *Journal* replies to, 327.

Transcript, Lynn, publishes Wallace Wright's contentions concerning Mrs. Patterson's teachings, 181.

Traveller, Boston, summarizes defence in "Conspiracy to Murder Case," 252-253; describes Mrs. Eddy's Chicago visit, 336-337; reports Woodbury lawsuits, 411.

Tremont Temple, Boston, heading Chapter 32, 315-323; lectures held in, 320; Mrs. Eddy replies to opponents in, 321-323, 327; Christian Scientist Association meets in, 334-335.

Tuttle, George H., member of Mrs. Patterson's first class, 169; Arens' suit against, 237.

Twain, Mark, makes onslaught on Christian Science, 206, 388, 426-427; admits growth of Christian Science, 241, 413; publishes articles in *Cosmopolitan* against it, 426; heading Chapter 45, 426-434; Mrs. Eddy's reply to attacks of, 427; Kimball answers attacks of, 427-431; publishes book, *Christian Science,* 428; later regrets attacks, 431-432.

Union, Lynn, publishes resolutions of Christian Scientist Association concerning seceding members, 281-282.

Unitarianism, position in America and attitude toward spiritual healing, 148.

Unity of Good, by Mary Baker Eddy, 483.

Vail's Water Cure Sanatorium, Doctor, Abigail Tilton sends sister Mary Patterson to, 106, 143; interest in Quimby of patients at, 110-111; Mrs. Patterson writes to Quimby

no more successful in securing evidence as to the existence of any plot involving Calvin Frye or anyone else at Pleasant View, while Mrs. Eddy's financial affairs were found to be in perfect order. In fact, the prevailing outside opinion as reflected in the press was that the petitioners' case was lost before it came to court.

After many delays the case was at last ready for hearing, and was opened at the Court House in Concord on August 13, 1907. A formidable array of counsel appeared on both sides, the action being heard by Judge Aldrich sitting as Master with two Co-masters, Dr. George F. Jelly (an alienist) of Boston and Hosea W. Parker of Claremont, New Hampshire.

From early morning on the opening day many people had been waiting to gain admission, and the limited seating accommodation of the court room was taxed to the uttermost soon after the doors were opened. Senator Chandler and his colleagues for the Petitioners had a difficult task. Again and again as the case was unfolded, the senior counsel for the Petitioners strove to broaden the issue but was brought back each time by Judge Aldrich to an admission of the fact that there was one question and one question only before the court, and that was Mrs. Eddy's competence on the 6th day of March, 1907, the day on which she signed the deed turning over her estate and its management to trustees. There was, of course, the question of misappropriation prior to the granting of the trusteeship, but although General Streeter in behalf of the defendants repeatedly challenged Senator Chandler to produce the slightest evidence of misfeasance in this respect, neither then nor at any time later were such charges advanced.

Driven thus into a corner, it became apparent that Senator Chandler intended to rest his case and build it up upon a charge of "general insanity", and that he sought to prove his point by showing that Mrs. Eddy was subject to delusion to a point where it "usurped the place of reason and controlled the will".

He set forth a chain of six delusions to which he claimed Mrs. Eddy was subject: (1) that the world does not exist; (2) that she was super-